Arnon Edelstein
Mass Murder and Serial Murder
An Integrative Look

Arnon Edelstein

MASS MURDER AND
SERIAL MURDER

An Integrative Look

ibidem
Verlag

Bibliografische Information der Deutschen Nationalbibliothek

Die Deutsche Nationalbibliothek verzeichnet diese Publikation in der Deutschen Nationalbibliografie; detaillierte bibliografische Daten sind im Internet über http://dnb.d-nb.de abrufbar.

Bibliographic information published by the Deutsche Nationalbibliothek

Die Deutsche Nationalbibliothek lists this publication in the Deutsche Nationalbibliografie; detailed bibliographic data are available in the Internet at http://dnb.d-nb.de.

ISBN-13: 978-3-8382-1224-1

© *ibidem*-Verlag, Stuttgart 2020

Printed in the EU

To my father, Professor Eliezer Edelstein,
God rest his soul;
To my wife and best friend, Yael;
to my children Roi, Shirly, and Gali;
may they live long!

Table of Contents

Chapter Three

Serial Murder and Murderers

Acknowledgments

I owe special gratitude to Prof. Menachem Amir, laureate of the Israel Prize in Criminology Research, for dedicating precious hours to reading the manuscript and suggesting his professional comments and clarifications which were priceless.

Thanks to Dr. Michael Matar, Senior Vice Manager at Beer Sheva Mental Health Center and lecturer at Ben-Gurion University who provided me with important insights into the depth of the human soul. I owe special gratitude to two scientists from abroad who helped me with their important insights on the issues this book deals with: Dr. Onno van der Hart from the Netherlands who is considered one of the world's leading experts in the field of *dissociative identity disorder* (DID); and Prof. Jack Levin, a sociologist and a criminologist from the US, considered a world expert in the field of multiple-victims murder.

Preface

About two years ago, my book *Criminal Career and Serial Criminality* was published by Ben-Gurion University Press in Beer Sheva. The book dealt with a renewed definition of the concept of the criminal career, as well as with the concept of serial criminality. In reference to serial criminality, a number of chapters were dedicated to serial murders. During the two years since then, I have given a course which dealt with the subject of the book and was amazed by the interest students showed in serial murders. As a result, my own interest has increased, and I have read recent articles and books on the matter. Through this research, I was exposed to different explanations on serial murders as a subcategory of multiple-victims murder. This exposure greater aroused my interest on this issue, and the discovery that theoretical and researched literature that deals with mass murders is inconclusive. I have also received important and enlightening reviews of the chapters in my previous book which dealt with serial murders. The reports on mass murders in schools and universities in the USA, led me to recognize that there is a lack of knowledge on mass murders, although numerous myths are expressed in the general media, by the public, and among students, as well. These facts convinced me that there is a need to present this issue in a structural way to the reader in order to clarify the overall picture. In my attempt to arrange the theoretical aspects of the phenomena, I will suggest new aspects for understanding them, some of which are multidisciplinary.

Introduction

The attempt to categorize criminals and crimes is not new to criminology. Since Lombroso up to now, some criminologists have attempted to establish distinctions among different kinds of crimes and criminals. This book chooses to deal with the most severe crime—taking the lives of others. As opposed to a "regular" murder in which one person murders another in a spontaneous and unplanned way, much more frightening is the phenomenon of multiple-victims murder, either by taking the lives of several people at the same time, or the life of one person at a time in a pattern that repeats itself.[1]

Toward the end of writing this book there was a news item which read: "A police officer murdered his wife and two children, and committed suicide" (23.10.08). A few months earlier, a murder of nine pupils in a school in Australia had taken place. In 2007, a mass murder was committed by a student at Virginia Polytechnic Institute, USA. There were students and lecturers killed in the incident, including a native Israeli lecturer who heroically defended his students.

Another event, which took place in Israel in the mid-nineties, refers to an emigrant from the former USSR, Nikolai Bonner, who murdered four homeless people one at a time in Haifa, and was sentenced to 120 years of imprisonment by the District Court in Haifa. These events are nothing new, and they accompany us through the years emphasized by the consistently developing mass media presently available in every home. Various scientists in the fields of psychology and criminology include these phenomena under the definition of multiple murders, extreme killing, and other definitions (Fox and Levin, 2005).

A hearing conducted by the American Senate Committee in 1983 regarding "patterns of murders which have been executed by one person with large numbers and no motive or reason," established quite a new taxonomy of violence. Multiple murder was recategorized according to the question of whether the actions of murder happened more or less at the same time and place, or stretched over a long period of months or years. The first type of a multiple crime, such as a massacre at a school, was called a "multiple murder," whereas crimes executed over a long period of time and in various locations were categorized as a "serial murder" (Jenkins, 2002).

The issue of multiple murder (a relatively small number of criminals causing the death of many, and fear in many others), has attracted the attention of criminological research and theory in the last three decades. The concept of "multiple murder" has risen also as part of the debate on the different definitions of a murder that is not of a single victim as in mass murder, serial murder, and so on. Until recent years, there had not been a criminological reference to a multiple murder as a separate category. The tendency was to refer to it as a special kind of murder, and as such, examine it according to traditional criminal theories. Alternatively, some regarded it as a case of a severe mental disorder (psychosis) and left the explanation to psychopathological theories. In other cases, it ended up with the claim that this was an arbitrary and rare category which does not justify a separate reference except for the determination that multiple murder only be considered as such if it is a case of at least four victims (Fox & Levin, 1998).[2] DeLisi and Scherer (2006) define multiple murderers as MHOs (Multiple Homicide Offenders), stating that they are: "Criminal defendants who murdered more than one person during a criminal episode" (Ibid., p. 367).[3] The main reference in defining the concept is the different components of a multiple murder, both serial and mass murders. Various scientists (DeLisi & Scherer, 2006; Holmes & Holmes, 1998; Fox & Levin, 2005) regard it as a concept that encompasses three different kinds of murder:[4]

The first is a mass murder, and it deals with cases in which the action of murder involves a large number of victims in a relatively short period (minutes, hours) during a one-time event.

The second is a serial murder which describes cases in which the action of murder involves one victim at a time, but the total number of murdering actions attributed to the same murderer, or murderers, amounts to a large number of victims.[5] These actions can last for days, weeks, months and even years, with a "cooling-off period" between one event and the next.

It is obvious then that the main difference between the two types of murder, mass and serial, is apparently only the duration of time in which the murder takes place, and the existence or non-existence of a cooling-off period between one murder and the next (DeLisi & Scherer, 2006). Delisi & Scherer (2006) have not emphasized sufficiently, however, the essential difference between the two types of murder: While a mass murder refers to a case in which a number of victims are murdered at the same time and place; in a serial murder, one person is murdered in each event.

Another essential difference stems from the fact that the mass murder may take place among acquaintances. For example, an armed man who murders his co-workers or colleagues when he feels they have hurt him and he feels anger and revenge; while most of the cases of serial murders are characterized by unfamiliarity between the murderer and the victim.

The third type, called a spree murder in the literature, is a journey of murder. In this case, there are two possible situations: One, an armed man on an undistinguished killing spree of strangers and/or innocent acquaintances without a cooling-off period between one murder and the next[6] ending up with the suicide of the murderer, or else killed by the police. An event of this kind lasts, in most cases, up to a few hours. The second type is the murder of strangers in the location of an armed robbery, killed in order to prevent them from being witnesses of the event.

Fox and Levin (2003, 2005) argue that both kinds of spree murder do not set a distinguished type of multiple murder, but a subcategory of mass murder. Therefore, it should not be presented as a separate category of multiple murder, but included within the subject of mass murder.

In this context, one must refer to a common mistake dealing with the acquaintance of the murderers with the victims. Among the erroneous myths this book deals with, there is a perception according to which the victims of mass murderers are always strangers. As a matter of fact, one can find cases where the murderer kills relatives at the beginning of the spree murder, and then turned to murder others, strangers and/or acquaintances.

In addition, the spree murders of the second type does not actually denote a mass murder as argued by some scientists. Although the murder is of a number of people in one event, the murder is not a one-time event, and it is probable that the same murderers would murder witnesses of their crime in the future. Therefore, it is a special form of a serial murder, rather than a mass murder. However, defining the serial murder as one in which one person is murdered at a time created a problematic obstacle which makes it difficult to regard the spree murder as a serial murder. A murder of this kind is actually not different from a murder of sect members belonging to a certain social category; from organized killings among gangs and organized crime, or from some acts of terrorism when a bomb is set and the terrorist escapes from the scene.

Two solutions to the problem of definition have been established: One, categorizing these cases as a separate category of multiple-victims murder which is neither a mass murder, nor a serial murder according to the definitions one finds in the literature (or alternately, both mass and serial). Two, including these cases under the term of "serial murder," while changing the definition of a serial murder. The new definition determines that a serial murder is an event in which at least one victim is murdered at each event, and between one event and the next there is a delay, or the cooling-off period. In this situation, one can define, for instance, the elimination of witnesses of a robbery as a serial murder for the sake of material benefit, with a number of victims each time, and a cooling-off period between one murder and the next. This kind of change would alter the essence of the serial murder as a murder of one-on-one, and, therefore, I prefer the first term option.

In any case, scientists came to the conclusion that a third category of a spree murder is unnecessary and confusing, and hence, the multiple-victims murder includes only the two types I have mentioned, although there are intermediate definitions, like a mass-serial murder. One of the problems in the literature in this context is a mixture of concepts when the same phenomenon is called both a mass murder and a serial murder, with no clear distinctions between them.

As I have indicated, one of the problems of understanding the phenomena of serial and mass murders stems from determinations—that have never been proved—becoming erroneous generalizations made by the mass media. For example, the common myth is that a mass murder is a spontaneous murder committed by a young man who shoots indiscriminately at people who are total strangers to him. As I will show, this is an incorrect and unrealistic generalization.[7] As a matter of fact, most mass murderers murder people they are familiar with, but due to a wrong distinction between serial murderers and mass murderers, different categories of serial murder have been acknowledged as mass murder, and vice versa. Alternatively, the media tend to emphasize a certain kind of mass murderer or serial murderer, even though they are the minority in these categories.

Sometimes the definition of a multiple murder excludes crimes between states (war crimes and ethnic purification like those which have been executed under the leadership of Hitler and other leaders in history). On the other hand, sometimes there is reference to institutionalized and organized crimes executed by criminal organizations, criminal gangs, and sects. In the case of sects it refers, for instance, to multiple murders as part of racism or hatred based on ethnic background, like the murderous acts executed by Manson and his believers. In this book, we will come to know the attitude toward multiple-victims murder executed by organized crime with a criminal background, and by terrorists with a nationalistic background, but reference to this kind of multiple-victims crime will be made just for definition and distinctions purposes, with no thorough reference to these fields, since, as we have seen, it is problematic to include these categories within mass murder.

Generalization Versus Distinction

Even if I accept the argument that a multiple murder is composed of only two kinds of murder, one can still ask why we should distinguish between mass murder and serial murder. Both cases deal with multiple-victims murder, and only the timing, duration of the act of murder, and the cooling-off period distinguish between them. Fox and Levin (2005) reinforce this claim by saying that the typology of the kinds of multiple murders is more theoretical than practical (Ibid., p. 18). Their attitude is influenced by the attitude of the FBI which aspired to solve cases of multiple murders by way of actually composing the portrait of the criminal, and less interest was placed on the theoretical differences and aspects among the kinds of multiple murders. Moreover, Fox & Levin (2005) claim that, in fact, one can see common motives for mass murder and serial murder even if the modus operandi is significantly different. Their conclusion is that one has to put the mass murder and the serial murder under one category. For strengthening their argument, they suggest a typology of five categories of motives which are relevant for both serial and mass murder: Power, vengeance, loyalty, benefit (economic), and terror (Ibid., p. 20). In summarizing their arguments, they say that even with different typologies for mass murder and serial murder, the problem was that these categories do not utilize all the options to the fullest (Ibid., p. 19).

DeLisi and Scherer (2006) present a similar approach that harshly criticizes any attempt of differentiating among the different kinds of multiple murders. According to them, the wider scope may provide more fertile and economical information than unnecessary separate insistence on each and every type. DeLisi and Scherer (2006) examined murderers who committed multiple-victims murder (mass or serial), and found that the common denominator among the different murderers was a combination of the following factors: Criminal record, an older age than that of "regular" murderers, white (in most cases), and commencement of a criminal career at an early age. The problem in this research is that these scientists sampled 654 convicted murderers, out of which they examined only those who committed at least two acts of murder. This condition contradicts the different definitions of a serial murderer or a mass murderer.

DeLisi and Sherer (2006) refer to multiple murders in general, but unintentionally show the problematic nature of doing so since on the one hand they talk about murderers who committed more than one crime—which is relevant to a serial murder and not to a mass murder. On the other hand they refer to the literature that deals with mass murder. Hence, the lack of agreement on the number of victims can lead to flawed theoretical distinctions, and as long as it is an arbitrary decision of the law and the legal authorities, there will be no uniformity among the theoreticians.

In spite of the claims on the importance of including different kinds of multiple-victims murder, the scientists who supported this inclusion dealt with distinctions, definitions and motives of mass murder versus serial murder (such as Fox & Levin, 1998, 2005; DeLisi & Scherer, 2006). Therefore, they definitely need different terms, although they argued against the fundamental distinction between them.

In view of the attempts at inclusion, the scientists alternately used the terms "mass murder" and "serial murder" to describe the same phenomenon—multiple-victims murder. The scientists used the title of "multiple-victims murder" when dealing with a mass murder or a serial murder, and by doing so, often ignored the essential differences between these two kinds of murder (US Department of Justice, 1996; DeLisi & Scherer, 2006; Messing & Heeren, 2004).

Even if there is justification for including serial murder and mass murder under one entirety with similar characteristics, there are still some essential problems in including these two kinds of murder which must be differentiated:

One problem refers to the motive for the murderous act. Even if the motive is allegedly the same, for example, a material motive, in a serial murder, the characteristics of murder for the sake of a material motive differ to a large extent from a mass murder from the same motive. An example for a material motive in a serial murder can be seen when a woman is married time and again to rich men and murders them in order to inherit their money ("the Black Widow"), or a woman who establishes a retirement home, and murders an old person in order to receive his social security payments. Nevertheless, a material motive for a mass murder can be a case of eliminating witnesses of an armed robbery so the murderers would not be caught and arrested, even if it does not lead to actual material profit.

A second problem is the modus operandi. How can one compare between someone who equips himself with firearms and ammunition and exposes himself to the public, part of which would be killed by him, to someone who is always very strict of not exposing his identity? This is the essential point which distinguishes between the two types of murderers.

Third, a mass murder is a one-time action, but the death toll can be high, up to tens of victims in each event. After the murder act, the murderer tends to commit suicide, to be arrested, or even to be shot by the police, while in a serial murder the murderer is very strict not to arouse suspicion, and in this way he can go on murdering, even for years, one victim at a time until the number of victims can be higher than that of a mass murder.

The fourth problem in this comparison between types of murder is the fear of the public: Although a mass murder arouses public horror, the event ends quickly and the anxiety becomes part of the past, whereas a serial murderer who has not been caught, and every now and then another body is discovered; hundreds of thousands of people are in a state of anxiety and worry for an extended period of time which influences the way of life and the quality of life. In this context, one should emphasize the central point that distinguishes between a mass murder (including a spree of murder) and a serial murder: In a serial murder, there is a cooling-off or latent period between one murder and the next which is not the case in a mass murder.

Fifth problem: While a mass murder takes place with a fire-arm (in order to hit maximum victims), it is rare that a serial mur-der would be executed with the use of a revolver or a gun. In most cases, the murderer would execute the murder through strangling, poisoning, using a knife, and other modes of cold-blooded murder.

The sixth problem has to do with the issue of choosing the victims. While the victims of a serial murderer are, in most cases, unfamiliar to the murderer, the victims of the mass murderer, un-like the myth, are known to the murderer (family members, friends, employers or co-workers, fellow students).

To sum up, a mass murder is mostly a one-time action stem-ming from the murderer's inability to cope with a certain situa-tion, such as a divorce and transferring custody of the children to the wife, or being fired from work. This person sees a certain cate-gory in society, or even society as a whole, as an enemy who is responsible for his failures and difficulties. The murder meets the murderer's psychological need of vengeance and publicly regain-ing power. On the other hand, a serial murder is by definition a repeated action intended to meet the psychological or material impulses of the individual over weeks, months, and even years. The fact that one can identify, in part of the cases, similar motives in both types of murders, is insufficient for determining that there are similar behaviours and characteristics. Therefore, there are enough justifications to refer separately to each type of multiple-victims murder as having unique characteristics. This situation is similar, to a large extent, to a situation in which we would refer to all property violations as one type of violation, ignoring significant differences among the types of various property violations. Steal-ing from an employer is not the same as breaking into a business location or an apartment, and these violations are very different from the violation of using a vehicle with no authorization. On a practical level, there is a significant difference between a case in which the police receive a report of a single body in a certain sce-ne, and a report of an armed attack of one or more armed people. When the police have information about a continuous shooting action, the assumption is that it is a mass murder, and the police must send forces and secure the environment while aspiring to neutralize the shooter in the shortest period of time by locating him (a restaurant, campus, or a shopping mall). The situation is quite different when receiving information on finding a body. There is no need to send mass law enforcement out since the murderer has already left the scene. The main task of the police would be to collect evidence from the scene; compare it to previous murder cases; begin profiling in order to study the characteristics of the murderer and those of his victims; compare DNA samples from different scenes, and so on, in order to determine whether this is a case of a "regular" murder of one victim, or a serial murder.

Another problem which caused confusion among theoreticians has to do with cases of repeated mass murders. These are cases in which sect members, gang members, or crime organizations commit repeated murders with a number of victims in each murderous action. The scientists referred to these phenomena as types of mass murder, or alternately, as types of serial murder. But these cases are unique because they have characteristics of a mass murder (several victims in each event) as well as those of serial murder (repeated murders). Therefore, I suggest the new category of "mass-serial murder."

Although this category does not exist in the literature, reality dictates this third type of multiple-victims murder.

Table 1: Distinctions among types of multiple-victims murder

Type of Murder	Duration	Number of victims in each event	Location of the event
Mass	Sequential event	More than three	One
Serial	A single event each time, repeated after a cooling-off period	One	One, not necessarily constant
Mass-Serial	A single event each time, repeated again and again	More than three	Changing, not necessarily constant

In view of the above, is there room for a comprehensive concept of "multiple murder" in criminology? The answer is positive, with a reservation. As a comprehensive concept, it presents an important distinction between a murder of a single victim and a murder of many victims executed by one person. The life of every person is precious, but a murderer who takes many lives is more dangerous than a murderer of a single victim. Therefore, it is important to understand the different aspects and motives of a multiple murderer (in this respect, it does not matter whether we speak about a serial or a mass murder). In sorting violations, criminology, as with the law and the justice system, tends to classify felonies according to their categories: Property, deceit, human life, moral, drug-related, and so on. In such classification, there is room for multiple murder, as well.

But just as the different kinds are divided into subcategories, a multiple murder must also be regarded as a title under which there would be sub-categories: Serial murder, mass murder, and mass-serial murder. The problem is that the majority of the scientists tried to refer to multiple-victims murder as a specific type of crime with no sub-division, and hence they confronted inaccuracies.

In Israel, for example, penal code 1977 specifies the types of violations in a general way: Chapter 10, Article A of the law entitled "causing death," and causing death is divided into sub-types: Killing (para. 298), murder (para. 300), soliciting or helping to commit suicide (para. 302), causing death through negligence (para. 304), and so on. One should refer to multiple murder cases in this way.

One of the central goals of this book is to examine multiple-victims murder thoroughly, characterized as: Mass murder, serial murder, and a repeated murder with more than one victim in each episode. Within this examination, there will be a reference to definitions, sub-typologies, motives, and characteristics of the murderers and the victims. This kind of distinction for each type would provide important information enabling the reader to get to know the types of a multiple murder and the problematic nature that arises from the existing literature. In addition, there will be an attempt to examine the question presented in the focus of the discussion so far: To what extent is there a justification to distinguish among the different types of multiple murders?

Definitions of Mass and Serial Murder

After having suggested insights about the need to distinguish between the two main types of murder the book deals with, there is room to deepen the theoretical aspects. Science is based on definitions of a phenomenon, variables, assumptions, research and conclusions. The ambition is that scientific research would be able to reach empirical generalizations and even forecast phenomena in the future. In the case under discussion, our scientific process was stopped already at a relatively early stage, since there is no agreed definition regarding serial murder and mass murder. Chapter one and chapter two, which deal with these types of murder, present a variety of definitions that have been suggested by different scientists until today.

The lack of agreement on a precise definition of the central concepts of multiple-victims murder caused confusion and inclusion of different types of murder under the categories of mass murder and serial murder. For instance, the annihilation of a family by its father was erroneously defined as a serial murder, while it meets the criteria of mass murder. On the other hand, a repeated elimination of enemies by sect members or a gang was defined as a serial murder, although in each event there were several victims. But there was no definition for cases that fall into the category of mass-serial murder, and these cases were once incorrectly sorted as a mass murder, and, at other times, as a serial murder.

Hence, the problem of defining the concepts and the disagreement about their theoretical aspects caused great confusion. For example, a serial murder is defined according to the number of victims in each event (one), and the time period between one event and the next (cooling-off period). On the other hand, the definition does not refer to a maximal period between one event and the next.

There are two criteria in defining a mass murder: An event in which more than three victims have been murdered, and a one-time event. But in different definitions there are distinctions between a "civil" murder and other cases of murder with an ideological-political background. There is still debate among theoreticians on each of the definitions and their criteria. And if there is no agreement on the definitions, it is very difficult to create distinctions and the sorting of these phenomena.

One has to understand that the problems in defining murder cases are not just academic. They have significant implications on budgets, formal statistics, and other factors. If a state defines a serial murder as a murder of only two victims, then the number of serial murderers in this state would increase, and the law enforcement authorities would present a harsh picture of the increase of affliction and would demand additional material and human resources. On the other hand, a definition according to which a serial murder is a murder of five people and more presents an opposite picture.

Theoretical Aspects of Multiple-Victims Murder

Human beings are one of the only species in the animal kingdom in which members of the species murder one another. While most animals are content with a symbolic demonstration of power, human beings, for different reasons, are satisfied only after the "enemy" dies. The enemy is defined in different social and cultural ways. He does not have to wear a uniform and bear the flag of a state at war. The human enemy changes its appearance throughout history. He can appear as an image of an innocent person the church defined as a witch; he can be defined as the laborers' class constituting a danger to the higher classes; he can have a different origin or skin color, and he can be an innocent person who belongs to a social sector which society has defined as unworthy of living, or his life deemed worth less than those of others.

The phenomenon of a person who for no apparent reason systematically murders a large number of other human beings who have come to do their shopping, or students and lecturers at school or in a campus; or the phenomenon in which a husband and a father murders his wife and children and commits suicide, led to a variety of "theories" that have become known in the mass media which is very influential in shaping beliefs and opinions, even if they are not properly based, or not valid at all.

In view of these horrible phenomena, the scientific explanation given was almost naturally among the professionals who deal with mental health—psychologists and psychiatrists. These fields of knowledge hurried up to appropriate themselves to the explanations of these phenomena without any significant competition on the part of other fields of knowledge. One of the reasons for this state of affairs was that, until the sixties of the twentieth century, psychology was the central field of knowledge in criminology (as part of the positivist school of thought).

As sociology gained esteem in the criminological field, sociologist-criminologists have started to show interest in such phenomena, but most of them tended to adopt the psychological theories which have sustained their status for a long time. The sociological interest in multiple-victims murder started at a relatively late stage, and only in the nineties can we find the first buds of disappointment in the psychological theories, a disappointment that stemmed from the fact that the different psychological theories did not enable a resolutely agreed upon theory, or a theoretical model.

The will of each of the fields of knowledge to present itself as having the only explanation to the complicated phenomenon of mass murder caused a lack of cooperation and a relatively narrow viewpoint on the issue from a theoretical aspect. I will try to overcome this limitation by using a combination of different fields of knowledge in the behavioural and social sciences. This can enable a comprehensive and clearer integrative and theoretical explanation for the phenomenon. One should remember that a person does not live in a social vacuum, but is educated within a certain culture and society with many social interactions, largely influenced by the socialization process. The sociologist Emile Durkheim presented an example for it in referring to the issue of suicide. He claimed and proved that although a suicide is a totally private act, the rates of suicide differ among different societies, that is to say, society has an influence over the individual, even in an absolutely private act.

The book surveys and critically examines existing theories in relation to the phenomenon of mass murder in different fields of knowledge and suggests a comprehensive and integrative explanation for it. This explanation also encompasses the phenomenon of serial murder, in which one person in each event is murdered by the same murderer, as well as regarding the suggested new category of mass-serial murder.

Typologies of Mass and Serial Murder

Science in general and criminology in particular aspire to establish classifications of cases connected to a certain phenomenon by way of similarities and common characteristics. Classification enables us to try to understand a certain phenomenon better by relating to its various and specific components. In the field of multiple-victims murder, the first source for constructing typologies was the FBI which did it mainly for purposes of investigation and catching murderers. It is recommended to divide the typologies of multiple-victims murder, especially those of serial murder, into typologies determined or suggested in the course of investigation aiming to enforce the law, and those determined by a theoretical purpose to understand the phenomenon.

One of the central problems in constructing a typology in this field is the lack of general agreement on the definitions of the phenomenon. Moreover, some of the typologies examine the characteristics of the murderer, some examine the victims, and others deal with motives or a combination of the above-mentioned characteristics.

But how should we examine the motive of a mass murderer who did not leave a suicide note and was shot by the police, or committed suicide? In such cases, the scientists' conclusions are done retroactively in an attempt to expose opinions, feelings and beliefs of the murderer from family members, acquaintances and so on. But concluding an obvious motive from such evidence is problematic and can be mistaken.

Alternatively, many biographies have been written about famous serial murderers, and many scientists tend to refer to the murderer's words as if they were an absolute truth. Sometimes, the investigators play a part in a manipulation the murderer operates on them, aiming to present his unique world. This issue depends, among other things, on the question of whether the murderer's sentence is a life imprisonment with no release on probation; does he expect a death sentence, and whether the processes of appeal and amnesty have been terminated. All these conditions are taken into consideration by the murderer, but not always by the investigators. In these situations, there is a high probability of making a mistake in concluding the true motive. Due to the multiplicity of the serial murderers and the great variety among them, it is difficult to establish a thorough typology which would refer to every event. On the other hand, we might reach highly generalized classifications which have no real theoretical significance. After surveying the central typologies in this field, I have chosen to present a new typology which would enable the use of the integrative theoretical explanation suggested in this book. In this manner, one can classify the cases as they are reported by the legal authorities and the mass media, but also try to explain the motives as well as the characteristics of each and every type.

Profiles of Mass and Serial Murder and Murderers

Profiling in criminology is a field which deals with characterizing criminals and constructing profiles according to different evidence from the scene of the crime, both from victims and eyewitnesses. The profiles deal with the psychological and social nature of the criminal while aiming to find his whereabouts and identifying him among many suspects. The goal of the profile is to help the police arrest the suspect of the crime. Profiling plays a central part today, not only in law enforcement, but also in academic institutions. Typologies made by legal authorities intend to enable the investigators to reduce the list of suspects ultimately to reach the murderer (mainly the serial murderer). But profile construction is not an accurate science. It can only provide the investigator with tools for a better understanding of the motive and administration of the scene, and little information about the character of the murderer, for example, if the murderer is an organized person, did he bring his own weapons to the scene of the murder, or did he take care of hiding the evidence. If the answers are positive, the investigators conclude that this is not a case of a spontaneous murder; that the murderer is levelheaded, possibly educated to a certain extent, or a professional who has studied under excellent professional tutelage. However, from the point of getting this information and up to the point of finding the suspect, the way is still very long, and conclusive evidence is extremely difficult to find. The main reason is that in a serial murder, for instance, most of the victims are unknown to the murderer.

If we think of how many people are levelheaded and organized planners, we would understand that the information from the scene of the murder cannot help the law enforcement authorities find the specific murderer, especially when there are no remnants of evidence at the scene.

Typologies serve as an important theoretical tool that helps us understand the phenomenon under investigation. It can also help, to a certain extent, in police investigations when it supports a prediction that tries to identify the next murder based on the evidence. At the same time, profiles based on typologies must have a solid theoretical and empirical basis. But even then, the rate of finding serial murderers, for instance, is relatively low. This book will try to overcome the problems of the existing typologies, and will suggest its own typologies in order to improve the field of profiling in relation to multiple-victims murder.

The Goals of the Book

The first and main goal of this book is to examine the concept of multiple-victims murder, while deepening each of its components in a way that would enable us to answer the central question: To what extent is this concept valid and important as a general concept? To what extent should one refer to the concept as an umbrella, under which there are several concepts, each one of them valid and important in criminological thinking?

The second goal is derived from the first one. In examining the arguments for and against the generalization, there has often been confusion among scientists. Such confusion takes place when the concepts are not properly defined and clear, for instance, attributing a serial murder to a person who commits a mass and/or mass-serial murder, and vice versa. The second goal consists of a more clear definition of the central concepts included within the wide concept of multiple-victims murder, while establishing a new category that enables referring to special cases which until now have not had a proper conceptual definition.

The third goal refers to the different typologies, especially those which deal with a serial murder, while emphasizing the fact that the existing typologies are not exclusive and exhaustive. That is, they do not include all the conceptual variety, and do not include only the typology itself. This situation damages the significance of the typologies. In addition, there is often a redundant and maybe even confusing duplicity among the various categories in a typology. Therefore, I want to suggest a more correct typology on the basis of the existing typologies, while investigating thoroughly complicated psychological concepts which sometimes star in this field, without the psychologists seeing the problematic aspects of overlapping and confusing explanations.

The fourth goal, which stems from its predecessors, is an attempt to suggest an integrative theoretical explanation to phenomena of multiple-victims murders, especially the phenomenon of serial murder. The various explanations suggested for these

phenomena are characterized by a varied list of the different characteristics of serial murder and murderers, or the variety of explanations of different fields of knowledge presented separately from
one another until the connection among them became unclear. An
integrative and theoretical explanation helps in understanding the
phenomenon as a whole with reference to its different aspects in
the fields of psychology, sociology, and criminology, as well as
additional fields of knowledge. The fifth goal of writing this book
is coping with a highly complicated academic issue which is often
influenced by ideological, economic and dominant aspects of regimes and factors within the law enforcement system. We have
seen that there is a critical perception toward the reports of the
FBI, according to which one gets the intended impression that
there has been a significant growth in the rate of serial murder in
the USA since the fifties and the sixties, an impression that is
aimed at receiving manpower and budgetary resources. Throughout the book, one can see the sociocultural structuring of mass
murder and serial murder through definitions, typologies and
other criteria. While every behaviour becomes criminal due to a
legal-political decision, the reference to the multiple-victims murder has been deeply influenced by the culture we live in, but the
leaders of the states in which these events have taken place were
not interested in admitting that this is the cultural legacy of their
state, i.e., the American culture.

The sixth goal of writing this book is to present to the interested public, especially the public of academicians, teachers, scientists and students in the fields of the social and behavioural
sciences and criminology, the behaviour which is considered the
worst among people—the loss of respect toward human lives on a
massive scale.

The Innovations Presented in the Book

This book, dealing with multiple-victims murder, presents to the
reader the option of getting to know issues and concepts that
currently occupy criminologists in the world, and enables the

reader to get to know the large scope of literature in this field, mainly in the two recent decades.

The book deals with issues which have been studied before, and quite a great body of literature has been written about them. The main innovation of the book is in the attempt to establish a common basis of knowledge which would be agreed upon in the criminologist community. This basis of knowledge starts with the attempt to define and better clarify the concepts we deal with. Such basis would enable a more fertile discussion and progress in the acquired knowledge in these fields.

The book opposes the attitude to the concept of multiple murders, or multiple-victims murder, as one comprehensive concept. The central argument is that when we examine the types of multiple murders, we can find essential differences among them, even though their common factor is multiple victims who have lost their lives. Including different concepts under one concept often leads to confusion and a mixture of concepts. Therefore, another innovation of this book is the clear distinction among concepts which are included under the general title of multiple-victims murder. For example, referring to a suicide bomber as a serial murderer is not correct. Due to the very fact that he murdered a number of people and died in the process, he is defined as a mass murderer. On the other hand, a terrorist who sets a bomb and runs away is not defined as a mass murderer, in spite of the large number of victims he killed. But he is not a serial murderer either who, according to the definition, kills one victim per event. Hence, there is a need for a new category that is called mass-serial murderer. This category enables including the cases in which a murderer murdered more than one person at a time, but would go on doing it again, like, for instance, a terrorist who sets a bomb and runs away, members of a sect who murder those who are defined by them as unworthy of living, executions in the underworld, political assassinations, and so on.

Scientists such as Fox and Levin (1998; 2003; 2005) claim that one can see similar motives in mass and serial murders, motives like power, vengeance, loyalty, material benefit and terror. But the general categories they suggest do not distinguish clearly between mass murder and serial murder. On the other hand, scientists like Skrapec (2001) claim that the decision, whether a specific action would be defined as a serial murder or a mass murder, is arbitrary.

I have found indeed equivalents in some fields between mass murder and serial murder, in the context of the characteristics of the social environment of the murderer. In both cases, there are events which have to do with the family (annihilators of families versus the Black Widow and the Blue Beard); to sectors in the population (an assignment-oriented murder, which can be a mass or serial murder), and a general attack against humanity (the mass- and psychotic-serial pseudocommando).

But similarity between the social environment of the mass and the serial murderer is not sufficient for claiming that it is a case of one type of murder rather than the other. There are most significant differences between the mass murderer and murder and the serial murder and murderer. These differences make a clear distinction between them, and therefore they are two totally different phenomena which cannot be included under one concept. For example, the serial murderer would never reach satisfaction by the murder acts, and therefore his personality structure and its contents would motivate him to repeat this act again and again. On the other hand, the mass murderer with suicidal tendencies performs a one-time act which is the peak of a process. In addition, most of the serial murderers murder strangers, while most of the mass murderers murder acquaintances. The margins of the pseudocommando among the mass murderers (total unfamiliarity), and murder of spouses for the sake of material benefit among serial murderers (high intimacy) are the exceptions to the rule, rather than the rule. Therefore, an additional innovation in this book is the unequivocal distinction between the two phenomena that the mass media and the myths it has brought about created a great confusion. For example, it has been found that mass murder events include, in most cases, murder of acquaintances, rather than a random murder of strangers as claims the accepted myth.

The main innovation of this book is the presentation of an integrative theoretical model for serial murder which has been missing in the theoretical and research literature until now. This model enables a proper theoretical connection among different fields of knowledge which complements one another. This theoretical model enables referring to each type of serial murder within a typology and to see how it can be implemented properly to each of the types. In the past, models have been suggested from different fields of knowledge, but there has not been a theoretical attempt to link the separate explanations to a comprehensive model.

Summary

The multiple-victims murder has a high toll of victims and often it creates significant anxiety in the public, but at the same time, the rate of finding the murderers in these cases is relatively very low, especially in serial murders, and the murderers are usually caught many years after the execution of the murders, if at all.

The book presents and criticizes the most up-to-date research and theoretical literature in this field, and suggests an integrative theoretical model. This book is intended for criminologists, psychologists and sociologists who are interested in this field, as well as students and any reader who is interested in trying to understand the complicated aspects of this field of investigation.

Chapter One
Mass Murder and Mass Murderers

It should be noted that the theoretical and research literature about mass murder is relatively limited, and the number of books and articles published about it is much less than those dealing with serial murder. Later on, I will refer to part of the reasons for this phenomenon.

Definitions

In certain cases, multiple murders are referred to as a "massacre," e.g., Mullen (2004). One would expect that the term massacre would be used in cases in which there are indiscriminate murders in a shopping mall, a campus, and so on, mainly in cases with a high number of victims, since a mass murderer is described in the media as a lunatic who shoots indiscriminately at people he is not familiar with. In fact, various scientists use it in relation to mass murder within the family.

The number of victims—when speaking about mass murder, the formal requirement is for more than one victim, but the term "mass" can consist of tens, hundreds, thousands and even millions of people. For instance, when dealing with the mass media, the reference is to television or radio broadcasts which can reach millions of people at the same time, like broadcasts of the Eurovision Contest or the Mondial games.

The number of victims bears great importance, since it determines whether the murder would be considered a murder of one victim or a mass murder. It seems that the term "mass" received different definitions by different scientists, but in any case, they do not refer to large numbers. For example, DeLisi and Scherer (2006) define a mass murderer as a person "who has murdered at least four victims" (Ibid., p. 396). Fox and Levin (1998) raised the same claim, but withdrew from this stand in their book from 2005, in which they speak about a murder of a number of victims. The US Department of Justice also chooses not to indicate the number of victims in a mass murder when it says: "A mass murder is defined as a murder of a number of victims ..." (US Department of Justice, 1996: Ch. 16). Another requirement regarding the number of victims comes from Meloy and Felthous (2004) who raise the bar to at least three victims, while others reduce the requirement to two victims or more (Mesing & Heeren, 2004).

From the short literature survey, one can see that there is no agreement regarding the required number of victims in order that an event would be defined as a mass murder. Anyway, the term "mass" is not obvious when the minimal required number of victims is between two and four.

What is more important is that the different scientists, who speak about a requirement for a certain number of victims, do not explain the logic that supports this requirement. One can accept the requirement of at least two victims, since it is the basic distinction between a single murder and another kind of murder, whether mass or serial. The thing is that the distinction between the requirements for two, three or four victims undermines the rational basis that has been formulated. One can agree that a murder of two victims can still be accidental, as opposed to the murder of three or more which testifies of a certain pattern. But this definition is sometimes problematic. For example, there are mass murderers who exterminate their family for various reasons. Let's say there is a divorced father who fears losing the custody of his children, and as a result murders them with the hope of uniting with them in the future, in another world. This father is defined as a mass murderer in the literature because he murdered his children and committed suicide. In this case we have a clear motive and action. But according to the definitions of those who require a murder of at least four victims, how would we define a father who has murdered his two sons? Do we not call him a mass murderer?

The problem with the different definitions is that they deal with a small number of required victims without providing a logical explanation or argument which supports this requirement. Some of the scientists went further by suggesting the definition of "a murder of a number of victims" instead of dealing with the problem. Eventually, the result is that each state determines arbitrarily, or out of pressures from the security services and the police, what the definition for a mass murder is in relation to the number of victims. This is a totally arbitrary aspect which can stem from different bodies and interests that are not relevant to this book. It is interesting to see that, statistically, the average number of victims per event of a mass murder was four to eight (Blackman et al., 1999).

Succession and the Continuity of Murdering—different scientists agree that a mass murder is a one-time event because in many cases the murderer does not think about the outcome of the event for himself, or does he care about them. He does not try to cover his identity, and in many cases would end the event by committing suicide or being killed by the police force (suicide by proxy). Hence he does not have an intention of committing other crimes in the future. Therefore, he is not defined as a serial murderer. There are cases of multiple-victims murders that have unjustifiably been categorized as a mass murder, like cases of terror, or murders within sects and criminal organizations (US Department of Justice, 1996). In these cases, the murderer disguises himself, is not caught, and is expected to commit mass murders in the future. These cases would call for a special reference since one cannot refer to them as a one-time event, and they do not meet the characteristics of a mass murder. This is the first problem in defining a mass murder: If the criminal is a suicide bomber, it would be a mass murder, but if it is a case of planting a bomb and escaping from the scene with the intention of committing similar actions in the future, then it is a kind of serial murder.[8] The same goes for actions of sects and organized crime.

As to the issue of defining what is a mass murder, the definition has to include different options: A planned one-time event defined in specific time and place, or an event that goes on continuously for hours or days and can take place in one or a few locations close to one another, provided that there is no cooling-off period between one murder case and the next. Such a murderous spree has often confused the investigators in the field of multiple murders. According to the average definition, one can include the term of "murderous spree" within the spectrum of mass murder, since it is a one-time event. This is an example of the scientists' tendency to prefer generalizations by using the term "multiple murders" rather than coping with vague situations which do not fall exactly in line with the definitions.

According to the literature survey, one can define a mass murder as "A one-time criminal event in which a number of victims (at least two) are murdered deliberately." The event is delimited in time (from a few minutes up to a few days), incessant or with no cooling-off period between one murder and the next,[9] and is also delimited spatially (house, academic campus, a shopping mall, an entertainment center, or a former place of work). The event might seldom take place in several locations close to one another, usually at the same defined area (campus). This event is initiated and planned by a single murderer or a few murderers; they do not bother to hide their identity and are not afraid for their lives. The murder is executed out of different psychological motives, like vengeance, loyalty, expressing power and other motives. In cases of murder for the sake of terror among sects, or in discord within the underworld, a mass murder would be included in the definition only if the operator intends to execute a one-time act at the end of which he would be killed or commit suicide, like a suicide bomber, or members of the sect of David Koresh. This definition brings together different viewpoints of scientists in the field, such as Fox and Levin (1998, 2005) and DeLisi and Scherer (2006).

One of the conclusions at this stage of the discussion is that a murder by sect members, terror organizations, crime organizations and even individuals, can be defined in certain cases as a mass murder or as a serial murder, or as a third type of multiple murder. If it is a one-time act and it ends up by depriving the murderer's capability of executing more crimes, it is a mass murder. If it is a case in which the murderer camouflages himself by taking measures to prevent his being caught or killed by the security forces, enabling him to continue killing, then it is a serial murder or another kind of murder. Those who side with including mass murder and serial murder under the category of a multiple-victims murder would hurry to show these facts as justifying a generalization. I, for one, think that the differences of the characteristics that categorize these acts once under a mass murder, and at another time under a serial murder, or another type, emphasize the differences among the different types of multiple-victims murders.

Characteristics

The Phenomenon and Its Analysis

After having defined the phenomenon under discussion, we have to examine its main characteristics. First, one can see that mass murder gained relatively small reference in the mass media, as well as in theoretical and empirical studies versus a serial murder, and this fact influences the knowledge and understanding we have on this issue. Fox and Levin (2003) enumerate five reasons for the small reference to mass murder, mainly in the USA:

First of all, mass murderers do not present a great challenge to law enforcement because the murderer is at the scene of the crime and is shot or commits suicide. Secondly, a slaughter does not tend to raise the level of anxiety and fear in the public. Although it is a disaster, eventually we speak about a one-time event which ends quickly. Thirdly, a mass murder tends to be limited in time and place, and hence the impact on the public is generally local. Fourthly, since many mass murderers do not survive the crime, the access to interviews and investigation of the case is relatively low. Fifthly, a mass murder does not involve sadism and sexuality, and hence does not cause a significant sensation in the media and the public.[10]

Scope of the Phenomenon

According to the title that has been given to this type of murder, we expect hundreds and thousands of victims as a result of its occurrence. One version claims that from the seventies up to the late nineties, there were about 600 cases of mass murder executed in the USA. The number of murderers who took part in these events was 826 (sometimes there is more than one murderer in one event) and 2800 victims were killed. That means 2–2.5 cases of mass murders on average per month, and the annual average number of victims is 100 (in their article from 1998, Fox & Levin quote data from FBI research that point to a similar picture). For the sake of comparison, the total number of murder victims in the USA per year is about 16,000 (statistical data of the FBI). It follows that the number of victims of a mass murder out of the total number of murder victims in the USA is 0.62%.

The average monthly number of mass murder victims is eight. This datum expresses the feeling that maybe the title given to this type of murder is a little dramatic.[11] On the other hand, the data show that every month one murderer murdered four people on average. When one relates to the data in this way, the feeling changes. If we assume hypothetically that every month a father exterminates his family of three children and a spouse, then the data would have become appalling. Hence, the absolute number of victims does not bear great significance as long as it is not attributed to the kind of victims. It is obvious, for example, that a murder of family members is more shocking than a murder of bank customers.

Duwe (2004) opposes the prevalent perception in the USA that there has been a dramatic increase in the frequency of mass-murder cases since the sixties. In his study, he examined more than 900 cases of mass murder taking place between the years 1900–1999 and did not find a justification for this assumption. From his data, every year, nine events of mass murder occurred on average—a datum that is three times higher than the data Fox and

Levin (2003) reached. The sense that a plague of mass murders broke out developed mainly in the eighties for several reasons: First, due to its conspicuousness or greater prominence in the media; secondly, due to an increase of interest by the general public, journalists and academics. The formal criminal statistics are not always a reliable source for gathering data because sometimes it unjustifiably classifies unsolved murder cases as mass murders or serial murders. For instance, the American Ministry of Justice (1996) indicated that 25% of the unsolved murder cases each year are classified as multiple murders. According to the ministry, an event of mass murder takes place every week (a datum that contradicts the data of Fox & Levin [2003], according to which such murders take place, on average, once in two weeks). The third reason there is a sensed increase of murder cases stems from law enforcement interests to increasing human, technological, and other resources by presenting the phenomenon as becoming more severe, and referring to it as a plague.

Hence it becomes more important to reach an agreed determination about the number of victims in an event of a mass murder. If one scientist defines a minimum of two victims, and another defines a minimum of four victims, it is clear that in the general counting of victims of a mass murder in a defined period of time (week, month, or year), there would be significant gaps shedding quite a different light on the scope of the phenomenon, and impacting the allocation of resources.

Demographic Characteristic of a Mass Murderer and his Victims: Myth and Reality[12]

According to Walsh (2005), mass murder generally does not take place in the big cities of the USA, but rather in suburbs and rural areas. The south is known for the large number of one-victim murders, and there are fewer cases of mass murder. The mass murderer tends to be a man (in 94.4% of the cases),[13] white (in 62.9% of the cases), and over thirty. Some claim that the age of the criminal is higher: Between his forties and upper-middle age. But due to the slaughter cases at schools, the averages went down. Black people have a greater representation among mass murderers versus their proportion to the general population (three times more; Ibid. p. 273), but this fact did not gain special coverage.

The victims of mass murder are usually white (71.6% of the cases), relatively young (34% are under the age of 20), and there is an over-representation of men. Blackman (1999). Men have a higher risk of being victims due to the kind of activities they are involved in, like being employers. In addition, the scientists found that a mass murder in public takes a similar toll of male and female victims (Petee, Padgett & York, 1997; Hempel et al., 1999; Blackman et al., 1999; Walsh, 2005). As with the case in a "regular" murder of one victim, mass murder also takes place in most cases, within the ethnic-racial group, since usually there are family members and friends involved (Duwe, 2004). The only example of femicide in mass murder may be among men who killed their family.

The mass murder gains exposure in the media which leads quite often to the establishment of inaccurate stereotypes in characterizing the events of a mass murder, or in describing the mass murderers. The media draw their profiles as "crazy murderers," who choose their victims randomly or symbolically in public places. Although in the data the age of the murderer and his gender are generally correct, it is found that part of the myths created by the media do not characterize the phenomenon of mass murder and murderers (Petee, Padgett & York, 1997). The myth of the mass murderer is one of a fully-armed person who slaughters his victims indiscriminately. According to this myth, an armed man enters a place where people assemble and shoots indiscriminately until at last he shoots himself or is shot by the police. According to this myth, the victims are people the murderer is not familiar with and are in the wrong time and place. But reality presents a different picture: 30–40% of the cases of mass murder were executed against family members in private space, and another 30–40% of the cases were executed against victims who had been known to the murderer. Hence it appears that only about 20% of the total cases of mass murder were aimed at strangers due to their belonging to a certain sociocultural category, like an ethnic-race or gender origin, or were meant to eradicate witnesses for another criminal act, mainly of an armed robbery (Fox & Levin, 1998, 2005). That means that a massacre that falls in line with the mythic description in the media is quite rare.

Mullen (2004) claimed that, in fact, the massacre cases have to do with specific aims that stem from the psychopathology of the murderers. Blackman et al. (1999) did not find a clear and structured pattern of the mass murder in the spatial aspect. The distribution of murder cases in public places was as follows: Restaurants (16%), shops (14%), governmental facilities (13%) and education institutions (10%, half of them universities). The scientists indicate that 40% of the mass-murder cases took place in a commercial location, and 31% in the workplace. They also found that a mass murder tends to take place on Mondays, mainly between the hours of nine and five. These data correspond to the routine activities theory, as these are the regular working hours in most working places.

The contradiction in the data presented by different scientists should be attributed to the fact that part of them referred to all the mass-murder cases, while others referred to murders in only public places (Holmes & Holmes, 1994; Levin & Fox, 1991; Meloy & Felthous, 2004; Rappaport, 1988).

Methodological and Theoretical Problems

The main problem of the different explanations has to do with the lack of distinction between a mass murder, a serial murder, and murder of a third type—mass-serial murder which characterizes murder by sect members, members of organized crime, or other affiliated groups. The mixture that has been created out of a will to preserve the framework of multiple murders created problems in understanding the causes for a mass murder.

The second problem has to do with the fact that the scientists ignored a mass murder that takes place at schools and on campuses by youngsters. This murder stems from a deep sense of depression, from a feeling of social rejection, and from regarding a certain social category as undeserving to live (Levin, 2008).

The third problem has to do with methodology. Since we speak about a relatively rare phenomenon, different scientists indicate possible factors for a mass murder, factors taken from the fields of psychology, biology, and sociology, but their explanations are not based on empirical research which makes a comparison between the group of murderers and the control group.

The fourth problem has to do with a lack of distinction between motives and characteristics. Different scientists tend to present the characteristics of the mass murderer, but they do not explain the reasons for his behaviour.

Biological Explanations

Just as the psychological school was dominant in the past, so was the biological school. The general assumption in criminology was that a crime is caused as a result of a deviation or a biological abnormality in the brain, hormones, chromosomes, and so on. Along these lines, Fox and Levin (2003, 2005) argue that there is documentation that a violent and uncontrolled outburst has to do with a head injury, epilepsy, and brain tumors. But one has to investigate if, and to what extent, biological catalysts lead to mass murder which is a systematic crime rather than an accidental outburst.

The problem with the biological explanations is that after executing a postmortem on the body of the mass murderer and a tumor is been found, the assumption is that the tumor caused the murderous behaviour. On the other hand, when other mass murderers were autopsied after their death, no such tumor was found. That is to say, not everybody who suffers from a brain tumor becomes a mass murderer, or, in other words, there is no systematic theory regarding biological explanations in relation to a mass murder, mainly due to the lack of a control group.

Cultural and Social Explanations

Fox and Levin (2005) focus on the various motives for mass murder in the cultural aspect. A mass massacre by murderers through a severe outburst of violence was acknowledged for the first time in Malaysia some hundred years ago as a syndrome of "amok." This refers to "Penamoks"[14]—ambitious youngsters lacking education. Amok was a mechanism that served youngsters who had gone through public humiliation, and the way in which they died was proof of their courage and power (Mullen, 2004; Fox & Levin, 2003). The literature refers to these men as having psychological and social deficiencies, but one cannot ignore the cultural aspects of this behaviour. A similar phenomenon was found among the Vikings in the years 830–1030 (DeLisi & Scherer, 2006).

There are scientists who compare the running amok to current mass murders: Angry and desperate young men who choose to die a death that would bring them glory and a halo of power and evil through which they settle an account with the uncaring world for rejecting and humiliating them. For them, mass massacre enables them overcome social segregation and isolation by taking control of public attention and causing fear in the whole of society (Mullen, 2004). The running amok was also the psychiatric basis for explaining mass murder under the assumption that a person with an amok attack is actually under a psychotic attack. He is disconnected from reality. Therefore, he murders indiscriminately. As a matter of fact, it seems that the murderer does make clear distinctions and chooses specific victims rather than random ones (Fox & Levin, 2005). As aforementioned, this perception involves a distortion of reality: Only a minority of the mass murderers murder strangers indiscriminately, and most of them are men in middle age, rather than youngsters.

Culture, Society and Gender

Mass murder is relatively common in the USA, but it exists in other countries as well. For instance, in 1987 a man called Ryan murdered 16 victims in England, Lapine killed 14 victims in Canada in 1989, Hamilton murdered 17 people (the vast majority of them were children) in Scotland in 1996, and Bryant murdered 35 people in Australia in the same year.

The fact that a mass murder is common in the USA more so than in other countries, points to unique cultural aspects of the American society, taking into consideration the overrepresentation of men in mass murder.[15]

Men have greater access to firearms (pistol, gun, submachine gun) which are used as the main murdering weapons in this kind of murder (over 80% of the events),[16] due to its efficiency in killing many victims in a short period of time. Although the use of explosives has a more destructive effect, the murderer is interested in choosing his victims selectively which he cannot do by explosives (Fox & Levin, 2003). This fact reinforces the argument that it is not a case of indiscriminate murder.

The history of American culture[17] shows that the use of fatal violence is legitimate as long as the threatening factor harms the individual's right for happiness, prosperity and so on. Furthermore, American culture praises and glorifies the culture heroes who come out strongly against what is considered injustice in their eyes. In this context, there is even admiration toward those who take the law into their own hands and avenge those who have hurt them, their family members, or the American dream in general.

About 40% of the mass-murder cases in the USA are related to the extermination of a family—the children of the murderer, and sometimes also his ex-wife. The sociocultural explanation for this stems from the fact that when couples get divorced, beyond the emotional crisis of the separation, usually the man is the one who leaves the house and is left to live by himself and so for him there is a significant emotional and economical loss (Fox & Levin, 2005; Duwe, 2004). In this context, Messing & Heeren (2004) indicate that in a mass murder executed by men, one can see clear indications of the patriarchal ideology: The man is the "owner" of the family and has absolute control over it (in Hebrew the same word signifies both owner and husband). When he is confronted with a situation in which he loses this control, the patriarchal response is the use of violence, up to a mass murder, in order to reestablish his dominant position. In other words, the man, as he sees it, is forced to murder his family in order to re-establish his control over it. Only upon the death of the family members can he establish this authority because he is not capable of assuming such a role if they remain alive.

Another 40% of the cases of mass murder in the USA have to do with murders executed by workers who have been fired from work who murder the employer and part of their former co-workers. This also has a sociocultural explanation, and the loss of work influences men and women differently. In spite of the rise of women's status in the USA, men, more than women, are defined by others and by themselves according to their occupational position (what they do defines what they are). When men are fired and unemployed, their self-esteem is damaged significantly in their own eyes, as well as in the eyes of others, and they suffer from it psychologically more than women. In addition, men, more than women, tend less to enjoy the advantages of support and encouragement when they experience a familial or employment loss (Duwe, 2004; Fox & Levin, 2005).

Fox and Levin (2005) describe the economic situation in the USA and its impact on certain men. There are several factors lately which might get together in establishing a fatal mixture of despair and resentment. An increasing number of men in their middle age lose their meaning of life and support, i.e., their family and work. The contracted and more competitive labor markets have caused thousands of men to feel helpless and unworthy. Higher rates of divorce, greater mobility in living, and a general lack of a sense of a neighbourhood and community have made many men very lonely. Part of these men feel that they do not have a place to go back to, and they do not have the means to solve their problems other than through deadly violence. This explanation seems to reinforce the claim of the increase in mass-murder cases in recent years, but as has been said, no empirical basis has been found to this increase.[18] The sociocultural explanation that has been presented explains why there is an over-representation of men in cases of mass murder. Nevertheless, it is my opinion that the fact that women reached the stage, after so many struggles, of being accepted for working positions outside the traditional "female" professions, we would expect that a woman who gets fired would feel a will to avenge her employers. But this has to do with the different socialization processes of men and women. Women go through a socialization which does not accept a violent behaviour as legitimate, and often tend to blame themselves, even when they are the victims (for example, raped women have guilt feelings, battered wives look for a justification for the beating husband's behaviour in their own behaviour). Therefore, they tend, more than men in similar situations, to commit suicide instead of murdering. This is why the ratio of women in mass murder is much lower to that of men (Messing & Heeren, 2004).

On the other hand, Kellher and Kellher (1998) argue that current society looks up to women who use violence as culture heroines and role models. For example, the media bring programs of women's boxing, and there are television series, movies, and fantasy computer games in which the violent hero is a heroine (like Lara Croft, and others). According to Kellher and Kellher, it would lead to a greater acceptance of violent behaviour on the part of women in the future. But one has to refer to this prediction with necessary caution in light of the fact that the count of women in mass murder is still lower than their count in regular murder cases.

According to the routine activities theory, we would expect to see an increase in the rates of women in mass murder as they come out of their traditional gender roles. But it is interesting to see that mass murder executed by women is still done in the defined field of their biological and gender social surrounding, that is, motherhood, nursing, medicine etc. For this reason, a case in which a woman murders her former employer gains a special publication. For instance, in 2006, Jennifer Marco, 44, was fired from her work in the post office in California. In June 30 she started her day on a murderous journey: First she murdered her neighbour, and afterwards she came to her place of work and murdered her former employer and co-workers. All in all, she murdered five of the post office workers.

This conclusion is correct, as mentioned above, mainly in relation to a mass murder of an employer and co-workers. On the other hand, Messing & Heeren (2004) found that between the years 1993–2001, 32 women committed mass murders of their children. It has been found that the characteristics of the women mass murderers are similar to those of men, that is, social isolation and an event that serves as a catalyst for committing the murder. Instead of trying to adjust to the new reality, they turn to murderous violence in order to solve their personal problems. Like male patriarchy, these women believe they have indisputable full ownership over the lives of their children, but they do not attribute this right of ownership to their spouses. We know, for example, the story about Medea who killed her children because of the infidelity of her husband.

The scientists like Messing & Heren (2004) defend themselves against criticism by saying that many women who have divorced or been betrayed by their husbands, turned their back to the crisis and started building their lives anew. Alternatively, women who could not raise their children gave them away for adoption and did not hurt them. On the other hand, the murderers who took the lives of their children, acted out of a matriarchal response to the patriarchal ideology, that is, the mother is the owner of the children. Therefore, they can decide their destiny, including their death.

To sum up, there are societies and cultures which encourage externalizing emotions up to a level of violence, while blaming the environment for the situation. A different picture can be seen in the Japanese culture, for instance. The individual learns to assume full responsibility for his deeds and conditions. It means that in different cultures the individual's reactions to similar events would be different. For example, while in the American culture which emphasizes individualism, there is legitimacy to blame others and avenge them in order to regain one's respect; in the Japanese culture which emphasizes the sense of community, the individual blames himself and would "avenge" himself in order to regain his respect (harakiri[19]).

One can find support for this assumption in Durkheim (1897) in his book *Suicide*, in which he demonstrates empirically how different cultures dictate different behaviours for the individual, even in a decision of a suicide.

Characteristics

DeLisi and Scherer (2006) and others survey the literature that deals with multiple murder. This analysis brings up several characteristics of mass murderers which sometimes contradict each other:

- Mass murderers are characterized by a personal history of psychopathology, including psychoses, depression, paranoia and antisocial behaviour. They perceive society, or part of its members, as responsible for their personal suffering, and the outcome is a sense of being a victim and a sense of alienation.
- Mass murderers are isolated people that only seldom established themselves in mature roles in an efficient way.
- They have a personal history of being victims of harassments and loneliness in childhood, show affection for weapons and violence as well as suspiciousness and narcissism.
- They have no criminal or antisocial history, neither a severe mental disorder, and they do not use drugs.
- Mass murderers are sane men who have clear and predictable target victims.
- Mass murderers combine mass murder with other criminal activity.

- Mass murderers are men in their middle age, single or divorced, who have suffered recently from a loss or a defeat in their work, or in their interpersonal relationships. They have suffered from mental problems, like depression and paranoia and part of them were psychotic at the time of executing the murder.
- Half of the mass murderers had previous convictions, but only 16% of them had a criminal record of violence (Blackman et al., 1999).

Delisi & Scherer (2006) summarize the characteristics of mass murderers in the following way: The popular image of an indiscriminate massacre of strangers by a lunatic murderer is the exception and not the rule ... In spite of the difficulty in predicting, different scientists found similarity or common characteristics in the social background of the murderers, like abuse and familial deficiencies, a severe variety of mental problems and involvement in antisocial behaviour prior to the murder (Ibid., p. 372).

One of the problems presented by Delisi & Scherer (2006) is the combination of mass and serial murder together which influences the reported characteristics of the murderers. For example, they refer to rape and robbery cases together with mass murder. In all the research literature that has been surveyed for writing this book, no evidence was found that mass murderers committed a rape in a context of a mass murder, only felonies of armed robbery.

We can summarize by saying that the outstanding characteristics among mass murderers include a history of failures. The failures can be in the educational, occupational and interpersonal fields, and they are accompanied by loneliness, and in especially extreme cases, paranoia as well.

These men blame the close environment (spouse, family, friends, and co-workers), certain social categories (feminists, people of certain origin) or society as a whole for their failures. Usually, social rejection, including dismissals or separation from the spouse, serves as a psychological catalyst that increases the murderer's loneliness and pushes him to execute a mass murder act. The mass murderer tries to regain control over his life through the murder, through meticulous planning and equipping himself with weapons.

The fact that the murderer is socially isolated prevents him from sources of guidance and social support, especially in these difficult situations of loss. Since the murderer knows very well who is responsible, according to him, for this unbearable loss (his former employer, ex-wife, or schoolmates), he has some kind of prepared list in his head of the victims he wants to avenge. In most cases, he does not hurt strangers who happen to be at the scene of the event, except in cases of terror, sects and psychotic murderers which are relatively rare. Among some of the mass murderers, there is a history of fascination with weapons and even collection of firearms. In many cases there is no history of contact with the law or the mental health system. In a few cases it was found that the murderer adopts an existing scenario of a murder from the mass media, trying to imitate it (Copycat; See: Duwe, 2004; Messing & Heeren, 2004; Fox & Levin, 2005, 2003; Mullen, 2004).

From the literature survey, there appears an outstanding disagreement among the scientists in a number of fields: First, in the field of mental pathology: While certain scientists regard the mass murderer as having a history of severe mental disorders, up to a state of psychosis (disconnection from reality), others indicate only a phenomenon of depression. Secondly, in the field of criminal history: Some scientists found a criminal history among half of the mass murderers they assessed; whereas others claim that mass murderers do not have a history of an encounter with the law.

Psychosocial Explanations

Unlike the myth that says that an episode of mass murder is characterized by suddenness and unplanned extreme violence, this description is the exception, not the rule. In most cases, the mass murderer has a clear motive, such as vengeance. His victims are chosen because of their deeds (real, symbolic, or imagined) in relation to the murderer, or because of what they represent for him. Since he plans the murder meticulously and equips himself with the suitable weapon, he usually cannot claim insanity as a line of defense. And indeed, an absolute majority of the mass murderers are not defined as mentally ill. Hence, attributing the mass murder to a state of psychosis is a sweeping generalization, taking into consideration that only 15% of the murderers were diagnosed as schizophrenic, for instance (Fox & Levin, 2003).

The question is: What are the causes which led McIlvane, a former post office worker in Michigan, USA, 31, to murder four post office workers and commit suicide? Why did a graduate of the University of Iowa, USA, Lu, 28, murder five university workers and commit suicide? Or why did a man, 55, murder his wife, two children and two grandchildren and commit suicide? What made a policeman, 32, from Israel, murder his wife and two children and commit suicide? Peled, Salztman & Apter (2001) argue that most of the people who suffer from mental disorders do not execute violent crimes, but when it happens—the tendency is to hurt family members and acquaintances. The scientists attribute the violent outbursts, in the population at large as well as among mental patients, to other factors, like traumatic life events in childhood and adulthood, such as the loss of one of the parents in childhood, and life in a single-parent family. It was empirically found in the USA that the majority of mass murderers murdered victims who were familiar to the murderer, like family members (familicide) and acquaintances, and the murder took place in the living area of the murderer and his victims; while the media emphasized and stressed the mass murder which takes place in public places, like working places (Petee & York, 1997; Fox & Levin, 2003).

The Psychosis Explanation

Psychosis is a "severe disorder in judgment of reality and in creating a new reality."[20] A psychotic person is incapable of differentiating between reality and imagination due to disruptions in his thinking and perceptual capabilities. This disorder may lead to exceptional, incomprehensible and unpredictable behaviour which might be aggressive and dangerous.

A psychosis is not a specific illness, but a mental state that can be a symptom for a variety of mental disorders. The most common symptoms of a person in a psychotic state are delusions and hallucinations. In addition, a person in a psychotic state would behave inconsistently and incomprehensibly, not be attentive or concentrated, look unkempt and neglected, and would behave without social and impulsive inhibitions.

A paranoid personality disorder is a sub-type of psychosis having to do with distrust and the suspicion of individuals toward others. People who suffer from psychosis feel that they have been wronged and are perceived as inflexible, hostile, and aggressive which leads to their social isolation.[21] This explanation only partially meets the characteristics of mass murderers, and it is consequently difficult to accept it.

Another psychological explanation which could have been attributed to mass murder is schizophrenia which is a sub-type of psychosis, but from the literature survey it seems that it rather expresses passive behaviour and disconnection from reality. All these negate the possibility of explaining mass murder by it since the murderer is characterized by a high planning and organization capability, there are no reports of disconnection from reality, and the murderer is usually selective in choosing his victims.

So it follows that the explanation of a psychosis can suit only a small part of mass murderers. These mass murderers are called "pseudocommando." They murder in public places, like shopping malls and entertainment centers, and they do it indiscriminately. Their behaviour can be explained, indeed, as a psychotic attack, but one can diagnose their mental state only in retrospect because these murderers do not survive. In this context, Leyton (1986) claims that we have to bear in mind that a psychotic person brings contents from his culture into his mental illness, and there are inter-cultural differences in psychoses.

The explanation of psychosis is less relevant for murderers who annihilate families, or avenge an employer and co-workers after being fired from work. In these cases, the organization, planning, and execution capability do not correspond to a disconnection from reality. Therefore, my conclusion is that regarding these mass murderers, it is a deep depression that pushes the murderer to commit suicide, or be killed by a foreign factor like the police. But the suicidal thoughts and intentions are accompanied by a will to get even with those individuals who have brought the individual to his state, as he perceives it. He does not take responsibility for his condition (familial or occupational), and blames others for it. These individuals develop a defense mechanism of the self which neutralizes guilt feelings and responsibility, while negating the victim and turning to "higher loyalties."[22]

In this situation, the individual feels socially isolated and perceives his situation subjectively as being under a severe and immediate threat, and therefore his action would be more extreme, after reformulating or constructing his situation (Lofland, 1969).[23] In the course of this construction, personal factors enter the picture, as well as sociocultural ones.

The Frustration-Aggression Explanation

Another theory which is worth dealing with in this context comes from expanding the theory of frustration-aggression that was suggested by Bandura, and gained several versions. One version claims that frustration means blocking the individual from achieving his goals. As a result of his frustration, the individual might use violence which can be directed directly toward the frustrating element, or against innocent others against whom the individual uses displacement or symbolization of the frustration he has gone through because he cannot be violent directly against the frustrating source.

On the basis of this theory,[24] Hale (1998) argued that the murderer releases, through the murder, feelings of humiliation he has gone through in his past, and the murder actually enables him to regain a sense of power he has lost. The assumption is that the murderer experienced humiliation in his childhood which was an attack on his self-worth or his moral worth. This kind of humiliation motivates him to act, aiming to restore what he considers as "good/right/just." Hale blocks the criticism on his arguments, a criticism that says that many people experience humiliation but do not become mass murderers. That is to say, that an early humiliation might become a murderous act only if the murderer knows and internalizes the humiliation as a motive for his murderous action for a certain psychological reason. Moreover, the murderer identifies certain signs in the humiliating and frustrating experience and relates them to his past humiliation. This situation is called "the violent cue," and it pushes the murderer into action.

It was found that the murderer usually does not turn to the origin of frustration, but to innocent substitutes. The explanation for this is that the feeling of aggression toward the frustrating or humiliating object was blocked due to an objective danger (like being caught and punished), or, as in most cases, out of a psychological fear of expressing aggression toward the frustrating/humiliating factor due to physical and psychological reasons. For example, the murderer is still under control, supervision, or dependency of the frustrating/humiliating factor, and therefore would not murder the source who caused his humiliation or frustration. Such blocking raises the level of frustration in future murders, and when the option of a direct release is blocked, his aggressive impulse must be released indirectly through a substitute. By so doing, the murderer uses displacement or a "learned analogy," which enables the violent response to be displaced from one object to another through generalization. The outcome is that innocent victims serve as scapegoats when the murderer finds similarity between the source of frustration and the victim.

Although the concepts of displacement and generalization were found as correct in a variety of behavioural responses in the field of psychology, there are a few fundamental criticisms about this theory in general, and in the context of mass murder in particular. First, not every person who has experienced humiliation or frustration responds by way of violence, especially fatal violence, toward the original frustrating object, or toward any substitute. Secondly, the above-mentioned scientist, like others, uses the terminology "for certain psychological reasons," without explaining what was the reason or the psychological process which damages the reliability of the explanation. Thirdly, while it is easy to accept the explanation that a small child cannot, emotionally and even physically, oppose a humiliating and frustrating parent; it is much more difficult to accept such an explanation regarding a young man who feels less dependent on others. Fourthly, there must allegedly be an expected pattern, or a theoretical stereotype, according to which there is something in the mass murderer's childhood which is the variable that explains his murderous behaviour as an adult. Even if this etiology is true, the central question that was left unanswered is: What is that element or psychological process that makes the humiliation or frustration the murderer has experienced in childhood into a murderous behaviour later on? It is also not clear why this behaviour appears only at a relatively late stage in his life.

The fifth point of criticism is why the frustration and the humiliation are expressed in a later stage of the murderer's life specifically through a mass murder, rather than a single murder. The answer can be that exactly because the murderer cannot hurt the original source of frustration, he would feel satisfaction only by murdering a large number of people who have similar characteristics to those of the frustrating/humiliating source, while presenting an ultimate power that brings back his respect through significant publication.

A second version of the theory connects between psychology and sociology through the use of the social learning theory (Wright & Hensley, 2003; Singer & Hensley, 2004).[25] The scientists present the theory of Dollard and Miller (1950) which claims that every individual goes through socialization in order to seek affection and confirmation from those he loves. When he gets a confirmation or a positive opinion, the individual and his significant others are satisfied. On the other hand, when there is no confirmation or such successful solution, the individual experiences frustration. He tends to transfer the frustration toward others who cannot retaliate. The reason is that the frustrated individual is under control of the frustrating object, and therefore cannot avenge him directly.

These scientists refer to the frustration theory of Amsel (1958), according to which humiliation is an outcome of a non-reward situation. A non-reward situation is defined in the following way: "Any situation in which no reward is given, while in the past in the same situation some kind of reward was given" (Singer & Hensley, 2004, p. 465). Being rewarded in a certain situation establishes an expectation for a reward in similar situations in the future. Therefore, when the individual confronts such a situation with no reward, as it was in the past, it arouses in him a reaction of frustration or humiliation. Individuals, who suffer from humiliation, tend to connect certain situations with humiliation. Since the original humiliation created frustration, then the situations which are connected by the individual with humiliation, lead to a sense of early frustration. In order to prevent further situations of humiliation, the individual acts violently. In relation to mass murderers, studies show that they experienced an abundance of humiliating situations during childhood, mainly situations with no reward. The mass murderer, in the course of his maturation, starts perceiving all situations as non-rewarding, and loses the capability to distinguish between rewarding and none-rewarding situations. He learns to expect humiliation in almost all circumstances.

One should bring the central criticism of this theory: Theoreticians of the frustration-aggression theory do not explain why a murderer would start murdering at a certain period in the future. Is there a particular stimulus that pushes him to act? At this point, the catalyst introduced pushes the murderer to execute the murder.

Fox and Levin's Explanation of a Mass Murder

The scientists refer to three factors that contribute to mass murder: One is early disposition. According to Fox and Levin, there are preliminary conditions that exist in the individual for a long time until they become part of his personality. An early disposition can include a violent temperament which may come from frustration and the externalization of guilt. This component stems from a long history of frustration and failures, since the individual has a low capability in coping with these factors. This history starts at a young age and goes on to adulthood. It can be accompanied by depression on different levels. This factor explains the fact that most mass murderers are middle age, rather than a relatively young age: It takes time, many years, to accumulate the disappointments of childhood and maturity (Duwe, 2004). For example, Ruppert murdered 11 family relatives in the state of Ohio in the USA in the seventies. He had a history of learning difficulties at school and a lack of social skills throughout his adolescence. In addition, he lost his father at a young age and felt uncomfortable in the company of women, up to the point that he had never experienced sexual intercourse. As an adult, he did not manage to hold down a job.

The scientists defend their position against criticism by claiming that many people, who suffer from frustration and depression for a long period of time, might commit suicide without hurting other people. They perceive themselves as worthless but responsible for their failures in life, and therefore their aggression is internalized. The mass murderers, who feel depression and frustration, differ because they perceive others as guilty and responsible for their own problems. For this reason, their aggression is externalized, and, as a result, they physically hurt others. They always see themselves as victims, rather than responsible for their disappointments. This reaction style is acquired through learning from their sociocultural environment or the mass media.

Even though the authors avoided criticism, such as "so why do frustrated and depressed people murder while others don't?"

their argument does not prevent another criticism: Why is it that one person has learned to blame others for his troubles, while another takes responsibility for his troubles? In addition, if the mass murderer externalizes his aggression, and therefore murders and does not commit suicide like others, why is it that at the end of the murderous spree, mass murderers tend to commit suicide, either by themselves, or "suicide by proxy"?[26] It should be mentioned, though, that from the research of Duwe and Vronsky (2004) it appears that in this context there is also a certain myth, and only 30–50% of the cases of mass murder would result in the murderer's suicide or his being killed by security forces.

Furthermore, the scientists do not explain why such a person would be a mass murderer, rather than a serial murderer, or a murderer of individuals, due to a violent outburst following an external stimulus. It is unclear as to why he accumulates the frustration and depression until the outburst of a mass murder. Another criticism is that this explanation does not suit part of the mass murderers who are students at school, college, or university. For instance, in 23.9.2008, a student aged 20 murdered nine of his classmates in Finland, and in the previous year, in the same country, a youngster murdered eight of his schoolmates (the evidence reported that the student planned his actions and spoke in a way that pointed to depression and a most pessimistic perception of the future).

The second component is catalysis, meaning certain events or situations might urge and accelerate the arrival of a violent fury. In most cases, the murderer experiences a sudden loss or a threat of such loss which for him is disastrous. Usually it is a case of losing a job or an undesired separation from loved ones, like transferring the children for guardianship or custody of the wife following a divorce, or dismissal of the man from work (Duwe, 2004). As I have mentioned above, the current explanation is supported by statistics which state that about 80 percent, out of the total cases of mass murders, take place among relatives and acquaintances.[27]

The authors claim that external examples and models can serve as a catalyst or inspiration for a mass murder, mainly by way of a copycat. This phenomenon stands out especially in mass murders at schools, where mass murderers inspire those who follow them. Sometimes the imitation or the inspiration can be even stronger from a long-term frustration, and then we would find young mass murderers, and even children. The scientists argue that while a mass murder at school causes most of the children to identify with the victims, part of the pupils who feel frustration and alienation, identify with the power of the murderer, and this is a basis for imitation (Fox & Levin, 2003).

The problem with this explanation is that it can explain the phenomenon of mass murder, but it cannot explain why certain people would turn to a mass murder, whereas the majority of those who are in similar situations would not do so.

The third component is promoter/assistant: Promoting elements increase the probability and extent of the use of violence. For example, mass murderers are usually disconnected from sources of emotional support. They are defined as lone wolves. They are characterized as being detached from people who could have supported them in bad times, or as those who live by themselves for long periods of time, away from their homes, experiencing anomia. The authors argue that it is probable for people with no sources of guidance and support to be more inclined to use violence or externalize it. At the same time, they argue against this claim by saying that people who feel anger, helplessness and isolation do not commit a mass murder, nor do they have the means to do so (firearms).

In my opinion, their claim that mass murderers are characterized as lonely people who are disconnected from social and emotional support is correct, and the literature supports it (Petee & York, 1997; Mullen, 2004). My claim is that specifically lonely, socially and psychologically helpless and lacking social support people would feel more than others that they have nothing to lose, and therefore, there is a higher risk that in certain circumstances they would tend to commit a murder.[28]

The thing that the authors do not explain is why lonely people, who lack social support, would tend to externalize their violence rather than commit suicide. One could attribute such behaviour to a rational behaviour on the part of the murderer. The neo-classical school of thought in criminology regards a criminal as a person who acts out of free will and choice, especially as one who acts rationally: Maximum gain and minimum loss. Therefore, when the individual has nothing to lose, as he thinks, any act would lead only to gain. The gain in such cases can stem from various psychological motives, like vengeance, or a martyr acquiring respect, or causing inconvenience to others. This approach is supported by the frustration-aggression theory, as the mass murderer aspires to regain, even if it is for a moment, a certain control over his life, when his deeds seem to him rational versus the frustrations he has experienced.

This approach emphasized two motives for a mass murder: A need for control and vengeance. In addition, the American Ministry of Justice, in its instruction for the courts, refers to morbidity and even to a lack of mental balance as motives for these actions, but there is no reference or psychological explanation for these statements. What is worse is the logical contradiction by claiming on the one hand that the murderer acts rationally and at the same time referring to mental morbidity. I would formulate it in other words: The murderer acts rationally according to his mental disorders. If he hears voices and hallucinates (psychosis), then he reacts rationally to these stimuli (the American Ministry of Justice, 1996).

Mullen's Explanation (2004)

Mullen opposes approaches that present a list of common characteristics of mass murderers as an etiological explanation for a mass murder. According to Mullen, our understanding of the phenomenon should come from the connection among the different components in the potential mass murderer's life experience. For instance, the social limitations of lack of interpersonal social skills, isolation and active detachment from relations with others which are partly an outcome of deeper elements, and partly the reason for the psychological limitations of suspiciousness and resentment toward the familial and larger social environment. Characteristics, like narcissism and a will to impress, may direct the resentment the individual feels to a struggle or an active fight, whereas obsessive characteristics contribute to persistence which is essential for planning and executing the murderous act. His opinion is that despair, regarding their lives and the world they live in, is an important part of the motive of mass murder. On the one hand, the murderers' (men) access to firearms provides the means, while haphazardness and chance provide the final ignition that leads to action, on the other.

One can see how the researcher integrates in his approach the concept of catalysts, as used by Fox and Levin (2005) in presenting the three characteristics of a mass murder. Nevertheless, it is difficult to accept his perception about haphazardness and chance, versus the data that show meticulous preliminary planning prior to the execution of a mass murder. Therefore, the more suitable term would have been opportunity which leads to the realization of the action.

Mullen refers to mass murder as self-generated: A mass murder that has been created mainly out of the personal problems and positions of the murderer. Holmes and Holmes (1998) called it an "internal motive." Hence, a mass murder is not a sudden and haphazard event of violence, although it is presented as such in the media. Most of the mass murderers have a clear motive of vengeance, and they choose only victims who have hurt them, according to their perception. Alternatively, they would look for victims who symbolize for them the original factor which had abused, humiliated or frustrated them, according to their random availability. In this context, one can refer to the explanation of the rational choice theory and the routine activity theory, when the murderer chooses the most vulnerable and available victims for committing his acts.[29]

As much as the element of vengeance is specific and focused, the outburst is expected to be planned and systematic, rather than spontaneous and haphazard. Furthermore, as the targets for vengeance are more specific, it is less expected that the murderer's anger stems from a severe mental disorder, like a psychosis (Fox & Levin, 2003). There seems to be a contradiction here: On the one hand, it is about a self-generated murder, and on the other it says that the murderer's anger does not stem from a severe mental disorder.

A central component that is missing in this explanation is the linkage between the environment and the personality of the murderer, like the reference to the issue of catalysts by Fox and Levin (2005). An external event, like a divorce or a dismissal, should have been linked with a certain kind of personality so that the individual would react with a fatal fury. This kind of explanation could have prevented the criticism: Not everyone who is fired or loses custody over his children becomes a mass murderer, but only in those whose personality structure supports a fertile ground for it. This analysis enables us to see how the whole of the features or characteristics that have been described integrate together in creating the final event of a mass murder.

One of the outstanding problems of the psychological explanations for a mass murder stems from the very small number of events of this kind and the lack of sufficient research and theoretical literature. When there is an attempt to present a psychological explanation for the phenomenon, it is done on the basis of a single case study. Looking for the common denominators of different single cases is the only basis for an etiological explanation of mass murder.

When examining the cases presented in the literature, one can see three factors that integrate together in a mass murder:

- Difficult situations of frustration in the familial, academic, social, or occupational fields, when the individual blames others for his failures and feels depressed;

- A dramatic event that is perceived as a loss or a threat of losing a close person;
- Lack of social support which would have been enabled coping with each of the aforementioned events or with a combination of them.

The central component that is missing in order to distinguish between those who experience these three components and do not become murderers, and those who commit a mass murder, exists in a personality disorder among those individuals, so that these components fall on a distorted personality to begin with. In addition, there is a theoretical problem that stems from the fact that people with a suicidal disposition that comes from depression, do not tend to be violent toward others, while in the cases under discussion, there is a combination of internalized and externalized violence due to the murderer's readiness to commit suicide, either by himself or by proxy, after executing the murder.

Summary of the Characteristics and Explanations

One can see that the phenomenon of mass murder is not a new one, and its roots existed in ancient cultures, but its highly frequent appearance in certain cultures points to the cultural connection. There is a chart of external events which serves as the main cause for most mass-murder cases (divorce, loss of custody over children, dismissal). But a mass murder would take place only among individuals with a certain personality structure who suffer from psychological and social deficiencies. This serves as a background for perceiving these events as unbearable and despairing, until they feel they have nothing to lose by executing the murders. That is, the important thing is the murderer's subjective perception of the threatening situation, rather than an objective view of the threat (Lofland, 1969). The psychological autobiography of the individual, together with sociocultural aspects, would dictate the perception of his situation over a given period of time, especially after a meaningful traumatic event in his life.

The rise of individualism, together with the decrease of communality, tends to lead the mass murderer to blame others, especially those who are connected in his consciousness with failures and difficulties in his life, as the ones who prevented him from achieving the goals of society.[30] Therefore, unlike the myth, most victims were known to the murderer. This aspect led many scientists to refer to the motive of vengeance and settling accounts as the main motive in a mass murder. According to Brantley and Hosky (2005), when a depression is externalized, together with symptoms of fermentation and thoughts of hurting others, there is a greater chance that the individual would execute a murder and would not commit suicide.

One can say that the murderer externalizes his anger and despair by blaming others, and due to his feeling that he has nothing to lose he would tend to commit suicide on his own accord, or as a response to the security forces. Therefore, one can attribute mass murderers an egotistical act of suicide,[31] when the mass murderer plans to die and take many people with him.

Only a fifth of the mass murderers murder strangers because they belong to a specific social group, or to humanity as a whole, a group they regard as responsible for their troubles. In these cases they would choose victims who belong to the same social group, or indiscriminately hurt every human being. The psychosis explanation is valid only for this phenomenon.

The picture that appears from studies on this subject (Levin, 2008) is that the absolute majority of the mass murderers have an interest in controlling and restoring a certain order, following an event that serves as a catalyst. The catalyst makes the murderer feel a loss of control over his life (divorce, dismissal, loss of money in the stock market) up to a level of a personal tragedy. In order to return to a state of control, the murderer eradicates the people who, to his understanding, are responsible for his personal tragedy. However, the prevailing assumption among scientists is that the source of frustration or humiliation is not in the immediate victim; the victim is the one who physically, socially and emotionally is available for the murderer while the murderer has no practical or emotional option of acting against the original frustrating factor.

It is clear, then, that we can assume, with a certain extent of probability, that the mass murderer accumulated frustrations and humiliations throughout his life, mainly in his childhood, and that a dramatic event served as a catalyst for the outburst of the anger and frustration which accompanied him for a long time beforehand. In certain cases, like a mass murder of pupils and teachers by pupils, it is probable that these pupils experienced frustration and social isolation for a relatively short period of time, but it influenced them in a dramatic way and they expressed it within a short period of time, and maybe even against the object of frustration itself.

In this context, one can refer to the routine activities theory in criminology (Felson & Cohen, 1979), according to which the murderer would choose a victim with the highest vulnerability and availability. This is enabled when more people are active outside of their homes in modern life.

Summary

According to the pattern of the mass murder explanation, there are three components—early disposition, catalysts and promoters; this pattern was found to be correct, and the discussion can be about the content of each component. Nevertheless, one can find agreement among scientists regarding the early disposition (frustrations and humiliations throughout childhood), catalysts (dismissals, divorce and sociocultural contexts), and promoters (detachment from a supporting social system). These characteristics distinguish the mass murderer from other people, and only the combination of the three components, together with a mental distortion, presents a full picture of the etiology for a mass murder.

Table 2: A theoretical chart of the creation of the mass murderer

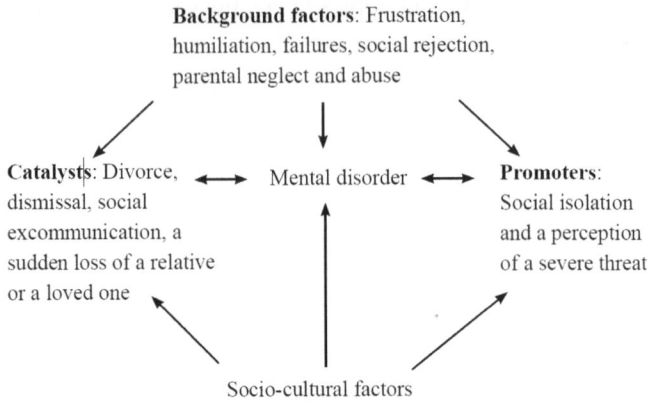

Background factors: Frustration, humiliation, failures, social rejection, parental neglect and abuse

Catalysts: Divorce, dismissal, social excommunication, a sudden loss of a relative or a loved one ⟷ Mental disorder ⟷ **Promoters**: Social isolation and a perception of a severe threat

Socio-cultural factors

The theoretical model summarizes in fact the existing knowledge in the literature.

The background factors may lead to catalysts like dismissal and divorce, due to the experiences and mental disorders that have been created in the mass murderer throughout his childhood. His mental disorder might influence the kind of relationship he would be able to establish in the future with a spouse, and his functioning at work. The catalysts, in turn, might aggravate his mental state.

The mental disorder he suffers from stems from his childhood, but it can influence, and be influenced by promoters, such as social isolation and a severe perception of the threat of every catalyst in his life. At the same time, there are social and cultural factors which influence the catalysts, that is, a tendency toward a high rate of divorce, or a harsh socioeconomic condition which leads to dismissal. These factors also influence the mental disorder from which the murderer suffers, and it has been found that it is culture-dependent. The sociocultural factors influence promoters as well, since certain people perceive their dismissal from work as a significant threat over their identity and their lives, being socially isolated. The same refers to divorce. Both can be perceived as a failure for which the murderer would blame society or specific people in it, rather than himself.

Typologies of Mass Murder

Typology has a theoretical as well as practical great value. It ena-bles a better understanding of a complicated phenomenon, of the motives and the ways of action.[32] Criminology has always aspired to establish a classification of crimes and criminals. Such classifi-cation can be done according to any criterion the researcher de-termines as appropriate: Motive, the criminal's characteristics, the victims' characteristics, the relationship between the criminal and the victims, location, and others. Typology is actually construct-ing a profile. It cannot predict future cases, but it enables us to identify a common denominator of a certain type of crime or crim-inal.

It is problematic to conduct a typology, since in order to make it worthwhile, it has to be reliable in the statistical termi-nology. That is to say, it has to include all the possibilities of the studied phenomenon, but only its obvious characteristics and not beyond it. This problematic nature stems from three origins: First of all, when trying to include all the possibilities, we end up with complicated and highly detailed typologies, and by so doing they do not reach a significant common denominator and make it diffi-cult to identify the phenomenon under discussion. Secondly, some categories overlap, when the case suits more than one group. For instance, when there are several possible motives. Thirdly, some cases do not fit into the different types that have been determined, and then the scientists create a general category which does not tell us anything. Another problem is that sometimes the scientists confuse between motive and characteristics of the criminal when they do not stick to the criterion that was chosen for the typology.

The outstanding scientists in the field of typology of mass murderers are Fox and Levin (2003, 2005). Their argument is that there are typologies for serial murderers (for example, Holmes & DeBurger, 198; Holmes & Holmes, 1998) which are applicable for mass murders. It is clear, then, that they think that one should not establish separate typologies for mass murder and serial murder, but present a typology for multiple-victims murder in general, and show how this typology is applicable for the sub-types of multiple murders. Regarding separate typologies, they criticize overlapping cases of both mass and serial murder, and hence a redundant duplicity is created.

It is my opinion that duplicity does exist, but it should not be defined as such. We have seen that a murder based on an ideological and racial background (sects), nationalistic (terror), or criminal (organized crime), belongs to a separate category of a mass-serial murder. There is a significant difference in motive, mainly in the way of action of a suicide bomber on the one hand, and a terrorist who sets a bomb and escapes, on the other. The same refers to similar actions such as terror, hurting people of a certain origin, and other criteria. There is a difference in the factual basis, the way of action, and the criminal thinking, as they are intended to be a one-time event, at the end of which the murderer would lose his ability to continue his action, versus a serial action of a murderer who sees to it that his ability of action would not be denied. The fact that the motive is similar and even identical is not the main characteristic. The way of action and the murderer's characteristics play a much more important role.

My claim is that instead of dealing with these differences, the scientists who support the concept of a multiple murder as a criminal action, preferred not to cope with the problem that was formed by what they call duplicity.

In relation to the question this book presents regarding the justification for including or preferring a distinction between a mass murder and a serial murder, I will present at first typologies which have been suggested by different scientists regarding a mass murder with the criticism of these typologies. Most typologies aspire to classify the different motives of mass murder, while others classify the cases according to different characteristics, such as frequency, victim-criminal relationship, and others (Petee, Padgett & York, 1997; Levin & Fox, 1991, 1994, 2001; Holmes & Holmes, 1996; Dietz, 1986; Rappaport, 1988).

Petee, Padgett and York (1997) survey two early attempts of establishing a categorization of a mass murder, and later they suggested their typology. They published their article eight years before the publication of Fox and Levin's article (2005). Hence I will compare their typology with that of Fox and Levin which will be presented afterwards.

Dietz (1986) was perhaps a pioneer in an attempt to establish a typology of a mass murder. According to Dietz, most mass murderers fit into one of the three types. Dietz's types do not deal with motive, but with the characteristics of the murder and the murderer.

- Family annihilator—these mass murderers murder every family member in their environment at the time of the murder, and tend to commit suicide afterwards. They express symptoms of depression and paranoia, and may be drunk at the time of executing the felony. But the use of drugs and alcohol has not been found as a characteristic of mass murderers. This type suits the type of vengeance or loyalty, presented by Fox and Levin (2012), Bowers et al. (2010).

- Pseudocommando—these murderers are enthusiastic about weapons and execute the mass murder after a lot of planning. Some of them provoke the police to kill them (suicide by proxy), showing a suicidal tendency, although research has shown that an enthusiasm of weapons characterize many mass murderers, not just this type. This group mainly suits the type with a motive of power (and excitement) that was determined by Fox and Levin (2012), but it can suit other types of terror and vengeance as well.

- Set-and-run or hit-and-run—mass murderers who belong to this group use techniques, such as demolition charges or poisoning so that they would be able to escape before the victims actually die. This type suits, to a certain extent, to what Fox and Levin classified as terror. But it was found that most mass murderers, even those who act as terrorists, tend to watch the death of their victims while they are at the scene of the event.

As I have indicated, this category does not characterize a mass murder, but a mass-serial murder. The motive and the goal are identical, but the way of action is totally different.

When we speak about murderers who leave bombs rather than suicide bombers, there is a high probability that the terrorist would repeat his actions again and again.

Holmes and Holmes (1996) developed two categories of an allegedly mass murder, but they, too, do not refer to the motive.

- Admiring follower/pupil—this murderer is under the influence of a charismatic leader and commits the murder out of a need to be accepted by the leader. This type suits the group of loyalty according to Fox and Levin (2005) which characterize mainly sect members. The members of the sect are prepared not only to murder others out of unrestrained loyalty to the leader, but even commit suicide, as did the sect members of David Koresh. Originally, this category was rightfully determined by the scientists as a kind of a serial murder rather than a mass murder. If the sect members, for example, family members of the Manson family, execute repeated actions out of obedience to the leader, or as attempts to appease him, then it is a serial murder. On the other hand, a one-time action of injury within a certain social category out of readiness to die for this action would be considered as a mass murder. Therefore, this group suits more the third type of murder which I called a "mass-serial murder."

- An embittered worker—this mass murderer takes revenge after being fired from his job, or after he was treated badly by his employer, as he sees it. This group appears at Fox and Levin (2005) under the category of vengeance (and also an aspiration for power to some extent). The worker kills employers and co-workers alike, and, therefore, this case suits the type of a mass murder.

Petee, Padgett and York (1997) claim that the early typologies they have surveyed are not sufficient for several reasons: Only part of them deals with criminal-victim relationship and the execution technique. In addition, in part of them there is a merger of several types of mass murderers under one category. For example, the youngster who murdered 14 people and injured six others among the post office workers in Oklahoma in 1986 can be classified as a pseudocommando, but also as an embittered worker. On the other hand, there are mass murderers who do not fit at all into the presented categories, like a mass murder after executing an armed robbery, or a murder between gangs.

It is my opinion that these categories, as a suggestion for a typology that should classify all the characteristic or motives of mass murderers and mass murders, are indeed insufficient. But as we have seen, this problem is typical not only for the early typologies, but for the most up-to-date ones as well (for example, Fox & Levin, 2005). In addition, part of the suggested categories belongs to a mass-serial murder and not to mass murder.

Petee, Padgett and York (1997) suggest a typology of their own which refers solely to cases of mass murder that have taken place in public places in the sixties of the twentieth century. The rationale is that a murder that meets this definition gained great exposure, and therefore we can know many details about the event and the executor. They add that a mass murder in the family is always motivated by reasons of vengeance or conflict. These scientists present a typology of eight categories of mass murderers which is based on a motive.

Prior to presenting the typology, there appears a significant problem. Pete, Padgett and York (1997) refer to a mass murder solely in public places. Therefore, according to their assumptions, the typology cannot be a comprehensive typology. Here are the categories these scientists specify:

- Avenging specific people—it was found that 12%[33] of the mass murderers tried to avenge specific people, people who were known to the criminal and wronged him, as he perceived it.

- Avenging a specific target—about 13% of the mass murderers chose a defined place for executing the murder in advance. Instead of designating a specific person, they designated a specific location for executing the vengeance. The site which was usually chosen as the target was an agency or organization which had authority or control over the criminal, or that he was subjugated to them in the past. The murderer makes a symbolic connection between the site and the anger he feels, and chooses to conduct the murder specifically in this place (campus, school, or a place of work).

- Vengeance of diffused targets—about seven percent of the mass murderers chose diffused and general targets with no special classification. In certain cases the linkage the criminal had to the victim or to the location was quite indirect. Although anger consists as a motive for murder, the target is diffusive. For instance, some mass murderers choose a category of people. In these cases, the designated victims are defined in terms of belonging to a certain social group. They do not have any connection with the murderer; they are just a convenient target (for example, eight random prostitutes in a certain city).

In the three first types, defined by the scientists as "vengeance," we can see how an overspecification might be problematic in a typology. The specification was meant, and rightfully so, to ensure that it would include and represent reality in a reliable way. I expanded on it when discussing the primary and secondary motives for a mass murder. But the scientists created a redundant classification in the general type of vengeance or anger, for example, the second type of mass murder, suggested by Petee, Padgett and York, that occurs in a specific place or a site. It is clear that in the chosen location there are targets and the murder is directed at them, but why do the scientists need such a category? If it is about a place, like a workplace, then it is included already in the first category, and even in the third (workers whom the murderer does not know who are victims just because they are part of the company from which the murderer was fired). The scientists' will to have a thorough typology is positive, but they created an over-specification that is unnecessary. In addition, they do not bring examples for demonstrating the different types, and by so doing they make the classification awkward and damaging its reliability.

- Familial/Romantic—it was found that five percent of the mass murderers direct the murder against family members or against people for whom they have a romantic interest. In spite of the similarity to anger or vengeance, we can still refer to these cases as a distinguished category. The gap between the known rate of murder of families (40% out of the total mass murders) and the low rate that is reported here is explained by the scientists as a result of the fact that they refer only to mass murders that have been executed in public places. They claim that a murder with a romantic background is relevant also to this type, because it is similar to a murder of families. The "fatal attraction" focuses though, in most cases, on a specific person, but it is expanded sometimes to friends or relatives of the victim and even witnesses that happened to be there.

It is my opinion that there is room to refer to the annihilation of families as a separate type of mass murder, not only because it is, as has been indicated, about 40% of the total cases of mass murder, but due to its clear and special nature. Nevertheless, one can see the problematic nature of this typology when the scientists confuse diagnoses classified according to motive with those related to victims. If we deal with criteria of motive, then the classifications of vengeance or loyalty already encompass the killing of families as types of mass murder. On the other hand, if we refer to victims, then the killing of families appears already as a separate type in relation to the specific choice of the victims to whom the murderer attributes hurt, insult and so on. Therefore, the scientists should have decided in advance the criteria for the classification of mass murder with no duplication.

- Immediate Conflict—about four percent of mass murders have a background of an immediate conflict, like a debate or a quarrel. This situation differs from a situation of anger/vengeance, in which the murderer postpones the execution of the murder. This category speaks of a simple and immediate confrontation, like a dispute between drivers. This category contradicts, to some extent, the explanations given by other scientists who indicated that unlike an interpersonal conflict which develops quickly, a mass murder requires relatively long planning and preparation. All the same, this category is important in relation to cases of an especially violent person, who suffers from severe mental disorders, and reacts by an immediate mass murder that is ignited by an interpersonal conflict. Unfortunately, the scientists do not bring examples for their argument. As far as I know, even when there is a dispute based on an interpersonal background, in most known cases, at least in Israel, there is no mass murder, but a murder of a single victim. The dispute can ignite over parking, a romantic issue in a pub, and so on. Alternately, such an event can take place among gangs, but then the classification is of a mass-serial murder.

- Mass Murder in Connection with Another Felony—thirty-six percent of the public mass murders have been executed in connection with property felonies (mainly robbery). The murder stems from a will to kill the witnesses of a robbery, or as a result of a loss of control and entering a state of panic. Usually, these murder cases are executed by a few criminals, and therefore this type was ignored in the past.

This category is also problematic as being classified as a mass murder. The fact that the murderer murders the witnesses in order not to be identified and caught proves his intention to continue his criminal behaviour in the future. It is obvious, then, that this category better suits the definition of a mass-serial murder rather than a mass murder. Sometimes the murder follows another felony, so the murder was not the goal in the first place.

- A Gang-Style Motive—This mass murder consists of about six percent of the total cases of mass murders in public places, and it is characterized mainly by murdering while driving. It is distinguished from a murder that is based on an interpersonal conflict when the murderers belong to a gang. It is usually executed by a number of murderers and is characterized by organization and planning which are common in gang activity.

This type of mass murder can stem from a number of reasons: A quarrel between gangs about a territory of influence (like drug trafficking and collecting protection money); vengeance of one gang against another due to a previous murder, and other reasons. That is to say, the motive can be expressive, like vengeance; or instrumental, like the control over a zone of action. Beyond the fact that there are several motives, this type is similar to the previous one by being connected to another felony. One solution could be to create a category of murder that includes a criminal background. Then we would be able to generalize the previous type and the current one under one category, or alternatively, both types can be classified as murder executed by an organized crime organization, as in a murder following a robbery. There are usually several perpetrators.

But the scientists ignore here an additional type of mass murder which can be attributed to organized crime, i.e., crime organizations which have a permanent team, a hierarchical conformation, compartmentalization, and so on. All these make crime organizations operate on a continuous basis, allowing organized crime to deliver ad hoc for the purpose of executing a single felony.

Hence, we see that the solution is to distinguish between organized crime which leads to a mass murder, and the crime organizations which cause such a murder. In both cases the motives can be similar, expressive (like vengeance for disrespect) or instrumental (taking over a territory). But this solution is also problematic, since a gang is also an organization, and then we have to speak about a different range of organization in a gang and in organized crime, like the Mafia or other organized crime.

In any case, we speak here about a mass-serial murder based on the execution of another felony, and its sub-types could be: Single, team, gang, representative of members in a crime family, and a crime family. One has to notice that this is the same trap the scientists have fallen into unintentionally: If the typology we conduct is according to motive, then we have to decide whether these felonies stem from vengeance or from a will to gain a material profit. After determining the motive, we can indicate the characteristics of the operators. At this stage, for instance, under the type of vengeance, we could find a variety of mass-serial murder cases which have been executed by individuals, teams or crime organizations. The same refers to murder events which have been executed for the purpose of profit. The important thing is to define the index for creating a typology and make the classification consistently. Therefore, I tend to define a murder of this type as a third type of a multiple-victims murder which is not a mass murder but a mass-serial one, and hence it does not suit this typology.

- A Political Motive—the scientists claim that an absolute majority of the mass-murder cases belong to terror acts, but an accurate examination shows that terror holds only about ten percent of the cases. They did not refer to the fact that in a terror event the number of victims can reach thousands.

A unique characteristic of these events is that the criminal is not always at the scene at the time of the murder. According to Mullen (2004) and Petee, Padgett and York (1997), this is in sharp contrast with the previously mentioned mass murder events, in which the criminals were personally involved in the act of the murder. They distinguish between a personal involvement when personal attendance is or is not obligatory (organized crime/terrorists' distributors).

I think one can find many examples of cases in which a mass murder was an act of terror, when the murderer was at the scene and intended to commit suicide, as in the attack on the Twin Towers in the USA, Palestinian suicide bombers in shopping malls and entertainment centers in Israel, and others. These mass murders are based on terror, but in many cases terror can be classified as mass-serial murder, especially when the murderer is not at the scene, since his intention is to go on executing such actions in the future. That is, only terror events at which there is a suicide bomber would be defined as a mass murder.

- Unclassified Cases—about seven percent of the cases have not been classified due to obscurity of the motive of the felony. The mass murderers in these cases are defined as irrational and as suffering from psychopathology (Non-Specific Motive).

The scientists' argument about a Non-Specific Motive is accepted well, because only the criminal knows his motive for the action. Often scientists draw conclusions about the motive, although the murderer committed suicide, and in many cases it is impossible to identify the real motive. Looking for a motive for the suicide through a post mortem: We can assume what the motive was based on conversations with friends and relatives, but generally speaking, we would never know for sure what the catalyst was that caused the materialization of the suicide. All the same, the scientists' claim that this is a case of a mental pathology seems a little ridiculous. In most cases, where a person murders his beloved children, or his former co-workers, after having planned his acts meticulously and waited for the right opportunity, there must be some kind of pathology, otherwise it would not have been an exception, but the rule. It is true that there are situations of a momentary anger which is not pathological, but then it would not have been a case of planning and equipping with arms in advance.

Another problem with this category is that its general definition—unclassified cases—can become a tool for putting in all cases which do not fit into the suggested typology, and when you have such a situation, the typology does no longer exclude, neither it is thorough.

In surveying the typological development of a multiple murder from the mid-eighties, Mullen (2004) indicates similar typologies to the aforementioned, but the classification he conducts is not done according to motive, but according to the characteristics of the murderers: Family annihilators; taking advantage of a criminal opportunity, an avenger in class, and pseudocommando. As a matter of fact, it is hard to see significant differences between these categories and their predecessors, as, for instance, it is not clear what the difference is between family annihilators as a "motive" or as a "characteristic." Kelleher and Kelleher (1997) suggest a typology of three categories, in which the criterion for classification is the choice of victims:

- Specific Victims—cases in which murders have been planned in advance in order to hurt certain victims. For example, murder of a family, murder by sect members and murder by gangs. The scientist does not refer to the motive, but there is a hint of a motive of vengeance.
- Mass Instrumental Murder—mass murder consists of a means for promoting the goals of the murderer. Even if certain victims have been selected, it is due to their belonging to a certain social category.

This category encompasses murder for the purpose of terror, or a mass murder which is secondary to other criminal activity. The scientist speaks about actual cases where the murder was executed out of a motive of profit or terror. The victims were unknown to the murderer yet they were not random, but selected due to their belonging to a social group of witnesses, or a certain ethnic group. According to this type, it is unclear whether the criterion for classification is selecting the victims or the motive.

- Massacre—an indiscriminate killing with the central goal of murdering people as people. The victims are selected randomly, but they can belong to a large social group. The term massacre is supposed to serve cases in which there is an indiscriminate shooting, like in a shopping mall or a campus. But the literature survey shows that this is quite a rare phenomenon. In most cases, of shooting in concentrated population, a major part of the victims were known to the murderer.

We have here a typology with an innovation of trying to distinguish among the types of mass murder according to familiarity or unfamiliarity between the murderer and the victims, as well as according to the selection of the victims. But as a typology, it does not enable identification and a clear distinction among different types of mass murder, both in light of the motive and in light of the characteristics of the murderer. It confuses sometimes between motive and characteristics, and between both of them and the selection of victims.

Fox and Levin (2003, 2005) present a typology of a multiple murder and conduct a comparison between a mass murder and a serial murder. According to them, one can create a common typology that is based on five categories of motives which have been presented in different typologies in the past: Power, vengeance, loyalty, material profit and terror.

- Power—in part of the mass murderers, the sense of power and control is dominant as a motive for murdering. The expression of this motive is especially outstanding in the category of pseudo-commando. The mass murderers who belong to this category go out dressed up in fighting uniform, armed with firearms, expressing a passion for the symbols of power. Sometimes, the motive of power accompanies a motive of excitement. For example, Knight, 19, executed in 1987 a murderous armed attack in Australia, killed seven people and injured 18 others. This youngster was obsessive about power, and pictured himself as a war hero.

In my opinion the existence of two motives at the same time harms the typology's distinction capability. In reality there may be combinations of a few motives in a mass murder, but the goal of a good typology is to separate among the different motives. In fact, we may argue that each motive implies that there is excitement involved. Hence the questions that come up are: What is the main motive, and whether excitement is a motive for a mass murder per se, or it is just an accompanied feeling to the motive of power. I think that excitement is a motive in and of itself. We can find support for this in quite another field of criminology. In the sociological theories of the positivist school, Miller (1958) describes the criminal behaviour of adolescents from the low class as built on several "focuses of interest," which compose their unique culture. One of the focuses of interest is a search for excitement as a motive for the execution of felonies. In addition, presenting power as a distinguished motive is problematic in relation to mass murder, since many times the motives involved are power and vengeance at the same time, and one cannot always distinguish between them. The opposite is also correct: Cases of mass murder committed allegedly out of a motive of vengeance also conceal a motive of achieving a sense of power, as happens sometimes in a mass murder at school. A pupil, or pupils, perceived as "square" or weak, executes a mass murder for the sake of vengeance, but also for the sake of creating an image of power and control. For instance, in April 1999, Harris, 18, and Klebold, 17, armed themselves with pistols and explosives and arrived at the high school in Colorado where they were studying to celebrate Hitler's birthday. They murdered 12 pupils and a teacher, and the students they murdered were considered highly popular at school. Again, one can see two motives playing a role at the same time, and as has been mentioned, we should refer to a primary and a secondary motive accordingly.

A more recent case is the one of a Finnish student, aged 20 who murdered nine students in 23.9.09. He tried to commit suicide afterwards but did not die of his wounds. A filmstrip that was distributed by him on the Internet said: "All life is a war and all life is pain, and you fight alone your personal war."[34] In November 2007 a Finnish high school student, 18, shot to death eight students before committing suicide. He was described as a rejected child, a lone wolf who received a "hooligan and humiliating attitude" on the part of his classmates.[35]

Vengeance—Mass murderers are motivated by vengeance as well, vengeance that can be directed at individuals (individual specific), or at society as a whole (nonspecific). The mass murderer is usually interested in getting back at people he knows, such as family members, a former employer or co-workers, teachers and classmates at school or at the university. When dealing with the killing a family, we speak about a concept of murder by proxy, meaning that the victims are selected because they are identified with the main goal against which the vengeance is directed. For example, a father may slaughter his children since he sees them as an expansion of his ex-wife whom he wants to avenge. For instance, in 1987 a man called Simmons murdered his entire family, including his grandchildren, aiming to avenge his wife for rejecting his attempt to have sex with her. The classical play of Medea, mentioned above, also belongs to this context.

Regarding a mass murder in a workplace, a worker who has been fired may murder his employer, against whom the vengeance is directed, but also his co-workers whom he sees as an expansion of his employer. In 1986 for example, in Oklahoma, USA, a postman named Sherrill murdered 14 post office workers because he was reprimanded and threatened of being fired by his employer. He aimed at exterminating everybody who was identified with his employer.

While the two types described above have to do with the selection of specific victims for specific reasons, part of the mass murderers who are motivated by vengeance feel enmity toward a whole category of individuals, especially in the domain of race, nationality, religion, origin or gender which is perceived by the murderer as responsible for his difficulties in life. For example, in 1989, 14 female engineering students were murdered at the University of Montreal in Canada by a man named *Lépine*, an engineer that held a grudge against feminists. In April 2007, a massacre took place at Virginia Tech, taking 32 victims, both students and lecturers. The mass murderer, Seung-Hui Cho, 23, was born in the USA to South Korean parents. His classmates at the university and at high school described him as a loner. He murdered two students in the dormitories, and after a short while went on to the class buildings and murdered 30 other victims. In his room there was a letter in which he attacked the corrupted and the privileged. In this case we can see that the murderer did not shoot at everyone who was in his way, and spared the lives of those whom he regarded as not belonging to the hated category. In 1973–1974, fourteen white people were murdered in the USA by a group of black Muslims. These Muslims defined the victims as "blue-eyed devils." A similar murder with a racial background was executed in 2000 by Baumhammers, an unemployed lawyer with severe hatred toward immigrants from developing countries; he murdered five immigrants.

Very seldom do mass murderers execute a murder as a result of a paranoid perception of society as a whole. In these cases there is a psychotic personality, such as with Hennard, who hated humanity at large and suspected that almost everyone had evil intentions toward him. In 1991, he drove his distribution truck deliberately into a window of a cafeteria in Texas, and started firing indiscriminately at the customers who were having lunch. Twenty-one people were murdered in this event.

Vengeance is also the main motive in a number of massacres which have taken place at schools, as of 1996. In the absolute majority of the cases, the young mass murderers (a relatively rare phenomenon) felt rejected and alienated from their peers and decided on revenge. In 1998, for instance, Golden, 11, and Johnson, 13, pressed the fire alarm button at their school. When pupils and teachers started running out of the classes, these two started shooting at them. Four pupils and a teacher were killed in the event. One of the murdered was a girl of 11 years old who had separated lately from Golden. In May, 1998, Kinkel, 15, arrived at his school armed with a semiautomatic gun, and turned the school cafeteria into a murder scene. It happened the day after he was suspended from school. In the morning he murdered his two parents at home, after having accusing them for arguing that he was not as brilliant as his big brother, and at school he murdered two pupils.

Another mass murder took place in a high school in Cleveland, USA, in 10.10.07. A boy of 14 with a history of mental problems, murdered two pupils and a teacher and then committed suicide. Coon had been suspended from school two days earlier, and arrived with two pistols. He had tried to commit suicide a year prior to the event. A few pupils reported that the boy threatened to blow up the school a few days before the murder. One of the boys even said that Coon had said that if he would execute a murder at school, he would not hurt some of them.

Fox and Levin (2003) indicate that a mass murder takes place at schools for several reasons: First, the long learning hours can cause the development of risks and problematic issues. Secondly, the children are gathered in great numbers and it might cause a conflict. Third, the school system can, sometimes, nurture feelings of inadequacy, anxiety, fear, hostility, rejection, and boredom. For extremely alienated or vengeful children, school can serve as an ideal place, logistically and symbolically, for expressing vengeance. One should remember that school is a place of learning, but there are also characteristics of power and control.

It is my opinion that mass murder at schools gets nonproportional publication in the media, in the same way that school violence has started to receive more and more exposure. From this respect, one may speak about a phenomenon of a "moral panic" the media arouse in the public. When examining cases of mass murder, according to the total number of victims, the events at schools do not stand out in their large number of victims, but rather the other way around. The media magnify these events, maybe because they deal with children. The same attitude can be seen in relation to serial murder: When the victims were from the margins of society, the coverage was poor, while when the victims were from the middle class, like girl students, the coverage was very dramatic. Furthermore, vengeance as a category is indeed a significant motive for murder, but as has been mentioned, not always can one distinguish between vengeance and other motives, like power and control.

- Loyalty—Fox & Levin, 1998, 2003, 2005 refer to the following motives as instrumental rather than expressive. That is, in the eyes of the murderer, the murder serves as a necessary means for achieving a desired goal. Part of the murderers get inspiration to murder by a distorted idea of love and fidelity which is expressed as an ambition to save their loved ones from misery and difficulties. For instance, some of those who murder their families are separated husbands or fathers who are depressed due to the lot of the family unit. As a result, they murder their ex-wives and children aiming to protect them, as it were, from the pain and suffering they are about to experience in their lives. For example, in 1990, a father, Elizalde, was fired from his job. He was described by his friends as a dedicated father. He was afraid that the dismissal would bring about transferring the five children to the custody of his separated wife, and therefore he murdered them in their sleep and afterwards committed suicide. This concept is called, as has already been mentioned, a murder by proxy. It can be assumed that the murderer's assumption was that murdering them would bring about their spiritual reunion in a better life after death.

The argument of Fox & Levin, 2003, 2005 is that this category expresses an instrumental motive rather than an expressive one, is problematic. One can indeed refer to the extermination of the family out of a hope for a united life after death as a goal, but the claim that there is no significant emotional motive here is a mistake. Moreover, Fox & Levin define the motive as the will to save the family members from suffering and pain. So, does it not express a deep feeling toward the family members? A feeling can be positive or negative.

According to Messing & Heeren (2004), and Fox & Levin (2003, 2005) part of the cases of familial massacre confuse, to a certain extent of ambivalence, both vengeance and loyalty. Like the case that took place in 1991, in which Colbert, 39, strangled his wife to death, and then murdered their three daughters in order to prevent them from becoming orphans, and then committed suicide. At the end of October 2008, a police officer in Israel murdered his wife who was a police woman, his little son and his baby daughter, and then committed suicide. The background for this deed has not been found yet.

One of the outstanding questions that appears here, as in other motives which are presented in the typology, is how do the scientists know what the motive was and what were the thoughts that passed through the murderer's mind in a case of suicide. In almost all cases, the murderer did not share his decision and motives with others, and therefore we speak only about assumptions. Furthermore, the scientists argue that part of the cases belong to two motives. Reality is, of course, more complicated than any typology which has a large extent of artificiality, but why do the scientists not choose to expand the typology so that it would include integrated motives as well? Alternately, why do the scientists not try to define what is the primary motive and what is the secondary one in these cases? In this way, every typology would have a primary and a secondary motive. In cases where there is no secondary motive, it would be simpler, whereas in the aforementioned case, for instance, the primary motive would be loyalty and the secondary would be vengeance. In a similar way, in the vengeance category, one can see vengeance as the primary motive, with different secondary motives.

Hickey (1992) claims that a multiple murder that is executed by sect members reflects, partly, the will of the followers, or the pupils, to express their loyalty to the leader they admire. In these cases they would murder because their messenger dictated it. This loyalty cab be expressed in a mass-serial murder, like the case of the Manson family, or the collective suicide in the case of the

Koresh sect in 1993, when 80 of the sect members committed suicide upon the instruction of the leader.

In this category it also does not necessarily seem either instrumental or expressive. Loyalty, like vengeance, expresses an emotion toward the other person, and therefore it can be seen as motivated by an expressive motive. The Koresh sect members, for instance, did not expect that their suicide would do something positive, but they did it as a demonstration of admiration and love to their spiritual leader. Although this book does not discuss terror as a motive, it should be indicated that even suicide bombers who execute terrorist acts against Israeli population, do so under the inspiration of their spiritual leaders, their goal being to kill as many Jews as possible which can be called an instrumental motive. It is true that their suicide also has to do with feelings, like hatred toward Jews and loyalty to the leader. Their motive and act of mass murder are intended to defined goals: Terror, protest and vengeance.

In addition, as I have mentioned, part of the cases are cases of mass-serial murder, rather than a mass murder, when out of admiration to the leader, the sect members would perform repeated actions of hurting a certain social group.

- Material Profit—in this category the motive of the mass murderer is financial profit. The assumption is that the murderers kill the victims after robbing them, but most cases deal with armed robbery, and then they murder the victims who witnessed the crime. This is what happened, for example, when three robbers burst into a club in Seattle in 1983, robbed the owner and murdered systematically 13 people by shooting them in the head. These people just happened to be there and witnessed the robbery.

It is my opinion that a murder meant to get rid of the witnesses of a criminal act (mainly an armed robbery) is not done for the sake of material or financial profit, but for the sake of preventing being caught by the police after the witnesses give identifying details about them. Therefore, this motive should have been called a murder as an attachment to another crime (mainly robbery). Moreover, the action points to the fact that it is a mass-serial murder, and not a mass murder, since the robbers kill the witnesses in order to be able to execute other robberies in the future. When a murderer takes the lives of company workers in order to steal a great amount of money, we can say that this is a mass-serial murder from a material motive, since in this case, the murder is the only way for the robber to get rid of the armed workers and execute the robbery, whereas killing witnesses of a crime is not meant to enable the execution of the crime. At the same time, it is agreed that the motive is instrumental and not expressive.

- Terror—Newton, (2006) and Fox & Levin (2003, 2005) indicate that certain cases of mass murder are actually terror acts, when the murderers "send a message" through the murder. For example, members of the Manson family tried to inflame a racial war between blacks and whites when they wrote with the blood of the victims, in the estate of the actress Sharon Tate in 1969, "Death to the pigs" intending to make the authorities think that the murder was committed by black people

The motive here can be called hatred based on racial background, or as a primary motive of xenophobia, indicating vengeance as a secondary category. In any case, it does not seem right to use the term terror here, especially as it is known to us in Israel. Furthermore, this action characterizes a mass-serial murder rather than a mass murder. To sum up, when examining the different typologies that have been suggested in relation to mass murder, one can identify a few problems:

Some of the typologies that have been suggested classify cases of mass murder according to motive. The problem in these cases is that one motive, like vengeance, appears in several categories. For example, a man who murders his family and commits suicide avenging his separated wife; a man who murders his employer and co-workers after being fired, a gang avenges another gang by shooting while driving, and a terrorist who commits suicide in order to kill many Jews because a relative of his was killed by Jews.

Defining the motive: The motive of loyalty, as can be seen in the following cases: A father who murdered his family out of loyalty to his children after losing custody over them, or a suicide bomber who murders out of loyalty to his dispatchers. The problem is that the scientists do not bother to define the motive, and so in many cases there is neither agreement nor understanding of the nature of the motive under discussion. There is no clear definition of motives like vengeance, power, and so on.

In some cases the scientists claim that in addition to a motive like vengeance, there is another motive of excitement (Fox & Levin, 2003, 2005). This claim is also deficient: Is there no excitement in a fight between gangs? It seems that the scientists confuse between motive and feelings or emotions that accompany the execution of the crime.

A more serious problem is the determination that a mass murder took place, while what actually happened was a mass-serial murder. When a robber kills the witnesses of a crime, his intention is to go on executing robberies, and hence it is a mass-serial murder. This behaviour points out a pattern according to which the robber is not afraid to go on murdering whoever interrupts him in his actions, and the same goes for assassinations among crime families and gangs, as well as some of the activities of terrorists and sects.

The confusion that appears from the typologies reflects the difficulty of referring to the complexity of the phenomenon which consists of a very wide range of motives, victim-criminal relationship, ways of operation and others. It seems one has to suggest a typology which would summarize in a clearer way not only the motives of mass murder, but also the different possibilities of each type. For example, as has already been indicated, one has to relate to the fact that there could be a main motive and a secondary one.

Another strategy used by scientists, was their preference not to choose the motive as the main criterion for classifying cases of mass murder, but rather choose to use clearer and simpler criteria, such as the choosing of the victims, or the murderer-victim relationship, in order to present the common characteristics of mass murder and the mass murderers. Such a typology does not deny the motive as a significant factor, but it enables the creation of a classification free of unnecessary complication. All the same, there is no doubt that the motive of vengeance is one of the outstanding motives for mass murder.

Toward a New Typology of Mass Murder and Mass Murderers

Explaining the Motive

After numerous attempts to create a typology based upon a motive, I realized that the task is very difficult and leads to falling into the same traps or the same flaws I warned from. The main reason for this is that when the motive is the guiding criterion of the classification, it seems that one can attribute one motive to many cases of mass murder, and then the distinction among cases loses its significance. One of the reasons for this is that the existing typologies do not provide a detailed and explicit explanation for each motive. For instance, the will to achieve power or dominance is explained generally as coming from a sense of insult, the individual's lack of control over his life, and so on, but what about vengeance? Vengeance is an abstract and complicated concept, but it is clear that through vengeance the individual experiences a feeling of power and dominance. That means that the motive of power and the motive of vengeance are integrated in one another and one cannot separate them, even if one can distinguish between them. All the same, in the existing typologies they are presented as separate motives. Let us examine, for example, a murder case of an employer and co-workers.

A person who has been fired from his work feels a loss of control over his life. He feels insulted and even humiliated by his employer, and he is afraid of the implications that this dismissal may have on his personal, economical, and familial situation. By murdering his former employer and co-workers, he regains a sense of power: It is not his employer and co-workers who determine his destiny; he is the one who determines the destiny of his employer. Things turned the other way around, but the sense of power the murderer feels is accompanied by a sense of vengeance. The account was settled. If we go on in this way, we find that power and vengeance, as main motives for a mass murder will appear in most types of mass murder: Family murder, murder due to a broken heart, a social category which the murderer blames for his personal failures, murder among gangs, and others. The resulting typology classifies according to the motive among the different and distinguished types of mass murder. This is a disappointing situation, since it does not meet the central question of criminology, as well as in other fields of science, the question of why. What is the motive that makes the individual or individuals arm themselves and kill others? In addition, when there is no option of questioning the murderer about the motive that moved him, as it is in most cases, the motive is concluded through assumption, and there is vast room for error which certainly does not promote our empirical knowledge.

The Law and the Motive

When we turn to the criminal law in Israel, as well as in other countries, we get an interesting picture. The legislator does not refer, in most cases, to the issue of examining the motive for the felony, except in cases in which the motive is explicitly indicated as part of the definition of the felony. The motive for the felony plays a part in the arguments of punishment, but not in determining whether the felony was actually executed. A criminal felony consists of two essential components: One is the factual basis of the felony (actus reus), an act that is included in the definition of criminal felonies, and the second is the circumstance or the result which was caused by the act (paragraph 18 of the criminal law, 1977). In our case, we refer to paragraph 300 of the criminal law which defines a murder felony as prohibited according to the law. The second component is the mental component in the felony, or the demand for a criminal thinking: "A person executes a felony only if he did it with a criminal thinking ..." (paragraph 19 of the criminal law, 1977). That means that in order for it to be considered a criminal felony, there must be a behaviour that is forbidden by law (a deed or a failure to do it), an intention to execute the felony, and the criminal being punishable (sane, not mentally handicapped, and above the minimal age determined by the law).

Let us have a look at the criminal law, paragraph 30037, and examine the attitude of the legislator to the murder felony. Paragraph 300 (2): "Causes deliberate death of a person"; 300 (3): "Causes, with an evil intent, the death of a person through the execution of a felony, or through preparations for executing it, or in order to facilitate its execution"; (4): "Causes the death of a person when another felony was committed, in order to ensure himself, or the one who participated in the execution of that felony, a getaway or an escape from punishment." We can see that short paragraph 4 refers to a motive, such as the elimination of eyewitnesses of the crime the criminal has committed, but on the other hand, short paragraph 2 does not examine at all whether the motive for the murder was out of vengeance, or an ambition for power and control, for example.

Reinforcement to this approach comes from another problem we find in the literature, to which I have referred beforehand: In many cases the motive for the felony is not known for certain, but is concluded or assumed in retrospect. This conclusion can be at times clear and at other times completely vague. Did a student who murdered female engineering students do it out of hatred for feminists? Did he do it due to a broken heart and due to regarding all women as one undesired social category? Did he do it out of motives of achieving power?

As far as the law is concerned, it is sufficient that a mass murder was executed and that the shooter is indeed the murderer. Criminology does not deal with this aspect of the law, but aspires to understand why the mass murder was executed. Therefore, the legal field does not help us in creating a typology, except in the distinction between a mass murderer who kills for purposes of material profit, versus the one who acts out of some psychological motive.

The question is how we can create a typology of mass murder and mass murderers, a typology which would not refer to the motive as the main criterion for classifying the cases, and would enable clear distinctions among the different types. The suggested answer is that the typology would be based upon the different victims of the mass murderers, of their being selected by the mass murderer and their relationships with him. Such typology would enable us to classify the mass-murder cases in more clearly, and through which, it would be possible to find common characteristics and patterns of the victims and even of the murderers in the different categories. It would enable a better and more correct conclusion of the motive for the murder, provided that the typology is exclusive and exhaustive.

The typology would include a terrorist who operates a demolition charge which kills him as well, family annihilators, murderers who kill former employers and co-workers, or a murder of pupils, students, lecturers, and so on. But it would not include murder by sect members, a terrorist who detonates a bomb and escapes, an assassination of regime opponents, eliminations based on an ideological or other background, assassinations by intelligence agencies, and murders among gangs and crime organizations. All the cases that are not included in this typology, and their number of victims exceeds three, would belong to a third type of multiple-victims murder, a mass-serial murder.

The New Typology of Mass Murder and Murderers: According to the Murderer-Victims Relationships; According to the Selection of the Victims

As opposed to the common perception which claims that a mass murder is characterized by the fact that the victims are unknown to the murderer, we can suggest a typology that is based on murderer-victim relationship, a relationship that runs on the range between a close personal and even intimate acquaintance, through to general acquaintance, knowing that the victims belongs to a certain social category, and up to a total stranger.

Holmes and Holmes (1998) created a typology of a serial murder, while referring to a deliberate selection of the victims, versus a random selection. This typology, or at least part of it, can also be adapted to the field of mass murderers. There can be a deliberate selection of victims who are known to the murderer, a selection of strange but specific victims (belonging to a social category), and selecting random strangers (pseudocommando).

The suggested typology can be constructed also through reference to the range of the social units the victims belong to, since everyone belongs to some social unit. Through the way of selecting the victims, one can see how the murderer refers to the range of social units, from the individual level, up to society at large. The typology would include the following types:

- **Individuals in Romantic Relationships with the Murderer**

This group includes broken heart cases that lead to a mass murder of the object of love, but is expanded to the victim's family and friends. The familiarity between the murderer and his victims is high, and the victims are selected in a deliberate and specific way.[36]

The main motive behind this mass murder stems from vengeance for pain experienced by the victim or her family, but there can be an additional motive of achieving power. The murderer annihilates the one who rejected and disappointed him and those who are related to her. The rejection may have strengthened by the family objection of this relationship, and therefore the vengeance is directed toward the family members as well. After the rejection, the murderer wants to avenge not only the one who has rejected him, and her family members, but indirectly other men as well: "If she is not to be mine, no one else would have her."[37] The murderer might commit suicide after his deed, because according to his perception, he lost the object of his love, and there is therefore no reason for him to go on living.

- **Individuals with Family Relations with the Murderer**

This type includes a mass murder of the murderer's family, children and wife. The reason for the murder can be the wife, and the murderer expands it to the children. Sometimes the source is the children, for instance, in cases of murdering mothers. The selection of victims in these cases is deliberate and specific. The main motive is the murderer's feeling that he loses his most beloved ones due to a divorce, infidelity, or shifting custody of the children over to the wife. This murderer is characterized by committing suicide after murdering the family, and hence the component of vengeance still exists but to a smaller extent. He aspires to exterminate the family which is not a family for him anymore, and establish it afresh in another world and under different circumstances. Therefore, the outstanding motives here are power and renewed control.

For example, at the end of June 2008 in Australia, a grandfather murdered his wife and grandchildren with an axe, and wounded his daughter. The background for his act was not clear. In another incident in Australia in the same month, a father murdered his three children and committed suicide.

In October 2008, a police officer in Israel shot his wife, his three-year-old son and his daughter, a baby of two months. The background for the act was not clear, but it was found that the father fired three bullets at his wife, who was a police officer herself, and it is probable that his act was directed mainly against her, maybe due to a suspicion of infidelity or some similar accusation.

- **Individuals who Belong to a Defined Social Group by an Academic-Occupational Status**

This category includes classmates at school or on an academic campus, and former or present co-workers. The source for the mass murder can be a teacher, certain students in class or on campus, or an employer, following a conflict or an insult on the part of the employer or the teacher. The selection of the victims is deliberate and specific, and the murderer would usually spare those he does not regard as having the negative characteristics or behaviours that characterize the rest of the victims. This phenomenon is known mainly in the killing of former employers and co-workers, and it includes victims who are known to the murderer.

The motive for this mass murder stems from a sense of rejection or lack of self-worth which was transmitted to the murderer by his co-workers, classmates, and so on. Through the murder, the murderer regains his self-worth and a sense of power, even if momentarily. Hence the outstanding motives here are vengeance, power and control.

- **Individuals who Belong to a Social Category Which has a Conflict with the Group to Which the Murderer Belongs**

In this case the murderer not necessarily knows his victims. He looks for individuals who belong to a certain social group, toward which he shows a fatal hostility, a hostility which can come from ideological, national, or personal motives. The selection of the victims is random but specific, as in the case when a student murders students or pupils and teachers who are strangers to him just because they are perceived by him as undeserving to live.[38] The outstanding motive in this mass murder is an ideological-social motive.

- **Individuals who are Murdered Due to Citizenship of a Country Which is Perceived by the Murderer as an Enemy**

In this category, the murderer acts out of nationalistic, ideological and even religious motives, as in terror acts. These individuals are strangers to the murder and are murdered only due to their national belonging. In this case, the selection of the victims is also random, but specific. In this category we see suicide bombers, booby-trapped cars that Irish terrorists posted against the British, the terrorist act on the Twin Towers in New York, and the like.

- **Individuals who Belong to the Human Race in General Which is Perceived by the Murderer as an Archenemy**

In this category the murderer perceives all human beings as threats, or those who have actually hurt him. He can be a person who suffers from a paranoid psychosis or from other severe mental disorders. In this category we find the cases of the pseudocommando, in which innocent citizens are murdered in populated concentrations. The victims are total strangers to the murderer, and are selected absolutely randomly. There is not any common denominator that connects them except being human, and the murderer does not spare any one.

Criticism

One can argue, apparently, that the categories of belonging to an academic-occupational status, to a society which is in conflict with the murderer, and to humanity at large, overlap each other. The answer to such criticism is that one can enforce the typology so that it would combine the three categories into one category, but the price would be an over generalization, while obscuring unique phenomena of each category. Belonging to the academic-occupational category is different in its nature from belonging to a group which is in conflict with the murderer which is a wider group than the first one. However, beyond this, there is another important fundamental difference between them. While in the category of belonging to an academic-occupational group, the point is the dismissal or social rejection on the part of people who the murderer knows, and in the category that deals with a conflict, the victims are strangers to the murderer. The fact that the two types of mass murder can take place in an academic institution is misleading and seems duplicitous, and therefore one has to examine the components of familiarity and motive. In addition, there is a significant difference between mass-murder cases which are directed to a certain social group, or humanity as a whole, as a perceived enemy. Therefore, there is no overlap between the categories, although they could have been included as sub-categories of a more general category which could have been called: Belonging to a group that the murder sees as an enemy. If we go on in this approach, then a family is also a group who is in conflict with the murderer, and so on, and we would digress from the guiding principles of the typology, and lose more than we gain. Moreover, there is a difference in the level of familiarity between the murderer and the victims in the different categories.

Another criticism can be about the separation between a murder with a romantic background and one with a familial background. Both cases deal with intimate relationships between the murderer and the victims, but there are significant differences between the two types, differences that stem from a different legal status (a divorced man and a father versus a friend or a lover), and from the fact that in the second case, a person murders his children who are his flesh and blood, versus the first case in which he hurts someone, and her relatives, who do not want him. Hence, including these two groups together would camouflage unique differences between them.

In order to examine the typology, one has to answer a few additional questions: Is the typology exclusive and exhaustive? In other words, through this typology, can we refer to all cases that have happened in reality, and only to them? Would all the cases of mass murder necessarily suit one of the components of the typology? And, is there no overlap among the different categories?

In order to answer these questions we will present the categories of mass murder which have been mentioned in the literature, and will examine whether they can be integrated in the components of the typology. A mass murder with a romantic background is included in the first group. "Family exterminators" are included in the second, and so are mothers who murder their children in one action, as opposed to serial murderer mothers. Murdering an employer and co-workers is included in the third type. A mass murder at school or on campus is included in the third category, but it can be included in the fourth as well, according to the familiarity of the murderer with the victims. Terror is included in the fifth category, and a mass murder in a shopping mall or entertainment center is included in the sixth.

Examining the typology according to the criterion of reliability was found positive. It is interesting to see that in a case where there is a personal acquaintance between the murderer and the victims, it is easier to classify the different types of mass murder. The problem appears when the murderer and victim are unknown to one another. In this context, one has to bear in mind that in the social and behavioural sciences it is difficult to present reality in a dichotomous way, and therefore it is more correct to look on a sequence or a range. It is especially true regarding the extent of acquaintance between the victim and the murderer and the selection of the victim.

After examining the typology and finding that it meets the two basic requirements, we can present it more elaborately. It would then include the presentation of a possible motive for the murder, the selection of the victims, and the relationship between the victims and the murderer.

Table 3: Typology of a mass murder (Source: Edelstein, 2008)

Type	Selecting the victims		Extent of acquaintance between murderer and victims		Motive	Examples
	Deliberate	Specific	High	Low		
Romantic	+	+	+		Vengeance, power	Murder of a spouse and their relatives
Familial	+	+	+		Power and control	Murdering the children of the murderer and sometimes the ex-spouse as well
Academic/ Occupational	+	+	+		Vengeance, power and control	Former employer, co-workers, or students known to the murderer
Conflict				+	Ideological-social	Murdering people of a certain social group perceived by the murderer as hostile or not worthy of living
Terror	-	-		+	Ideological-nationalistic/ religious	Mass murder of strangers due to their belonging to a nation which is at war with the murderer and his people
Psychotic	-	-		+	Paranoid psychosis	Indiscriminate murder of strangers in public places against humanity as a whole

We have to bear in mind that typology is an attempt to describe reality and classify complicated phenomena that takes place in it. As such it is a tool for understanding the phenomenon of mass murder. Science aspires to understand phenomena and with this understanding to predict their recurrence in the future. But from this typology we cannot derive the capability to predict, and there is no such aspiration. It is interesting to see that when we shift from the interpersonal level within the individual level to wider social spheres, the motive shifts from vengeance, power and control to ideology, and therefore the victims shift from acquaintances to strangers. All the same, statistically, most of the victims belong to the interpersonal level, where there is a personal acquaintance between the victims and the murderer.

Summary of the Phenomenon

The research and theoretical literature in the field of mass murder is quite poor. This is a widely varied phenomenon which could be characterized through dividing it into typical groups and creating sub-classifications of the general phenomenon.

A mass murder is defined as a murder of a number of people (more than one), depending on the definitions of the researcher and the law enforcement entities, which takes place for different motives. These motives can be emotional (expressive), like vengeance, ambition for power, even if momentarily, or a sense of loyalty; or target directed (instrumental), like promoting racial ideologies[39] (acts executed by sect members), or national and others (terror acts). A mass murder can be executed by an individual, a team, or a terror organization. A motive of material profit does not characterize mass murder, because the murderer, in most cases, would not be able to enjoy the money he has gained. The most outstanding characteristic of mass murder is the one-time event, in which the murderer is not afraid to expose his identity publicly, as he intends to commit suicide or to be shot by the police. One may say that in many cases the murderer has reached the point of no return, in which he feels he has nothing to lose anymore. The same goes for events with a romantic background and events directed against co-workers or classmates. In this respect, mass murder is meant to meet a one-time goal of the mass murderer. Part of the myths, regarding mass murder and murderers, stem from attributing biological and psychological theories to this behaviour. For example, the murderer is perceived as one who entered a psychotic state, and therefore shoots indiscriminately at strangers in a public place. In fact, it has been found that mass murderers selected their victims specifically, and in most cases, the victims were known to him. In addition, a major part of the mass-murder cases were not executed in public places, like the family home or the working place.[40] In recent years the sociological explanations are more outstanding among researchers regarding the murderer (a man) whose social relations do not provide him with support and direction in a time of distress. The man is still measured and measures himself according to his economic-social status, his occupation and capability to make a living, rather than according to his personal characteristics. These factors play a central role in motives that have to do with the mass murder of families and that of employers and co-workers. If we combine the social and personality factors, we may understand better the motives and behaviour of mass murderers, as only a very small part of them suffer from paranoid psychosis. We can also see that sociocultural explanations provide better insights of this phenomenon than general vague explanations.

The fact that mass murder is much more salient in the USA[41] suggests a sociocultural explanation to the phenomenon, rather than just a psychological one. In a society in which the individual is measured and measures himself according to his occupation, dismissal or a humiliating attitude from the employer constitutes a significant trigger for a fatal response. At the same time, not everyone who is fired or gets a humiliating attitude from his employer, or loses custody over his children responds with fatal violence.

The routine activity theory and the theory of rational choice can explain the mass murder acts in most cases that have been presented here. On the other hand, psychological theories can explain the phenomenon of mass murder, even without a diagnosis of a severe mental disorder like a paranoid psychosis. Hence we can conclude that the combination of psychological and sociological theories, instead of competing with each other, can provide a better explanation for this phenomenon, although it has not been seriously used until recently.[42] The combination would explain the social factors which push people to conflict and distress situations in the American society, while the psychological factors would clarify why specific individuals, who are in these situations, would act by way of mass murder, while others would tend to act in normative ways.

To sum up, the different typologies that have been suggested for classifying mass murder and murderers dealt mainly with the motive of the murderer through a classification which caused the typologies to be too general or lacking reliability due to duplicities.

The suggested new typology tries to classify the mass murderers according to the victims and the groups they belong to which is a novelty that enables the typology to be exclusive and exhaustive.

Part of the cases defined in the literature as mass murders do not meet the central criterion of the definition which is a one-time murder.

Mass Murder in Israel

The penal code 1976 does not refer to mass murder. Paragraph 300 of the law defines the murder felony and determines the obligatory punishment for it—life sentence. In a case of a multiple murder, the legislator tends to impose accumulated life sentences to equal the number of victims.

There are not many mass murders within the family in Israel. When such murder takes place, it is usually executed by husbands due to a suspicion of treason, separation, and receiving custody over the children by the wife, and other factors. In August 1995, Yshay Galizky strangled to death his two sons, aged a year and a half and five years old, and committed suicide by hanging himself. In the letter he left, he explained that he wanted to prove to his wife that his threats of hurting the children, if she does divorce him, were serious. In July 1999 a husband murdered his wife and two children because he suspected that his wife was having an affair through the Internet. In August of the same year, Amnon

Cohen, 43, murdered his wife Lea and his two sons, aged two and four years old. He was sentenced to three accumulated life sentences. At that year, Yaakov Cantor electrocuted his wife and son, and afterwards put their bodies on fire in the car and pushed it down into an abyss. Recently a police officer shot his policewoman wife and their two children and then committed suicide by shooting himself, maybe due to a suspicion of treason.

There were in the past very few cases of a mother who murdered her children and was found insane (*Haaretz* newspaper: 1994–2007).

Most of the cases of mass murder in Israel have been done with an ideological-nationalistic background by terrorists. On the one hand, there were the suicide bombers who blew themselves up in populated centers, like buses, shopping malls, cafes and restaurants, while on the other hand there were individuals from the right-wing ideology who murdered Arabs who were waiting in a station to go to work, in a plant, or in a praying place. We will survey here the outstanding cases in this field:

Amy Popper—a young man, 21, from Rishon Lezion who murdered seven Arab workers from Judea and Samaria. In 20.5.1990 he arrived at the transportation station which was situated in a rose garden, in the junction between Rishon Lezion and Ness Ziona, equipped with a gun and magazines he had taken from his brother. He gathered the Arab workers who were in the junction, stopped a car with a Palestinian license plate, and instructed the Arab workers who were on it to join the ones who were in the junction. Popper made them stand in a row, cocked the Glilon gun and shot them to death.

Baruch Goldstein—a physician who lived in Kiriat Arba (Hebron), murdered 29 Muslim prayers in the Cave of Machpelah in Hebron and injured another hundred. In 25.2.1994, at five o'clock in the morning, Goldstein entered the Izhak Hall in the cave, waited for the prayers to kneel down in the direction of Mecca, and started shooting everywhere. He managed to change five magazines until the crowd threw on him a fire extinguisher, made him fall down and killed him. Goldstein worked as a physician and treated both Arabs and Jews. At the day of the murder he left his car at home and asked a friend to drive him to the Cave of Machpelah.

Eden Nathan Zada—was a young man who deserted his army service, claiming that he was not prepared to participate in the evacuation of the settlements of the Gush Katif in the Gaza Strip. Zada left his parents' house in Rishon Lezion, and moved to live in the settlement Tapuach in Samaria, and became an extremist believer. In 4.8.05, after five o'clock in the evening, he opened fire on bus No. 165 in the Druz neighbourhood in Shefaram. As a result of the shooting, four people were killed and nine injured. The crowd in Shefaram lynched the shooter and killed him.

Asher Weisgan—a driver of workers, 40, married and a father of two who lived in the settlement of Shvut Rachel. He murdered four Palestinians who worked in a plant in the settlement of Shilo, and injured another two. Weisgan snatched the weapon of the guard by threatening him with a knife, and on 17.8.05, at 17:00 killed two workers he had taken in his car. From there he went on to the industrial zone, murdered another worker and injured two more (one of them died of his wounds later on). The security officer of the settlement caught him and transferred him to the security forces. According to him, Weisgan executed the murder as a response to the evacuation of the settlements of Gush Katif.

As has been mentioned, the common denominator of the four cases of a mass murder in Israel, executed by a Jew, is the nationalistic motive: Eliminating Arabs because they were Arabs as an expression of a nationalistic hatred and an ideological vengeance. The four murderers held political positions held by the extreme right wing in Israel. From this aspect, this type of mass murder can be referred to as terror. The victims belonged to a certain group which the murderers regarded as an enemy, and they can be classified as a pseudocommando. Nevertheless, in Weisgan's case the murderer knew his victims. In the other cases the murderers did not know the victims who were selected just because they were Arabs or Druz.

The outstanding characteristic of these cases is the murderers' feeling that they could not take it any longer. This feeling led them to go out and murder. An outstanding example for this is Goldstein who treated Arabs as a physician, and suddenly, in spite of being a religious person, murdered Arab prayers in their place of worship. Still, the unique situation of Israel in relation to terror makes it difficult to compare it with other western countries. In addition, one should bear in mind that not every extreme activist of the right wing in Israel goes out and murders Arabs, and therefore one has to take into consideration the personality characteristics and processes they have gone through which brought them to the point of executing a mass murder spree. Additional outstanding characteristic is the fact that these mass murderers did not think about their personal destiny, and Goldstein and Zada indeed found their death in it.

On the part of the Palestinians, the number of suicide bombers increased versus terrorists who lay demolition charges and ran away from the scene. Both cases are a one-time mass murder with a nationalistic background, aiming to murder as many Jews and Arabs as possible just for being Jews or Arabs. Among the motives we can find national aspirations, religious considerations, obedience to religious representatives, and a promise for a better life in paradise. All the victims were strangers to the suicide murderer, and his main goal was to murder indiscriminately as much people as he can.

Part of the terrorists belonged to terror organization, while another part committed the mass murder on their own and were shot by the men of the law, or by citizens carrying weapons, like, for instance, in the terrorist act in the Mercaz HaRav Yeshiva in Jerusalem (March, 2008), and in running over people with tractors in Jerusalem.

Profiles

The central assumption of profile makers is that if we find the common characteristics of mass murderers, then we will have an important and reliable tool for predicting the behaviour of people with these characteristics, or be able to identify murderers who have not been caught yet. But the vast majority of men who lost their source of living or their custody over their children, did not murder their families or their former employers and co-workers. On this point, we have to look into the psychological aspect. There should be a specific infrastructure in a person's personality in order to react in a fatal way as a result of being fired from work, or losing custody of his children. Most scientists indicate that there is no proper predictability for a future mass murder, and therefore the explanations for this phenomenon are in retrospect.

Mullen (2004) thinks that a list of common characteristics of mass murderers cannot provide us with a profile of a mass murderer, as far as the capability of identifying individuals with a high risk of committing such a murder in advance is concerned. The reason for this is that there is not enough data about the distribution and frequency of the critical elements in the general population in order to conduct a comparison. In addition, these people do not tend to enter into specific psychological and/or social situations prior to committing the murder so that we would be able to assess the extent of risk. Mullen presents two appropriate criticisms: First, the fact that there have been found characteristics of mass murderers, like loneliness, enchantment of weapons, repeated failures from childhood up to adulthood in the professional and the interpersonal fields is not enough, since there are people who do not become mass murderers due to these characteristics. Secondly, even if we find that mass murderers started acting following a catalyst event, like a separation from a spouse and her receiving custody over the common children, or being fired from work—these events happen to many people in the general society, and do not make them start a murderous spree.

Fox and Levin (2003) raise the following questions: If there is a profile of the typical mass murderer, would we be able to identify him properly and predict the next mass murder? Usually after events of mass murder, acquaintances and neighbours recall that they had concerns about the criminal, prior to the violent event. In other cases, witnesses tend to report that they had heard the criminal scatter direct or indirect threats of violent acts. Nowadays, there are consulting companies which market a variety of tools for predicting trouble makers, aiming to prevent them from being hired for work. In a similar way, school teams receive lists of warning signs in order to help them prevent severe cases of the shooting at their classmates by children and young adults. The problem is that these lists include items that reflect mental disorders, but not a tendency to a future mass murder, or items that have nothing to do with a mass murder, like the use of alcohol and drugs. Even if potential mass murderers share common characteristics, only a few of them become mass murderers. Furthermore, one has to take into consideration that different means of interference might be interpreted negatively, and by so doing increase the individual's feeling of being persecuted. Generally speaking, the authors argue that most of the prediction strategies have failed, since they saw the criminal as the exclusive source of the problem, instead of referring to the issue of how the environmental factors are connected to his personality characteristics. Such a connection may reinforce his will to hurt, and create situations in which this intention might be materialized.

Chapter Two
Mass/Serial Murder and Murderers

There is a certain difficulty to refer to the term "serial murder," even if indirectly, before we can deal with this phenomenon in detail. In order to conclude the discussion of mass murder, we must refer to these cases which do not meet the characteristics and definitions of mass murder in its "pure" form. Examples include repeated mass murders by a sect member or reproduction of acts of terror in which the terrorist plants a bomb and escapes the scene; repeated killings of gang members or organized crime members by other gangs or criminal organizations; the recurrent act of eliminating the witnesses to a crime, mainly a robbery, and ideological assassination with a political background.

For the sake of the discussion we will define a serial murder in short. A serial murder is a murder of at least three victims, with one victim murdered in each event, and with a cooling-off period between one murder and the next, a period that can last days, weeks, months, and even years.

If we go back to mass murder, two conditions have to take place so that we would be able to define the event as a mass murder: The number of victims in the event is more than one, the act is a one-time event, and when it ends the murderer is incapable of going on to committing more felonies. This incapability can stem from the murderer's suicide, his being killed by the security forces which is considered also a kind of suicide—suicide by proxy, or his being caught by the security forces and being imprisoned for many years, or a death sentence in certain states in the USA.

The above examples meet only one criterion: The number of victims is more than one. This is why they are defined as a mass murder. On the other hand, they do not meet the second criterion of a mass murder since it is not a one-time event. These are repeated cases: The terrorist who laid a bomb would do it again, the gang members would go on acting in light of the ideology of the leader and murder members of social groups who are perceived as unworthy, and the robbers would go on murdering witnesses of their crimes in order to avoid being caught.

Hence, and as has been indicated already in the previous chapter, there is a problem: These cases cannot be referred to as a mass murder, at least they cannot be defined as a mass murder according to the existing definitions, since they are not a one-time event; On the other hand, one cannot refer to them as a serial murder, since they deal with more than one person murdered in each event. Therefore, we have to determine that this is another type of multiple-victims murder which meets part of the definitions of a mass murder, and part of the definitions of a serial murder.

As has been indicated in the previous chapter, the existing definitions constitute an obstacle which often makes it difficult to refer to a complicated reality. In this situation there are two options: According to those who are in favor of the concept of a multiple murder as a central concept, the existing definitions of a mass murder or a serial murder can be changed in order to include the above-mentioned cases. For instance, a serial murder can be defined as a murder of at least one victim in each event, and then we would be able to include a murder of three victims and more in each event within serial murder. But as we will see later on, such a change of serial murder would not match reality, since a serial murder deals, by definition, with a murder of one victim at a time. On the other hand, if we change the definition of mass murder, then here, too, it would not match reality, as a mass murder is, by definition, a one-time event, rather than a serial one. In this state of affairs, the only choice we have is, as aforementioned, to create a third category of a multiple murder which would include the cases of murdering a number of victims at the same time, then after a cooling-off period, another murder of a number of victims, and so on and so forth.

According to my assessment, this is one of the reasons why different scientists (mainly Fox & Levin, 2003, 2005) aspired to include the different cases under the term of multiple-victims murder. Such concept could solve part of the problems we have encountered until now, but this generalization misses the differences among a mass murder, a serial murder and a mass-serial murder. This is one of the problems of the confusion among the concepts that have been presented regarding a mass murder when a murder by sect members, terrorists, and assassinations with an ideological background were repeatedly defined as examples for a mass murder. This approach prevented these scientists from making a clear distinction among different behaviours within a multiple-victims murder, and made it difficult to create clear and unambiguous typologies.

If we deal with the policy implemented toward crime, then the cases of mass-serial murder are exactly the cases that endanger the public, and the fear of them is the highest. We can see how terrorist acts in different countries, like Japan, England, the USA, and Israel which have been executed for the sake of terror, influenced the sense of personal security up to a state in which citizens experienced PTSD which led in turn to different disorders and behaviours, such as depression and consuming alcohol and drugs (Schiff & Benbenishty, 2004; Vlahov et al., 2002). In addition, we can see to what extent terror acts call for recruiting human, economic and technological resources, and influence daily life of the population.

In a similar way, the fear of crime, expressed in armed robbery and murdering the witnesses of another event, might create anxiety in the population up to the point of avoiding going to places which might be a focus for such an act. The attempts of the security services to penetrate into different sects stem from the same reasons.

It is obvious, then, that even if this mass-serial murder is not of the common type of a multiple-victims murder, its continuation creates fear in the public, and in certain countries this type of multiple-victims murder is the most common one, like in Israel.

A salient type of a mass-serial murder is a murder committed by sect members, especially the ones which are based on a background of racial and religious ideology. Walsh (2005) indicates that while such a murder is committed in a small number of cases by whites against blacks, the opposite is quite common: A murder of white victims by black sect members. For example, California's Death Angels murdered in the seventies more people than did all the serial single murderers who operated at that period. Five black Muslims committed most of the murder cases which were attributed to this sect, due to their conviction that their Islamic belief would free the world from the "white demons." Another sect, Yahweh Ben Yahweh which was known in its nickname Death Angels, operated in Miami in the eighties. Its activities, like those of California's Death Angels, were directed against whites. Its members received an instruction to murder "white demons" and bring parts of their bodies to prove the execution. This sect was accused in 22 murder cases. While these two sects operated mainly on the basis of a religious Muslim background, another sect called The De Mau included at least eight black army veterans who lived in Chicago and shared a common grudge against white society. Unlike the religious groups, this group did not endure and was less cruel, but all the same it committed 12 murders by randomly shooting white people. We can see that in a mass-serial murder there is an expression of hatred with an ideological, religious or racial background, more than in interpersonal conflicts, as in a mass murder (Newton, 2006).

But the place of gangs and crime organizations was not left outside the list of the mass-serial murders, and events of settling accounts in the underworld have become part of our routine. A certain crime family hurts another crime family due to a competition over territories of control, or fields of occupation. As a result, the aggrieved family retaliates by eliminating the "soldiers" of the attacking family, and these processes repeat themselves over and over again.

Ideological-political assassinations are common especially in non-democratic regimes, but they are less represented in the research literature. Loyalty to the leader or to the party in power establishes objection to any threat coming from an overt or hidden opposition. Sometimes it is difficult to separate between an ideological murder with a political background and an elimination of the opposition and its supporters by dark regimes, as has been the case in Russia, the former Yugoslavia, and part of the African countries.

Sometimes the distinction between terror and another kind of murder has to do with the definition. For example, the Hamas which was elected in democratic elections in Gaza; should we classify its activities against the state of Israel as acts of war or terror? We are used to distinguishing between the shooting of Kassam missiles and laying demolition charges, an explosion in a bus, or a restaurant by a suicide bomber. But is there a difference among these actions? The answer has to do with political definitions rather than criminological ones. Nevertheless, in regards to terrorism, one can find many cases of mass-serial murder, when the terrorist does not blow himself up, but plants the bomb and runs from the scene, or, alternatively, cases of shooting by a terrorist attack.

To sum up, murder cases of two victims and more, which often take place by a certain person or group, are not included in the definition of mass murder. On the other hand, cases of murder of more than one person which take place by the same murderer more than once, are not included in the definition of serial murder, although there is a cooling-off period between the cases. Therefore, these cases would be included in a third sub-group of multiple-victims murder which I call mass-serial murder. This is a new category that does not exist in the literature of multiple-victims murder.

We can, already at this stage, see reinforcement to the claim that there is a need to distinguish among the different multiple-victims murders, and that they cannot be put together in one group, in order to reflect reality in the most appropriate way and distinguish significant differences of motive, the way of operation and so on.[43]

Explanations and Characteristics of Mass-Serial Murder and Murderers

One of the most important characteristics in the discussion about mass-serial murder is the fact that it deals mainly with actions of individuals who act under the mission of a leader and his blessing. These individuals belong, in most cases, to some social group or an organization. The organization can be an ad hoc organization, like the Jewish Underground which aimed at assassinating mayors in the West Bank. Alternately, they may be a stable and defined social organization, like crime families, sects, gangs and terror organizations. One of the salient characteristics of acts of mass-serial murder, especially in relatively stable organizations, is the need of the individual to belong, to be accepted and even develop a reputation. The loss of congregational life and the rise of individualism have not developed equally among all individuals in society. Part of these individuals do not manage, or are not interested in achieving the social goals in legitimate ways, and part of them do not accept the goals of society and pose for themselves goals and means of achieving them in a way which deviates from society's ordainments.[44]

In such an organization one can find people who have not managed to achieve social goals, and feel a decrease of their self-worth, anger toward society at large, or toward certain sections in it which prevented them, according to their opinions, from achieving these goals. Getting connected to the organization, especially when it is led by a charismatic leader, enables them an alternative for achieving these goals, retrieving their self-worth, and even some kind of vengeance. It is interesting to note that usually these people are not in their middle age, after having experienced repeated failures, but rather young people who look for, I think, borders and acceptance they do not find elsewhere, including in their families. For instance, many young people joined the Manson family who saw in Manson the charismatic image whom they missed in their lives, together with a message against blacks. It is my opinion that the search for belonging and acceptance is the psychological motive that pushes such youngsters to the different organizations, while the goal facilitates the sense of cognitive dissonance that develops following the need to belong to such an organization.

But one has to distinguish among the different organizations. Joining crime organizations is different from joining a sect with a certain ideology. Joining crime organizations enables these young people to establish a course of career, acquire reputation, and gain social acceptance in other ways than those of the normative society. These are the "innovators," according to the classification of Merton (1957). They accept the goals of society, but cannot, or would not, use the legitimate means society put at their disposal for achieving them. This fact, together with a high financial temptation, influences the youngsters to join these organizations. One can see their joining these organizations as an implementation of the theory of the rational choice: A high profit in the long run and getting professionals which would prevent them from being caught, versus living a life of chronic crime with no real career (Edelstein, 2006).

Another explanation refers to the theory of frustration-aggression by Dollard & Miller which was presented previously. The scientists claimed that frustration experienced in childhood does not disappear from consciousness without the release of aggression, and this aggression can come out in any time in the future. One of the assumptions, suggested by Wright & Hensley (2004) which gained only a partial empirical confirmation, is that humiliated and frustrated people take out their frustration on weaker creatures, including animals. The assumption is that children and adolescents become, through being cruel toward animals, insensible and violent, or learn to enjoy causing suffering and pain which might deteriorate in their attitude toward people. The rationale is that aggression toward animals does not meet their needs any more. The scientists argue that such a behaviour can predict a serial murder in the future, since whoever experienced frustration must take it out through violence, even if it is prospective and indirect (Singer & Hensley, 2004).

This theory, as well as reference to antisocial personality disorder,[45] can suggest an explanation to violent behaviour, mainly among members of crime organizations, but also among sect members, and terror organizations. Certain members in such organizations can execute, on behalf of the leader, most cruel acts against innocent victims, without feeling a moral or any other problem about their deeds, and even repeat them in the future when it would be required of them. An example of it can be seen in the mass media which presents the image of the ugly giant who carries out his master's commands not only without hesitation, but even with some kind of enjoyment from the sadistic acts he is required to do.

To sum up, the salient characteristic of mass-serial murder is murder actions which stem from obligation to others, mainly to a charismatic leader, unlike other types of multiple-victims murder which will be discussed in this book. Under this category one can include terrorists who lay booby-trapped cars and other demolition materials, members in crime organizations, sect members, and others. The common denominator to all of them is the loyalty to the leader, but this loyalty has to do with an ideological, religious, or other belief. Although the salient characteristics are expressive, in this type of murder there are also other instrumental and material components which not always can be disconnected from the emotional ones.

It could be that individuals with severe mental disorders would find in these organizations a convenient solution for satisfying their needs, together with gaining secondary profits, like money, prestige, and especially belonging.

Although the individual enjoys the technique of "neutralizing guilt"[46] ("I only filled an order") which allegedly removes any responsibility, I think that these individuals operate additional personal neutralizing techniques in order "to live in peace" with themselves and with their murderous behaviour. Part of the guilt neutralization is structured in a sociocultural way to ensure obedience.

A Typology of Mass-Serial Murder and Murderers

Since this type of murderers has not been known yet in the theoretical literature, there is no classification for them. Classifying the murderers who belong to this group is significantly different from the classification of serial murderers who are not mass murderers.

The types of mass-serial murderers can be classified according to the main motive for their activity, although there are problems of definition that make univalent classification difficult.

- **Mass-Serial Murderers who Act on Behalf of an Ethnic-Racial Ideology**

These murderers are organized in a clear, separated social framework. At the head of the organization is a charismatic leader who addresses mainly those who are in a low socioeconomic status, and feel threatened by other groups in society, especially ethnic-racial groups (immigrants and others). The social organization that characterizes this group is the sect. Examples of such social organization can be seen in the case of the Manson family who aimed at creating a confrontation between whites and blacks, and its way of operation was to leave hints in the murder scene which would raise suspicion that blacks had executed the murder acts.

Another example is the KKK organization which operated in the USA against blacks and whoever fought for their rights. The main characteristic of this group was acting in the local level, although the organization may have branches in several cities in the same state, or in several states in a federal administration. The main goal of these murderers was to murder the members of the social group or groups which had been defined by them as unworthy of living. First of all they would conduct a process of dehumanization and depersonalization against the unworthy group. These murderers generally direct their actions against foreigners, but the murder can be directed also toward specific people who help the unworthy group.

The gains of the murderers who belong to this category are varied. They experience a psychological profit by hurting the object of their hatred, and feel a sense of belonging by the very existence of the leader's instructions. At the same time, their reputation goes up in the eyes of the group members, something they could not have achieved elsewhere. These elements were missing in their lives prior to joining the sect. Anti-Semitism also fits into this type, but I do not intend to deal with it here.

- **Mass-Serial Murderers Who Act on Behalf of a Nationalistic or Religious Ideology**

The main difference between this type and the previous one is that the motive is not an ideology that deals with origin, but refers to different nations at the same country, or between countries and religions. In this category we can include a few types of mass-serial murder: Terror, wars, Crusades, commando operations beyond enemy lines, assassination by intelligence agency, and others. In my opinion, a systematic removal of opponents of the regime can also be included in this category, for example, the Iranian regime which persecutes Salman Rushdie.

As I will show here, part of the definitions which dealt with serial murder, focused on acts that have been done on a civil background which means that they excluded from the definition most of the examples indicated in this type of mass-serial murder.

The most outstanding field in this category is terror. Terrorists execute mass-serial murders in order to kill as many members of the other nation or religion as they can, out of hatred and vengeance, aiming to instill fear in the population that is under terrorist attack and to gain political power. The execution of these acts is enabled by penetrating an ideology of hatred toward the other nation or religion, with the help of political, military, or religious charismatic leaders. Outstanding examples for such acts are the terror acts of Bin Laden's organization on behalf of Islam; terrorist acts of Islamic organizations against western countries; terrorist acts which had been done by the Irish underground against England; terrorist acts by the Basques against Spain, and terrorist acts in Israel and in Jewish communities around the world by Palestinians.

When religion is involved, together with a nationalistic ideology, the sense of fulfilling a mission is not just a national mission of hurting the conqueror, a will for independence, and so on, but a feeling that they act on behalf of God which makes the process of neutralizing guilt and responsibility for their deeds is much easier.

These people, who would not achieve society's goals in an ordinary way of life, become heroes and culture heroes in the ethos of that nation or religion.

- **Mass-Serial Murderers Who Act Out of Material Motives**

While in the previous two types of murderers the salient motive was allegedly emotional (expressive), one cannot deny the fact that the motive can also be goal-directed (instrumental). Regions and countries often achieved independence due to repeated terror acts, including the acts of the Israeli organizations against the British regime. On the other hand, one may say that the main motive is an emotional one, when it is obvious that terror acts would not change the national or religious reality. For instance, the Islamic organizations do not really believe that they can remove western culture and impose Islam, and therefore the emotional element is dominant in their actions.

The third type of mass-serial murder is characterized by instrumental motives in an outstanding way. These murderers belong to the organized crime, like gangs or crime organizations, and are involved in the killings of other crime organizations for the sake of control over territories, aiming to operate illegal businesses which provide them with a lot of money (drugs traffic, prostitution and so on).

Another way in which the mass-serial murder is connected to material motives is through organized actions of murder, including armed robberies, elimination of businessmen who refuse to pay protection money, and so on. One may argue that there is ideology in organized crime as well, but still, the instrumental component is dominant in this type of action.

To summarize, this is a preliminary suggestion for classifying this type of murderers which has no reference in the theoretical literature. As we will see later on, this classification differs from most kinds of serial murders, although one can see two categories within the serial murder which are similar to the suggested classification.

The first is the mission serial murderer who murders individuals who belong to a group which he perceives as unworthy of living (prostitutes, nomads, and others). The second one is the hedonist serial murderer who is motivated by profit. This murderer acts in a planned and calculated way for the sake of achieving material profit, and he acts against familiar victims (spouses) as well as against strangers, like in the case of the "professional assassin."

Chapter Three
Serial Murder and Murderers

Background

While the amount of research and theoretical literature as well as coverage by the mass media of mass murder is relatively poor, the academic literature that deals with serial murder, as well as the publication in the media are quite large. This phenomenon was dealt in movies, serials, prose and a wide variety of academic research. If earlier I brought Fox and Levin's (2003) explanation why mass murder has not gained publication, we can see a number of reasons explaining why serial murder gained great publication: This is a repeated event which raises the level of public anxiety until the murderer is caught, something that can take place a long time after the execution of the murders; part of the murder cases have to do with sex and raise public interest and curiosity; the murderer is a challenge for the police which again raises great communication interest. The murderer is perceived as a sophisticated criminal who conducts a mental fight with the police, with the elements of a good thriller. After the murderer is caught, the public is eager to know his life story.

Clarifying Concepts

Serial murder versus other multiple-victims murder—the only similarity between serial murder and mass murder is the large number of bodies in their cases and in both types the murderers are usually planned and methodological. They plan their attack a long time before executing the crime, get equipped accordingly and wait for the proper moment to attack. In all other characteristics of the murder and the murderer, they are opposite to those of the mass murder and murderer: In a serial murder we deal with repeated and planned events of one victim at a time, and between one case of murder and the next there is a cooling-off or latent period of time. A murderer who murdered at least three victims[47] is considered serial. On the other hand, in a mass murder there is a one-time event in which the number of victims is more than one.

While most serial murderers murder in a "personal" way, and use a weapon which expresses intimacy with the victim, mass murderers use firearm which increases the emotional distance and efficiency of killing a large number of victims.

The serial murderer sees to it that he and his deeds are well camouflaged, and by so doing he is a kind of a "professional criminal," who tries to prevent being caught, so that he would be able to go on doing his deeds. He would clean the scene from physical pieces of evidence, like semen, blood or DNA, remove weapons, and generally get rid of the body or camouflage it. On the other hand, the mass murderer executes a one-time act, at the end of which he commits suicide, shot or arrested. The situation of the scene after his execution does not interest him, and he does not try to camouflage his identity. While the serial murderer chooses his victims according to a characteristic, gender, or certain status, with an emphasis on foreign people, most of the victims in a mass murder are known to the murderer (former employer, co-workers, classmates and so on).

While most of the victims of serial murders are women, and most of the serial murder cases include a sexual element, a mass murder does not involve sex, although there can be an element of malice (sadism) which comes from a sense of omnipotence regarding the victims.

Although the motive in the serial murder is generally sexual, as has been noted, it can also have material motives. On the other hand, in a mass murder the motive is not material in an absolute majority of the cases.[48] In addition, in a serial murder there is nothing the victim has done, while in a mass murder there can be such contribution, like dismissal from work, divorce, mockery on the part of co-workers or classmates (Kraemer et al., 2004; Meloy & Felthous, 2004; Vronsky, 2007; Levin 2008; Holmes & Holmes, 1998).

A serial murder differs in its characteristics from a single murder. Most single murderers are honestly sorry for the murder they have committed, and they would rarely murder again.[49] On the other hand, serial murderers are exactly the opposite: They are usually aware of their intentions to murder, and deal with planning it, though this planning can take years of fantasies. They become "addicted to murder," and after each case they do not regret or feel pangs of conscience, at least not in a sufficient extent to change their behaviour. Furthermore, they learn from one murder to the next, aiming to improve their execution (Vronsky, 2007).

To sum up, different scientists present a number of components which distinguish between serial murder and other types of murder: It is a repeated murder.

This is a case of one-on-one, and only in rare cases there is a team. According to Fox and Levin (2005), serial murderers usually operate as individuals (81%), and only in a few cases as couples (12.2%) or as a team (7%). Part of the cases of serial murder is executed by a pair of relatives, like brothers and cousins. For example, the brothers Carr murdered five victims in Kansas in 2001; the cousins Bianchi & Buono were convicted in the eighties for murdering ten young girls. When there is an operation in teams, the tendency is to operate in a defined geographical area, while one of the partners is the dominant one. The number of victims of teams does not differ from that of single serial murderers, and in each murder there is one victim.

In most cases, the victim is unknown to the murderer, unlike a regular murder, in which most of the victims are known to the murderer. The reasons for this have to do with the motive for the murder, as well as with the will to avoid being caught. Among serial murderers in a murder based on a sexual background, the rate of foreign victims is still higher, since the murderers choose victims like prostitutes, female hitchhikers, single women like single students, divorcees or widows, wandering or foreign boys and girls who have come to town. That is, they deal with foreigners whom they can seduce, catch, control and murder in order to satisfy sadist impulses and violent fantasies, especially people who live by themselves. We have to bear in mind that a sexual serial murder is committed against men as well, in about 15% of the victims (Fox & Levin, 2005).

The serial murderer is motivated to kill: He operates out of motives that differ from the traditional motives among people with intimate relationships, or from the motive that causes a murder among foreigners as a result of a conflict, vengeance, and so on. The victim symbolizes something for the murderer, and generally belongs to the weak layers of society: Prostitutes, nomads, wandering youth, and so on. In most serial murders, there are no overt and clear motives. The motive can be pathological-expressive, such as sex, power, control, sadism, or greed, like a hired or an independent murderer who assassins for a financial profit, or a murder of tenants for the sake of financial profit.[50]

Most of the serial murderers are older than regular murderers, and are in the age group of 25–35, with the median age of 27.5. On the other hand, the victims of serial murders are similar in their age to those of regular murders (20–29).

Unlike a regular murder, in which most of the victims are men, most of the victims in serial murder are women, and most of the murderers are men. Among serial murderers with a sexual background, 70% of the murderers murdered only women, 15% murdered men only, and 15% murdered men and women. On the other hand, in a serial murder which is not based on sexual background, the rate of women is twice as much as that of men among the victims (Ibid., 2005; this datum stems, though, from including family annihilators in the field of serial murder).[51]

Race: Among serial murderers, whites have a little lower representation than their proportion in the population, versus regular murders (80%), whereas black serial murderers have a little higher representation in serial murder (20%) versus regular murder cases, regarding their proportion in the general population. A serial murder takes place more within the ethnic group and less among different ethnic groups.

A tenth of the victims in serial murders are children, unlike regular murders where the number of murdered children is very small. Again, these data include data about family annihilators.

Half of the serial murderers who were caught, had a criminal record in the field of property felonies, violence and sex, but only 7% had a record of psychological treatment following mental problems or addiction to psychoactive substances.

In a serial murder there is a higher use of "cold," manual methods of killing, as opposed to a regular murder which is usually executed with a firearm. In a serial murder with a sexual background, the rate of using manual killing is even higher, due to its slow nature and the control the murderer has on the whole process of seducing, torturing, and so on, rather than a quick killing act.

In a serial murder there is similarity between the locations of the different murder events, whereas in a regular murder there are a larger variety of locations (Holmes & Holmes, 1998, Holmes et al. 2004; Hickey, 1992; Kraemer et al., 2004; Vronsky, 2004; Fox & Levin, 2005).

The History of Serial Murder and Murderers

According to Newton (2006), the first documentation of a serial murder is from 331 BC, when the Roman authorities convicted 170 murderous women for poisoning many men. In Roman time, a serial murderer was known as the Blue Beard (Bestia) who murdered his seven wives by penetrating poison into their sexual organ during having sex with them. At that time it was publicized that a man murdered his pregnant wife, his two sons, his brother, his father-in-law and others, each one separately.

In 69 AC, a serial woman murderer, under the name of Locusta, was known for poisoning her victims for money, and in 70 AD Asperenas was accused of murdering 130 victims. Four hundred years later, in Yemen of the fifth century, Zu Shenatir was accused for seducing young boys to eat at his home for money, subjecting them to acts of sodomy and throwing them from a high window to their death.

In Europe of the fifteenth century, serial murder was common among nobility and peasants alike. The count De Rais murdered a hundred children in 1440. In 1542, a cook in England named Davey, murdered by poisoning a few of her employers, with no clear motive. At the same time at least five cannibals were put to death in France and in Germany. In the seventeenth century, a Hungarian countess under the name of Bathory was convicted of torturing and murdering hundreds of girls and women. She even bathed in their blood. In the eighteenth century, a serial woman murderer by the name of La Totania, was executed in Italy as she was accused of poisoning six hundred victims.

The tradition of serial murder in Europe continued into the nineteenth century, when the German Gottfriend was accused in 1828 of poisoning 20 victims. At that year two serial murderers were convicted in England for the murder of 11 people. In Austria Swiatek was accused of the murder and cannibalism of six children. In France a cook, called Jegado, was accused of poisoning 60 people. The Englishman Dyer was convicted in 1896 for the murder of 15 babies, and the French Vacher was accused of four cases of murder and necrophilia during three years.

The brothers Harpe operated in the USA in the eighteenth century, and murdered an unknown number of victims. They threw their organs to the river in order to avoid being caught.

One of the classical figures of serial murder, who has been well known up to our time by the mass media, is the Romanian Dracula.

Creating the Myth of the Serial Murderer

Before going on with the discussion of the characteristics of the serial murder and murderers, it is worthwhile referring to the concept of serial recurrence which has implications on the myths that have been established about serial murders and murderers. Jenkins (2002) presents an interesting approach in his article "Seriality as Modern Monstrosity." He claims that although seriality means just recurrence, it has carried recently a much richer meaning, including pathological, obsessive, and uncontrollable behaviour. Jenkins (2002) argues that the concept serial which is an allegedly mathematical neutral term, has gained a meaning that hints of monstrous violence. He goes on accusing the eighties, when it was a necessity, both rhetorically and politically, to present the existence of aggressive, dangerous and unique criminals, against whom no means was too extreme. The appearance of the serial murderer as an authentic creature whose existence was confirmed by the behavioural and social sciences, materialized for us the superhuman mythical role which nightmares present. The inhuman and monstrous image given to the serial murderer included a total lack of self-control, so that the murderer has no actual chance of stop doing what he does. The concept of serial murder had an essential and unique characteristic which is the evil of seriality per se. If someone executes the same murder action two or three times, then we speak about accusing him twice or three times. In the case of serial murder, one and one equal much more than two. The emphasis on the sexual aspect in serial murder presented brutal men who hunt defenseless women. Serial murderers were described as wolves that are out there to prey "the silent sheep." The serial murderer has become a "wolf-man" of modern times. Like wolves, the serial murderers prowl for prey, wander the country and attack once here and another time there, until the number of victims reaches hundreds.

Jenkins (2002) claims that the formal mythology holds that the monstrous behaviour was unique in a certain time and space: It did not happen up to the end of the seventies, and it is very rare outside of the USA. He criticizes the arguments as if this phenomenon was part of the establishment of the mythology of serial murder, by saying that this kind of murder has always existed and was not unique to the USA. On the other hand, this phenomenon is relatively rare and it is not, as has been argued, an epidemic. In addition, in spite of the myth that has been presented here as if it deals with white men only, blacks and women have also part in this phenomenon. Hence the stereotype of the eighties owes its existence, and even its invention, to a social ideology and bureaucratic needs and interests. This myth fell into line with the political and cultural mood at that time, and therefore was not criticized, as this scientist does.

According to Jenkins (2002), the exclusive source for the mythology of the serial murderer was the FBI which presented the problem of the serial murder as a problem that collects many victims and is spread all over the USA. By presenting the serial murderers as wanderers who cross borders between states, the organization demanded a legal authority to deal with felonies beyond its legal jurisdiction. Although in fact, most of the serial murderers operate in a certain city or county, attention was turned deliberately to those few cases of wandering serial murderers in order to increase panic.

Jenkins (2002) claimed that one could explain the gap between myth and reality by the fact that the FBI aspired to establish fear in the public by presenting statistics which created awe and panic. It was done, according to Jenkins, by emphasizing a few cases in which serial murderers kill a large number of victims. He thinks that these cases, especially those which had a sexual background, are the exception and not the rule. But the impression that has been established in the American public and administration led to the allocation of very large resources to deal with "the social problem," as it was presented by exaggeration.

The moral panic in the public continued and increased with the help of the media which show respect and reliability toward the FBI and the information it provides. The question why did the public believe these data so quickly and created, within months, a popular culture on this thin basis, can be understood only within the political context of that period, taking into consideration the threat of national degeneration which the Republicans used in the elections of 1980. Throughout the eighties, the conservative political rhetoric dealt with external threats, and a fear of national vulnerability and internal degeneration. These worries were nourished by external and internal forces as representing severe threats for the American nation: The USSR, serial murderers, Satanism, drug dealers, terrorists coming from within and from outside, sexual abuse and pornography which endanger Native Americans. According to Jenkins, these different groups fulfilled the same social and rhetorical function: Personalizing evil and immorality following the decline of morality and politics of administrators and system managers. These "outsider" factors were presented as a product of the collapse of the family and the raise of hedonism in recent generation. The personalization was done by focusing on a notorious individual or an unpopular figure, like Ted Bundy. Like the panic of the war against drugs and the abuse of children in those years, the movement against serial murderers seems as part of a general moral structuring, as a kind of vengeance in the field of devils in the sixties and the seventies.

This political agenda was presented versus the victory of the liberals in the elections, and it was difficult to gain public support which would demand control or regulation of behaviours. Therefore, the political emphasis was on the threat of innocent groups in the population, mainly women and children who were presented as victims of lascivious men. Serial murder enabled promoting this logic up to the point of a violent death, and in this way, hedonistic America became a society of wolves and sheep (Jenkins, 2002).

The American Congress referred to serial murder as a matter of masculine violence, up to the point at which experts denied the very existence of serial murder by women. Consequently, serial murder and murderers suited, or adjusted to, other images at that time regarding the nature of violence and the social danger.

After the serial murderer has been invented, the concept developed momentum of its own, due to an inner logic of essential elements which were built one on top of the other, mainly with the help of theoreticians from the field of psychology. In fact, one can see differences, and even contradictions, between the psycho-logical assumptions and actual cases.

Compulsiveness: A serial murderer is defined as compulsive, not only because he repeats the murder again and again, but due to the fact that he is incapable of avoiding murdering again. From this assumption it is understood that these crimes would go on forever, as long as the murderer is not caught, and the rates of this crime would escalate in the course of time. This is the explanation for the large number of victims. Expressions of compulsive vio-lence have deep roots in the American thinking since the twenties, when a figure of a demon was prevalent in public culture, a demon who was a sexual psychopath, and caused a great deal of damage due to the distortions of his personality. One of his characteristics was compulsion and inability to stop his deeds. This concept has been preserved through the concept of addiction. Addiction was attributed at first to drugs, but paved the way for the panic which aroused serial violence. The outcome was that the Reagan admin-istration announced the "drug war," while drugs, sexual abuse, and murder were united by a central theme of compulsion until the serial murderer became addicted to murder. My argument against the psychological perception, in the context of obsession, is that there is a difference between inability to control impulses and the lack of will to control them which bring psychological and other benefits to the one who uses them. Presenting the serial murderer as obsessed enabled not referring to this argument at all.

Obsession: The central idea of seriality is the recurrence of a behaviour and the inability to avoid it. And so, by definition, serial murderers repeat their actions again and again, not being able to stop, and hence serial murder is much scarier than mass murder. The idea of an uncontrollable recurrence is very scary in many cultures, since it denies the ability of choosing which is essential for materializing free will and humanity. This characteristic is also common in mental diseases and in situations of insanity, and in this way serial murder has become a compulsive obsession. Again, we can see how the "medical model" in psychology has made the serial murderer into a person who is perceived as a victim of himself, by claiming that he is not able to control his impulses. Such perception suits the positivist school of thought which presented the criminal as a victim of his social, biological and psychological elements, and if the criminal is a victim, then it is hard to accuse him for his deeds.

Lack of roots and instability in social relationships: Serial murderers lack the constraint that keeps normal people from entering a compulsive recurrence of their behaviour. As has been noted, the bureaucratic interest of the FBI demanded emphasizing the characteristics of wandering, lack of roots and social instability among serial murderers which prevent them from staying in one place. The murderers were described as people who do not have a conventional sense of home and family, and their lives are defined as a journey on the railways and the roads rather than having roots and stability regarding a geographical place and relationships. And so they actually symbolized the failure of the traditional ideals of the American community. As wandering murderers, the threat they pose is very great, because they can hit anywhere and at any time, with no reference to the behaviour of the victims. As I will show later on, most of the serial murderers are not unstable wanderers at all. These are people who live at one place for years, are employed and known by the community as "normal" people. In addition, most of them do not change the location of the crime, and do not wander from one place to another for executing their murders.

Irrationality: Serial murderers cannot prevent their actions and lack normal standards of behaviour and constraint. Therefore, they also do not respond to the same stimuli which motivate regular criminals. The American Senate Committee determined that the serial murderer is irrational, and therefore is considered as a person who murders for an unknown motive. This is why the Committee removed from the list of serial murderers those male and female murderers who acted for the sake of material benefit. According to this perception, a serial murderer who acts out of a rational motive, like money, is not considered a real serial murderer, since his actions are rational and have a clear motive.

Passion/lust: Describing the murder as a move that has been done compulsively out of passion, mainly by men, explains why a woman cannot be a serial murderer, unless she is lesbian.

Violence: Losing the capability of choosing denied the serial murderer his full humanity. This dehumanization which was described as a withdrawal to a sub-human condition, or as a return to a bestial condition, is confirmed by the extreme nature of the crimes. Therefore, women were taken out of the category of serial murderers, since they usually did not use physical violence in their actions. A "real" serial murderer is a bloodstained type who stabs his victims or cuts them and mutilates their body.

Jenkins (2002) claims that if we bring together the six elements, we would receive the perception that serial murderers differ from normal people, and even from the cruelest criminals. In other words, these are the beasts of prey of modern era, the vampire and the wolf of the time. Jenkins (2002) uses the term "predator"[52] as a metaphor which served the political and bureaucratic ideology. This predator survives by hunting and eating other animals. According to him, at the early nineties serial sexual criminals were called "predators" so commonly that states formulated special rules against "sexual predators," or "sexually violent predators." The serial murderer was also called a "monster," as the metaphor was that serial murderers have supernatural and demonic characteristics. One has to shoot or hunt these predators, but the journey to the land of monsters is full of dangers.

To sum up, Jenkins (2002) indicates that the concept of serial murder is shaped by a sophisticated and planned process of combining the so-called real world of the legal system and the imaginary world of the popular culture. The irony, as he sees it, is that the popular structuring of serial murder mixed several characteristics of the mythology of this seriality: The constant and cyclic creation of the media produced more and more images, until it seems that seriality is a product of seriality.

Another example of this myth is presenting the murderer as a loner who lurks for prey. In fact, most of the serial murderers have a regular work, a family, and they even go to church on Sundays (Fox & Levin, 2005).

These descriptions can be related to Vronsky's (2007) reference to the phenomenon of serial murderers. According to his claim, serial murderers, especially those who are motivated by a will to achieve power and control, have been since the beginning of documented history. In the ancient world they appeared in the shape of emperors, dictators and aristocrats who had the power to determine the lives and deaths of their subjects. This is exactly the power that serial murderers today aspire to in relation to their victims. At the same time, there were serial murderers from the simple folk who were described as cannibals, vampires, monsters, and so on.

Vronsky (2007) argues that the modern serial murderer is a secular monster. In the 18th and 19th centuries monsters were given a specific name and human identity, or alternately nicknames with an unknown identity. The appearance of the mass media brought about a situation in which the monsters have started to be identified as real people rather than a mystic animal hiding in a dark forest.

For about a hundred years Jack the Ripper was the serial murderer of the industrial era, and he shaped our popular perception about serial murderers up to the seventies of the twentieth century. At that time Ted Bundy brought the serial murderer to a new, postmodern era: The neighbour next door, the handsome man with the academic degree—someone who did not fit the image of the serial murderer, as he resembles many of us!

Characteristics and Definitions of Serial Murder and Murderers

Some attribute the coining of the term serial murderer to the scientist Ressler (1992) from the FBI who wanted to distinguish between a murderer of familiar people and a murderer of strangers

(Ibid., p. 46). But historically it was the psychiatrist Brophy who wanted, in 1976, to distinguish between a mass murder and a serial murder. Another claim says that the term surfaced in 1936 by Wakefield who described a criminal who was afraid of being caught and deported, and therefore became a "serial murderer." Another scientist, Lindsay (1958), used the term "series of murders."[53]

The large amount of literature that deals with serial murderers and murders often indicates the problematic nature of the definition of seriality, serial murder and serial murderer. We can see that the number of definitions for serial murder is like the number of people who deal with this field, while many critics suggest new definitions of their own.[54] Brantley and Hosky (2005) argue that like the behavioural classification which tries to label complicated systems of variables, so the attempts to establish a standard definition of a serial murder have not succeeded in achieving agreement. Nelson (2007) agrees with this claim, and indicates that without a universal and accepted definition it would be difficult to understand the complexity of the phenomenon of serial murder and serial murderers.

For instance, Harbourt and Mokros (2001) claim that the most quoted definition for a murder is the one formulated for the FBI by Ressler et al. in 1988: "Three separate events or more with an emotional cooling-off period between murders, while each murder takes place in a different location" (Ibid., p. 139). These scientists claim that this definition raises more questions than provides answers. For example, to which cases of murder they mean by the term events? Is one attempt of murder and two actual murders, or three attempts of murder would suffice to be called a series of murders? And why do the murders have to take place in different locations? The criticisms can be divided into a few types:

First of all, there is the issue of the total number of victims which is required so that the murder cases, executed by the same murderer or murderers, would be considered as a serial murder. It is obvious that in order to distinguish between a one-time murder and a serial murder, the number of victims of a certain serial murderer must be more than one. The dispute among the scientists is around the total number of victims. Some maintain that two is enough. On the other hand, Harbort and Mokros (2001) argue that the reference to three cases of murder is not random, but is based on the lexical definition of the term series. According to Webster's Dictionary, a series is a group of three items or more which are arranged in a certain order and have relationships with each other.

The rationale which differentiates between three victims versus one is obvious, but the rationale of those who differentiate between three and four victims is more difficult to understand. For example, "a serial murder involves a chain of four or more cases of murder which were executed by one or more murderers, in a period of days, weeks, months, or even years" (Fox & Levin, 2005, p. 31). As if the dispute about actual cases of murder is not enough, Skrapec (2001) expands the dispute over the definition by asking: Would an attempt of murder be included in the definition or not. Eventually, like in the definition of a mass murder, the law and legal authorities determine the criterion arbitrarily, according to their viewpoint and interests (Harbort & Mokros, 2001).

The second criticism refers to the period of time that distinguishes between one murder and the next. The scientists agree that what distinguishes between a serial murder and a mass murder is the cooling-off period, but there is no agreement about the length of the required period. According to the existing definitions, the cooling-off period can move from three whole days (72 hours) up to a month. In addition, there is no agreement among the scientists about the duration of the maximal cooling-off period between the murder cases. For instance, can we call a man a serial murderer who murdered a person when he was 20 years old, and after 30 years, murdered another victim, and after another 20 years, murdered another victim? According to the existing definition the answer would be positive, but practically it raises a significant problem.

The third criticism deals with the content of the definition. Does the definition have to include the motives for the murder, the location of the murder, the number of murderers, and so on? Skrapec (2001), for example, claims that the ten most quoted definitions for a serial murder do not represent at all the components of the phenomenon. Even when we try to expand the definition so that it would include the maximal cases, arbitrary decisions about the inclusion of certain kinds of cases on the one hand, and excluding others on the other, makes the definition more problematic. Furthermore, there is no consistency in the definitions: Part of them deal with the characteristics of the criminal (gender, relationships with the criminal, motive, psychopathology), while others describe aspects of the felonies (the method of murder, the minimal number of victims, the type of victims). According to the scientist, we can solve part of the problems of the definition by formulating sub-categories of serial murderers by referring to the motive. For example, separating between a murder that is executed while executing another felony, in which case the murder is secondary to the central goal which is achieving a material benefit, and a real serial murder, in which the murder is the main motive. In this context, Skrapec argues that the myth of a murderer who operates with no motive is a severe mistake. According to Skrapec, as has been noted, the existing definitions are very problematic because they do not refer to the motive, and as a result the definition includes serial murders that are executed by mercenaries, terrorists, assassins on behalf of organized crime, and others. This kind of generalization adds a political motive which has a very different dynamic to those murders committed from other motives. Accordingly, adds Skrapec (2001), some of the definitions exclude certain categories from the definition, like acts executed by soldiers during battle, terrorists, people of the organized crime, and gangs. In spite of the change of definitions and the emphasis they put on "civilian" serial murder, a new situation has been established, in which the definitions determine what is not a serial murder, but do not explain what is one.[55]

A serial murderer always has a motive, and it is his lust to kill. The term comes from the German word *lustmord*, i.e., a murder that was done for the sake of enjoyment. Later on, this term was used in a sexual connotation. This is a type of serial murder that is different and distinguished from a series of murder for the sake of achieving other goals, like a financial benefit.

From his viewpoint, Skrapec (2001) suggests the following definition: "Three or more murders which are forensically connected and take place in separate events by the same person or persons, along a long period of time whose primary motive is personal satisfaction" (Ibid., p. 22). Skrapec (2001) adds and indicates that the death of the victims is the intention and the primary goal of the series of murders.

An example of the problematic nature of the definition of serial murder can be seen in the definition by Keeney and Heide (1994): "A serial murder is a premeditated murder of three or more victims which is executed in the course of time, in separate events, in a civilian context, and the method of murder is determined by the criminal." This definition emphasizes the civilian nature of serial murder, versus actions with a military or political background. Nevertheless, it is not clear why does the definition exclude political assassinations, but leaves assassinations of the organized crime, while both of them are actually a mass-serial murder. Moreover, the definition might suggest that every action of serial murder that takes place in a military basis would not be included in the definition of serial murder, even though a soldier, who systematically murders his commanders or POWs, can absolutely be labeled as a serial murderer (Ferguson et al., 2003).

Salfati and Bateman's (2005) definition for a serial murder, a reducing definition in its nature, emphasized the motive for the murder. According to them, a serial murderer is "a person who murdered three persons or more in separate events who is motivated by a different combination of hedonism, sexual lust, ambition for power and control, or zeal and a fanaticism to rid the world of the unwanted." Salfati and Bateman's (2005) claim that a serial murder appears as an expressive crime rather than an instrumental one. Therefore, the definition they suggest does not include serial murderers who are motivated by achieving a material benefit, people of crime organizations, like serial professional assassins, or a serial murder executed by groups, due to political or religious reasons (Ibid., p. 277).

Although allegedly there is a shift from defining a serial murder to its motives, it is important to elaborate this point. The definition of a serial murder would influence later on the classification and the typology, as well as the understanding of the motives for these fatal activities. Therefore, the definitions of the phenomenon would often influence the theoretical reference to the phenomenon and its motives. Salfati and Bateman's (2005) determine: "Expressive actions of aggression focus on the victim as a specific person and make him suffer. Instrumental activities of aggression focus in achieving material commodities, with no reference to the price the person, who is perceived as a hindrance for achieving the goal, pays" (Ibid., p. 277).[56]

The above definition differs from the previous ones due to its reference to possible motives, with an emphasis on the serial murderer rather than on the serial murder, and since it is so, the definition is reductive compared to the other definitions which include a wider range of cases. Reduction has an advantage, as we restrict the concept we deal with into clear limits, and in this manner we determine what is included in the concept and what is not. On the other hand, a reducing definition is not valid because it cannot be considered as 'exhaustive and exclusive'. For example, Salfati and Bateman determine that a serial murder is an expressive act which is not motivated by material-instrumental motives. This point of view is influenced by the serial murderer who acts out of a sexual motive, and does not represent fully the phenomenon as a whole. A serial murderer is also motivated by material motives, as part of the scientists determined, when they included hedonistic motives (Holmes & Holmes, 1998). In addition, "The professional assassin" is the most outstanding example of an instrumental murder, rather than an expressive one. He receives instructions and money, executes his job, and then his connection with the victim and the issuer of the assassination is terminated. There is a difference if we define a phenomenon with all its aspects and say that we do not intend to refer to certain domains included in the definition, and a definition which does not include all the possibilities in advance.

On the other hand, other definitions tried to expand the range as much as possible, like the definition of the FBI. Such definitions, according to Brantley and Hosky (2005), do not refer to motive, behaviour, and psychological characteristics, as they have been deliberately formulated in an expanded version in order to include a wide range of serial murderers. That means that there is a decisive point of disagreement among the scientists whether to include the motive in the definition or not. Morton (2005) supports the definition without reference to the motive, arguing that if the definition refers to the motive, it would become too complicated.[57]

Beyond this issue, it is worthwhile referring to a more serious claim that a few scientists raise, that part of the problem of the definition stems, like in the mass murder, from different perceptions and stereotypes. Hickey (1992), for example, indicates that for the law enforcement system, a serial murder is usually perceived as a murder which includes a sexual assault. Therefore, many cases of serial murders were not included in the definition because they did not meet the stereotype. For example, hospital nurses who murdered hospitalized patients, serial murderers with material motives, people who are not perceived as cruel, bloodthirsty monsters, and male and female murderers who do not torture their victims and do not attack them sexually. These are the "silent murderers," married men and women who hold a permanent position at work, like the next door neighbour. Although Hickey (1992) raises the aforementioned problematic nature, he does not suggest a wider definition (Hinch & Scott, 2000; Ferguson, et al., 2003).

The American Ministry of Justice took up the gauntlet (1996) and suggested a wide definition, according to which a serial murderer is every criminal, male or female who kills over a long period of time. Generally, there are three to four victims. The murder is characterized by the pattern of selecting the victims, the method of murder and its motives. The definition includes people who murder within their home, town, or the state they live in, or even travel to another state in search of victims.

To summarize, one can see that even today there is no agreement among the scientists regarding the three problems that have been presented: Number of victims, the cooling-off period between one murder and the next, and the question whether the motive should appear in the definition, or not. Some of the recent definitions choose to reduce the definition by referring to the motive and the framework (civil, political, and military). For example, Ferguson et al., (2003) are in favor of a definition which would comprise three components: Number of victims (at least three); causing death to the victims was considered an enjoyable stress release for the murderer and suiting his set of values; and the fact that the murders have not taken place within a political or criminal organization. On the other hand, some of the scientists choose to avoid referring to the motive and the framework in order to include the maximal possibilities in defining serial murder. It is interesting to see the most up-to-date definition for a serial murder which Vronsky (2007) suggests: "A murder of two people or more, as separate events, for whatever reason, is a serial murder" (Ibid., p. 20). According to Vronsky, this definition can include the assassin who works for organized crime, as well. For him the psychopathology of a mercenary, as well as that of a war criminal, does not differ from that of "regular" serial murderers. He refrains from the dispute about the duration of the cooling-off period by referring to "separate events," but the maximal range of the time period between one event and the next may be an issue of disagreement.

To sum up, one can see definitions of serial murder not comprised only of criteria of time and number of victims, but largely influenced by populist perceptions of the media, as well as by interests of the law enforcement system. This is the reason why we would find differences between the definitions suggested by the people of the law enforcement system and those of theoreticians in the field. Moreover, especially in the academic-theoretical domain, the definitions refer sometimes to the field on which the scientist is interested. Hence, many cases, which fulfill the "regular" definition of serial murder, would be excluded from the definition if the scientist is not interested in explaining the phenomenon as a whole, but prefers to focus on a certain aspect of it. For instance, a scientist who is interested in explaining the phenomenon of a sexual-sadist murder would exclude a murder for the sake of material benefit from the definition.

After distinguishing between a mass murder and a mass-serial murder, I can now suggest the following definition for a serial murder: A serial murder is a series of at least three murder cases, executed by the same murderer (or murderers), over a period of months and years; the murder cases are separated from one another in time and number of victims, and can take place in one location or in several locations; only one victim is murdered in each event, the motive for murdering repeats itself in all cases, and it can be for the sake of psychological benefit which stems from pathology and/or for the sake of material benefit; the way of operation is usually similar in all cases, but can be changed deliberately in order to make it difficult for the law enforcement authorities.

The Scope of the Phenomenon

One of the outstanding difficulties in examining the rate of serial murder cases and the number of victims stems from the fact that unlike mass murder, a major part of the serial murderers is not caught, or caught after a very long time. Some scientists (Holmes & Holmes, 1998; Mitchell, 1997) assume that as of the seventies, the rate of serial murder cases in the USA increased 22 times in relation to single murder cases. The scientists base their opinion on the assumption that about 20 percent of the unsolved murder cases were executed by serial murderers.

The scientists indicate that according to their assessment—at the time of writing the research—there are thirty-five active serial murderers. In the same year Levin and Fox (1998) argue that the numbers presented by their colleagues were exaggerated and influenced by overblown numbers which were meant to achieve budgetary goals. For example, Hickey (1997) speaks only about some tens of victims per year, while in the same year Mitchell (1997) evaluates the number of serial murderers at about 200–300, and the number of victims at about 5,000 per year.[58] Mitchell found in his research that during 1960–1991, 357 serial murderers operated in the USA murdering 3,169 victims. His assessment is that the annual number of murder cases amounts to two hundred. These data are confusing and unclear: If in the thirty-one years of the scientist's examination there have been 3,169 victims, how can it be that the number of victims per year was 5,000? Furthermore, if there are 200 murder cases per year, how does the number of victims amount to 5,000? The meaning of this datum is that every year 25 victims are murdered in every murder case which is of course impossible, as it has been determined in the definition that in every murder event only one victim is murdered. That is, the data are undoubtedly exaggerated. The annual number of victims, in a rough estimate, is about a hundred at the most.

In 2005, Fox and Levin presented new research in which they claim that since 1900 up to the time of their research, there operated in the USA only 558 serial murderers, and the number of victims in this period was 5,650 people. That is, the average number of victims per year comes close to sixty which is about ten victims, on average, per serial murderer.[59] The scientists explain the immense gaps versus the previous data by a mistake that stemmed from the fact that the different scientists attributed all the victims of the unsolved murders to serial murders. In addition, they indicate that at the height of the eighties, the average number of victims amounted to 120–180 victims per year. They suggest two explanations for the increase in the reported number of serial murder cases in the eighties. The first one is that like in the case of mass murder, the FBI has inflated the numbers, aiming to receive material, human, and technological resources by establishing a public panic. Secondly, Fox & Levin (2005), refer to a concept which was coined by Egger (1988), called "linkage blindness." According to Egger, the scientist cannot always link murder cases which had been separated in time and space to the activity of one murderer, especially if the murder cases occurred in different states, and therefore the number of victims is actually higher than can be seen in the statistics.

Although the implications of both explanations on the number of serial murderers and their victims are very different from one another, one can assume eventually that its scope is about a few hundred victims per year.

A partial answer to the gaps between the different assessments was given in 2007 by Quinet. This scientist claims that the American authorities exaggerated the number of victims of serial murders, because they referred to each victim who was murdered by a foreigner as if he was necessarily murdered by a serial murderer. Quinet (2007) argues that the real number of victims of serial murders is a product of what we know (arrested murderers), plus cases we assume are included in serial murderers. The exaggeration of the number of victims moves between 182, up to 1,832 per year. But such a gap in assessment not only does not contribute anything, but even adds confusion.

Vronsky (2004) supports the approach of Holmes and Holmes (1998), and argues that the frequency of serial murder in the USA increased in the last three decades. According to Vronsky, 80% of the total number of male serial murderers appeared during the years 1950–1995, and in these years the frequency of serial murder increased according to the formal statistics by 940%. The author connects it with over-reporting in the media which is influenced by inaccurate formal statistics. He assumes that since the seventies, right up to the nineties, about 365 serial murderers operated, and the average annual number has been found at about seventy. In addition, the author emphasizes that the reports in the media about a "plague of serial murders" stem from a public panic the media create rather than from reality.

After the peak in serial murder cases in the eighties, one can see a decrease in this phenomenon in the nineties in parallel to the decrease of murder cases in general. Fox and Levin (2005) attribute this decrease to several reasons: An increase of the number of imprisoned people keep potential violent criminals and serial murderers restrained; the techniques of predicting the exposure of serial murderers who have not started operating yet were improved; and serial murder has become part of regular public awareness, so that the phenomenon does not receive the hyped attention and conspicuousness it once received in the past.

I disagree with the arguments of the scientists mentioned above: Serial murderers do not have a criminal record of violence or anything to do with the law enforcement system, and the predictability of a serial murder has not improved over time. Hence the increase of the number of inmates does not influence the number of serial murder cases. In addition, the scientists do not present empirical data from the nineties to support their argument.

At the same time, Fox and Levin (2005) claimed that in spite of the quick increase in the rate of serial murders in the eighties, one cannot speak about a plague, but about an increase of serial murders together with an increase of violent felonies, including murder in general.

The significant differences in the number of serial murder cases and their victims can be explained by the use of a different operational definition of different scientists for defining serial murder. For example, it is obvious that if one scientist refers to a threshold of two victims, and another to a threshold of three victims, there would be a significant gap in the data they would find and present. Furthermore, one may say that the formal criminal statistics create significant distortions in the number of murder cases, murderers, and victims. As for the contradicting data, we would have to assume that there are about 100–180 victims per year, and the scientists' supposition, like in mass murder, is that it is about one percent of the total number of murder cases in the USA which amount to about 18,000 victims per year.

It is very important to emphasize that empirically, researches have compared serial murder cases in the past and in the present in relation to the number of victims, but there was no research which compared between the number of victims according to socio-demographic characteristics, or other variables. The problem is that while in the past we could find cases in which one nobleman murdered 800 children of vassals, today we speak about more murderers, and every one of them murders less victims. Therefore, it is important to refer also to the status of the victims. Let's look at another example: While in the past, prostitution was usually located in guarded brothels, today there are more prostitutes roaming the streets and city centers. This lack of protection contributes to the increase in murders of prostitutes. It is well explained by the criminological theories of rational choice and routine activity.[60]

Demographic and Geographic Characteristics of Serial Murder and Murderers[61]

Most of the demographic characteristics of serial murderers have been presented already at the beginning of the chapter, in a comparison between serial murderers and one-time murderers. Therefore, only part of the characteristics will be emphasized.

As far as world distribution is concerned, 76% of the serial murder cases take place in the US, 21% in Europe (mainly in England, Germany and France), and 3% in the developing world countries.

Statistically, it was found that 86% of the serial murderers are men, and 82% are white, with a higher intelligence than the average that have started murdering in the 20s and 30s of their lives. The average age is 30 which is higher than the average age of regular murderers.[62] The serial murderers operate as individuals (81%), in pairs (12.2%), and in a team (7%) (Vronsky, 2004; Fox & Levin, 2005).[63]

Serial murder is characterized by murdering people who are strangers to the murderer:[64] 61% murdered only strangers, and 15% murdered at least one stranger among their victims[65] (Fox & Levin, 1998). The main reason for this is the motive and the will to avoid being caught. Part of the serial murderers operate with a sexual background, and in these cases, they choose prostitutes, women, and sometimes even children as their victims, strangers they can seduce, catch, and murder in order to satisfy sadistic impulses and violent fantasies. According to Fox and Levin (2005), two thirds of the victims of the serial murderers fall into these categories.

It is necessary to discuss black serial murderers, since referencing has met with some distortion, an extent of media interest, and statements from the academia toward the murderers and their victims. Walsh (2005) surveys the issue elaborately, starting at the end of WWII up to 2004. A serial murderer by the name of Bird murdered forty-four victims—almost a record number in the USA. After WWII a few other black serial murderers stood out, like Carl Watts, "The Sunday Morning Slasher," who was related to twenty-one murder cases at the end of the seventies and the beginning of the eighties. In the recent decades another black serial murderer appeared: Wallace who murdered at least nine women in the mid-nineties. All the victims were known to him, an exceptional phenomenon in serial murder; Francois was arrested at the end of the nineties for the murder of eight white women which is an exception to the pattern of murdering within the ethnic group, and at the beginning of 2000, other black serial murderers were arrested; all of them murdered white victims. Walsh argues that although black serial murderers, in recent years, murdered less victims than white serial murderers, like Ted Bundy (20 victims), or Gacy (33 victims), they murdered more victims than famous white serial murderers, like Berkowitz and others. Walsh (2005) argues that in spite of this fact, black serial murderers remained without publicity, while the white murderers gained vast publication. Walsh (2005) enumerates a number of reasons for the lack of publicity: A political apprehension of an allegedly racial attitude in the media by emphasizing members of a certain ethnic group in a negative context; until recently, the law enforcement authorities tended to refer less seriously to crimes executed by blacks, unless their victims were whites; there is a perception saying that mass media is less entertaining when they cast black people in negative roles, and therefore there have not been movies about black serial murderers, as opposed to whites.

Walsh (2005) mentions that criminology ignored the overrepresentation of black people in serial murders due to the apprehension of being accused of racism, as it ignored organized crime executed by blacks. Another reason he mentions for this ignorance is the apprehension that a group that suffers anyway from weakness and deficiency, would go through additional labeling and maligning by discussing its felonies. Walsh (2005) claims that these serial murderers are almost unmentioned in papers about serial murder, and this is in fact an expression of racism.

Geographically or spatially speaking, in spite of the common myth that the serial murderer travels for long distances in order to find his victims, these cases are the minority. There are indeed such murderers, like Ted Bundy, Lucas, and others, but most of the serial murderers operate in a geographical area in the proximity of their home or work ("comfort zone"). Gacy, for instance, murdered 33 victims at his home and buried most of them there. From data presented by Fox and Levin (2005, 1998), it appears that half and up to three quarters of serial murderers operated locally, about 15% operated in one specific area (work, home) on the regional level, and a tenth up to a third of the serial murderers traveled for long distances throughout the country.

As far as education is concerned, while the sophistication of some serial murderers created a myth of people with high education, it was found that actually they have low to average levels of education (ten years of study), and they mainly worked blue-collar jobs (Kenney & Heide, 1994). Furthermore, not always was there found a correlation between the number of years of education and the sophistication in executing the murder.

The time intervals between the murder cases, the cooling-off periods, intrigue several scientists, and eventually they achieved no agreement, but Lange (1999) proved that there is cyclicality in the murder cases, and that one can predict, to a certain extent, the time intervals between the murder cases among specific murderers. But he found three different models on this issue. One is stability at the times of the murders, and then an increase in their frequency; the second shows an increase in the frequency of the murder cases and then a decrease; and the third is a combination of the previous two.[66]

Psychological and Social Characteristics of Serial Murder and Murderers

This issue will be discussed elaborately with reference to the motives of serial murder. Kenney and Heide (1994) summarize some of the outstanding findings about male serial murderers:[67] We speak about the eldest sons in their families who grew up in destroyed families: Separated/divorced parents, or one of them died. In their childhood they were victims of abuse or neglect by their family which explains the fact that part of them grew up outside their biological family in institutional or semi-institutional frameworks (a fostering family).

From the data examined by Kenney and Heide (1994), there is no clear picture regarding the use of psychoactive substances or contact with the law and legal systems in adolescence. Part of the serial murderers suffered in their childhood and adolescence from the Macdonald triad which includes bed-wetting, pyromania, and cruelty toward animals.[68] Their psychiatric diagnosis shows an antisocial personality, but not psychosis or schizophrenia.

Until now I have tried to answer two questions: What is a serial murder according to the different definitions, and what are the characteristics of serial murderers?[69] The third question, maybe the most important and intriguing of all, is why—what are the reasons or the motives for serial murder? While in mass murder the motive of vengeance in different ways is outstanding, in serial murder the different motives are different from vengeance and are much more varied.

Explanations of Serial Murder and Murderers[70]

Methodological Problems

We may characterize the explanations of serial murder according to different approaches: Biological-physiological, sociological, and psychological. According to Holmes and Holmes (1998), the assignment of understanding a serial murder, that is, what motivates the serial murderer is almost an impossible assignment, because the mind of the serial murderer is unique and different from that of regular murderers, so the use of traditional theories would not suffice.

Holmes & Holmes (1998) are correct in assuming that it is very difficult to explain this phenomenon, but I claim that the criminological-sociological theories, combined with traditional psychological theories provide a good explanation for serial murder and murderers. Unlike scientists who have looked for new theories for explaining this phenomenon, I will claim that rivalry among fields of knowledge prevented a fertile cooperation in order to achieve an interdisciplinary, or a comprehensive multidisciplinary explanation.

One of the outstanding problems in investigating serial murder is that the scientists, mainly psychiatrists and psychologists, presented a single case and according to it created theoretical generalizations. Later on, the scientists used a collection of cases, and one central research, conducted by the FBI on a small group of serial murderers, aimed at finding common characteristics about them, mainly in the sado-sexual field. But this research was conducted, as has been said, on single cases, and their main empirical deficiency was the lack of a control group.

The outcome is that even if there are outstanding characteristics among serial murderers, it was not proved empirically that these characteristics exist only among them. The criticism claimed that the same characteristics, like trauma and abuse in childhood, exist also in the general population. In this context, Pino (2005) suggests to refer to a concept, or an idea, of a Criminal Event Perspective, meaning that every criminal event involves the murderer who has a history and a motive of his own; the time, place and situation in which the serial murderer and the victims met; the interaction between them that focuses on the murderous act; and the implications the event has on the behaviour of the murderer. According to Pino, the roles and relationships the individual has in one stage of his life influence his later relationships. Hence, we have to investigate the entire life history of the criminal. Pino's perception is that criminal events, like a serial murder, are a process rather than something which stands alone. The scientists who were aware of the criticism, moderated their generalization a little and referred to a collection of factors that characterize the serial murderer, but the criticism claimed that the same factors exist in the general population as well. Some of the scientists argued that a certain mixture of the different characteristics is what makes a certain individual a serial murderer, but again, they gave too general a list of characteristics, and it is not clear how they are linked to one another and in what "dosage" so that the individual with these characteristics would become a serial murderer, while another person would not.

One of the results was attempts, mainly by people from the mental health disciplines, to construct theories and explanations about the creation of a serial murderer, relying on the DSM-IV and DSM-V manual of diagnoses as a tool for validating their explanations. We have to bear in mind that even if an individual suffers from a certain disorder, this disorder cannot be defined rigidly. At the most, one can see that the individual has some of the characteristics which exist in the manual as an ideal model. Hence, there is a very wide range within the different disorders regarding the existence of the disorder: Low, medium, and full level. Another problem has to do with the fact that the determination that a person suffers from a certain disorder is done according to a number of symptoms regarding several parameters. This is an arbitrary and problematic determination that creates labeling and rigidity which provides mental health practitioners with a diagnostic direction for treatment, but one cannot conclude from them unequivocal determinations regarding the diagnosis and the etiology. For example, an individual can suffer from certain symptoms which exist in a few definitions of mental disorders, like an antisocial personality disorder and narcissism. The question is which label was determined for this individual. Alternately, and against the rigidity of labeling, we could say that a certain individual suffers from symptoms which are characteristic to several definitions.

Another problem stems from the fact that research on serial murder and murderers is based on different sources of information: Police, mass media, and biographies with different levels of reliability. It damages the capability to build a meaningful basis of knowledge, and by so doing makes it difficult also to present explanations to the phenomenon, especially when the number of the diagnosed cases is very small (Skrapec, 2001).

Hence, we have two options: One is claiming that each case has to be examined individually, and then we would not be able to make theoretical generalizations in order to understand the phenomenon. On the other hand, we may claim that the psychological and the sociological explanations and the combination of them have some insight which does not exist in each of the disciplines when it stands alone. These insights enable us to explain in a more general way the reasons why an individual becomes a serial murderer, even if we should do it carefully, without being able to generalize and predict unequivocally. Unlike the instigator of a disease, like a virus or a microbe, one cannot find exactly the same "instigator" in two serial murderers. Moreover, the great diversity and variance of serial murderers do not enable generalizations, even with an "ideal" theory. In this book I have chosen the second option, in spite of its limitations. Another problem in explaining serial murder stems from the reference of the mass media to these murder and murderers and to the myths that have been established in the public eye. As of the eighties, the media, movies, television series, books, reports, investigations and interviews dealt a lot with serial murderers. The image which has been established in the public was that the serial murderer is indeed a wolf who is on the prowl for prey, mainly a feminine one. The image of the serial murderer created a frightening and threatening figure of a mentally disturbed man, and it led the public to be aware and concerned of such men, but not from serial murderers who live among us and do not meet the image: The nice next door neighbour, the dedicated family man, the permanent and punctual employee who comes to work every morning, the man who pretends to be an injured academician who asks for help, and so on. On the other hand, Bonny and Clyde, Billy the Kid, and a variety of westerns' heroes were actually psychopathic serial murderers, glorified by the media until they became culture heroes.

The different descriptions by the mass media created myths and images which distorted reality and influenced the explanations and definitions of serial murder. For example, the serial murderer who kills for the sake of material benefit does not appear in part of the definitions, since he does not suit the myth of the sexual attacker.

The explanations for serial murder, like a mass murder, stood out at first in psychology and psychiatry, since the acts of serial murder could not be perceived as "normal" acts of "sane" people, and therefore these fields of knowledge appropriated, to a large extent, the explanation of the phenomenon. The dispute among scientists was mainly about the origin of the mental disorder which brought about the murderous behaviour,[71] and about the question of whether one can define the serial murderer as a sane person who suffers from a mental disorder, like psychopathy, or has to be defined as insane and as suffering from psychotic mental illnesses (dissociation), and hence has to be acknowledged as one who is not accountable for his actions.

As I will show, the lack of satisfaction from the psychological explanations, which relied mainly on case studies, brought about developments in other fields of knowledge, including sociology and criminology which tried to suggest better explanations to the phenomenon. Due to competition among the different fields of knowledge, and the lack of cooperation among them, one can find sociological explanations which are similar to the psychological ones, complement them, or suggest a theoretical substitution for them.

The hypothesis of this book is that the combination of knowledge between these fields of study could enhance under-standing the phenomenon better than the singular understanding that each field suggests. In other words, the whole is greater than the sum of its parts.

Biological Explanations of Serial Murder and Murderers

The general title refers to explanations from physiology, genetics, neurology and biology of the human being.

Mitchell (1997) surveys the main explanations in the fields of biology and neurology for serial murder. One explanation is bor-rowed from the animal world: The will for power and control is rooted in the world of nature. Darwin's theory regarded the pro-cess of natural selection as a competition among males in the ex-clusive access to females. In order to ensure the rights of mating and reproducing, the animal world is conducted according to an aggressive and enforcing behaviour which includes violence among males and between males and females. If we go back to serial murder, we may conclude that a murder with a sexual background stems from the will of the murderer to force himself on women for the sake of mating, and therefore he murders them.

In nature, males fight among themselves over females in order to mate with the female, either by force or willingly, in order to ensure the reproduction of their species. A serial murder in which the murderer kills the woman ensures the opposite result. Even if the murderer rapes the victim, murdering her prevents her getting pregnant and giving birth to his son. Alternately, if the murderer is not interested in a sexual act, but in control, like the leader of the herd who feels satisfaction after driving away his competitors, or hurting them, the fact that the murderer kills his victims does not enable him enjoy the sense of the power of the leader, because his subjects do not exist anymore. Furthermore, why do serial murderers not murder the husbands or lovers in order to have the woman they desire? It is problematic to deduce a conclusion from the activities in the animal world compared to the human world as far as murder is concerned.

Today more and more scientists assume that in the background of a serial murder there is biological-brain damage that comes from a defect or head trauma, but the assumption that a person becomes a serial murderer as a result of such a factor is not true. A brain defect might bring about violent behaviour, but such a connection to serial murderer was not proved (Anderson, 1999).

Another explanation deals with the correlation between a head injury and abnormality of the brain, and serial murder. Some serial murderers show these findings. There is abnormality or deficient development in the brain of the murderer, and it can be seen in many characteristics which demonstrate immaturity. There are some outstanding characteristics of a psychopathic personality: Sexual immaturity, emotional impotence, emotional outbursts, and others (Mitchell, 1997; Anderson, 1999).

It is true that most of the serial murderers can be described as psychopaths, but not because of a defect or defects in the brain. As far as head injuries in childhood are concerned, the argument is very inaccurate, since it does not explain why many children who have suffered from head injuries in childhood, have not become serial murderers in their adulthood. This criticism is true in relation to the other biological characteristics which were found among serial murderers as well, because they have not been compared with a control group of people who were not serial murderers.

Another explanation deals with hormones, arguing that most of the serial murderers suffer from some kind of psychomotor brain damage, like epilepsy or a serious hormonal imbalance which may stem from a dysfunction of the hypothalamus. Alternatively, a genetic explanation was suggested, according to which the serial murderer suffers from an excess of chromosome Y—"the crime gene."

Mitchell (1997) and Holmes and Holmes (1998) criticize harshly the biological explanations which have been suggested for serial murder. They raise three arguments: First, there are law abiding people who suffer from the same symptoms and disorders; second, scientists have not yet exposed the full potential of the brain, and the correlation between brain activity and fatally violent behaviour has not been proved; and third, an evidence of a biological disorder among serial murderers has not been found. According to Holmes & Holmes (1998) and Mitchell (1997), even today, there is not even one clinical picture in which biology indeed plays the main or the secondary role among serial murderers.[72]

Psychological Explanations of Serial Murder and Murderers

While just a fifth of the serial murderers had a history of mental illness,[73] psychiatry has still been the dominant paradigm in explaining serial murder (Mitchell, 1997). Appropriating serial murder to the field of mental illnesses, as has been said, was an outcome of the inability to attribute this phenomenon to sane people. The basic tendency was to regard the serial murderer as a person who is controlled by the impulses of his id with no control of the superego.

In the field of psychological explanation, there is no reference to all kinds of serial murder, and certainly not to those which are connected to professionalism and/or to the motive of material benefit, like the professional assassin. Most of the psychological explanations present serial murderers as people who act out of different personality disorders, like identity disorders and others. Only a small minority of the serial murderers is presented as psychotic.

Freud's theory of personality—Freud claimed that the human soul is composed of three parts. The first part is the id, a biological component which includes impulses and bestial instincts, like hunger, sex, surviving instincts and others. The second component is the superego. This component in the personality expresses the internalization of moral and social norms, and its role is to repress the bestial impulses and instincts within the person. The third component, the ego, is a rational component which expresses the principles of reality, and its role is to express the impulses and instincts that have been repressed by the superego in a normative and socially accepted way.

When the superego is weak, defective or with some flaw, it cannot repress the bestial impulses and instincts. The individual actually lacks a mechanism of self-control, and in this situation he might commit a serial murder from a variety of sadistic, sexual or other instincts (Mitchell, 1997).

The criticism of this theory is that one cannot examine and measure scientifically-empirically the components of personality, the relationships between them and their very existence.

The theory of humiliation-frustration-aggression—this theory has been presented and discussed in the previous chapter, and therefore it is only mentioned here. Based on this theory, Hale (1998) claimed that the serial murderer releases, through his murder actions, feelings of humiliation he has experienced in his past. The murders enable him to achieve again the power he has lost. The assumption, accompanied by empirical evidence, is that the murderer experienced humiliation in his childhood which was an attack on his self-worth or on his moral worth. Such humiliation motivates the individual to act, aiming to retrieve what is considered by him as "good"/"correct"/"right." Hale responds to the criticism that many people experience humiliation, but do not become serial murderers, by arguing that a previous humiliation might become a murderous act only if the murderer knows and internalizes the humiliation as the motive for his murderous act from some psychological reason.[74] Furthermore, the murderer identifies certain signs in the humiliating and frustrating situation in the present and connects them to the humiliation in the past. This situation is called "the violent cue," and it pushes the murderer into action, or prevents him from entering similar situations in the future.

In my opinion, this claim suffers from a logical and empirical contradiction, since such a serial murderer wishes, in fact, to enter situations in which he would be able to achieve the power and dominance he lacks.

In fact, the serial murderer does not usually turn to the source of frustration, but to innocent substitutes. Like Ted Bundy, for instance who did not murder his fiancé after she canceled the engagement, but instead attacked and murdered tens of women who looked like her. The explanation for this is that the feeling of aggression toward the frustrating or humiliating object was blocked for the hurt individual, due to an objective danger, like being caught and punished, and much more so, due to a psychological fear of an expression of aggression toward the frustrating or humiliating object from a variety of physical and psychological reasons. For example, the murderer may still be under control or supervision of the frustrating or humiliating object, and therefore would not murder the person who has caused the hurt he suffered. Such blocking raises the level of frustration in the future murderer and his aggressive impulse must be released through an indirect substitute: Abusing animals in part of the cases, or humans, and murdering less threatening objects in relation to the murderer. In doing so, the murderer creates a displacement, or a "learned parallelism," which enables the violent reaction to be displaced from one object to another through "inclusion." The result is that innocent victims serve as scapegoats when there is similarity between the source of frustration and the victim, in appearance, occupation and so on.

Although the concepts of displacement and inclusion were found true in a variety of behavioural reactions in the field of psychology, there are, all the same, a few principal criticisms of this theory in general, and in the context of serial murder in particular. First, not every person who experiences humiliation or frustration reacts violently, especially with fatal violence toward the original frustrating object, or toward some kind of substitute. Second, Hale (1998), like others, uses the terminology "for a certain psychological reason," without explaining what that reason is, or what the psychological process is, and it spoils the reliability of the explanation. Third, while it is easy to accept the explanation that a little boy cannot emotionally and even physically come out against a humiliating and frustrating parent, it is much more difficult to accept this kind of explanation for an adult. Fourth, when examining the childhood of serial murderers, one can find a variety of positive and negative experiences which are not significantly different from those of other children who have not become serial murderers. Fifth, there is allegedly an expected pattern, a theoretical stereotype, according to which there must be something in the childhood of the serial murderer which is the explaining variable of his murderous behaviour in adulthood. Even if there is some truth to this etiology, the central question that has still remained unanswered is what is that factor or psychological process that makes the humiliation or frustration in childhood into a murderous action later on. In addition, it is not clear why such behaviour appears only in a relatively late stage in the murderer's life. Sixth, the theory does not explain why the frustration and humiliation are expressed in the later life of the murderer as a serial murder and not as a one-time murder. The answer can be that just because the murderer cannot hurt the original source of frustration, he does not achieve a full sense of satisfaction from the murder acts, and as far as he is concerned, he has not settled the score yet with the original frustrating or humiliating object. This is why he murders over and over again, aiming to achieve this feeling, a feeling which would probably never be realized.

A second version of the theory connects psychology and sociology through the use of the social learning theory (Singer & Hensley, 2004; Wright & Hensley, 2003).[75] The scientists present the theory of Dollard and Miller (1950), according to which every individual goes through socialization in a search for affection and confirmation from those he loves. When a positive confirmation or opinion are received, the individual and his meaningful others feel satisfied. On the other hand, when there is no confirmation or a successful solution for such search, a frustration is established in the individual, and he tends to express this frustration through violence toward others who cannot properly retaliate. He does not direct his violence toward the frustrating object, since that object is in a control position toward him and therefore he cannot directly avenge him.[76]

Studies on serial murderers show that they experienced many humiliating situations in their childhood, mainly non-rewarding situations and only a few rewarding ones. In the course of his maturation, the future serial murderer starts to perceive all situations as non-rewarding, and loses the ability to differentiate between a rewarding and a non-rewarding situation. These people learn to expect humiliation in almost all circumstances. In this context, Dollard and Miller (1950) claim that frustration does not disappear from consciousness without the release of aggression, and this aggression can be expressed some time in the future. Wright and Hensley (2004) suggest an assumption, which was confirmed empirically only partially, that humiliated and frustrated people take out their frustration on weaker creatures, including animals. According to this assumption, people who abuse animals develop more severe ways of violence. The children and adolescents under discussion become, through cruel treatment toward animals, insensitive to violence, or learn to enjoy causing suffering and pain, and later on expand their activity toward people as well. The reason for this is that aggression toward animals does not answer their needs any more. Wright and Hensley (2004) argue that such behaviour can predict future serial murder, since a person who experienced frustration must take it out through violence, even if it is in the future and indirect (Singer & Hensley, 2004).

There are a few points of criticism on this theory as well: First, one cannot ignore the fact that many serial murderers have gone through humiliation and abuse on the part of their parents, but one has to be very careful in regarding being cruel toward animals as a predicting factor for a serial murderer, for a number of reasons:

a) not everyone who has experienced abuse or humiliation in childhood has become a serial murderer or a person who abuses animals;

b) not everyone who abused animals in childhood has become a serial murderer. The scientists examined just five cases of serial murderers who have abused animals prior to becoming serial murderers, and therefore the empirical component for basing the theory and the correlation between being cruel toward animals and serial murder is not sufficient.

Secondly, if, according to Singer and Hensley (2004), serial murderers experience only non-rewarding situations, why do they experience humiliation? The theory claims that humiliation is a situation in which there was a reward, and afterwards there was no reward in the same situation. In addition, the theory claims that serial murderers learned to by-pass non-rewarding situations, so where do the humiliation and frustration come from?

Thirdly, the theoreticians of frustration-aggression theory do not explain why the murderer starts murdering in a specific period in his future. Is there a certain stimulus or catalyst which pushes him into action, or is it maturation of a process that involves fantasy?

Vronsky (2004) suggest a slightly different explanation in the context of frustration and humiliation, and he attributes it mainly to serial murder based on sexual background. His claim is that the creation of a serial murderer is rooted in gender identity which has to do with the child's capability to negotiate successfully with his mother about his masculine autonomy.[77] When a son cannot achieve such autonomy, or when there is no solid basis from which he can conduct his negotiation about his autonomy, a sense of anger develops in the child which he then carries to adolescence and adulthood. Unlike the act of penetration or oral sex, many times it is found at the scene that the murderer has shifted to sexually secondary mechanisms, substitutes for the primary act which bring him to a later satisfaction. In this way, the murderer expresses maximal control over his sexuality and over that of his victim. For example, piquerism (pleasure-cutting/"overkill") of the victim by many stabs after he has been dead can express a symbolic penetration which, together with the screams of the victim and the presence of blood,[78] creates a harmonic sexual experience for the murderer.

As we will see in the following explanations, a serial murderer operates usually on the basis of a certain fantasy which matures in the course of time, until it is materialized in reality. His difficulties from frustrating experiences in childhood are not solved by a one-time murder, since there is an essential gap between fantasy and reality. Since the murder does not meet exactly what he has imagined in his fantasy, he feels frustration, and therefore goes on murdering out of a hope to materialize his fantasy. I assume there is something more to it: As long as the murderer uses substitutes for unloading his frustration in relation to the original source of frustration, he would never feel the satisfaction he hopes to find through serial murder.

Psychotic, psychopathic, sociopathic and antisocial personality disorder—Most of the serial murderers are defined as having a mental disorder which has received different labels over the years. This disorder calls for an elaborate reference in order to understand its origins and characteristics. Vronsky (2007) surveys the development of the serial murderer while using the terms psychopathy, sociopathy, and *antisocial personality disorder* (ASPD).

Most of the researches show that the serial murderers experienced a childhood trauma which was accompanied by physical and sexual abuse. Most of them experienced unstable family life with no order, and the majority comes from destroyed homes, with a history of high frequency of delinquency and use of drugs and alcohol by their parents. Research on *post-traumatic stress syndrome* (PTSD) shows that children who have gone through abuse can develop psychological situations like psychopathy which enhance or enable the occurrence of serial murder. In addition, abuse accompanied by a physical and emotional attachment disorder to his mother and/or father can manifest in behaviour disorders throughout life.

But Vronsky (2004, 2007) claims that these factors do not provide a satisfying explanation to the psyche of the serial murderer, because there are hundreds of thousands of adopted children who have gone through abuse and have not become serial murderers.

A more moderate claim assumes that there is a fine balance between abuse in childhood, disorder in the attachment with parental figures and peers, and a lack of chemical balance in the brain. Such an explanation can show why part of the children would become serial murderers, and others not.[79] In the psychological-social aspect, Vronsky (2004) indicates that loneliness and the inability to create an attachment with his peers, social rejection and isolation, together with abuse in childhood, can bring about fantasies with violent content that characterize the childhood of many of the serial murderers. But the Vronsky (2004) restricts his words by saying that even today it is not clear what came first: Does behavioural disorder brings about social isolation, or vice versa?

According to Vronsky, most of the serial murderers are diagnosed as psychopaths, sociopaths, or having an ASPD. A psychopath is a popular term which has become the "miscellaneous" drawer in psychology to some extent.[80] It does not have a formal and clear psychological term, and it does not appear in the DSM.[81]

There is a common mistake of not distinguishing between a psychopath and a psychotic. An individual with psychotic disorders suffers from hallucinations, delusions, or an organic illness of the brain, like schizophrenia.

Psychotic serial murderers are very rare since their illness does not enable them to have a long career of serial murders. The psychotics are insane clinically and legally, and are usually more dangerous to themselves than to others. The psychotic is not aware of the reality of his situation or the acts he commits, and he is motivated by voices and fantasies in his head. He has difficulty maintaining that psychiatrist Hervey Cleckley called the "mask of sanity"—an appearance of normality which is required from the serial murderer between murders (Vronsky, 2007, pp. 52–53).[82]

Unlike the psychotic, the psychopath is quite another type: He is aware of reality and understands very well the damaging nature of the actions he commits, but he just does not care. The closest element to insanity in the psychopath is his fantasies, and his inability, according to Vronsky, to object to the impulse to materialize them. But these fantasies are not delusions. Serial murderers are totally aware of the criminal and murderous nature of their fantasies.

Psychopaths are basically incapable of feeling a normal range of feelings, but they are capable of pretending or imitating feelings for a long period of time. They give a convincing show of sympathy, love, attachment and concern, while they do not feel anything or feel the opposite. This is the mask of sanity. The French psychiatrist Pinel identified the phenomenon already in 1700, calling it "insanity without madness" (Ibid., p. 52).

Regarding the issue of sanity, in the nineteenth century, psychopathy was described as "moral insanity," and was the basis for the claim of insanity. In the seventies, due to the increasing number of serial murderers, American courts started rejecting the claim of insanity on the basis of an "irresistible impulse," up to a point that the claim of insanity for serial murderers has become very rare (about 1% of the total number of serial murderers).

The modern definition of a psychopath was termed by the psychiatrist Cleckley (1941). According to Cleckley, the psychopath is grandiose, arrogant, manipulative, exploitative and tough, has a hot temper, gets bored easily, is incapable of establishing strong emotional connections with others, lacks empathy, guilt feelings and regret, and behaves in an irresponsible and impulsive way while violating the social and legal norms.

Vronsky (2007) presents the etiology of psychopathy. Bowlby (1969), the founder of the Attachment Theory in psychology, explains that the hunger of the young child to his mother's love is more meaningful than his hunger for food. A healthy development of the child totally depends in the confidence and trust he has in his primary caretakers. If this access is disturbed, the child develops defense mechanisms which may help him emotionally survive the separation, but it might cause an irreversible damage to his ability to connect with others and develop a normal range of feelings as an adult. In other words, the child uses the instinct of "fight or flight," but he cannot fight, and instead he stores, bypasses or represses the anger, and enters a state of escape by an emotional detachment or by losing control of the pain of separation, or the trauma.[83] The human brain cannot connect or disconnect the switch of this emotional detachment selectively, and so this process is connected permanently to the individual's personality, together with a number of other defense mechanisms, like fantasy. The soul of the psychopath is re-wired for good, the same as certain feelings are cut off forever, and this is why there is currently no cure for psychopathy, and it is expressed through a lack of empathy toward people. There are six main characteristics of the sociopath or the psychopath:

- Asocial: The sociopath does not feel guilt when he violates social norms. Social laws and rules do not prevent him from a deviating or destructive behaviour on his part.
- The sociopath is motivated by uncontrollable desires: He enjoys achieving his desires, but does not take into consideration the desires of others.
- A strong tendency to impulsivity: The sociopath tends to ignore obligations and limitations. He does what seems to him enjoyable or attractive at that moment.
- Aggression: The sociopath tends to react to frustration with fury. He hurts others during the increase of his frustrations and draws enjoyment from it.
- The sociopath feels guilt feelings or regret to a very small extent, if at all. He is unscrupulous.
- The sociopath has a small capability of loving. He is cold and emotionless, and refers to others as objects and means for achieving his goals or desires. Even if he establishes an attachment with others, it is an attachment with no depth or empathy.

Vronsky (2007) emphasizes that this personality component is a necessary condition, but not exclusive for creating the serial murderer. This component becomes a significant factor when it is involved with other circumstances. For example, a combination of a child with a disorder in his attachment to his parents, together with abuse in childhood; rejection on the part of his peers; a head injury or chemical problem in the brain—can create a monstrous serial murderer. At the same time, Vronsky (2007) claims that not all psychopaths become serial murderers, and not all children who have suffered from a trauma or a detachment, become psychopaths.

There are a few common characteristics to serial murderers, like the search of excitement, lack of guilt feelings or regrets, the need to control and a predatory behaviour. These characteristics and behaviours are compatible with a psychopathic personality.

But the conclusion is that psychopathy alone does not explain the motives of the serial murderer (Morton, 2005).[84]

Vronsky (2007) concludes that between trauma and abuse in childhood and the creation of a serial murderer there is a mediating variable, psychopathy.

The road to a serial murder is long and twisted, with side ways, stopovers and many by-passes. Not all psychopaths arrive, but those who do, are especially fatal (Ibid., pp. 60–61).

Later on Jenkins (2002) presented a more complicated definition, when he integrated psychology and sociology. According to Jenkins, psychopathology is not a personality disorder, but a defect in the personality, when a set of defenses are built around the defect. The defect refers to the most central element of human personality: Its social nature. The psychopath is, basically, an asocial or antisocial individual. As a result, the American psychiatrist association changed the term "psychopathic personality" into "sociopathic personality," and the psychopath has become a sociopath (Holmes & De Burger, 1988).

But disagreement on the definition of the disorder brought, in the nineties, the creation of a new term: *Antisocial personality disorder* (ASPD), and now it is the formal psychiatric definition to what used to be called psychopathy (Ibid., pp. 56–57). In so doing, the social emphasis of this disorder has increased.

According to some psychiatrists, the diagnosis of antisocial personality disorder is based too much on behaviour, and ignores permanent personality characteristics. As a matter of fact, part of the psychiatrists claim that this disorder is a disorder that only part of the psychopaths suffer from, and hence it is a symptom of psychopathy and not identical to it. While all psychopaths can be diagnosed as having an antisocial personality disorder, not everyone who suffers from this disorder is a psychopath (Ibid., p. 57).

The connection between antisocial personality disorder and serial murder occupied mainly Holmes and Holmes (1998), Levin (2008), and Mitchell (1997) who claimed that many serial murderers are unscrupulous and lack empathy to the suffering they cause to their victims. Sociopaths never feel regret for their actions, and therefore can go on murdering with no conscience. In this way, they emphasize the social or interactional sources of this mental disorder. Although one can see this argument as an explanation taken from the field of psychology (personality structure, mental disorder, and so on), we have here a shift to the direction of an integration of psychological and sociological theories.

In an earlier version, Fox and Levin (2005) claimed that the anti-social personality explanation is problematic, especially in reference to serial murder out of sadism. According to them, in order that the murderer would be able to enjoy the suffering of the victim, he has to feel some extent of empathy toward him. Following this claim, the authors claimed that there are two kinds of sociopathy: One is expressed through a lack of empathy and a lack of planning of one's behaviour, while the other is characterized by planning and a high level of empathy. Fox and Levin (2005) argued that in fact we speak here about a borderline personality, rather than an antisocial personality disorder. But the definition of a borderline personality disorder is not compatible with many of the characteristics of serial murderers, and therefore we should better remain in the field of antisocial personality disorder.

The main criticism of this theory focuses on the fact that it deals too much with the description of the serial murderer's characteristics, and less with the explanation of his behaviour. The Attachment Theory is well accepted in psychology, and it certainly may explain the development of a psychopathic personality, or the antisocial disorder. But the question of why does the psychopath choose to murder others serially has not been cleared. In addition, the theory does not explain which children would become psychopaths, and which not, and who of the psychopaths would become serial murderers and who not. As has been mentioned, there is no link between psychopathy and turning to serial murder instead of turning to some legitimate occupation in which the individual can express the characteristics of his personality.

Narcissism: As I will argue later on, relying on the DSM causes sometimes more confusion than unequivocal certainty.[85] An example for this is the narcissistic personality disorder which is often similar to the borderline personality disorder. Schlesinger (1998) reported of studies which found a connection between pathological narcissism and serial murder. Narcissistic personality disorder, lack of self-worth, and fantasies of self-empowerment to compensate humiliation were all found connected to serial murder. It is important to emphasize that the studies which found such a connection referred only to sexual serial murder toward women.

The problem in this explanation is that narcissism has become part of our culture. The decision when narcissism is pathological is very problematic, like, for instance, watching Snuff films which present real events of rape, murder and so on. There is no prohibition on watching these films, although the people who watch them know that the photographed events are real. It is similar to clients who visit brothels in which the workers are kept or were smuggled in against the law, their passports were taken from them, and they are in fact enslaved workers.

In the past, dissociative identity disorder was called multiple personality disorder—a dissociative condition is a state that can be absolutely normal, and most of us experience it in daily life. For example, when a person reads a book that fascinates him. We may say that beyond being concentrated in the content of the book, the reader dissociates himself from his personal and external environment, from his needs, his feelings and sense of time. For example, this reader would suddenly distinguish that the sun has set already, that his leg "fell asleep," that the weather has become cool, or that he is hungry or thirsty. His dissociation was the reason that he was not aware of these changes. When he comes out of the state of dissociation, he pays attention to all these phenomena, but that "diving" into the book he had felt stops because he cannot experience these two conditions at the same time.[86] The psychiatrists call this state a normal state of dissociation or detachment.[87]

But a dissociative state might become pathological, and this is what is important for our discussion. According to Van der Hart et al. (2005), a trauma is defined as a subjective response of the individual or the victim, and it is not a derivative of the quality of the event which has caused it. The trauma has to do with a void of the pre-traumatic personality structure which interrupts the development of a cohesive and consistent personality structure in children. Van der Hart et al. (2005) claim that in every individual there are two states of operation: One intended for daily functioning, while the other is for defensive acts as a response to a threat. They differ from one another, and in a time of threat the daily-life state of operation would not respond. But in order that a cohesive personality should be created with a continuation of the sense of self, there must be some kind of integration between the two states. The assumption is that such integration would fail when the individual is in a state of extreme stress which decreases his integrative capability. Such a state can stem from physical and sexual abuse, as well as from the lack of attachment to meaningful others. The outcome is an alternate shift between daily functioning and preventing situations which might arouse the trauma and re-experiencing the traumatic event. In other words, a disconnection is established between the two states, and there may be even a disconnection within each one of them. The result can be a different perception of the self in the dissociative parts, including viewpoints and beliefs highly different from those that exist in the "neutral" (the "normal") personality. Van der Hart et al. (2005) report of a situation in which a woman was aware of two different viewpoints in her relationships with other people, but she could not do anything to change this situation. That is, there is evidence that there is awareness among the dissociative parts, and it depends on the extent of dissociation.

The conclusion is that a dissociative situation enables the individual a regular functioning in daily life when the trauma he has gone through does not damage his capability of conducting normal life.

The situation in a mechanism of suppression is different. In this case, the individual avoids, consciously and unconsciously, being exposed to unpleasant and traumatic experiences he has gone through in his life. In a state of dissociation, the individual shifts between the different identities. This is a pathological situation, because there is disconnection from the "neutral" identity. In addition, unlike a state of suppressing an event, in a dissociative state, the "other" identity has a life of its own. Experiments under an MRI test[88] found that when the individual shifts from the "neutral" identity to another one, other centers in the brain start operating, the sensorimotor reactions are different, with changes in both systems of cognition and emotion. Moreover, it was found that handwriting changes, as well as the quality of sight. These findings are unequivocal empirical evidence of the existence of another identity or identities which have an independent existence that is disconnected from the neutral identity.

We can summarize by saying that following a trauma or hard life circumstances there are established in the individual at least two identities. One identity, which can be called the central one, received a few labels from the scientists: *Apparently normal part of the personality* (ANP); *neutral identity state* (NIS); *neutral personality state* (NPS). It refers to the part of the personality that is responsible for the normal functioning of the individual in daily life (in the family, at work, and so on), through operating a censorship—blocking access to the traumatic memories or supervising them. The label "neutral" in reference to the identity of the individual is a little problematic (Van Der Hart, Nijenhuis, Steele, 2005; Reinders, Nijenhuis et al. 2006; Reinders, et al., 2003; Porter et al., 2001).

At the same time, there appear other identities or parts of the personality which are in a state of dissociation. These parts or identities include the traumatic memories, or react to the trauma in different ways. This identity received a few labels: *Emotional part of the personality* (EP); *traumatic identity* (TIS); *traumatic personality state* (TPS).

A dissociative disorder includes allegedly three components: Fantasy, dissociation, and compartmentalization. Compartmentalization means lack of awareness of the existence of the other identity (which was not proved), or alternately, a state in which elements of one identity do not penetrate the other, or at least there is an attempt of blocking this kind in the individual's personality.[89]

Fantasy is defined as a process in which the individual tries to achieve satisfaction by being involved in imaginary actions that he cannot or does not dare to execute in reality. Fantasy enables the individual experience feelings of hatred and bitterness and other negative feelings, while being dissociated from the moral aspects of his thought. Coming out of fantasy might cause the individual a sense of disappointment or frustration, because then he returns to the painful, depressing or hollow reality from which he tried to escape through fantasy. Furthermore, since the individual has no tools of coping with the harsh reality, it is probable that he would tend to escape again and again to the fantasy world he has created. This is why fantasy might become pathological when it receives a higher and higher level of "reality," or a desire to materialize it in reality.[90] The outcome of these processes is a "dual identity": One identity is related to the daily reality and to the people with whom the murderer associates in his daily life. The second identity is a "secret identity," where aspirations of power and control in relation to others can be expressed, together with the fantasies he has about himself and others. An attempt to illustrate a situation like this was done in the movie "Dr. Jekyll and Mr. Hyde," although in this case, the secret identity was uncovered to the spectators in all its grandeur.

There is a constant dynamic between the two identities within the individual. I have described already how the individual escapes to and from the world of reality and fantasy. But beyond this, one identity is suppressed by another identity: At the time of fantasy the real world is suppressed, since it disturbs fantasy which cannot be normative. On the other hand, fantasy suppresses the real world in which the individual experiences hardships, pain and so on. This is the evidence that there is awareness, but a certain compartmentalization is kept between the two identities that are presented in the theory.

The discussion that interests us in the context of serial murderers is the identity, or the part, which dissociated from the personality. Serial murderers described it as a "shadow" or as "the dark side" in their personality.[91] This identity can serve as a refuge from those memories or from harsh circumstances, but beyond this, it can also provide the individual with an inner world which is not limited by moral or social norms, and this is the point of pathology that has to do with this process. The linkage between sociology and psychology enables us to explain the violent contents that reside in that dissociated identity. My claim is that these contents do not stem only from murderous motives that have developed in the individual because of great fury, but are influenced by the violent sociocultural environment of the murderer.

Carlisle (1988) showed interest in the connection between this disorder and serial murderers.[92] He argues that just as those who suffer from dissociation disorder are not defined as psychotic, the same applies to serial murderers who suffer from it. Moreover, the fact that there are two different identities among serial murderers—functioning at high and regular levels and committing horrible murders at the same time—points to the possible existence of two identities which are detached from one another, although they may be aware of one another. Let us take the case of Ted Bundy as an example who is considered one of the most severe serial murderers. Bundy terminated his studies in college, went on to study law, and achieved good results. He worked as a help-line phone assistant, helping people, and even volunteered for the election campaign of a senator. Yet at the same time, he murdered tens of women.

Reinders et al., (2006) claim that people who suffer from the above-mentioned disorder learn to establish a rotation between the two states of identity in a controlled way, as opposed to previous claims as if these individuals are carried away without control to and from their dissociative identity. Van Der Hart's words consolidate a perception that these identities are indeed well aware of each other.[93] According to Carlisle (1988), there is no equality or balance between the two identities, and the fantasy identity would overpower the real one, and it happens for two reasons: First of all, the fantasy identity was meant to meet the strongest needs of the individual, and therefore it would become dominant. Second, the real-normative identity experiences the guilt feeling that come from the thoughts and fantasies of the fantasy identity. The individual who experiences guilt feelings represses the normative identity more and more, after having realized that it is difficult for him to repress his fantasy identity, especially when it helps him emotionally.

The dissociation between reality and fantasy and the dynamics between the identities continue their existence for a long time, and as far as serial murderers are concerned, it has two expressions: First, the serial murderer continues functioning normatively after the murder, going to work and maintaining his family life; second, while we would expect that the fantasy would make him go on murdering continuously, it does not happen because the normative identity is the dominant one after the murder until the next one. Carlisle (1988) tries to explain these points later in his theory.

Carlisle (1998) claims that the serial murderer runs again and again in his imagination a scenario in which he murders and at a certain stage he might go beyond the fantasy world into the real world, and the imaginary murder would become a real one. The scientist argues that in suitable circumstances,[94] the murderer would materialize the murder automatically after having "trained" on doing it in his imagination for a long period of time.

I have two comments on this argument: Serial murderers usually do not operate automatically and impulsively, as if driven by the devil. Most of them operate in a planned and organized way. Moreover, Carlisle (1998) does not bother to explain the critical point of the shift between a murder in fantasy and a murder in reality. It is unclear what he means by the words "in suitable circumstances." Does he mean an opportunity? Does he aim at some sort of process the future murderer goes through, through which he removes a normative block which enables him to murder?

My claim is that while fantasy provides a relief and excitement to the serial murderer for a certain period, one can compare these feelings to the feeling a drug user gets from drugs. At a certain stage, the psyche develops tolerability to the sights of fantasy, up to a point in which the individual cannot feel the same excitement he used to feel in the past, and therefore he would want to materialize his fantasy in reality. My second claim is that from the moment in which the serial murderer neutralizes the influences of society, or the influences of the normative identity by using techniques of neutralizing guilt or defending the self, no normative block would hold him from committing the murder.

Carlisle (1998) claims that after the murder, the murderer may dissociate the event partially or fully from his consciousness: His thought returns to the normative identity and he experiences a surprise, guilt and despair. This is how Bundy describes his deeds, in the third person, when he speaks about the experience after the murder: What he did frightened him and he was full of regret ... he started crying. After the first time ... he swore to himself that he would not do such a thing again, or something that would lead to it ... for months the impact of the event dwindled slowly and lost its deterring value, and within three months, he withdrew to the old routine [fantasies which led to another murder].[95]

Carlisle (1998) explains the cooling-off period between one murder and the next as the individual's struggle against the dissociated identity with the murderous contents, like the struggle against addiction, while trying not to return to the same excite-ment and fantasies which led him to commit a murder the first time. But since the murder did not solve his problems and feelings, and the impulse to feel again the power and control he experi-enced in the first murder becomes stronger, it is expected that the murderer would give in to this impulse and murder again, and then would again feel guilt, and would enter a cooling-off period, and so on and so forth.

Since the murderer feels self-hatred following the deed, he has to defend himself through idealization of the pathology, by positioning himself at a level with God, worshipping his self-images. According to Carlisle, to be divine means be clean of sin and hence guiltless.[96] In this context, Carlisle (1998) refers to seri-al murder as some kind of obsessive addiction, like an addiction to drugs, when the murderer must, due to his addiction to murder, escalate his actions by committing a murder in an increasing fre-quency. In the same way, if he acts out of a sadistic motive, he would escalate his behaviour.

There is room for the comparison Carlisle (1998) conducts between a serial murder and addiction to drugs, although it may influence the ideology which I mentioned at the beginning of the chapter. But we may see the murder from a different point of view: In the murderer's fantasy world he is the main actor. He has in his mind a detailed scenario which he memorized by heart in his fan-tasies, and at the same time there is a second key-actor in the situ-ation, the victim. But since the victim is not aware of the scenario, he cannot behave as is expected of him. As a result, the murderer feels disappointment and even frustration from the comparison between his feelings during fantasy and his feelings during the murder and afterwards. This can be a significant reason for re-peating the murders aiming to materialize the fantasy verbatim. But this is useless, since reality forever differs from fantasy.

The central criticism of this theory is that it is not exhaustive and exclusive. It suits part of the serial murderers, especially those who are motivated by a sexual and sadistic fantasy, as the Carlisle

(1998) himself testifies. It does not suit all serial murderers who are motivated by hedonistic motives of material benefit. On the other hand, this theory can explain a variety of criminal deeds which are not related to serial murder, mainly according to the positivist approach in criminology. The murderer "is not guilty," but there are forces which push him to do it. In our case, it is fantasy. Nevertheless, that "other identity" that exists in the murderer, pushes him to murder again and again, does not serve as an excuse or a justification for insanity, and therefore the murderer is responsible for his deeds legally and psychologically, especially as he knows, according to the Carlisle (1998), how to distinguish between good and evil.

Another criticism of this theory is much more meaningful theoretically and empirically speaking: Why is it that among most people, day dreaming and fantasies can be a convenient and non-pathological niche for a temporary escape from a harsh reality, while among serial murderers this normal phenomenon of fantasy becomes pathological and fatal? The theory does not answer this question.

We should bear in mind that this theory was not formulated for serial murderers, but we conclude from it and can apply it in relation to this issue. Hence, the theoretical answer can be highly complicated psychologically. There are people who, although they have gone through a severe trauma, repress it and go on with their lives even if they suffer from psychological scars; while others whose personality does not enable them to cope with the traumatic memories, develop a dissociative identity in order to manage.

In spite of the negative criticism, one has to remember that this theory is one of the only psychiatric theories which have an empirical confirmation in the laboratory, and we have seen how it is expressed among serial murderers. For this reason one can accept it to a certain extent in the theoretical explanations to serial murder.

Holmes and Holmes (1998) summarize the knowledge in the psychological field in a similar way as they refer to the biological field by saying: "Even today there is no absolute or simple answer to the question what makes people murder over and over again, and even today the etiology for it is unknown."

I think that this statement expresses the frustration of the fact that one theory has not been found which can explain all kinds of serial murder and murderers. Nevertheless, there is no basis to disqualify all the given explanations. Since we deal with a very complicated phenomenon which is finally expressed by individuals, it seems that part of the explanations can explain part of the phenomenon. In addition, one should bear in mind that a serial murder is not a homogeneous phenomenon: There are different types of serial murders, and in each type there is a variety of individuals. For this reason, Holmes and Holmes (1998) suggest to look at the phenomenon of serial murder and murderers from another point of view. According to them, one should not ask what the characteristics of all serial murderers are, but rather examine what are the benefits they achieve from committing the serial murder. Their intention is, while a minority of the murderers does so because they are psychotic and hear voices which instruct them to commit the murder; others do it for a material motive or a sado-sexual motive. In this way, Holmes & Holmes (1998) assume that we would be able to arrive at a theoretical and empirical generalization in relation to different groups of serial murderers, and by so doing they negate the approach that there is a one and only theory which can explain all serial murder cases, although they did not refer to the integrative model which incorporates several theories.[97] It is important to mention that Holmes and Holmes' book was published before the development of the dissociation theory, but there is no later reference on their part to this theory.

Psychosocial Explanations of Serial Murder and Murderers

Fractured social identity—this theory resembles the theory about the dissociative identity disorder, but refers also to social aspects, and so it is a kind of a psychosocial theory.

Holmes et al., (1999) criticize previous attempts to explain serial murder, including their own attempts, claiming that while attempts have been made to classify characteristics of serial murderers, constructing a profile of the murderer and the victims, a proper theoretical etiological explanation is still missing.

Holmes & Holmes (1999) present the theory of the Fractured social identity, basing it on two psychological-social theories: "The Looking Glass Self" (Cooley, 1902), and "the virtual social identity" (Goffman, 1963). Cooley's theory deals with the notion that the individual has an active role in his personality development. He examines himself and conducts subjective value judgments by trying to examine how "significant others" perceive him. This information makes the individual decide whether to introduce changes in his behaviour according to the worth of his significant others who judge him.

Goffman's theory, which is based on Cooley's theory, claims that the individual may change his behaviour when he goes through an especially vulnerable period in his life. Goffman suggests two views about the social identity: The social "virtual" identity and the actual social identity. The virtual social identity is an aspect of the self as it is administered and presented to the public, while the actual social identity represents the real self as the individual knows himself. This identity is known only to the individual and his closest friends/family. Holmes & Holmes's (1999) assumption is that deviants in society are people who have gone through a trauma which can influence them in different ways. For example, part of the victims become criminals themselves, while a small part of the victims go through a process in which a schism is established which paves the way to the development of a personality of a serial murderer. The scientists do not specify what the characteristics of these people are, but one can assume that they are people with psychological or social disorders which serve as a convenient ground for the growth of a murderer. In such a case, the serial murderer would learn that there is an "innate stigma," and he would have to go through socialization to his actual social identity which might be deviant. This socialization can be done by the family, or by his social and cultural environment. For example, "the village fool" was born into a sociocultural environment in which he was labeled as such, and even has gone through the socialization of mockery from his social environment. It shows that society has an important role in the development of the personality. According to the theory, serial murderers seem and behave normatively in the first years of their personality development. However, during adolescence, a social event or a series of events are expressed through a crack or a split in their personality. The terms "crack" or "split" mean that the old personality is not totally destroyed, but a certain destructive part takes its place in the personality. The break is not seen by the external world, but is felt by the serial murderer. For instance, Bundy was socially and politically active because he concealed the broken part of his personality from the public. In other words, he exposed only his virtual identity.

The serial murderer cannot only feel the break that was caused by the traumatic event, but he also remembers the event. Holmes & Holmes (1999) claim that it is improbable that a single event would cause a break in the personality. They think that it is more probable that a single event would cause a small crack, whereas events which would come afterwards would expand the crack up to a state of a personality break from identity. Holmes & Holmes (1999) emphasize that they do not speak about dissociation which protects the personality of the serial murderer, but about a phenomenon in which there is an element that was damaged within the personality due to trauma during childhood or adolescence. They do not indicate where in the personality was this crack. I would humbly say that the crack is caused to the superego, and it enables the individual to behave in a murderous way again and again. Bundy, for example, conducted a normal life until at the age of 13 when he discovered that he was an illegitimate child. After this discovery, he turned to pornography, and two years later murdered his first victim.[98] Holmes & Holmes

(1999) defend their arguments against criticism by saying that it is obvious that there are many children who have discovered they were illegitimate and have not become serial murderers, except they felt or internalized the fact that there was a terrible hurt in the development of their personality. In addition, they claim that this pain may be real or imagined.

According to the authors, the continuity of events and the specific age in which the event of the break takes place are important. Their opinion is that it is not the experiences that everyone goes through that matter, but the unique and subjective experiences and the timing, stage in life, when the event or the break takes place.

Before I go on presenting the explanation, it is important to see its highly problematic nature. Holmes & Holmes (1999) assume that there is a sequence of events that are related to the event of the break, but their assumption remains an assumption which has not been confirmed empirically. Furthermore, their assumption has no other basis, and this is true for a number of reasons. First, the assumption that Bundy turned to pornography exactly after discovering he was an illegitimate child has no theoretical logic. We could just as well assume that he turned to pornography out of curiosity of an adolescent, and not because he was an illegitimate child. Second, one can find youngsters and children who have gone through a series of breaking events and have not become serial murderers; on the contrary, they have become depressive and suicidal. The third point of criticism stems from the second point and from the scientists' claim of an allegedly rational decision of the individual over the event that caused him a break in personality. We do not speak here about a rational decision, but about the impacts of this break on the personality. Apparently, Holmes & Holmes (1999) claim that if adolescents were under the same circumstances, part of them would become serial murderers since they decide they had a break in their personality, while others would not become such people because they would not assume they had a break in their personality. Such an explanation is not perceived as a proper theoretical explanation.

Another point of criticism is the reference to a sequence of breaking events. In this context, it would be appropriate to limit the events in time, like the example of the period of adolescence, a breaking event every year, and so on. According to the given formulation, there is no maximal time definition between the events: Can we call a sequence two events, one that took place at the age of five, and another at the age of thirty? In addition, even if there was a sequence of breaking events during childhood and adolescence (a sequence that different scientists tried to indicate as characteristic of a serial murderer's past), the presented explanation does not explain the gap of time between the events in childhood and the execution of the murder later in life. One should also indicate what kind of breaking events are concerned, for example, death of a relative, continuous abuse, social isolation, and so on.

According to the Holmes & Holmes (1999), the serial murderer, like everyone who is influenced by a break in his personality, learns to live with the pain, knowing that he is labeled. He learns how to hide it by investing a large amount of energy for doing so, while constructing and presenting a virtual identity in social interactions. This virtual identity would present him as a normative member in the "normal" society, while the broken identity is hidden from the eyes of the public. According to Holmes & Holmes (1999), one of the reasons for the serial murderer's avoidance from maintaining long-term social relationships is the will to diminish the risk that someone would find out his real identity.

The only place in which the serial murderer can expose his real identity is during the events of the serial murders. This exposure provides him relief and relaxation from the need to camouflage his real identity, but it makes him vulnerable. The serial murderer operates out of an impulse of control and dominance over his victims in order not be hurt, and the victims must eventually die. After the murder, the broken identity returns temporarily to relaxation until it exposes itself in the next murder.

As I have previously indicated, it is difficult to see this theoretical explanation as a proper one. Moreover, Holmes & Holmes (1999) use the term "personality" and "identity" alternately, although they are not identical. According to the description of these scientists one could think of an invalid rather than of a serial murderer, a child or an adolescent who was in an incident and lost an arm, his body is scarred, and so on. Outwardly he presents a virtual identity of a "hero," functions, studies, and dresses in a way that would hide his wounds. On the other hand, the traumatic event severely damaged his self-confidence and his body image. He may also suffer from post-traumatic syndrome and be treated by a psychologist. His inability to present his real identity, which in the above example has both internal and external signs, makes it difficult for him. But most of the people who have gone through traumas find the place where they can take off the misleading façade and present their real identity. It can happen in the psychologist's room, with his parents, with a friend, girlfriend, support group and so on. The theory does not explain why these people would function normatively, while others would become serial murderers. In other words, the theory which was supposed to fill the etiological void regarding the serial murder does not do so.

I would mention that in addition to the scientists' claim, according to which serial murderers avoid, due to the break in their identity, long-term social relationships, there are serial murderers who live with a parent, a spouse, and so on. It should be emphasized that the criticism does not deny the possibility that there are serial murderers who would meet the criteria presented in the theory, but as has been said, the theory does not explain why a certain individual would become a serial murderer, while another would not.

An additional criticism can refer to the very choice of serial murder. The claim of Holmes & Holmes (1999) is that after the murder there would be no witness to the real identity of the murderer. This is a true fact, but still it does not explain the murderer's choice to murder of all other things. For instance, there are rapists with veiled faces who cannot be identified afterwards. The explanation these scientists may have given as an answer is that the serial murderer can totally expose himself, without hiding under some kind of mask, only in a place where no one would survive, and this is why he chooses a serial murder. This kind of answer responds well to the criticism.

Summary of the Psychological and Psychosocial Theories

When examining the psychological and psychosocial theories that have been presented in the context of serial murderers, we can see one common empirical starting point: Traumatic events, such as sexual and physical abuse in childhood which are related to a lack of development of attachment between the child and the parents, especially the mother. These are objective events that happened to these children, and this is the factual part, for which there is no disagreement in the etiology of serial murderers. Mitchell and Aamodt (2005) claim that the rate of abuse in childhood among serial murderers is six times higher than it is in the general population. But as Van Der Hart (2005) indicated, the trauma is the subjective response of the individual for an objective event he has experienced. Such perception enables us to explain why part of the children who have gone through the same objective events would respond differently to similar events, and there is certainly relevance to the personality structure and the child's social environment. This is an answer to the central criticism which claims that there are many children who have gone through harsh traumas and have not become serial murderer.

Table 4: A comparison between the psychological and psycho-social theories for serial murder

The Theory	The explanation why trauma and a lack of attachment would lead to serial murder.
Personality Theory (Freud)	A lack of attachment or trauma lead to inability to identify with a parental figure. The outcome is lack of development of the superego. In this state there is no block that would prevent the murderer from murdering again and again.
Frustration-Aggression	A sense of humiliation and frustration following a childhood trauma and a lack of attachment lead to the release of violence against substitute innocent objects. Frustration due to the release of violence not against the original source of frustration and a gap between fantasy and reality lead to a repeated murder.
Antisocial Behaviour Disorder	Traumatic experiences and lack of attachment create an unscrupulous individual with no empathy to others. A rich fantasy world prepares the action of murder, and frustration of the gap between fantasy and reality leads to a repeated murder.
Dissociative Identity Disorder	A trauma in childhood leads to dissociation of one identity from the neutral identity. The dissociated part might act murderously as a response to the trauma.
Broken Social Identity	A trauma creates a crack in the personality which increasingly expands due to accompanied events, and creates a virtual identity and a real identity. The real identity can be expressed only during the murder, each time anew.

(Origin: Edelstein, 2009)

A summary and comparison among the theories enable us see a similarity between some of them. For example, in Freud's personality theory and in the theory of antisocial behaviour disorder there are similar characteristics. According to both of them the individual lacks empathy toward others, and therefore does not feel guilt or regret from his fatal behaviour.

The theory of broken identity and the theory of dissociative identity disorder refer to the existence of two identities within the individual: The normative one and the murderous one. All the theories except that of Freud refer to the existence of fantasy which precedes the act of murder. Freud did not refer to this fact, but maybe according to the personality theory the existence of such fantasy could be probable. The fantasy explains not only the first murder that takes place after the fantasy stops fulfilling the individual's needs, but also the next murders coming from frustration and the vacuousness of the individual after the murder did not meet the fantasy excitement.

Except for the similarity among theories, it seems that there is some overlap between some of them. For instance, Freud's personality theory and the theory of antisocial behaviour disorder overlap to such an extent that it seems that one could give up Freud's theory for this matter altogether.

Another overlap exists between the theory of dissociative identity disorder and the theory of broken social identity. Both of them refer to a break in identity which creates dissociated parts which can motivate the individual to murder. But one cannot say that one of the theories is redundant since they explain the murder differently. Likewise, the theory of dissociative identity gained an empirical confirmation in laboratory conditions, and although the frustration-aggression theory is similar in its components to some of the other theories, its unique explanation remains important and without competition.

It is important to emphasize at this stage that trauma and the lack of attachment to parental figures were found as the basis of the disorders which may lead to serial murder. But one has to remember that between the trauma and the execution of a serial murder there are many different important variables, like social isolation, the development of a fantasy world, neutralizing guilt and the use of a variety of complicated defense mechanisms which enable the execution of the murder, as well as a confrontation with the outcomes of the murderer's acts.[99]

We have, apparently, the theoretical tools for understanding the sources of the development of the serial murderer. But we have to bear in mind two things. First, not all the psychological theories that have been presented refer to all types of serial murderers.

Second, the individual does not live in a social vacuum, and as I have claimed, the contents of the fantasies, the motives and the attitude toward the victims are influenced by the culture and the society in which he lives. As a result, we can see in recent years more and more academic articles and books which deal especially with the sociocultural aspects of the phenomenon. As it seems, these explanations are not less true than those of the psychological explanations, and they can complement them and even substitute part of them.

Sociocultural Explanations of Serial Murder and Murderers[100]

It is important to see that psychologists preferred the use of the term "sociopath" and "antisocial personality disorder" over the term "psychopath." This preference demonstrates the acknowledgment that after all the psychological processes and personality analysis of the individual, he does not live in a vacuum. He lives, operates, influences and is being influenced in the sociocultural environments in which he has grown up, was educated and lived (Leyton, 1986; Hinch & Scott, 1986; Mitchell, 1997). One can compare this perception to the dispute about genetics and environment. A serial murderer is not an innate characteristic, but an acquired one. DeFronzo et al., (2007) found that cultural and social variables correlated significantly regarding the rates of serial murder by men. The main characteristics which were indicated were the geographical location in which the murderers murdered the highest number of victims, and the place in which the murderers went through the process of socialization. The central questions for which anthropologists, sociologists and scientists from close fields of knowledge try to answer are: What is the sociocultural background that enables the growth of this horrible phenomenon? And also, why is the phenomenon of serial murder more common in certain states (mainly in the USA) versus other countries?

A serial murder may be a social warning, a warning that says that individuals in society believe that violence toward their friends is a normal and accepted means for achieving goals or receiving satisfaction for their motives, impulses and needs (Holmes & Holmes, 1998; Holmes & DeBurger, 1988). Such approach enables us a wider and more comprehensive reference to the phenomenon of serial murder, as compared with the psychological approaches. The assumption is that there is something in the society and culture we live in which enables, and maybe even cultivates, the phenomenon of murderous violence. Even if there is a preceding psychological disposition in the serial murderer for a serial murder, the cultural and social factors increase the probability for this tendency to materialize. A similar approach argues that just as there are different expressions of mental diseases in different cultures, so violence in general and murderous violence in particular depend on culture.[101]

Vronsky (2004) argues that scientists speak, in fact, about the correlation between "normalization" or "legitimization" of violence in the cultural milieu and serial murder. In other words, there is social encouragement to kill the kind of person who is "less dead" than other categories of people. For instance, prostitutes, homosexuals, homeless people, youngsters who have run away from home, and so on, are located in a low position in the social stratification, and therefore their lives are "less" worthy. They are considered "less dead" after the murder, since they were "less alive" before it (Vronsky, 2004).

But a violent culture or cultural legitimacy for violence do not yet pose a factor in the etiology of a serial murder, unless there would be found significant factors in the individual which would join the cultural factors. In spite of the prevalent violence in the USA, an absolute majority of the inhabitants do not become serial murderers, of course.

Various scientists, like Holmes and DeBurger (1988) referred to the fact that the American society is a violent society, in which alongside the norms that prohibit hurting the other person, there are norms which confirm violent behaviour. These scientists assume that there is a correlation between the socialization process which is soaked in a potential of violence in the interpersonal relationships in the premodern, modern, and postmodern American society and the phenomena of harsh violence, including serial murder.

It is interesting to see that the same assumptions that were presented in relation to mass murder come up again in relation to serial murder. There is something unique about American society which pushes more people than any other culture to commit one murder at a time, at a number of events, over a long period of time. The statistical data confirm this assumption as three quarters of the serial murder cases in the world have taken place in the USA. On the other hand, the frequency of suicides in the USA is lower than that of other countries in the world. This strengthens the assumption that the influence of the American culture transmits legitimacy to interpersonal violence. Violence has been interwoven into American culture from its first days, when criminals were deported to America, and later on there developed an acceptance of violence as part of life in the frontier zones. The law enforcement system was very poor in these zones, together with a general weakness of the legal system. Lynching was often committed on a suspect through field trial[102] by taking the law into people's own hands, mainly by conservative leaders who aspired to maintain the existing social order. As a result of this policy, the victims of violence were groups perceived and identified clearly as dangerous and threatening to the ethnic-cultural hegemony whose only crime was to belong to the unaccepted social status (North American Indians, blacks, and Catholics).

Hinch and Scott (2000), who dealt extensively with the cultural issue, bring examples like Billy the Kid or Sally Skull the Black Widow who were outstanding serial murderers at that time, although not the only ones. According to the Hinch & Scott (2000), "serial murderers have become part of the heritage of the

American culture, but only in the seventies has there penetrated an awareness of this issue."

While violence as part of life was accepted and even legitimate in the Wild West, creating culture heroes of "the fastest gun drawers in the West," led this legitimacy to expand all over the USA, even after settling in the west was completed and an efficient law enforcement system was established. Today the ideology of the powerful people in the USA legitimizes the use of violence for the sake of defending American domestic and foreign interests.[103] At the same time, there is a general increase of violence in the USA, when urban minorities get armed for the sake of defending themselves against new urban "predators," who aspire to take their lives or property. An expression of this can be seen in the increase of the number of executions, and the number of killings claimed to be done out of self-defense.

It is my opinion that the historical Wild West comes back and exists, to a large extent, in the urban centers in the USA today. Expressions of this phenomenon can be seen by taking the law into people's own hands, the lack of will to testify to the police and the lack of will to intervene for the sake of preventing a crime.

One can speak about a "culture of sociopathy" that prevails in the USA, as serial murder actually reflects a state of affairs in which more and more people feel they are not limited by consciousness or social norms which could have prevented them from committing felonies against others. An increasing number of people are prepared to deceive their neighbour, lie in work interviews and so on, and acquire a massive extent of arms. The explanation is that socioeconomic situations brought about the decrease of altruism, and so what was left is only egoism and individualism. American society suffers from a kind of sociopathy with a moral decrease in all fields of life. One manifestation is that proper conduct is determined according to what is convenient and practical; not what is ethical, as is seen by achieving social goals through illegitimate means. From here the road is open to serial murder as well (Fox & Levin, 2005).

As part of the "competition" among different fields of knowledge for providing an appropriate theoretical explanation for the phenomenon of serial murder, one can see that the sociocultural explanations reject the psychological ones in order to be able to provide an explanation that does not exist in psychology. This is, as has been said, instead of looking for the integration of the fields of knowledge. Hinch and Scott (2000) claim, for example, that since the serial murderer is considered sane and rational, the psychological explanations are anyway irrelevant, and hence one has to give more weight to the sociological and anthropological aspects. Before presenting their arguments, it is important to point out the essential mistake in statements of this kind. The fact that a serial murderer is not defined as someone mentally ill who cannot distinguish between good and evil, or does not have any connection with reality, does not mean that the murderer does not suffer from severe psychological disorders, even if they are not extreme up to the point of a mental disease. Finally, it is about an individual who makes decisions based on a psychological, social, and cultural background, and this approach separates again among the fields of knowledge, instead of integrating them.

On the other hand, Mitchell (1997) expands the scene and creates the required connection with psychology. According to Mitchell, the social environment influences the individual significantly. This environment can include abuse or neglect on the part of the parents, and these acts can create, in turn, psychological disorders which would eventually bring about the creation of the serial murderer.

But in relation to the social environment, the scientists aspire to deal with the macro level, as opposed to the micro level of psychology, and present elements in the American culture which may contribute significantly to the cultivation and encouragement of even murderous violence. Mitchell (1997) refers to the following elements in American culture:

- Looking for excitement and a feeling of high spirits
- Emphasizing the wellbeing of the individual and his capability to achieve all the achievements he would like to achieve, through competitiveness among individuals over relatively rare resources
- Emphasizing the will for an immediate satisfaction
- Presenting violence as a "normal" way of coping with personal and interpersonal problems
- Emphasizing violent role models
- Blaming others when the individual suffers, lives in harsh conditions, or does not manage to materialize his aspirations[104]
- The huge urban centers create depersonalization and anonymity of the individual, as well as alienation on the part of the individual versus society. In this way, for instance, Bundy said in relation to the women he had murdered: They were not more than objects.
- Very high geographical mobility of inhabitants with different genders, beliefs, and origins influences the social order, the sense of belonging, and the general accepted beliefs. Durkheim's theory is based on this in relation to social anomaly.

There are those who claim that in the era of the big mergers, extensive government and global connections, a larger number of Americans feel helpless in all that has to do with their capability to influence their lives and future. After the terror acts, more individuals feel vulnerable and helpless. Furthermore, masculinity in the American society has to do with physical power and dominance over others. In order to feel strong, men express their authority through socially accepted ways: Senior businessmen who recruit and fire workers, politicians who attack their rivals and lawyers who "kill" at court by means of their words. As a result of all this, the popular culture is spread with sadistic images. For a small part of the people, this sadism is perceived as a legitimate and as a tool of retrieving power and dominance through serial murder (Levin, 2008).

The socialization process proposes to pass the values and norms of culture on to the next generation, and therefore the process may increase the chances of developing a murderous violence, or as it was formulated by Holmes and DeBurger (1988): "The serial murderer is not a crazy man who is disconnected from his social environment. On the contrary, he is connected to his social environment which has to be seen as the habitat for the growth of serial murderers."[105] There is no disagreement that in the American culture there is violent characteristics which sometimes even support violence as a legitimate means of operation. But like the criticism we have made regarding the psychological theories, in the socio-anthropological explanations there is also a rigid determinism: If all members of society go through the same socialization why is it that just a small part of them becomes serial murderers? Moreover, in a heterogeneous society it is difficult to say that there is only one socialization process for the entire population. Therefore, we have to moderate the explanation presented and claim that certain individuals, with a predisposition to murderous violence, receive reinforcement to this disposition through the violent contents of the American culture, and so the chance that they would become serial murderers, increases.

One of the outstanding scientists in the field of cultural explanation of serial murder is Seltzer (1998). He claims that there is room for the serial murderer in the public culture of the USA, in which addictive violence has become one of the central focuses of interest. The gathering of public around arenas of violence has created what he calls "the wounded culture": The public gets enthusiastic, curious, and converges collectively around scenes of torn bodies (car accidents, terror acts, and murder). According to Seltzer, if the private and the public spheres communicate through torn bodies of people during this crowding, this is a relocation of the public sphere which concentrates now around common pathological public violence. The mass attraction to horror in

the pathological public sphere receives a shape of magic and enthusiasm together with a shock from technology, as can be seen in
thrilling medical series like "ER" which are presented in the media. This shock indicates, in turn, the collapse of the distinction
between private and public, or between the individual and the
crowd. The crowding around the open and shredded bodies emphasizes the victory of survival, when the murderer becomes, in
our consciousness, "the only living witness," or as the Seltzer
(1998) puts it: "Death is the theater for the living." But what is
more serious is that this crowding involves depersonalization,
when everything becomes statistical, reports concentrate on the
number of victims in a terror act, one identity is exchanged with
another, the personal gets lost on the public stage, every injured
becomes anonymous, and the borders among strangers fall apart.
What unites them is their being in the wrong time and place, in
addition to the fact that they have been removed from private images to public ones. The serial murderer identifies with crowds within
a person, "he observes the commotion and sees himself in it."

It is my opinion that the crowding and the characteristics
Seltzer (1998) describes are more suitable for situations where
there is no single victim, but a mass murder rather than a serial
one. But the idea that there is no separation any more between the
private and the public can suit to a large extent also the crowding
around one body at a time (in reality—in the street, or in the media,
for example in television series that deal with medical treatment).
According to Seltzer (1998), this issue stands out mainly in sexual
felonies, as they are a shift from fantasy to execution, or making the
will of the individual (the performer) into a public show.

Pornography and Serial Murder

According to the scientists,[106] pornography makes people into
objects through an outstanding process of depersonalization, and
therefore they claim that there is a connection between serial
murder and pornography. People, mainly women who perform in
pornography, become objects without a personality, meant for use

and sale. Furthermore, these objects are described as if they enjoy the violence directed at them, and hence this violence becomes legitimate. It can be seen, for instance, in serial murder of prostitutes who are presented not only as an empty tool, but as someone who allegedly enjoys sexual intercourse with every client, and above all, one can do everything with them.

Vronsky (2004) refers to pornography in a more general cultural-historical context. His claim is that there are scientists who connect the increase in frequency of serial murder as of the nineteenth century with the pornographic literature and the Victorian society. The society of the nineteenth century referred to sex as a forbidden issue, and women became the object of a forbidden passion. This taboo could be by-passed only through voyeurism, control, aggressiveness, and rape. Hence, from this point of view, a woman could enjoy sexual intercourse only if she was attacked forcefully. The term sadism, for example, is a relatively modern expression which arrived at the end of the eighteenth century with the Marquis De Sade. Sadism, then, is not a personal characteristic, but a cultural element which can appear in the imagination of people as a part of fantasy.

The theoretical and empirical debate on the connection between pornography and serial murder has not ended yet, but one cannot say that there is a definite causative connection. There are consumers of "hard" pornography who do not become sadist serial murderers. The important point is that in the American culture, with its various components, humanity is taken off a person who becomes an object,[107] and as such he/she becomes a convenient and easy target for the serial murderer. We can find support to this claim in the fact that most of the serial murder cases take place between people who are strangers to one another.

On the other hand, Vronsky (2004) claims that even today, there is no clear connection found between the factors of sexual felonies and pornography, and some claim that pornography in fact releases sexual tension which otherwise would have led to sexual felonies.

Social Structure and Serial Murder

Another sociological explanation has to do with the social structure, and it goes from the micro to the macro levels. Hinch and Scott (2000) argue that serial murderers appeared on the scene as a result of stress factors within the social class which was threatened at that time. For example, at the end of feudalism, aristocracy was the threatened class, from which rose the Baron Gilles De Rais who murdered hundreds of the vassals' children due to his fear of the lower class and his hatred toward it. Another example is Bundy whose murders expressed dissatisfaction of the middle class from the norms of the lower class. According to Hinch & Scott (2000) the murderer who came from the middle class, murdered female students who agreed to take a lift in his car, because this behaviour was not appropriate in his eyes for girls of the middle class, and better suited girls of the lower class. Still another kind of serial murderer came from the lower class, and their victims were from the lower class as well. Leyton (1986) is an enthusiastic supporter of explanations of this kind, as he attacked the psychological explanations for mass murder and serial murder. He argues that such murderers come from the margins of the middle class, the lower class, or from the margins of the working upper class. He speaks about conservative figures who feel detached from the status they wish so much to have, and therefore the murder is directed toward victims who represent for them the class which rejected them. Hence, he says, there is vengeance and a settling of an account here, when the murders are a kind of a monologue that includes cursing toward the social order.

But if this is so, we would have expected to find a serial murder of girls from the middle and upper classes by serial murderers from the lower class which almost never happens in reality.

We can find an inner contradiction in Hinch & Scott (2000) words. On the one hand, he claims that the murderers are not radicals who go out to change the social order, but conservatives, and on the other hand, they avenge society due to the prevailing social order, while feeling rejected by the social class they want to be accepted to. This kind of explanation, as interesting as it could be, is not based theoretically, or empirically: Empirically, it was not found that people from the upper class murder people from the lower class, neither was it found that serial murder is directed against people from the upper class by people from the lower class as a kind of rebellion or affront, in the spirit of the neo-classical school of thought in criminology.[108] But we cannot ignore one social fact: The preferred victims are in the low social status: Prostitutes, nomads and homeless, wandering youth, children, and so on. The reason for choosing these victims can be for a few reasons. First, they do not attract attention or concern by family members and friends when they disappear. Second, they are a convenient target to be seduced and caught because of their social dependence on the murderer (the prostitute's livelihood, a lift for moneyless youths). Third, it is easier for a murderer to depersonalize these victims due to their lower social status. Society creates some kind of legitimacy for the inferiority of certain groups in the population which might be interpreted by part of the serial murderers as legitimacy to exterminate them.

Vronsky (2004) gives a sociological explanation on the macro level which connects the events the USA have experienced since WWII up to the terror acts on the Twin Towers in New York, through to Kennedy's murder, the Vietnam war, oil crisis, Watergate affair, and so on. These events, he claims, brought about a cultural collapse. He says that something in extreme cultural changes of this kind brings about the creation of serial murderers or enables their appearance. Maybe this is the collapse of values which have been established in the past, or the loss of some future vision, as people with an impulse to murder tend to act out in such times. In addition, according to Vronsky, the future does not have good predictions in store. The American dream that every generation would progress to an improved socioeconomic status does not materialize. A major part of the Americans went down, not up, versus the status their parents had, and the real income decreases together with the increase in unemployment. The middle class is not a safe goal any more, and it is not a guarantee for a better life. Even the span of the oceans do not guarantee safety, as was found in the 9/11 events. Therefore, Vronsky (2004) says, only one dream remained, and that is the dream of continuous murder.

This explanation is reminiscent of the sociological one given to mass murder executed by people who have lost their source of livelihood together with their self-worth. There are two problems with this explanation. First, Vronsky (2004) compares the moral collapse of the American society to the one that occurred in the former USSR after the revolution, or to the one that took place in Germany after WWII. But in these two states, the moral collapse was not accompanied by an increase of serial murder, so that there are still other unique cultural characteristics of the American society. Second, even if there is some truth to this explanation on the macro level, there is still the connection missing between the macro level (society) and the micro level (the individual)—and this is the important issue for our discussion.

To sum up, the sociocultural etiology of serial murder refers to a number of central factors: First, socialization to violence as part of the norms of general culture, in which violence is perceived as a legitimate way of solving personal and interpersonal problems, as a means of achieving goals and immediate benefit, as a way of looking for excitement, especially in a society that goes through moral chaos. Second, this is a culture that emphasizes the depersonalization and anonymity of the individual. Third, there is a sense of helplessness that makes certain people look for the power and control they miss in everyday life. Fourth, there is confusion up to a cancellation of the border between the private and the public by showing publicly torn and shattered bodies as part of the leisure culture. This issue takes the discussion to the mass media.

Mass Media and Serial Murder

The main criticism addressed toward mass communication deals with its responsibility for increasing violence in society, claiming that the violent contents presented in the media influence the interpersonal level of violence among the spectators, since the exposure to violent contents blunts sensitivity and empathy toward the victim up to a degree of indifference, and even accepting violence as an inseparable part of social life.

To defend themselves, the media argue that they do not operate in a sociocultural vacuum, and that they extract their contents from the social and cultural environment in which they operate. If the media present violent contents, they say, it reflects part of the culture and it is not their invention. It seems that there is a large extent of truth in both claims.

The different scientists who deal with serial murder tend to attribute to the media certain guilt. It obviously does not create serial murder, but the scientists indicate its secondary contributions to the etiology of serial murder. For example, Holmes and Holmes (1998) emphasize the fact that the media present violence which cannot be explained, and by so doing create an insensitivity to violence in all age groups. One can see it in violent films on television and video, and in performances of bands which use hammers, clubs and swords on stage. In my opinion, unlike these traditional claims, news broadcasts provide examples of the recourse of violence in politics, in interracial relationships, in terror and the war against terror, in working relationships and in family relationships in the USA.[109] All these events are not an invention of the media, but a presentation of the sociocultural reality in which we live.

The scientists refer also to the variety of imaginary and semi-academic movies and books on the issue of serial murder which make serial murderers into some kind of culture heroes. "The names of the serial murderers are used by law students like a list of non-sacred angels" (Ibid). According to Holmes & Holmes (1998), the serial murder and murderers have become a social issue. We know the names of the murderers but not the names of their victims. The serial murderers are presented in the media in a way that shows us a human and vulnerable aspect of their personality, while providing reasons and even justifications for their violent behaviour. These scientists' claim is that the media have created a social aspect in which the serial murderers have become cultural icons for the audience, and their lives have become an intimate target for public curiosity.

When serial murderers do not murder, they find other ways to feel control. One way for is to scatter fear and terror in the community or the state, and become famous thanks to mass media. The murderers enjoy appearing on the front page of newspapers and television reports, and become famous, even celebrities. They want to read about themselves in the newspaper and watch the results of their deeds on television, and are glad to get a famous nickname which would ensure that their deeds would permanently enter our collective memory. The media respond with quick creations of a nickname, such as: Jack the Ripper, The Boston Strangler, and others (Levin, 2008).

It should be added that when there were serial murders executed in small townships, its victims had low social status, it received less exposure in the media in relation to a serial murder carried out in big cities, and the victims were from the middle class. For example, The Boston Strangler gained immense publication in various media, although regarding the number of victims he is one of the less dangerous serial murderers. The same refers to Jack the Ripper from London. Hickey (1992) claims in this context that the media focus public attention on serial murderers because they look bizarre and extra ordinary. The serial murderers serve the media by creating headlines which sell newspapers, like The Child-Killer, The Boston Strangler, and so on. The media's treatment of the victims is also problematic: It reports the number of victims, and this is a news report, but it also focuses on the method of killing, and by so doing it feeds a morbid curiosity accompanied by the stereotype of the serial murderer: A man, generally white, who attacks sexually and cruelly women who cannot defend themselves. This stereotype damaged the understanding of the phenomenon because it did not refer to other types of serial murder that are not focused at sexual gratification. In addition, it ignores cases of serial murder executed by women.

The media focus more on the murderer's skills of misleading the police and on the nature of his actions, while the victims are just stage props in the story, or else, justify their own death. What is more severe, the public starts making distinctions between a good serial murderer and a bad one, and it paves the way to attaching a value to the serial murderer which elevates him to a higher status than that of the "regular" murderer. The murderer is not perceived as a law violator in the eyes of the public, but a person who has gone through over-socialization. The public sees him as one who executes the verdict of society against his will. All these connect to the concept of "the injured culture" (Vronsky, 2004).

Levin (2008) claims that since the beginning of the twenty-first century sadism has become more pronounced on prime-time shows in the mass media in the USA. The producers present more and more programs which attract the spectators by witnessing the pain and suffering of others, all presented graphically. The supply of sadism meets the needs of many Americans who are desperate to feel good about themselves. When the spectators get a chance to watch humiliated, tortured or murdered victims, they may feel superior and strong, they laugh at the losers, the miserable, and the weak as it often happens in the genre of reality programs, and even in stand-up routines which tend to brutally hurt the most vulnerable: Old people, immigrants and minorities. According to Levin, this leads the spectators, especially youth, to an insensitivity of the real influences of destructive behaviour. Due to the fact that the programs are broadcast in primetime, the spectators learn that enjoying the suffering of others is a socially accepted phenomenon. The acquired sadistic impulse becomes, according to Levin (2008), active in societies in which the needs of the individual are not fulfilled and he remains with a strong feeling of helplessness. These individuals, who feel weak, tend to be happier or enjoy the misery of others through a sense of sadism. This gives them a sense of power and control they cannot achieve in every-day life, and part of them turn to the serial murder of the same populations who have become legitimate victims.

In our dealing with the mass media, we have to distinguish between two concepts: Reality of the media and the media of real-ity. The media of reality, in our case, reports on an event of a serial murder with reference to the way of operation and the image of the murderer. On the other hand, the reality of the media has to do with the way the media work and the way they deal with issues, both in news reporting and in interpretation. For instance, the claim that the media emphasize the "graphics" of the murder and elaborately describe what the murderer did to the victim is not part of the plain news reporting for reasons of hurting the feelings of the public, respecting the dead, and the right for privacy. We saw an example of this in the Twin Tower disaster in the USA, in which the media did not show injured and dead people. The criti-cism against the media in relation to a serial murder does not refer to the "dry" concise news reporting, since its task is to report on such events. Making the murderers into culture heroes is what makes it outrageous and damaging. Figures who hurt the moral values of society become celebrities, and by so doing the media contribute to a number of negative phenomena: Empowering the criminal and hurting the reputation of the law; presenting and creating most negative images to be admired and imitated by oth-ers; and a severe damage of the role of the media to express and preserve basic moral values of society. For example, Billy the Kid, or movies about other "heroes" in the Wild West of the USA, praised these hooligans who were evaluated according to the speed of drawing the gun and killing the other person. The same refers to Bonnie and Clyde who are presented in a movie as a ro-mantic adventurous couple, while actually they were a couple of psychopaths who unnecessarily murdered people during rob-beries, committed murders just for fun, and murdered policemen just for being policemen. Moreover, serial murderers are often characterized by their passion for publication, and in this respect, the media serve their goal and are some kind of "school" for new serial murderers, while they learn from the media about past famous serial murderers. A small part wants to imitate them, but the majority wants to enjoy a greater publicity than their predecessors, and this might intensify their actions.

It does not mean that the media create serial murderers, but the messages it sends about them roughly blur the fact that they are criminals of the worst kind who enjoy not only a neutral news stage, but also becoming cultural icons that children and youth look up to. So, instead of condemning the phenomenon, the media make it "normal," if not legitimate. For example, in the movie "The Silence of the Lambs," the serial murderer who sits in jail for his despicable actions is the "good guy," the only one who is ready to and can help the FBI. The media emphasize the person behind the murderer, so that we can identify with him. It shows him as a person who materializes the absolute freedom, and so he becomes an object of admiration and may be even of jealousy, since this situation touches each one of us in one way or another, even if we are shocked by their deeds. The graphic exposure which specifies the horror acts causes the desensitization of the viewers. The shock and empathy for the victims is numbed as long as the public is exposed to more cases and more details about each and every case.

The linkage between the media and the violent American culture is obvious. When the days of the Wild West were over by enforcing law and order, the urban centers have become the new, modern Wild West. The gunman has become an urban attacker, a wolf. The gun led to horrible murder methods. The rationale that accompanied the Wild West as the arena of settling conflicts in violent ways led to allegedly irrational murder, murder for the sake of having fun in an act which meets the needs of power, control and sexual sadism. In this modern world, the media not only present reports about serial murderers, but also create genres of books, movies and music which deal with this phenomenon from the fictional aspect.

When I dealt with introducing violent contents into fanta-sies about serial murderers, it was indicated that it comes from the sociocultural environment the serial murderer lives in. Now it is clear as to how such contents are created and studied by the murderer.

Sociological Theories for Explaining Serial Murder and Murderers

It should be emphasized that sociological theories in criminology, like various theories in psychology, were not intended originally to explain serial murder, but were an attempt to apply them in order to explain this phenomenon. The goal was that these theo-ries would be able to explain a systematic, rational and serial vio-lation of the law over a long period of time, and even a "criminal career." This condition leaves us with many theories that can be applied to a wide range of serial criminality.[110] But not all the soci-ological theories which are applicable for explaining serial crimi-nality are necessarily applicable for serial murder, due to the se-verity of the felony and its uniqueness. Therefore, the number of the relevant theories is significantly smaller. Before presenting the theories, it is important to indicate that in criminology there are a few schools of thought that bear similarity and difference to the psychological theories.

Together with the increase of the medical model in psychol-ogy, there appeared a similar model in criminology. Since the peri-od of Lombroso up to the sixties of the twentieth century, the positivist school of thought dominated criminology. According to this school, biological, physiological, psychological and social factors influence the individual and his behaviour. The result is a delinquent behaviour that "is not under the individual's control," as the different powers that operate him push him to commit fel-onies. Some of the theories of the positivist school can be applied for explaining the creation of the serial murderer. The innovation in these theories is that unlike the psychological theories, they can explain not only a serial murder with a sado-sexual motive, but also a motive for achieving a material benefit.

It has to be emphasized: Although these arguments are presented by scientists who stand for the sociological explanation, one cannot conclude that psychology does not have a role in explaining the serial murder and murderers. At a later stage, I will present the possible connection between sociology and psychology in a multidisciplinary explanation of the phenomenon.

I will present four theories from this school: The strain theory, the differential association theory, the social learning theory, and the self-control theory.

In the seventies of the twentieth century there developed a new-old school in criminology, the neo-classical school. As opposed to the positivist school, this one claims that the delinquent is a person with free will who is motivated by a rational calculation of profit and loss from the felony and its outcomes. Hence, one should not refer to the powers that push the delinquent, except for his personal free will. From this school I will present two central theories: The rational choice theory and the routine activity theory which are more suited to serial murderers who have material motives and to which the psychological theories have almost no reference.

The Strain Theory—Merton (1957)

Merton uses a central concept, called "anomie." He claims that every society poses two systems for its members: One system represents the goals which are perceived as appreciated by society and the individual has to aspire to achieve. The second system is the regulating system. This system poses the normative and legitimate ways for achieving the appreciated goals by society. Through the socialization process, children and new members in society learn the essence of these two systems.

In fact, the unequal social structure makes it easy or difficult for individuals and groups in society to achieve the appreciated goals, according to the socioeconomic stratum they are in. In social classes or strata which lack the legitimate means, there may be a significant gap between internalizing the appreciated goals and their capability of achieving them. Merton describes this situation as a state of anomie which can show itself in different ways and what he calls "patterns of maladjustment or a social deviation." For our case, only the relevant patterns will be presented for discussion:

- The "innovator" takes upon him the goals of society, but lacks the legitimate means for achieving them. This is why he turns to illegitimate means, like crime, for achieving the appreciated goals.
- The "rebel" comes out against the social goals society poses as the appreciated goals, and, in addition, is not ready to take upon himself the legitimate means that society poses. Such people are revolutionaries who aspire to change the social order by determining appreciated goals of their own and the legitimate means for achieving them.

The question is how the different patterns that Merton presented are connected to serial murder. The serial murderer who acts for the sake of material benefit can be explained by the pattern of the "innovator." The murderer internalized the social goals which attribute great value to materialism, and aspires to achieve it in any way, but he does not get the legitimate means that society attributed for this end (hard work, entrepreneurship and others). As far as he is concerned, the end justifies the means. This is how a professional assassin behaves as he works as a freelance contract killer, and so does a Blue Beard who murders his wife in order to receive the inheritance and insurance money.

Another pattern that can explain the serial murder with a sexually sadistic background is that of the rebel: This murderer fantasizes of goals of his own. Outwardly, he seems as someone who took upon himself society's goals: He works, sets up a family, and looks like the next door neighbour. In fact, through his fantasy he creates new goals of fatal sexual sadism. He does not internalize the legitimate means for achieving his goals, because society did not pose legitimate means for such a murder. Therefore, he creates for himself the means which are legitimate in his eyes for executing the murder: Seduction, kidnapping, sexual abuse and murder, and sometimes even abusing the body by necrophilia, justifying his behaviour in different ways.

The question that appears as a criticism of this explanation is why should a specific individual accept the social goals and the legitimate means for achieving them, while others do not? Why should an individual who aspires to materialize the value of materialism choose a legitimate work, while another would become a professional killer? The theory cannot answer these questions, since the component of the micro level, the individual, is missing. In other words, the psychological explanation is missing, an explanation that would clarify why a certain individual would become a serial murderer for the sake of achieving material benefit, while another one would work from sunrise till sunset in a legitimate occupation. Furthermore, it is unclear why a certain individual would court a woman, fall in love and have sexual relationship with her out of free will, or turn to a prostitute who would meet his special needs, while another individual would materialize sadist-sexual fantasies with a strange woman and murder her afterwards.

Although this criticism allegedly points to the weakness of the theory in explaining serial murder, it enables a valuable generalization, and there is room for the integration of psychological theories. It is not deterministic and does not claim that everyone who lacks the legitimate means for achieving society's goals would become a murderer, but at the same time, it lacks the explanation why certain individuals go in this direction.

Differential Association Theory—Sutherland (1947)

This theory consists of nine principles. We will summarize the theory for our needs by saying that delinquency is an acquired behaviour, like any other acquired behaviour. Learning is done through attachment to other criminals in intimate groups and through interpersonal communication. Criminal learning consists of two components: The how—how they execute different kinds of felonies from the technical point of view, and the why—the justifications and excuses why the felony becomes legitimate. Sutherland applied his theory in his book *The Professional Thief*, in which he showed how a differential association to other professional thieves enables the apprentice learn the secrets of the profession and the professional norms from the veterans, go through a period of specialization under the supervision of their superiors and receive acknowledgment and "authorization" as a professional thief.

As far as serial murder is concerned, except for a small rate of murderers who operate in pairs or in a team, one cannot speak about socialization to serial murder, especially if the motive is pathological-psychological. All the same, one can assume that the "professional assassin," as a kind of a serial murderer, has gone through training by others, and has even gone through specialization with the help of others, since the murdering technique requires a professional learning of sophisticated surveillance, operating tools. Fighting means learning how to disguise, escape, forge and so on, at which point the professional assassin can work on his own.

Sutherland's theory denied to a large extent the influence of mass media on the creation of the serial murderer, since according to him, delinquent learning takes place in small groups and through interpersonal communication. But one has to bear in mind that the theory was suggested at a time in which mass media was at its beginning. Various studies which have been conducted since then, point to more significant influences of mass media than those Sutherland knew. It does not mean that a person who reads a book or watches a movie with contents of fatal violence becomes a murderer if he does not have a pathological predisposition for it.[111] It must be said, however, that the very exposure of violent contents by the mass media creates an additional stratum to the making of a serial murderer if the individual has such a pre-disposition. Moreover, the will to be famous, as has been reflected in the discussion on mass media, is also influential.

This aspect was improved by Glaser (1956) who added an-other component to the differential association theory, the Differ-ential Identification: The individual uses a delinquent behaviour due to his identification with people, whether real or imaginary whom he admires, or sees as heroes whose behaviour should be imitated. This attitude contributed to the explanation of the phe-nomenon of copycat among serial murderers, and to the under-standing of the individual's capability to become a serial murderer through his identification with "culture heroes" and his admira-tion of them, even if he does not know them personally. This un-derstanding supports the perception that mass media has a signif-icant role.

The Social Learning Theory—Akers (1973)

This theory enables expansion on the issue of socialization be-yond what was suggested in the theory of differential association. According to this theory, delinquent behaviour, including mur-derous violence, is a product of social learning and the influences of different groups with whom the individual socializes. Accord-ing to this theory, the basic development of the individual can be predicted according to the unique experiences he is exposed to throughout his life. For example, exposing the individual to vio-lence toward another can become a positive role model for him for future violence, if the individual would learn that violence is worthwhile in situations of interpersonal conflicts.

Another aspect of social learning of murderous violence is the experiences the individual goes through in his own life. For instance, a beaten child becomes very often a beating father, be-cause he has learned that this is the right or the proper behaviour. In this context, Holmes and Holmes (1998) argue that "exposure to violence at a young age might, for some, be a pushing factor toward later violence, but not for everyone ... many people are victims or witnesses of violence, but do not become serial murderers. On the other hand, for others, the violent experience as a child is never forgotten; it is repressed and later released against others ..." (Ibid.). Cater (1997) adds in this context that serial murderers learn the violent behaviour, and therefore have to be seen as a product of the society in which they grew up. A criticism of the claim that serial murder is learned as a means of solving conflicts is that the murderer is not in conflict with the victim. In most cases, the victim is a stranger for the murderer, and serves him as a means of materializing fantasy, vengeance of someone else, and so on. This criticism is not accurate for several reasons. First, if the victim serves as a means for vengeance of someone else, like a parent, for example, then the serial murder does serve as a means of solving interpersonal conflicts. Second, some serial murderers choose a specific victim, even though he is a stranger to them, due to the fact that he has a characteristic that makes him unworthy of living ("the assignment murderer") in their eyes. Third, although most of the victims are strangers to the murderer, there are specific victims who are murdered by contract, and in these cases the choice of the victim is not random, but deliberate.

Castle and Hensley (2002) show how one can apply the social learning theory in explaining serial murder by bringing examples of former soldiers who have been educated to hate, attack and kill. The soldiers have actually learned to kill strangers just because they have one specific characteristic—they are the enemy.

The Self-Control Theory—Hirschi and Gottfredson (1993)

In an attempt to suggest a general theory for explaining crime, the scientists present the term self-control, or to be more precise, lack of self-control, as what causes delinquency. According to them, when a child who goes through a process of socialization, does not receive positive reinforcement and negative reinforcement (punishment), for deviating or delinquent behaviour, he does not develop a mechanism of self-control which would instruct him as to what is permitted or forbidden behaviour. The outstanding characteristics of those who have not developed a self-control mechanism are the inability to postpone satisfactions, impulsiveness, lack of long-term thinking, and indifference to the suffering of the victim.

This theory is very much like the psychoanalytic theory in the context of voids in the superego and the characteristics of the sociopath. The question is whether everyone who has not developed a self-control mechanism might become a serial murderer. The answer is, of course, negative, although we may find among serial murderers those who lack a self-control mechanism. In other words, the theory can explain, at the most, why serial murderers lack a self-control mechanism, and from this aspect, the strength of this explanation is similar to that of the antisocial personality disorder.

The Rational Choice Theory—Cornish and Clarke (1986), Gibbs (1975)

This theory belongs to the neo-classical school in criminology. The classical school and the neo-classical school explain delinquency by saying that the criminal acts out of his free will for the sake of profit. He makes a rational choice because he knows what the punishment by the law is if he gets caught. Unlike the positivist school, the delinquent is a rational creature who acts out of free will and not from necessity or various powers which push him to commit a crime without being able to resist them.

The rational choice theory is based upon the principle of the "expected benefit" in economic theories. According to this principle, people would make rational decisions which would, according to their calculation, bring maximal profits and minimal losses. Beyond the aspect of economics in this theory, in a criminological context, the theory is suggested as a comprehensive and general explanation both for the decision to commit a specific crime and for the development of a criminal career, or retiring from it. The decisions are based on the expected effort and reward for the criminal, as compared with the probability and severity of the punishment and other prices the crime involves.

This theory, unlike the psychological theories which have taken from the criminal the freedom of choice, points out that delinquency is an act of choice, even if the calculation of profit and loss is irrational. This "rationalism" is expressed, in fact, as the criminal has a freedom of choice that the positivist theories (the biological and the psychological ones) have taken from him.

Beyond the question whether criminals make a pure rational calculation about effort, profit and loss, theoretically, the important point is in returning the responsibility to the criminal and to his choices. The psychological theories which have been surveyed emphasize, to a large extent, the disorder in the criminal's mind due to a trauma in childhood, and although they do not justify his behaviour or the serial murder in our case, they are quite deterministic, and see the individual as a passive product of his childhood. On the other hand, the theory that claims that the criminal executes a serial murder out of free will and his own choice, expecting to gain something, while doing everything to avoid being caught, presents the serial murderer in another light. They do not say that his choice to murder is not connected with his personality and his psychological background, and that this choice comes from a void, but the emphasis is on the capability to execute their choice. Morton (2005) contributed to this approach by summarizing a discussion that has been conducted in an international conference on serial murderers. According to Morton, the most significant factor for serial murder is the personal decision the criminal makes to continue with his crimes.

It is my opinion that the distinction between choosing and not choosing is reminiscent of the distinction between psychotic and psychopathy: The psychotic murderer is not free to choose between executing or not executing the deed, because he hears voices and sees delusions which neutralize to a large extent, his freedom of choice. The psychopath, on the other hand, chooses consciously and plans to execute the serial murders in order to receive a material or a psychological satisfaction. Although there are those who claim that the psychotic also has a freedom of choice, since he chooses to obey instructions that exist only in his reality, and can choose not to obey the instruction he hears in his head. But defining this situation as a rational choice would be cynical. One can say that the psychopath also has no freedom of choice, since he is controlled by impulses and obsessions he has difficulty to control.

As I will show later on, part of the serial murderers who are under obsessed thoughts do not murder every random victim, and wait until the "ideal" victim comes. Therefore, the conclusion is that they have freedom of choice, and they do not act out of an uncontrollable impulse. Outstanding examples for this freedom of choice among serial murderers can be seen in murderers who are motivated by a material motive. The professional assassin, for example, can choose to execute a murder agreement or refuse to do it, and similarly, the Black Widow, the woman who murders her husbands, one by one, chooses for her future husband the one who has the maximal material resources so that her benefit from murdering him would be the highest. Among the serial murderers who are motivated by a sadist-sexual motive we can also see some rationalism in their choice. They create a fantasy world in which they characterize the image of the "ideal victim." This is making a choice, even if it stems from a certain background in their child-hood. Afterwards they compose the plot of the fantasy out of their choice so that it would yield the maximal enjoyment from the act of murder and the sexual act that accompanies it. At the same time, these serial murderers behave professionally in order to avoid being caught. Therefore, we can see that the theory of the rational choice is applicable in explaining serial murder, because it includes a choice that yields the maximal benefit and minimal loss. We may assume that the "ideal" victim who is chosen by the murderer is a victim that is meant to increase the murderer's satis-faction from the murder he has committed due to his identity or certain unique characteristics.

Here is another example which demonstrates to what extent psychology and sociology complement each other, rather than oppose one another. The question why choosing a specific victim increases the psychological benefit the murderer produces depends on his past and personality, and this is the task of psychology to give this answer. Moreover, even among serial murderers with a sadist-sexual background there are those who, in spite of the impulse to commit their evil scheme, would not compromise on a victim who does not meet the criteria of their "ideal victim."

The Routine Activity Theory—Cohen and Felson (1979)

This theory, like the previous one, has developed since the rise of the neo-classical school of thought in criminology. The scientists claim that the probability for a crime increases when there is one person or more who is motivated to commit a crime; when there is a suitable target or an accessible potential victim, and there is no formal or informal protection which may have deterred the criminal. According to the theory, the risk of a crime changes very much according to the circumstances and the places in which people position themselves or their property.

Cohen & Felson (1979) assume that the combination of these three elements for executing a crime has to do with normal, legal and routine activity of the potential victims and their guards. The term "routine activity" refers to the common actions that meet the needs of the general population and those of the individual in particular: Work, shopping, leisure activity, social interaction, sexual intercourse, studies, and raising children. Their assumption is that changes in daily activities that have to do with work, studies and leisure have, since WWII, positioned more people in specific locations and times which increased their accessibility and vulnerability as victims, while distancing them from their relatively safe homes.

It is interesting to see that this theory does not try to explain the reasons for the crime, but the ease or difficulty in which it would take place. In other words, the theory assumes that the fact that more people are away from home, due to routine activities, makes them potential victims at a higher level than before, as they are defenseless in certain times and places.

As far as serial murder is concerned, the theory does not explain the reasons for it, but the increase in amount of victims of a certain status who stay in certain time and place without any protection, and so become potential victims more so than in the past: Street prostitutes, homeless people, wandering youth, and so on (Rossmo, 1995). Furthermore, the theory can explain the fact that college girls who travel by hitchhiking are murdered because when they enter the car they become defenseless, versus traveling in a group or traveling by public transportation. Similarly, the norm according to which a prostitute is called to an apartment or a hotel room makes her defenseless against a psychopath, a situation that was rarer in the past.

We may say that the routine activities theory cannot explain the motives for serial murder, but the greater ease in which it can be done today. In this regard it is connected to the rational choice theory, as the lack of defense of potential victims increases the probability that potential victims would become actual victims and potential murderers would become actual murderers, as part of the murderer's calculation of gain and loss.

To sum up, in spite of the challenge of building an integrative theoretical model, one should bear in mind that there are many types of serial murderers with different motives, and even within the same type there is a wide variety of serial murderers although they share a common motive. As has been said already, a theory that explains serial murder with a sado-sexual background which has been done for the sake of achieving a sense of power and control does not necessarily suit an explanation of serial murder from material motives. Therefore, an assumption is derived that maybe it is correct to suggest different explanations for different types of serial murders. For this end I will have to use the concept of "framing or reframing," with reference to theories that explain such behaviour in general, and among serial murderers in particular.

Framing/Reframing

Before going on to integrative theoretical models, I will recruit a perception to aid me that, although it is not new, has not gained proper use in the last decades. I refer to reframing. This term includes sociological and psychological theories which contribute to the explanation and understanding serial criminality that have lasted for a long time, and includes, in certain cases, a criminal career.

The term "reframing" serves as a set of techniques for neutralizing guilt and shame, or reconstructing of situations and behaviours. The criminal uses it when defining feelings and situations in his inner world through his subjective viewpoint and in light of his emotional and other experiences that he has gone through or would go through in relation to his deeds. But his inner world is influenced by social and cultural environments. Sometimes, this process is done within a differential association in which the future criminal learns, during the process of training from others, a set of justifications that enable him execute the felony, and see it in a positive light and justify his deeds afterwards (Sutherland, 1947; Matza, 1964). In other cases, the process is done without being aware of it. In this context there come up some significant explanations:

Techniques of Neutralization: Sykes and Matza (1957)[112]

The theory explains delinquent behaviour as a result of the use of techniques of neutralization by criminals. These techniques are justifications for executing criminal acts, and they are actually a distorted expansion of accepted justifications in the general culture.[113] It should be emphasized that it does not mean that criminals totally reject the values of conventional society, or that they have a set of values that directly opposes the conventional one.[114]

Scientists who referred to this theory, indicated that the intention of neutralization is to weaken internal blocks against delinquency, or a break in the individual's connections with society

(Akers, 1997, p. 85). It is important to indicate that the theory is applicable for delinquency in two time periods: Neutralizing guilt before the execution of the felony, and afterwards. The assumption is that the criminals have also gone through socialization to the norms of society, and therefore executing a felony is against the norms that have been internalized and creates a situation of cognitive dissonance. So, in order that the individual would be able to execute a felony, he needs techniques for neutralizing the norms which prevent him from executing the felony. But even if the criminal succeeds in neutralizing the norms or the self-control which stops him from delinquency, there are situations in which the criminal feels regret, guilt feelings, or psychological inconvenience[115] after committing the felony. In order to come out of the inconvenient psychological state, one option is to justify the deed in retrospect through techniques of neutralizing guilt and shame. The advantage of this theory is that it explains, by using the term "drift,"[116] the possibility that the criminal would enter into delinquency and come out of it to normative activity. In our case, the serial murderer conducts a normative way of life at the same time and as a disguise of the serial murder action.

Before presenting the various neutralizing techniques, it is important to emphasize that while most scientists referred to the stage after committing the felony, I think that the stage of using these techniques before committing the felony is not less important, and may be even more so. It provides an explanation of how the individual can commit horrible deeds like a serial murder by reframing the situation and the motives. The authors suggest five techniques of neutralizing guilt and shame:

- Denial of responsibility—the criminal refuses to take responsibility for his acts, and attributes them to powers beyond his control (harsh childhood, living in difficult conditions).
- Denial of the damage or the hurt—the criminal does not deny his act, but argues that nobody was actually hurt physically or economically.

- Denial of the victim—the hurt or damage caused by the delinquent act was appropriate, because the victim deserved it (stealing from a shop owner who overprices, hurting a teacher who insults her students, hurting minorities who forgot their "proper" place in society).
- Condemning the denouncers—blaming those who criticize the criminal as being hypocrites and have a hidden deviation (police officers who aspire for personal promotion through blaming the criminal, a teacher who abuses her pupils).
- Addressing higher loyalties—immediate demands of family and friends values overpower the values of society and its rules (Shoemaker, 1996).

Neutralization techniques were used also in the differential association theory (Sutherland, 1947) as part of delinquent learning. Sutherland called them "definitions," meaning positions or meanings that the individual attaches to a given behaviour. Definitions are orientations, rationalizations, definitions of situations and moral and value positions which define the execution of an act as good or bad, appropriate or inappropriate, justified or unjustified.

The criminal justifies himself by positive definitions or by definitions which have gone through neutralization. Positive definitions are beliefs or positions that make the behaviour a desired or permitted behaviour from a moral point of view. Definitions that have gone through neutralization support the execution of a crime by justifying it or finding an excuse for its execution. The individual sees the delinquent act as undesired, but in relation to the circumstances, it becomes appropriate, justified, or not terrible. The concept of "definitions" which has gone through neutralization in the social learning theory, combines the terms of "verbalization," "rationalization," "neutralization techniques," and "explanation." Such positions include justifications such as "I'm not guilty," "I can't control myself, I was born that way," "I'm irresponsible," "I was drunk and I didn't know what I was doing," "He deserves it." The immediate criticism against this theory's capability to help in understanding serial murder comes from the fact that it is very limited. It has been said already, in the discussion on the antisocial personality, that the criminal does not feel guilt or regret for his deeds, and therefore does need neutralization techniques. My answer to such criticism is that maybe the person with an antisocial personality has operated techniques of neutralizing guilt in advance, and therefore does not report of guilt feelings, shame or regret. A second claim is that part of the serial murderers feel guilt and regret for their deeds, mainly after the first murder, or at least this is what they report. In addition, when sociopaths were confronted with their deeds, they tended to use techniques of neutralizing guilt, and hence they were familiar with these techniques.

Fox and Levin (1998) suggest to elaborate on the concept of the dehumanization the murderer does in relation to the victim, as a kind of explanation that enables him to execute the felony. From this respect, one can see it as another significant component of neutralizing guilt techniques.

The technique of neutralizing guilt has to be attached to the concept of structuring or reframing. It is known, for instance, that prostitutes go through such process as a preparation for their work. In this process they learn from veteran prostitutes how to collect more money and how to attract clients, and hear justifications of their behaviour, like the possibility to help their children. The veteran prostitutes explain why their occupation is legitimate, and even help other people in society (Amir. In Bryan, 1965–1966).

The concept of reframing enables us a wide sociological and psychological reference, as it presents, in fact, how the murderer perceives subjectively his world; and this is, perhaps, the most correct explanation for serial murder. Even today, scientists try to attribute different objective explanations to the phenomenon of serial murder, but these explanations are not necessarily suitable. On the other hand, in interviews with serial murderers it is difficult to distinguish between truth and lie because the murderer structures a reframing in the interview so that his deed seems normative and obvious up to the point that it is difficult for us to know what he feels and what he tells us about it.

The most difficult problem in the concept under discussion is the inability to examine it empirically. This is a variable that cannot be measured, only assessed. It is true, indeed, for many variables which have been raised within the discussion of the sociological and psychological theories.

We have to bear in mind that the perception according to which one has to examine deviant and delinquent behaviour through the eyes of the criminal or the deviant, is not news, known since the sixties of the twentieth century. The labeling theory claimed that one had to understand the world of the deviant through his eyes and his perception of the world (Becker, 1963). Though criminologists continued to look for the objective empirical explanation, and hence this domain has not been developed in criminology as a scientific field of knowledge. In the behavioural sciences of today, however, accepted qualitative research techniques exist which are quite often based on the life stories of the interviewees, and the examination of the narratives they use (Shkedi, 2004; Flick, 1998).

Even the impossibility to examine the interviewees' words empirically, the narratives they use point to the way they perceive the world and the structuring of it in relation to the victims and the crimes they have committed. All the same, one has to re-emphasize that the level of sophistication of some serial murderers is very high so that even their life stories and the narratives they use are often a means to manipulate the investigator.

For example, Bundy refers to all the murders he executed in the third person: "He did ...," on one hand, suits psychological dissociative theories; and, on the other hand, it is a technique used to convince the murderer's insanity and incompetency to stand trial.

A relevant example for the concept of reframing used by the serial murderer is that of the mission serial murderer. This murderer refers to a social group or category as unworthy of living, and, therefore, they have to be eliminated. The reason for this belief can be a real or an imaginary event the murderer experienced regarding this category, or alternately, a rational explanation to a large extent in, for instance, removing the prostitutes from the streets in order to ensure a better environment for raising his children. The answer to the question of why not everyone who lives in a neighbourhood in which there are street prostitutes would murder them is that among most citizens, the will to kill does not exist. Furthermore, the citizen believes in the law and the rule of the law, and the most he would do is to address the police or the mayor. On the other hand, the mission serial murderer structures his subjective perception as if he, and only he, can solve the problem. He uses neutralizing techniques by addressing higher loyalties: The concern about his children comes before everything else. The question of why he structures his perception in this way and not another, can be connected to a variety of parameters: In his childhood his parents did not react to bad things that had been done to him by others; hating prostitutes with no relation to defending his children's innocence, but because his mother was once a prostitute and brought men home; a prostitute who scorned him, and so on. That is, the reframing process and the use of techniques for neutralizing guilt can serve as an envelope for a variety of other motives than those the murderer speak about. In the very process of neutralizing and reframing, the murderer uses a heroic cultural narrative which gives his deed some legitimacy in the eyes of the public: His goal is the most supreme one in a society which emphasizes the values of the family and the concern for the children. But as we have said, this narrative can be a cover for a variety of totally different motives. Therefore, the theory of neutralizing guilt and the explanation of reframing can be significant for understanding the behaviour of the serial murderer and his capability to execute the deed, but they do not enable exposing the real motive that hides beyond these techniques. Apparently there are no psychological components in these explanations, but I assess that the explanation of reframing holds a psychological reference in store by the individual in relation to the norms of society. In terms of the psychoanalytic theory, the self can cancel part of the conflict between the id and the superego. In addition, reframing can cope better with the explanation of antisocial personality disorder. Instead of arguing that the individual who has experienced childhood traumas, repressed feelings of anger and tried to cope with reality without internalizing norms and empathy toward others, one can argue that the individual reframed social norms according to the traumas he has experienced, and by so doing could ignore social norms without feeling guilt feelings.

The Self-Defense Mechanisms—Anna Freud

Theoreticians dealt with the connection between the deviation of the individual and society a long time before Durkheim. Durkheim showed how social norms influence the rate of suicide in different societies. Later on, Freud and his daughter Anna referred to the disharmony between the individual and society. The reason for this is that the impulses of the individual are repressed due to the social pressure for a behaviour that is considered normative. This process is done by creating the superego and consciousness whose task is to supervise the impulses of the id, so that the actual behaviour would be according to the accepted norms by society.

Anna Freud noticed that people do not act just to satisfy the impulses of the id, but aspire also to give meaning to the events they experience through active coping with the obstacles of life and overcoming them. She also claimed that one has to examine the individual's defence mechanisms and see to it that the person would be aware of the way he uses the defence mechanisms which contribute to adjustment.

We can see that the defence mechanisms in the psychoanalytic theory are basically not different from neutralizing guilt and shame techniques, suggested by sociologists and criminologists. According to Freud, the id consists of mainly two impulses: Sex and aggression. The self is hardly there because it has to satisfy the id and the superego at the same time. The self has few tools it can use in its role as mediator, tools that have been intended to defend it. These tools are called "the defence mechanisms of the self." When the self has difficulty to please the id and the superego, it would use one or more of the defence mechanisms. The operation of these mechanisms can appear before executing a certain behaviour, like a serial murder, and enable it immediately, or afterwards, and provide the individual with justifications for this behaviour and similar ones in the future. I will present here some of these mechanisms which are relevant for our case:

- Displacement—removing feelings or impulses which arouse anxiety that are directed at a certain object, to another, less threatening object. Examples include slamming the door instead of hitting a specific person, quarreling with the spouse after a dispute with the employer, or a child who feels aggression toward his little brother and hits a doll. In our case, the serial murderer addresses frustration and angry feelings experienced from the humiliating mother figure, and murders women who have similar physical or occupational characteristics.

- Intellectualization—dealing with a problem or an emotional situation by making them an intellectual issue, while ignoring the personal and emotional aspects that are involved in it, like focusing on the details of the funeral instead of dealing with agony of mourning. In our case, we can see this mechanism as depersonalization of the victim. For example, the mission murderer refers intellectually to the problem of the prostitutes, drug dealers, and immigrants, and decides to deal with the problem composedly. Similarly, the serial murderer has no difficulty in hurting those that society defines as "less worthy."

- Projection—removing threatening ideas or feelings for the self, and attributing them to others. For example when the individual loses a debate, we would claim: "You are just stupid." In our case, the serial murderer would claim, for instance, that he murdered the prostitute because she wanted him to do so.

- Rationalization/logic—the person provides a logical and probable explanation for his behaviour which stems from impulsive impulses which are not accepted by the self. Like a person who explains to himself that he was fired because he did not flatter the boss, while the real reason was his poor performance at work; or the serial murderer who draws satisfaction from the act of murder and the control over the victim, would claim that he murdered the person who had hurt society.

- Sublimation—channeling socially unaccepted impulses into a socially accepted channel, like sublimation of aggressive impulses toward a career as a boxer. In the context of a serial murder, this mechanism can be used in a phenomenon called Munchausen Syndrome which refers to cases in which a mother or a sister hurts a child by poisoning, and then they are the first who try to save him. In this way, they gain attention and even a sense of acknowledgment by others as heroines.

- Isolation —a separation the self makes between the emotional part and the contents of thought, memory or impulse. Isolating contents from emotion enables the self to reduce the intensity of anxiety, by showing indifference and coolness in relation to threatening emotional situations that threaten the person. In the case of serial murderers, one can see a similar mechanism in the phenomenon of a dissociative personality disorder, in which there is a deviant identity alongside a normative one, "the dark side."

- Internalization/identification—this is an opposite action of the projection mechanism. The self internalizes positions, feelings and the like from the external environment and attributes them to himself. This is an internalization of negative, distorted or exaggerated values which serve as compensation or cover for the real self. For example, a mission serial murderer perceives himself as a social hero, or as the man of justice who frees society from the presence of those who are unworthy, or else, he murders out of sexual hedonism and feels as if he is attractive and can have any woman he likes, and allegedly he makes her enjoy it as well.

From the analysis of the defence mechanisms of the self, we can see how non-normative behaviours receive a normative confirmation through a varied set of mechanisms which create a reframing of the behaviour.

The Vocabularies of Motives—Mills (1940)[117]

Another interesting connection to the neutralizing techniques and reframing we find in Mills who dealt with the vocabularies of motives. He deals with it from a sociological point of view, and disqualifies, in fact, the existence of unconscious motives in the individual. According to Mills, we have to relate to linguistic behaviour not by attributing it to early and private situations in the individual, but to see it as an index of future activity.[118] The motives are expressed by a typical vocabulary or in specific social situations, when the human actor expresses and attributes motives to himself and to others. In other words, the motives are not a constant component in the individual, but are terms through which social actors make interpretations. The motive does not indicate a specific element in the individual, but represents situational outcomes which other doubt. Motives are, in fact, names for situational outcomes and a substitute for the actions that lead to them.

Different groups have different vocabulary for motives, and a stable vocabulary of motives connects expected outcomes to specific actions. Turning to psychological terms, like "passion," "aspiration" and the like, as explaining motives is not appropriate, since these terms should be explained socially.[119] In this context, motives are, or express, relatively stable linguistic stages of distinguished situations. Hence, motives and actions are not created within the individual, but stem from the situation in which he finds himself. As a result of this situation, a vocabulary is developed which accompanies the type of situation and is a justification for normative acts in that situation. Expressing the motive verbally becomes, actually, an accepted justification of a set of actions or plans in the past, present and future. By using a word, the motive is an indisputable answer for the actor and other members who are in a certain social situation regarding the question of the expected or the appropriate social and linguistic behaviour in that situation. Expectations for accepted justifications also create a social supervision that is accompanied by asking questions, so that the decisions of the individual are answers to these questions. For example, if I do such and such, what should I say? What would others say? Mills argues that when a social agent verbally expresses the motive, he does not try to describe the social act he has experienced, nor does he simply formulate "reasons," but influences others as well as himself, since in many social actions an agreement is required on the part of others. The motive, in fact, serves as a justification for action or as a criticism of it, and connects between behaviour and norms.

A typical vocabulary of motives for different situations significantly determines the action and its nature. The motives which are the linguistic part of the social action are directed to actions or to prevent them. For example, adjectives like good, bad, or pleasant, can promote an action or prevent it. In this way, a vocabulary of motives is created, and it operates as guidance and incentive from the very fact of being a judgment of others in relation to the actor.

Generally speaking, motives are attributed to others before they are adopted by the individual, and together with rules and norms of action in a given situation, we learn the vocabulary of the appropriate vocabulary for the given situation. These motives are introduced for use because they are part of our language and build our behaviour.

To go back to our subject, we see that among serial murderers the phenomenon of admiration, copycat, and competition with other famous serial murderers stands out.

Mills argues that sociologists look for something more rational and real than something biological and abstract. Every group, culture and society has a vocabulary that expresses motives, and therefore a motive is culture-dependent. The linguistic motive does not serve as an index of something internal within the individual, but it is a basis for attributing a typical vocabulary of motives in a certain situational action. Therefore, when we look for the real motive instead of the rationalization the individual does, we actually look for a way of speech that is under social supervision which has been presented in an action in the past, or in a series of actions which the individual executed.

Miles (1940) says that the modern vocabulary has to do with money, sex and hedonism. Hence, if a businessman argues a religious motive to his actions, it would arouse distrust, since religious motives are not based on an accepted vocabulary and do not accompany business situations. When we analyze the actions of others, we attribute to them motives that are accepted in society today. In other words, what is considered as a reason for one is considered as rationalization for another. Hence the important variable is the accepted vocabulary in relation to the motives in every group the individual belongs to, and for whose opinions he is apprehensive or cares about. According to the Mills, various groups may have different motives, because the motivational structure of the individual and the pattern of his goals are connected to his social framework (occupation, stratification). Therefore, the linguistic connections that hold people together make them institutionalize a framework of motive and trends.

The vocabulary of motives is meant for different situations, guides the behaviour and expects the reactions of others to this behaviour. In the urban, modern, secular society, there are different and competing vocabularies of motives which operate at the same time and the situations for which they are suitable are not clear regarding their domains and borders. Therefore, motives that were obvious in the past in defined situations become doubtful today, and a variety of parameters can arouse similar actions in a given situation. People get confused in different situations and guess what the motive is that "operates" the individual. This is one of the problems that criminologists and law enforcement officers come across while attributing a motive to a serial murderer.[120] For instance, psychoanalysis characterized the patriarchal middle class as having a strong orientation toward sex and individualism, and therefore the patients used the only vocabulary of motives they knew. This phenomenon stands out in competing sectors of the individualistic society which is characterized by competition over vocabularies from the old style, like: Obligation, love, kindness. "Mixed motives" and "motivational conflicts" are competing or contradicting situational patterns, and so is the vocabulary of their motives which are unclear for different situations as they used to be in the past. For example, those who internalized an economic cluster of motives applied these motives for all situations, including the family. Alternately, in America today, behaviour goes through control and integration by a hedonistic language. Therefore, for a major part of the population, in certain situations enjoyment and pain have become unshakable motives, in the same way as religious motives characterized past motives.

Mills' conclusion is that motives are worthless without a distinguished social situation, for which they are the appropriate vocabulary. They must be situational, and therefore the motives change in content and nature in different times and social structures. He says that instead of interpreting actions and language as an external expression of subjective and deep elements of the individual, one has to allocate different types of actions within a typical framework of normative actions from a social aspect.

In summarizing up to this point, we may conclude that there is a significant connection between motive and justification and one of the factors we look for in explaining behaviour in general, and murderous behaviour in particular, is the motive.

If we refer to Freud's neutralization theory, and Mills', we can explain a murderous behaviour by justifications which explain the causes for action. These justifications are described through a vocabulary the murderer learns from his sociocultural environment. He does not invent this vocabulary. The justifications are part of the motivation. But if we regard justifications as motives, we still lack the tools for explaining the action. How is it that one person would become a serial murderer, while another would not, even if both have gone through similar humiliations, frustrations and traumas? Alternately, we do not have the answer why a specific serial murderer should murder women with a sexual context, while another would murder women who remind him of a humiliating figure from his past. Although this dead end brings us back to psychological explanations within the personality of the individual, and we can see that different scientists, like Mills and Lofland (later on) refer to motives and threats through the aspect of social situations, rather than as something that is hidden inside the individual's soul.

It is my opinion that it is true that social interaction influences the personality and the behaviour of the person, and therefore one cannot disconnect the individual from the environment. On the other hand, the structure and nature of the personality changes from one person to another. So, although every science aspires to generalizations, there is no other way but to determine that the attempts to find one comprehensive explanation for the creation of a serial murderer is not realistic and it is given, as we have seen, to significant criticism.

Excuses and Justifications—Maruna and Copes (2004)

The book of these authors, which deals with excuses, justifications and neutralizing techniques, is actually a repetition and development of Mills and Sykes and Matza's approach, and there is therefore no need to repeat it. Whoever is interested in the criticism of the neutralization theory will find it in their book.

Neutralization can be defined in the following way: An explanation or a justification that the individual gives to himself and others as an answer to why he committed a felony from reasons that are inside him or from external pressure, like the case of Etty Alon. Etty Alon was a senior bank clerk. Her brother was a heavy gambler and owed hundreds of thousands of NIS. He turned to her and told her that if he did not pay the money, he would be killed. Etty Alon embezzled client money in the amount of NIS

400,000, and passed it all to her brother. She was caught and sentenced to 17 years in prison. Her husband divorced her and received custody of their children. One of the outstanding explanations is the necessity, or the urgency, to commit the felony. Also in Israel, there was a case in which the husband of a woman who had cancer stole money from his employer. In court he claimed that because the life-saving medication was not included in the healthcare service, and he wanted that his beloved would go on living, there was an urgency to commit the felony.

What is important for our discussion is the conclusion of Maruna & Cops (2004) that neutralization has no role in the etiology of the crime, and it explains only the persistence of crime. This is not a new claim. It relies on the perception that neutralization does not lead to crime. The innovation is in the criticism of the neutralization technique by Sykes and Matza, since one could have assumed from their approach that neutralization leads to crime, but it is obvious that a normative person does not become a criminal just because he used neutralization, guilt, and shame techniques. Sykes & Matza have made a mistake in their assumption because the component of readiness for performing a crime has to do with the criminal's ability to explain and find excuses for himself and for others. On the other hand, Sutherland was right, as I have shown and will be shown further on here. Neutralization enables potential criminals to become actual criminals.[121] For example, a serial murderer would move from the stage of fantasy to the stage of execution only after having used techniques of neutralizing guilt. Hence, neutralizing techniques have a role, and sometimes a significant one, in the etiology of a crime, even if it is true only for people who have already a temporary readiness for delinquency. When looking at serial murderers, one can understand to what extent neutralizing techniques serve as a key factor in their murderous behaviour. It is true both before and after the execution of the murder, and the neutralization enables repeating it again and again.

Identity and Deviation—Lofland (1969)

An approach which is more similar to the neutralizing technique by Sykes and Matza was suggested by Lofland (1969), in her book about identity and deviation. Lofland (1969) refers to the individual's response to a threat. Except for a physical attack, what can be considered as a threat has to do with what the actor's[122] beliefs that would put him in a social risk or under a social disgrace versus a group or groups of people, in whose terms he structures his activity, and for its sake he plays a certain kind of self. By learning their social group, people learn in what situations they have to present shame or pride, respect or humiliation, self-esteem or lack of it.

Even if the threat-creating structuring is subjective, it does not mean that deviate actions are secret. The action becomes public and defined as shameful through a social definition of others. This is exactly the definition of deviation in the labeling theory.

The author uses the term "encapsulation" in relation to social norms or to the use of legitimate means. The appearance of a sense of threat facilitates the execution of deviate action later on. The threat as such is not sufficient for such an occurrence, unless it helps the actor to enter into a state of psychological encapsulation. A state of constant focus on the threat, during an increase in anxiety, seems to lead sometimes to the structuring of an alternate actions range, and then he responds by reducing the threats which are short-term, accessible and close, and therefore perceived as more threatening as well. The state of encapsulation is experienced as a different state of thought: "I didn't think," "You're in another place," "I've gone crazy"—these expressions seem as different ways of saying that somebody arrived at a state in which considerations of long-term influences, including punishment, become weakened (Ibid., p. 52). Hence, encapsulation as a reaction to a threat increases the individual's sensitivity, and strengthens his tendency to be involved in short-term, fast, simple and accessible actions.

I think that the explanation is relevant also for those who lack self-control and those who suffer from antisocial personality disorder, that one of its characteristics is the lack of long-term sight. One may say that in a state of encapsulation, among some people, there is a tendency, or a preliminary tendency, to choose an action out of a group of actions which in the American society tends to include deviate actions. For example, the serial murderer who has gone through humiliation and frustration in his childhood would experience a state of encapsulation when he is reminded of it, when he experiences similar feelings, or when he comes across, whether in reality or in imagination, a figure that arouses in him the painful feelings. It could be also that the existence of a fantasy arouses in him an urge to receive satisfaction through an action toward an "ideal victim" ("you're in another place"). The serial murderer who experiences these feelings lacks the mechanisms of social support and social resources which could have prevented or postponed his turning to fatal means.

Alternatively, his solitude prevents him from achieving satisfaction in some normative way.[123] This phenomenon would be appropriate mainly for those serial murderers who are called "disorganized," who operate out of an impulse without any consideration of the outcomes of their deeds, and who even leave physical evidence at the scene. Nonetheless, other serial murderers may aspire to execute a murder because it is the only means they have learned for achieving satisfaction and a sense of control, and they choose the "ideal victim" who meets their fantasy. However, this does not mean that they are irrational enough to plan and execute the hiding of physical evidence. Lofland (1969) connects the behaviour of the individual to sociocultural aspects, through reference to the lack of social support. The events that enable encapsulation, beyond the preliminary tendency of the actor to manage the threat, have to do with personal and social aspects. These variables are most important: First, the extent of previous experience of the actor with the current occurrence; second, the extent of active social support that can moderate responsive actions against the deviation. Rare or unique events which are not expected and are not well defined, can be especially threatening from the viewpoint of the individual. Under the circumstances of the new and difficult situation, people might be paralyzed, experience panic, or attack furiously and violently.

This explanation is more suitable for murderers who operate out of an impulse with no planning, or the first murder of serial murderers which includes fantasy, choosing the murder action as the only or preferred choice, and the choice of the victim which would yield the maximal satisfaction or a sense of removing the threat.

It could be that relatively unique occurrences would take place in the presence of other or others for whom the event is not unique, not threatening, or less threatening than for the actor. If such others are present and actively involved, they may intervene in directing the individual in taking into account a longer and wider considerations of alternative acts than he would have done had he coped with the threat on his own. Hence the others can prevent the threatened individual from entering a state of encapsulation which decreases the probability of a deviant act even more. This part in the explanation of the phenomenon of encapsulation is unknown in relation to serial murderers. The explanation suggests a situation in which the individual tends to operate in a course of a serial murder, but does not do it due to social influence. We have no empirical evidence on how many people with a tendency for serial murder have not acted in this way due to that social support. On the other hand, we know that solitude and lack of social support among serial murderers contributed significantly to a state of encapsulation as has been described. This situation, as has been mentioned, can encourage a response with no thought about its future implications, including choosing a serial murder as the preferred response.[124]

The absence of active intervention that inhibits encapsulation can be also a product of shame, guilt or fear on the part of the individual, due to the fact that he has put himself into the current difficulty. Others may be incapable of intervening on his behalf because he hides the origins and the characteristics of his problem. This kind of secrecy leads to encapsulation. In other words, these are problems that cannot be shared with others, as they relate to the threat and involve a fear of losing social reputation, like in many mental problems, or, for instance, when a girl becomes pregnant and fears from the reaction of her family and aborts her baby.

As I have shown, this situation takes place in the serial murderer who experiences fantasies prior to the murder in which he sees in great detail the different stages, starting from the seduction of the victim, up to the removal of the body. It is obvious that he cannot share these fantasies with others. I have demonstrated such a situation in the theory of the "cracked personality," when the serial murderer internalized the stigma about him. This phenomenon characterizes many of the serial murderers who live in both worlds—a normative world and a murderous one. It is also true for those who suffer from dissociation, when the individual is not exposed and does not share his other identity with others.

Encapsulation is built slowly, sometimes during hours, and in other times during weeks. In any case, as the actor has more time to gain before acting, the probability of encapsulation decreases, since there is a greater chance of interference by others. It means that in order for encapsulation to take place, the threat has to enable a very short time for a responsive act, unless the murderer is socially isolated. One has to bear in mind that interpreting the situation is subjective, and the actors can define the accessibility of these actions differently. When we speak about variance in defining accessibility or permission, we refer to the subjective perception of the person on the moral and objective implications of the various social actions. Individuals tend to perceive a wide range of actions as totally moral, and as having implications which are absolutely good or profitable, or at least natural (Ibid., p. 84). In this respect, again we can see the reference to neutralizing techniques which are adopted by the individual from his sociocultural environment. In our discussion, it can explain the transition from the stage of fantasy to the stage of execution of a serial murder that has not been explained properly in the psychological literature.

The individual does not tend to execute actions that he, personally, believes are bad or erroneous. He would not execute actions which are "subjectively inaccessible." Therefore, in order for a deviant action to take place, he must be capable of arriving at a state that such an action would be subjectively accessible for him.

This is exactly the proof that the mechanism of neutralizing guilt is not operated only after the action, but also before it, and so it enables the criminal to execute the murder.

Actions that others may regard as deviant seem to the individual as moral, conventional, or erroneous in some abstract way, but not unjustified. He may also arrive at a state in which he defines an action as morally positive, while others would define it as deviant. All the same, most individuals today would feel at least pangs of conscience and guilt feelings for a wide variety of actions that are defined publicly as deviant.

If an individual has already defined an action as moral as far as he is concerned, although it is publicly defined as deviant, then a reaction of encapsulation is expected as a closure. That is, the individual would adjust the justification and the excuse for what is accepted culturally. In the USA, private definitions which are contrary to the public policy tend to be heard especially in relation to felonies which are defined as "victimless felonies" (use of drugs, abortion, gambling, and certain sexual behaviour), and in relation to the white collar crimes, because they are considered as the private business of the individual. Even if the action is not perceived as positive morally, but as the private business of the individual, then he would define it as neutral, and as one that is not anybody else's business. In other words, he would use the justification of "denying damage."

It is interesting to see how actions that are defined by the individual as clearly immoral, or doubtfully moral, become—at least for a certain period of time—unclear from a moral point of view, or even positive. We can see an example in the case of physicians who violated a law against abortions. Or, a murder of every man is a serious felony, but when we witness the elimination of a leading criminal by a competing gang, we see the murder as something neutral and even positive from a moral point of view. That criminal is punished and is no longer able to hurt others.

The additional mechanism of neutralizing guilt can explain the transition from the stage of fantasy to the stage of executing the murder. This kind of change is accompanied by two strategies, or two mental mechanisms: Conventionalization or a special justification.

- Conventionalization—a belief that the definition of a certain deviant action (serial murder) is erroneous and is not accessible subjectively for the individual. The action is aimed at changing the definition of the certain action to be accessible. For example, a serial murderer would justify a serial murder of prostitutes, drug dealers and wanderers since they are a danger to society. By so doing, the serial murder becomes accessible for him.
- Conventionalism can be achieved also through tough and vaguer tactics of distinguishing between the spirit of the law and the letter of the law. These tactics enable making a deviant action into an accessible one through defining it as a case within a conventional category, or at least as being on the border between deviation and conventionalism. If we take a look at the previous example, we would see that a serial murder of prostitutes expresses, in the eyes of the murderer, a conventional action, because society and the law (in different countries) prohibit prostitution, and, therefore, the serial murderer carries out the spirit of the law by eliminating the people who operate outside the law to a certain extent, and who do not deserve to live.
- Special justification—In this technique the individual sees his actions as a certain kind of a deviant action, but chan-

241

ges it, subjectively, into an accessible one through his definition of it as not morally wrong and not totally erroneous, due to special circumstances. The action becomes permitted for execution by the individual through the excuse that a certain set of facts or other moral rules pressured him, and although his action may not represent morality, it is not clearly immoral either.

- Special justifications include claims that the victim deserved to be a victim; that the individual is not a responsible person; and that superior moral obligations cancel prohibitions against a certain action. These are the justifications that Sykes and Matza suggest:

- A fitting victim—if hurting another person is an expected result of a deviant action, the action can become available through the definition of the designated victim as morally notorious, and therefore he deserves what he gets. The victim can be considered as such due to the definition of his social category, or due to personal pain that is perceived by the individual as stemming from others against him. For instance, the way prostitutes and minorities are perceived in the eyes of the mission murderer. These are ready targets who "deserve" to be victims, since "everybody knows what they are." In other words, we have here a materialization of "the denial of the victim." Stained categories and local institutions are widely known as deserving of being victims. This is a kind of rhetoric of motives which are used by the criminal in order to justify his action against them.

- Lack of self-control—formulations of the person which are aimed to define himself and others as passive victims, or gaining from powers which are not under their control. There is a belief that these powers make the individual not responsible for what he is and what he does. Therefore, people may believe that whatever they have done, do, or plan to do is to a certain extent beyond the decision of their personal will. This is, in fact, the claim of "denial of responsibility," with reference to a future action, as well as to an action that has already occurred.

- Superior obligation—the claim of superior obligation is the most interesting and important among the special justifications. Throughout history, it has been the outstanding way of making actions which are considered deviant in a certain social system, accessible from a subjective viewpoint. This justification is more positive and moral than the others, and it is presented to the public post factum. The issue here is the order of preferences in obeying general rules in specific cases. The individual can support the general perception that it is forbidden to kill others, but in specific circumstances he can believe that his personal survival is preferable over the general rule which forbids murder. The state which claims for a virtual monopoly regarding settling insults and personal safety is perceived sometimes in the eyes of the individual as violating his right to act for his own defense. Therefore, there may be a feeling that the individual's obligation for himself overcomes his obligation to the state.

In the neutralizing theory this technique is presented differently. The reference to the individual and his action is justified due to his obligation to groups of belonging, like family and friends. Here, on the other hand, the justification for action is in the name of the individual only. To go back to our case, we speak, for instance, about a serial murder that stems from humiliation and frustration, from a will of vengeance, and even for the sake of yielding a material benefit.

According to Lofland (1969), it seems that most of the deviant actions can become possible and permitted subjectively for most people who are under pressured conditions, to a sufficient extent, of threat and encapsulation.

Sykes and Matza claim that the crucial idea of aggression as a proof of obstinacy and masculinity is highly accepted in many points in the social system. The ability to take something, get something and deal with it, defend the individual's right and reputation by force, prove his masculinity through obstinacy and physical courage—are all highly prevalent in the American society, and in our discussion it can explain a serial murder on a sado-sexual background.

The conclusion is that what people can find as possible for execution is a function of the moral justifications which make certain actions accessible for them. Every action is a product of the character, considering the range of rhetoric and the justification of the motives provided to the individual by the surrounding society. The crucial suggestion is that in a society of complexity and variance like the American society, there are moral justifications for almost everything. The question is not what makes people act, but what permits them to act in this way and not in another. One component of acting in one way and not in another is the selective power of the pool of justifications or possible motives. A complex culture with a large variance provides pluralism of morally confirmed motives, and therefore enables not only conformity and heroism, but also deviant actions.

To sum up, the serial murderer can suffer from a variety of mental disorders as has been described. But we cannot disconnect the murderer from his sociocultural environment, in which he lives, grows up and goes through socialization.

Part of the socialization process has to do with learning the justifications and excuses for a variety of behaviours, including murderous behaviours. My claim is that the guilt-neutralizing techniques and the verbal description of motives have a central role in the serial murderer's capability to neutralize the social norms and conventions in order to be able to execute the murder that he has experienced in his imagination so many times. Hence, the neutralizing techniques which are acquired from the murderer's surrounding society, are part of the etiology of a serial murder, after the murderer has chosen this way of operation, although they are certainly not the main factor for his choice. Moreover, after the murder, these techniques enable him to justify his deed for himself and for others, even if these others are not specific people but represent questions that could have been asked if he is caught ("imagined others"). The individual prepares these answers as part of the process of social supervision he has internalized. Guilt-neutralizing techniques, shame and responsibility, justify the act of murder and enable its execution in a serial manner. One can see how the psychological and the sociological theories interweave with one another in providing an answer to the question of what enables the existence of the serial murder: Psychological factors in the personality of the individual which push his choice toward a serial murder, and social factors which enable him to neutralize the social norms that prohibit these actions.

Law Violators as Culture Heroes—Kooistra (1989)

The scientist refers to the concept of "heroes" regarding law violators or Robin Hood figures. By this concept, he helps us understand the neutralizing technique not only from the criminal's point of view, but mainly from the viewpoint of society around him. In doing so he complements, I think, the theory of neutralizing techniques.

Kooistra emphasized the sociocultural atmosphere in the USA which enabled the development and existence of law violators who have been perceived as social heroes like Robin Hood. Throughout history one can find a variety of people who murdered and robbed through obvious violation of the law, but not only have they not been considered as contemptible by the public, they were defined as social heroes in their lives and also after their death. Their actions gained glorification in poems, movies and books like *Bonnie and Clyde* and *Billy the Kid* in the USA, and *Robin Hood* in England.

Although such criminals lived in different times and places, the set of legends that surround them is generally similar: They were "pushed" to criminal life as victims of injustice, and were considered in the eyes of a large part of the public, and even in the eyes of the law enforcement officers, as respectable and moral people. Their becoming culture heroes camouflage the part of their crimes which was intended for personal benefit, whether material or other.

The sociological explanations for the phenomenon focus on the fact that the hero criminal appears in times of social crisis, when the trust in justice and the political systems is broken. For example, in periods of a fast social change, high unemployment, and wide political corruption, deficiencies and other conditions damage the daily routine of many people. In these situations the law is not perceived as a tool of justice any more, and many find themselves "outside the law." In this situation, people turn to symbolic representations of justice outside the law, when Robin Hood and other criminal figures return a sense of justice. The criminal who meets these requirements gains public empowerment through guilt-neutralizing techniques which are operated on his behalf by the public.

The legends which make criminals into culture heroes contain the neutralizing technique components presented by Sykes and Matza; the law violators are motivated by criminal life (denying responsibility). They do not hurt simple people and steal only from the corrupted (denying the damage). The glorious criminals are some kind of personalization of an efficient court of justice, in which justice is done swiftly (denying the victim); and actually, the political system and its representatives are the bad guys, the corrupted ones, rather than the criminal hero (condemning the condemners). Robin Hood's criminals do not obey the law, but they are loyal to higher moral obligations. They work not only for the sake of family and friends, but defend an entire class of people—the oppressed (addressing higher loyalties). This phenomenon stood out especially in the time of settling the west, when the victims of the criminal hero were the oppressors of the agricultural society. The criminal became a hero since he was a symbol of a political struggle against the ruling class.

In modern society the communication was a central factor in creating a modern Robin Hood. One of the characteristics of modernization is the constant need of creating celebrities, and mass media industry adds and structures the legends of these glorious criminals. The idolized criminal receives noble characteristics that reflect admired cultural characteristics which contradict the less desired aspect of his delinquency.

From the above explanation, one can claim that the serial murderer adopts not only his own definitions which serve him as guilt-neutralizing techniques prior to executing the felonies and afterwards, but he also tends to adopt the neutralizing techniques that society poses in relation to the Robin Hood criminals. In other words, the serial murderer elaborates his neutralizing techniques as part of the existing sociocultural texture in society, in relation to the structuring of crime and criminals, and this makes it easier for him to commit his crimes while wishing to get famous and become a celebrity by his own accord. But one should not be mistaken: The serial murderer is not the same Robin Hood who hurts the exploiters and the oppressors of society. He does not operate against strong social groups; on the contrary, he operates in most cases, against the weakest groups in society: Prostitutes, wanderers and homeless people.

As part of the neutralizing techniques, he makes himself into another kind of Robin Hood, one who operates against the social groups which are presented and often labeled as unworthy of living. Such distortion undoubtedly serves his murderous tendencies, because murder acts against these populations ensure his safety from being caught and arrested, especially because the victims are not part of the strong and important groups in society.

Theoretical and Multidisciplinary Model for Serial Murder and Murderers

Introduction

The same arguments I have raised in relation to the multidisciplinary explanation of mass murderers hold for serial murderers as well. An interesting attempt to link between biology, sociology, and psychology was done by a few scientists who have seen that only the sociological explanations, as well as the psychological ones, cannot provide an explanation for the phenomenon of serial murder. The scientists assume that among serial murderers there is a predisposition—biological, psychological, or social—which might influence their behaviour. But scientists argue that this predisposition is not enough for creating a serial murderer, and so there has to be traumatic or destabilizing events such as abuse in childhood, a death of a parent, divorce, and so on. These traumas might hurt the individual's self-image and push him into a fantasy world as a means of achieving a renewed control over his life. Fantasy facilitates the transition to a murderous behaviour as mentioned in the theory of the dissociative personality.[125]

In this context, one can see two opposite theoretical directions: One is presented by Holmes and Holmes (1998) who argue that one had to examine the continuous exposure to activities, experiences and characteristics that have shaped the personality of the serial murderer. The combination of the biological, psychological and social factors is what makes us who we are. For instance, coping skills which exist in one child may not be accessible for another child who has experienced the same traumatic event. Likewise, the implication of a traumatic event on the continuation of life would be different for different individuals. Therefore, Holmes & Holmes (1998) think that two children from the same family may experience the same experiences and cope with them differently, up to the point that one would become a serial murderer, while the other would become a normative person. Therefore, their recommendation is to examine each case according to the structuring experience of the violent person: What was the way in which the murderer experienced certain events; what was his background before the experience and afterwards; how this experience and background operated in the process of becoming a serial murderer. The conclusion is that, in fact, one cannot suggest a comprehensive explanation for the development of a serial murderer, since we have to examine each case separately.

Furthermore, it seems that anyway it is impossible to provide one explanation that would give a comprehensive answer to the phenomenon of a serial murderer. We can raise two explanations for this: First, the kinds of serial murder and the motives for such a murder are so numerous and varied that there is no one theory which would be able to explain such a wide variety of phenomena; second, the theoretical experience in the course of years in the various fields of knowledge shows that it is impossible to explain phenomena of human behaviour by one theory, but there is a need of a wider theoretical aspect which combines several theories from different fields of knowledge.

An opposite theoretical direction is presented by Vronsky (2007) who tries to combine the different theories which have been presented into a comprehensive explanation for the creation of a serial murder. According to Vronsky, there is a fine balance between biological, psychological, and social symptoms, and when most of these components or all of them are out of balance, the outcome would be a development of a serial murderer. He claims that this comprehensive explanation explains why part of the children who have gone through harsh childhood experiences would not become serial murderers, while others would. For example, if we identify in a certain child one of the following elements (or some combination of them): Disorder in parental attachment; physical or sexual abuse;[126] rejection by their peers; biochemical imbalance or a head injury—we would be able to explain why the child has become a serial murderer in this case.

The central problem in this integrated theoretical attempt is that it lacks an empirical validity. Studies in this field have not examined control groups. One can see in the components presented by the scientist an inventory, but not a proper theoretical model. Moreover, scientists who spoke at an international conference on this issue argued that there is no one factor which leads to the development of a serial murder, a variety of factors contribute to it, but the most significant factor is the personal decision of the serial murderer to go on with his crimes (Morton, 2005) which is in fact a return to the theory of the rational choice.

Unfortunately, in the above two theoretical approaches one approach is missing, the one of reframing which is most important in regarding deviant and delinquent behaviour, including serial murder.

The Model

After having presented a collection of theories in psychology, social psychology, sociology, and biology, there follows the question: To what extent do each of these theories give a specific explanation for the creation of a serial murder, or in other words, can one create an integrative theoretical model for the creation of a serial murderer, so that the whole will be greater than the sum of its parts? I think that as one delves into the sociocultural aspects of serial murder, one can see that the combination of psychological and sociological theories contributes to the creation of serial murder and the behaviour of the serial murderer.

The central factors that lead the individual to this fatal behaviour are in his unique perception and processing of the personal and interpersonal events he has experienced, mainly in childhood. This claim emphasizes the unique and individual aspect of human behaviour of the psychological and subjective aspect, but does not ignore the influence of society and culture on the individual. All individuals who live in a certain society are influenced by its culture, including its values, but at the same time every individual has a unique personality which may interpret and formulate the cultural decree in his unique way.

Before entering the discussion of the theoretical models, we have to refer to a methodological problem of referring to a theoretical model. Part of the theoretical literature on this issue demonstrates inflexibility. Theoretical models in the social sciences try to reflect the social, cultural, and other reality. Since it is obvious that reality is more complicated than any model, the models are called "ideal," and the assumption is that we would not find the model as it is in reality, but we can base on the ideal model in investigating reality, meaning that an ideal model also needs some flexibility. This flexibility can exist when we present the characteristics of the social reality on a sequence or a scale, and not through arbitrary determinations that characterize mainly a dichotomous division of reality.

For example, it is easy to find out whether a person feels pain or not. This is dichotomy. But when we would like to find out the extent of pain, we would need a scale that expresses a sequence or a range of the phenomenon. Unlike certain opinions, such flexibility enables getting closer to reality than rigid models allow.

One of the central claims that came up against the various theories of explaining the development of the serial murderer was about the absence of empirical evidence, as similar characteristics have not been examined in a control group. This claim is still valid, but we can suggest a theoretical explanation as to why different individuals would react differently to the same stimuli.

According to the dissociative personality disorder theory, a certain individual who experienced abuse on the part of his parents makes this experience into a motive for escaping to a fantasy world as a defense mechanism through which he feels safe and disconnected from the threat. But if the threat continues, in the eyes of the individual, and he has no efficient ways of coping with it, then fantasy becomes a source of satisfying the needs of the individual, like escaping from difficulties, being able to feel control and power, and even satisfaction and excitement. Alternately, according to the broken personality theory, the same individual might develop two identities: The social and virtual identity and the actual social identity, while the latter, the real one, is known only to the individual, like the fantasy that is suggested in the first theory. These individuals who experience fantasy create contents they must know from some source. These are the contents of the culture they live in. They include violence, imitation of culture heroes, materializing personal aspirations, and other things. On the other hand, another individual who goes through similar abuse may perceive the behaviour as less threatening, since there may be friends around who help him cope with his reality. He would not need the same refuge in a fantasy world, and would not develop a violent perception as a basis for satisfying his mental needs, like vengeance, release of frustration feelings, and an aspiration for power and control.

In this way, two individuals who experience similar trauma may perceive it, or react to it, in quite a different way up to the point that one would develop a dissociative personality disorder with normative identity and a deviant identity at the same time, or develop a social broken identity disorder which would consist of two contradicting social identities; while another individual would not need this defense mechanism. This explanation answers the criticism regarding the comprehensive explanation about the creation of a serial murderer: Not everyone who experienced abuse would become a serial murderer, but it does not mean that abuse has no role in the creation of a personality disorder which would lead certain individuals to become serial murderers.

In this context one may say that a serial murderer has a developmental history which includes a childhood trauma (of different kinds). While most of the individuals who have gone through such trauma adjust and overcome the traumatic experiences, the ones who do not adjust, go on dealing with the inappropriate treatment they have received in childhood and live in their past experiences which might lead to a variety of disorders like frustration, anger and depression. One has to indicate at this point that serial murderers are mentally abnormal, but their disorders do not reach the threshold of a mental disease (Brantley & Hosky, 2005).

Perceiving an experience or a behaviour as threatening, like the contents of fantasy, is not experienced in a void. It depends on the cultural contexts of the society we live in (Mills, 1940; Lofland, 1949). A girl who goes through sexual abuse does not know she is going through abuse until she learns that the cultural decree forbids such behaviour, or until she shares her experience with her girlfriends, and then she learns that her experiences are unique. But perceiving the threat by the individual is given to a subjective interpretation.

While the first two theories explain violent personality content as a product of trauma, which can be expressed in violent fantasies as a cultural product or as a need of releasing frustration, other theories refer to the structure of the personality. Perceiving a threat on the part of primary caregivers hurts the individual's socialization process because he cannot identify with the significant figures in his life, and a lack of attachment is established. One can refer to this situation as damage in the development of the superego according to psychoanalysis, or the lack of development of self-control according to sociology. In these two explanations the individual does not internalize the cultural norms of society he lives in and develops an antisocial personality disorder. Among the characteristics of this disorder, we can see a lack of caring for the other person, an impulse for satisfaction without reference to the results, narcissism and a use of the defense mechanisms of the self. In other words, one may say that the individual operates according to the impulses of the id, without a control mechanism that comes from social norms of his society. In this respect, he is an antisocial person who perceives other individuals in society as a source of satisfying his impulses. The outcome can be serial murder, among other things.

At this point a certain doubt appears. How can we explain the behaviour of the serial murderer as someone who aspires to satisfy his impulses immediately with no consideration of the results, when part of the serial murderers are professional career criminals who plan their actions meticulously, choose their victims whom nobody would look for, and see to it that the scene of the murder would be left without any forensic evidence? (Gibbs, 1975). One explanation for it is that people with antisocial personality disorder tend to behave relatively rationally, although they are not perceived as such.

To sum up until this point, we can say that the basis for the creation of a serial murderer is the child's relationships with significant figures in his life, and later on, of his social relationships with his peers. The literature reports of rejection or social isolation of the individual. It is important to emphasize that not every isolated or socially excommunicated individual would become a serial murderer, but the childhood trauma and social isolation were found as characterizing most of the serial murderers.

When an individual perceives his environment as threatening, and does not have the psychological tools to cope with the feeling of threat, either real or imagined, then for him, reality is perceived as threatening (Mills, 1940). In addition, his inner world and personality are influenced by the sociocultural environment he lives in. There is apparently a logical contradiction: On the one hand, it is claimed that the individual does not internalize the norms of his culture which deal with respecting human lives, consideration of the other person, and so on; on the other hand, it is said that he internalizes other components of culture, like solving conflicts through violence. The answer is that in order to internalize cultural norms, we have to identify with significant figures in our childhood, while in order to internalize cultural contents,[127] the individual does not need these significant figures. For instance, children are highly influenced by the mass media when they are exposed to it by themselves, with no connection to significant figures in their lives. Alternately, the individual can create a differential identity with violent culture heroes in society who are empowered by the mass media.

Furthermore, the fact that the individual who has gone through a trauma cannot identify with the significant figures in his life, or has difficulty doing so, does not necessarily have to lead to a lack of development of the superego, the self-control mechanism, or the creation of certain flaws in them, as has been previously claimed. A child who has trusted his primary caregivers and they betrayed his most basic trust would feel a surprise, amazement, helplessness and a sense of betrayal. In such cases a split is established in the individual: On the one hand, he is aware in the most basic way that these figures are supposed to satisfy his needs, including his safety, love, and so on; while on the other hand, these figures have operated unexpectedly and hurt his basic trust. Hence, the individual internalized norms and developed a certain degree of consciousness and morale, but has experienced pain from the contents he had internalized, and then he acquires other contents (a criminal conscience), and the result is a development of an antisocial personality disorder.

Hence the question to the first doubt is: How is it that the individual with the personality disorder behaves strictly according to social norms, although he has not internalized these norms? According to psychology, individuals who are called sociopaths, or having an antisocial personality disorder have not internalized social norms until they have become a supervising element in their personality (superego or self-control mechanism), but people with this disorder learn what the accepted norms are in society. They internalize certain norms that serve them, what the norms they are expected to internalize are, and how they are expected to behave.

We find an example for this in the psychosocial theory of the cracked personality which has been presented previously. The individual has a real identity and a virtual one, as in the split of the dissociative personality disorder: The personality of the individual is split into two opposing identities which reflect the expectations he had as a child versus the trauma he had experienced. There develops in him a normative aspect and a pathological-deviant aspect, like the colorful figure of Dr. Jekyll and Mister Hyde. In addition, the individual complements the socialization process of his normative identity or the virtual one through learning the rules of the game according to which society permits to play. One can see it among serial murderers who play according to the social rules in order to avoid being caught: They work, help others, and acquire social skills which help them take the victims, and so on.

Both theories emphasize the fact that the individual strictly hides his real identity by presenting the virtual identity which created a normative image of him in the eyes of society. One of the reasons for the serial murderer's avoidance from long-term social relationships is the will to reduce the risk that someone would discover his real identity, exactly as a person with an antisocial personality disorder behaves. Therefore, at this point one can see a similarity, to a certain degree, of identity between the psychological perception and the psychosocial one.

An important question is why violent and murderous capacities develop in the individual within the fantasy component in his personality, and the answer lies in the cultural components in which he lives. A society that empowers violence as a legitimate means of coping with threats; society that empowers serial murderers and makes them culture heroes with the help of the mass media, casts the violent contents into the individual's fantasy, and it is true for the psychological theories as well as for the psychosocial one. This point explains, perhaps, the fact that in the USA there are more serial murderers than in the rest of the world. Moreover, the fact that American capitalism encourages the legitimacy of accumulating money, might lead to the increased number of cases of serial murder for the sake of robbery. Amir[128] calls it "murderous capitalism."

But this phenomenon can also be explained by sociological theories. For instance, in the context of the "innovator" type that Merton (1957) presents in the anomie theory. The innovator sees achieving the goals of society as the utmost important goal and for the end to justify the means, including illegitimate ones. According to his perception, the individual is judged in society according to his achievements and not according to the way in which he achieved them. A similar explanation is found in the neo-classical theories in criminology.

Until now, we have seen how the different theories explain the connection between a childhood trauma, social isolation, and cultural influence which might lead to personality disorders with violent contents. According to this explanation there is apparently a sequence between internalizing violent contents and executing a serial murder. But there is still the question of why would such an individual feel guilt, and why people who suffer from a dissociative personality disorder do not act immediately to materialize their murderous fantasy? This is a more significant doubt than the one we raised earlier, because we have here a more principal question: Why does the individual need the defense mechanisms of the self, according to psychoanalysis, or guilt-neutralizing techniques according to sociology and the social psychology, in order to move from the stage of fantasy to the stage of executing a serial murder which involves reducing shame and guilt prior to the execution of the crime in order to justify his behaviour for himself and for others after the execution?

If the individual has not internalized the social norms that prohibit hurting other people, and encourage compassion toward the life of the other person, he is not supposed to feel guilt feelings regarding his murderous behaviour (Akers, 1996, p. 85). Alternately, one can see in his behaviour a kind of release from the tie of social norms, as he is carried away to a murderous behaviour, and in this way he neutralizes the limitation of his antisocial behaviour (Matza, 1964). Furthermore, if the serial murderer suffers from an antisocial personality disorder, he is not supposed to feel guilt or shame due to his behaviour, or at least he is not supposed to need techniques to reframe or neutralize the situation, while actually the serial murderer executes these actions. This claim undercuts one of the essential perceptions in psychology which says that people with antisocial and narcissistic personality have not internalized social norms and therefore can act in a deviant and delinquent way since there is no inner constraint that would prevent them from doing so (conscience).

First of all, in a search for answers to this question, we go back to the theory of the dissociative personality disorder, to the theory of the cracked personality syndrome, and the defense mechanisms of the self: Most of the serial murderers are not defined as psychotic; they know how to distinguish between good and evil, and between permitted and prohibited. Therefore, the normative identity in the personality of the serial murderer would feel guilt feelings because he is aware that his deed is forbidden.

Second, attributing an antisocial behaviour disorder to a serial murderer in a general way is not correct. The deviant identity of the serial murderer has of course characteristics of antisocial personality disorder as well, but at the same time, there is a kind of disconnection between the two identities, when the normative identity in the personality internalizes the social prohibitions, like in the theory of the broken identity. This fact explains why after the murder, the murderer would feel guilt when the normative identity would be dominant. On the other hand, the feeling of guilt would motivate him to use defense mechanisms and neutralizing techniques in order to avoid guilt feelings until shifting back to the deviant identity; it is like the existing dynamics between the real identity and the virtual one in the cracked personality syndrome.

Such perception can explain the cooling-off period between one murder and the next. The insubstantial explanations that have been given so far, explained that the murderer received satisfaction from the murder, and would murder again only when he would feel that he needs a renewed satisfaction. This explanation is insufficient because there are murderers who murder in more frequently, while others murder once in a few months or years. My explanation about the dynamics between the identities is more correct, and it also explains the variance in the cooling-off periods the murderer needs, each one according to his individual case.

Another problem is that the formulators of the various theories have not yet explained what makes the serial murderer go from the fantasy stage to the execution stage. The integrative explanation that has been given here suggests an explanation to this transition: The defense mechanisms and the guilt-neutralizing techniques play a central role, and enable the potential murderer to become an actual murderer. For example, the cracked personality theory indicates that the only place in which the serial murderer can expose his real identity and experience it fully is in the serial murder events. Such exposure is a relief and relaxation for him from the need to cover his real identity, but makes him vulnerable. This is the explanation for his ambition to control his victims and bring them to death. On the other hand, Holmes and Holmes claim that even today, there is no clear explanation of the reason for the transition from the fantasy stage to the execution stage.

An up-to-date study has found that among sexual criminals, for instance, there is a rich mechanism of neutralizing techniques which includes denial, minimization, justification and refutation. Langton et al. (2008) found that among recidivist sexual criminals there is a correlation between future danger and neutralizing technique by minimization.

Therefore, the only explanation that appears from the various theories on the transition from fantasy to execution is the one I suggested about formulating or reframing that the serial murderer does with the help of the defense mechanisms of the self, guilt-neutralizing techniques, using a vocabulary of motives, perceiving the threat, and cultural influences. According to this explanation, the psychologists who claimed that individuals who suffer from an antisocial personality disorder lack a conscience, empathy with the other person, and so on, were mistaken in their diagnosis in relation to time. They reached these insights when they examined individuals and diagnosed them at a relatively late stage. My claim is that at that stage, these individuals have adapted to reframing already, and therefore could behave as they did and in front of others defend themselves for their deeds with various justifications. It is my opinion that it is not a matter of conscienceless individuals, or individuals who have not internalized social norms, but as a result of the trauma, impulses, and absorbing violent and antisocial contents they felt a cognitive dissonance which in turn led them to the need of reframing, so that they would feel a relief following the outcome of the dissonance.

This perception guides me, to a certain extent, to the phenomenological direction. Skrapec (2001) presented such perceptions in relation to serial murderers. According to Skrapec, the task of the scientist is to systematically examine the serial murderer through the portrait he draws of himself and of the world. For this end, we have to pay attention to the content of his words, instead of trying to understand the process through which he arrives at certain words and the feelings he attaches to them. Skrapec (2001) claims that conventional approaches tend to ignore the central aspect of the phenomenon. That is, they do not get us closer to the inner experience of the murderer in relation to the murders. The way of operation of the serial murderer includes behaviours which bear specific emotional significance for him, together with the events and circumstance of his life as he has experienced it. In this context, we have to bear in mind that behaviour is a product of the individual's subjective sense of reality, and it can be different from the objective facts of his life. Skrapec (2001) argues that we should ask ourselves what the significance of the repeated actions for the murderer is, and in this way expose the powers that motivate his behaviour. The aim is to identify the organizing principles of the murderer's thought, and so determine his perceptions, emotions and behaviour. For example, the technical fact that the victims are strangers to the murderer is different from the murderer's point of view, and he feels that he knows them intimately and therefore he chooses them. He chooses them because of what they are for him, because of the place they have in his personal structuring in relation to the world. In his summary, Skrapec (2001) argues that there are empirical problems in identifying the primary motive for serial murder. Even if it is a sexual motive, we have to distinguish between a serial sexual murder and a sexual serial murder. That is, a sexual motive exists in every case, but for part of the murderers the act of murder is the main thing, while for others the murder is secondary to the sexual satisfaction.

Even if part of the scientist's claims suit the perception of the suggested model, still one of the methodological problems in this context is the lack of reliability of the murderers. Many biographies have been written according to the stories of the serial murderers, but undoubtedly, at least in some of them, the murderer dictated the viewpoint that he wanted us to attribute to him, rather than his real viewpoint.

If in the phenomenological approach there are problems of reliability, relying on the psychiatric/psychological diagnostic manual, DSM, is also not so simple. It does not permit variance and a combination of several disorders,[129] and does not refer to the fact that a mental disturbance can be of quite a wide range, from a minor disorder to a significant one. For instance, Gabbard (1994) argues that there may be a psychopath who does not meet the definitions of the DSM for antisocial personality disorder, and vice versa.

An interesting psychiatric theory which supports the perception of formulation or re-structuring claims that destroying others, as well as the self, can be perceived as a choice of structuring (Winter, 2006). The theory sees serial murder, as well as mass murder, that are accompanied by a suicide as attempts of the individual to make his world more predictable, mainly in states with a sense of inner chaos. The theory sees the murder as a kind of dedication act which was chosen by the murderer. For example, a mass murderer described how the murder of his family would bring him glory. A murder of a family or a spouse with a background of parting is perceived as an act of dedication that was meant to preserve the relationships as they had been, as if to freeze them in time.[130] A similar perception is presented in the theory about those who perceive life as meaningless and death as nothingness. This perception sometimes characterizes a member of a medical team who saves life every day, and becomes a serial murderer, or individuals who were not afraid to kill and die or commit suicide because they wanted to introduce some "life" (action) into their world. An important and interesting point in this theory is the choice of murder as a way of life. This kind of choice suggests more structuring and being able to predict the chaotic world of certain individuals than any other choice.

Another important point in this theory negates the psycho-logical perception, according to which psychopaths cannot feel guilt. The author claims that the individual who uses structuring can feel guilt no less than any other person (Ibid., p. 160). For in-stance, the sadist feels guilt in relation to his sadistic role, and hence would act more sadistically. Likewise, a woman who suf-fered in her childhood from sexual abuse, and murdered her boy-friend, felt guilt for her role as a victim and became the aggressor.

We can see how a relatively recent psychiatric theory again connects criminology with psychology. Structuring characterizes many criminals who look for meaning and justification for their deeds which are defined by society as immoral. Rational choice exists in a meaningful way also among those who take the lives of others, not just for the sake of material benefit, as suggested by economists. The theory supports the approach of formulating or re-structuring of the individual's inner world, as has been sug-gested here, including a sense of guilt and other feelings that the traditional psychiatrists and scientists in the field of serial murder argue do not exist among psychopaths.[131]

To sum up this part, I would like to quote a key sentence in the comprehensive theoretical explanation that has been suggest-ed: Sometimes the answers to some of the most important ques-tions cannot be measured, even though their component parts can (Beeghley, 2003, p. 36).

The integrative theory does not have the pretense to explain motives of various serial murderers (mission, hedonist, material-ist, and so on), but one can assume that different kinds of motives stem from the process of early childhood. For example, the indi-vidual learns to connect between a violent and murderous behav-iour and sexual satisfaction; from absorbing cultural contents that have created specific contents in fantasy, like pornographic con-tents that again connect between sex and violence; or from an aspiration to materialism when the individual does not have the legitimate means to achieve it, like the professional assassin Blue Beard. In this way, the individual finds justifications for his deeds in the fact that this content is part of the culture in which he lives. In a similar way, the mission murderer chooses victims who belong to a certain sector in society, as society refers to this sector as unworthy. The mission murderer gets legitimacy from this attitude to hurt this sector. In this way, the serial murderer finds self-justifications for his actions in the spirit of the social justification. The same refers to an idealistic mission serial murderer.

In this context the importance of the routine activity theory stands out: This is a murderer with the competence and readiness to murder defenseless victims due to their social status, and their routine makes it easier for him to execute his act.[132] In addition, one can see how the choice of the victims points to a rational consideration of maximal benefit and minimal loss. The murderer can achieve satisfaction from executing the crime while his chances of being caught are small.[133] Personal background, which can be related to the biological background in a certain sociocultural environment, can create not only the contents of the personality or the contents of fantasy, but also the justifications for materializing the fantasy. All this is within a complicated process of formulating or reframing self and social perception of the murderer about himself. The suggested explanation until now presents five stages:

- Preliminary stage—a traumatic experience influences the personality and identity of the individual up to a crack in his identity or dissociation when the individual may have a predisposition to violence.
- The individual's inability to cope efficiently with the traumatic experience, or with additional traumatic experiences that aggravate the crack in his identity, enabling him to find refuge in an imaginary world.
- The development of a deviant identity in the individual's personality by learning cultural contents from the surrounding society which enable him to learn techniques of neutralizing responsibility and guilt which in turn would enable the execution of the murder.

- The stage of executing the murder, in which the individual expresses his deviant identity and enjoys a psychological or other benefit.
- The cooling-off, or latent period, in which the normative identity of the individual returns to be dominant. The individual behaves according to the norms of society and its expectations, while using techniques of neutralizing guilt and camouflaging his real internalized identity.

We may ask why the individual should go on murdering over and over again? The sixth stage in the theory focuses on this point.

According to the dissociative theory, the individual has built an imaginary world of his own, in which he plays the role of the scriptwriter, the director, the main actor, and the casting director. But in reality, the victims do not know the lines intended for them in the text, or the directing that the murderer has designated for them in this role. As a result, the individual experiences a gap between fantasy and reality which frustrates him. Therefore, he is repeatedly pushed to fulfill a realization of his fantasy with other victims. There is an element of obsession together with rationality: Looking for the suitable victim, being able to execute the act and leave the scene quickly which show his professionalism as a serial murderer.

According to the cracked personality theory, the individual has difficulty to keep his real identity hidden for long, and therefore he needs the murder which is the only circumstance in which he can expose this identity and feel relaxation afterwards. It means that according to the two theories, there is actually no hindrance that would stop the serial murderer, and one can only postpone the execution until the suitable conditions arrive.

Table 5: Stages in the development of the serial murderer (Source: Edelstein, 2009)

Stage	Content of Stage	Psychological Theory	Sociological Theory
Preliminary stage	Traumatic experience in childhood that might have hurt an individual with predisposition for violence. Pain of parental attachment	Adjusting/coping through "neutral" fantasy as a way of escaping from uncomfortable difficulties and memories	The creation of a crack in the personality of the individual, or inability to identify with primary caretakers for internalizing social norms
Coping stage	Continuation of the traumatic state, additional traumas and lack of tools for coping with this reality which leads to an antisocial personality disorder	Dissociation and split into two identities: Normative and sociopathic	Split into two identities: Virtual (normative) and real (deviant), and behaviour that is meant to achieve immediate satisfaction without considering the other person
Stage of absorbing cultural contents	Learning violent contents from the surrounding culture with justifications for the execution of a murderous behaviour and process of reframing that enables the execution of the murder (motive, justifications), with operation of a rational choice	Creating a script in the deviant identity which includes violent and murderous elements in relation to chosen victims	Creating expectations in the real identity for the experience versus the chosen victim. Referring to people as a means for achieving goals
Executing the murder	Executing the murder according to the fantasy of expectations	Benefit and satisfaction before, during, and/or after the act of murder	A sense of relief from the ability to expose the real identity. A sense of satisfaction from achieving the individual's goals, when the end justifies the means

Cooling-off/latent period	Transition from the deviant identity to the normative one while using techniques of neutralizing guilt post factum	The normative identity deals with techniques of neutralizing guilt and shame, ensuring oneself to avoid a similar act in the future and wandering to the deviant identity in order not to feel guilt	After exposing the real identity there is a psychological relaxation and ability to return to present the virtual identity. The individual enjoys the satisfaction he achieved until he feels the need to achieve a new satisfaction
The next murder	Transition from the cooling-off period due to impulses that motivated the murderer to execute the first murder	The murderer is reminded of a certain satisfaction in the experience of the previous murder, and, in addition, he feels frustration from the discrepancy between fantasy and reality. Therefore, he is motivated to another murder	The murderer feels difficulty to go on presenting his virtual identity and aspires to return to the experience he had upon presenting his real identity which can be done only by another murder

The conclusion that appears from the integrative explanation is that there are varied preliminary conditions for the creation of a serial murderer; most of them are necessary but not sufficient. For example, a childhood trauma, head injury, hormonal imbalance in the brain, abuse, lack of attachment, and others. The mistake in the large body of literature on this issue is that the scientists referred to each of the variables or to their entirety as independent variables which explain the dependent variable—the serial murder. As has been mentioned, these variables are a necessary condition but are not sufficient. Hence appears the criticism of the direct connection between these variables and serial murder which has never been proved properly in an empirical way.

The quoted sentence above clarifies this point. In the background of serial murderers there are the events and the situations (the variables) that each one of them can explain the phenomenon to some extent. As a result, various scientists suggested that a combination of all the mentioned variables would be the independent variable that explains the creation of the serial murderer. This theoretical approach is also unacceptable. For instance, what is the rate of abuse one should "add" to the combination versus the rate of hormonal injury? This question has no answer of course. The answer is that among children and adolescents with a personality and social background and a predisposition for violence, an experience of abuse and neglect on the part of the primary figures and with no support of others might lead to a disconnection of the personal identity of the individual into several parts. The disconnected part can include an identity with antisocial characteristics which the individual wants to hide from others in daily life, or alternately can contain fantasy contents which at first would serve as normal and healthy means of coping versus unbearable conditions of abuse. But later on, out of feelings of helplessness, together with absorption of contents that justify a violent response for discharging the frustration the individual has experienced, the disconnected part might contain fantasy murderous contents. In both cases, the process of formulation or restructuring, while neutralizing the accepted norms of society and adopting social legitimacy for a violent action, would enable the individual to execute such a murderous action.

This theory cannot be examined empirically due to the lack of a proper sample, lack of reliability of the subjects, and a variety of methodological problems, like quantifying and correlating immeasurable variables, but this explanation is still an appropriate alternative for understanding the creation of a serial murderer versus the separate theoretical explanations one finds in the literature.

An additional criticism of this explanation has to do with the question of to what extent it explains all the phenomena of various serial murderers who operate from different motives. The answer is in the question, and indeed, the variety of serial murderers is great and difficult to generalize. But the suggested explanation is relevant for a large part of the serial murderers, even if not for all of them. As I have indicated at the beginning of the chapter, the capability of generalizing in this case is very low. The bottom line is, in my opinion, that one can benefit from the integrative theory for an explanation of a major part of the serial murder cases and types of serial murderers.

Table 6: An integrative theoretical scheme for the development of a serial murderer

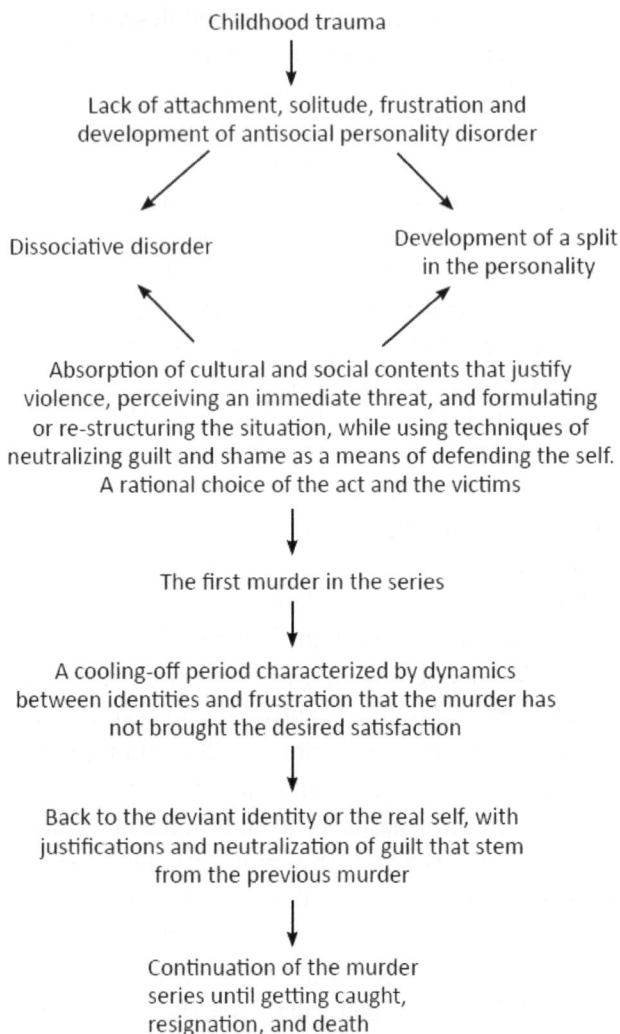

Childhood trauma

↓

Lack of attachment, solitude, frustration and development of antisocial personality disorder

Dissociative disorder

Development of a split in the personality

Absorption of cultural and social contents that justify violence, perceiving an immediate threat, and formulating or re-structuring the situation, while using techniques of neutralizing guilt and shame as a means of defending the self. A rational choice of the act and the victims

↓

The first murder in the series

↓

A cooling-off period characterized by dynamics between identities and frustration that the murder has not brought the desired satisfaction

↓

Back to the deviant identity or the real self, with justifications and neutralization of guilt that stem from the previous murder

↓

Continuation of the murder series until getting caught, resignation, and death

Chapter Four
Cooling off periods among serial killers

Although definitions of serial murder have changed over the years, there is a consensus that between every two murders there must be a cooling-off period. While psychological, sociological, and geographical theories of serial murder can be used to explain the cooling-off period, none of these theories used in an empirical study so far. Our study, based on the Encyclopedia of serial killers (Newton, 2005) in oppose to former studies, found that the longest cooling-off period is between the first and the third murders (i.e. a series). Some theoretical psychological explanations are offer to this pattern although we couldn't study it empirically.

Despite constituting only 1% of all murders, the issue of serial murder has attracted a lot of attention. There is, to date, no consensus on the definition of serial murder, mainly because of the different worldviews of academia, on the one hand, and law enforcement agencies, on the other (Bartol & Bartol, 2013; Burgess, Douglas et al. 1986; Douglas, Burgess, & Ressler, 2006;; Edelstein, 2014; Fox & Levin, 2014; Homes & Holmes, 1998; Morton & Hilts, 2008). However, common to all studies is the understanding that a serial murder is a unique phenomenon due to the fact that there must be a cooling-off period between every two murders. Various psychological, sociological, and geographical explanations have been offered for this time interval. The current article explores in more depth the reasons for the cooling-off period and presents an explanation based on our own empirical study alongside former investigations. We also examine whether this phenomenon is common among all serial killers or whether they vary in their cooling-off periods.

Serial Murder

Serial murder is a rare event that has nonetheless received much attention not only among law enforcement authorities but also within popular culture (Cater, 1997; Jenkins, 2002; Seltzer, 1998). Serial murder tends to be defined as two or more incidents of murder, each with one victim, by one or more killers at different times and with a so-called "cooling-off" period of at least three days between incidents (Fox & Levin, 2005; Holmes & Holmes, 1998; Kraemer, Lord & Heilbrun, (2004). et al., 2004; Levin, 2008; Meloy & Felthous, 2004; Vronsky, 2004).

There is, however, a major problem with this definition, and there is much debate about its various aspects. There are, for example, different theories about the number of victims required in order to define murders as serial. Some scientists have argued that the dictionary definition of a serial pattern is when it appears in at least three cases that relate to each other and have some sense of order between them (Harbort & Mokros, 2001). Consequently, scientists have also relied on arbitrariness to define this concept. See, for example, the debate on defining a minimum numbers of victims (Edelstein, 2006; Egger, 1998; Gerberth, 1996; Giannagelo, 1996; Hickey, 2002; Holmes & Holmes, 1994; Skrapec, 2001; Turvey, 1999). In addition, there is no required maximum time interval between the murders in order for them to be seen as serial, and thus a person who kills every 20 or 30 years can be automatically labeled a serial killer. This seems absurd and is clearly not the intention of those who set the criteria defining serial murder (Ferguson, White, Cherry, Lorenz & Bhimani, 2003).

Cooling-Off Period

What is the cooling-off period? The main difference between serial murder and other kinds of multiple victim homicide is the concept of a time interval know as a cooling-off period (Erdman, 2017). However, definitions of the cooling-off time also vary greatly, ranging from 72 hours to periods of years (Bartol & Bartol, 2013; Douglas et al., 1986; Douglas, Burgess, Burgess, & Ressler, 2006;; Edelstein, 2014; Levin & Fox, 2014; Homes & Holmes, 1998; Morton & Hilts, 2008).

The confusion over interpretation of serial murder led the National Center for the Analysis of Violent Crime (NCAVC) (Morton, 2005) to define it as the unlawful killing of two victims or more by the same offender at "different times." While this was an important attempt to overcome the problem of definition, it bypassed the meaning of the cooling-off period. As a result, new notions of short (less than two weeks) or long intervals (more than two weeks, months and even years) between murders have become accepted in interpretations of serial murder (Osborn & Salfati, 2015; Schlesinger, Ramirez, Tusa, Jarvis, & Erdberg, 2017).

From a psychological perspective, the cooling-off period should be long enough to enable the serial killer's psychological process both before and after the murder. This process is salient in the dissociative identity disorder theory, according to which the murderer moves between a normative and a lethal identity (Edelstein, 2017; Van Der Hart, Nijenhuis, & Steele, 2005). Others have argued, however, that this psychological explanation is too abstract; instead they have proposed other functions of this period of time. For example, Osborne and Salfati (2015) claimed that the geographical preference and selection of the victim or social involvement of the murderer influence the intervals between the murders (Greswell & Hollin, 1994; Hickey, 2002).

Thus far, there is no statistical baseline or empirical research that clearly shows which factors directly influences the length of the cooling-off period. On the other hand, the cooling-off period has been found to be universal, thus proving that it has some latent function (Osborne & Salfati, 2015), in other words, it either enables or facilitates the next murder (Douglas et al., 2006; Douglas et al., 1986; Edelstein, 2014; Levin & Fox, 2014; Homes & Holmes, 1998; Morton & Hilts, 2008).

Existing research on the cooling-off period. The debate over the explanations for the cooling-off periods convinced scientists of the need to study it in further depth without attributing psychological, sociological, or other theories (Osborne & Salfati, 2015; Simkin & Roychowdhury, 2018). While some research has been conducted, there is, however, still no empirically-supported theoretical explanation.

Not all scientists approved the neglect of the theoretical aspects. Of the few studies attempting to better understand and predict the cooling-off period, only one took into account variables such as the geographical distance between murderer and victim as influencing the interval until the next murder, and none addressed psychological explanations for the time intervals between the killings (Osborne & Salfati, 2015). An additional problem with the existing studies is their use of different operational definitions of serial murder.

These studies nonetheless revealed three important findings. The first finding is that the longer the interval between murders in the series, the lower the likelihood of an additional murder. The researchers also found that the time intervals between murders were smooth with no profound peaks of shorter or longer intervals (Simkin & Roychowdhury, 2018). Their findings contradicted an earlier study that claimed that as killers escalate their lethal behaviour, so the interval between the murders gets shorter (Holmes & Holmes, 1998). The first explanation for this pattern is the killer's increasing frustration. The second is that after the first murders, killers are likely to be in a state of panic or distress and will thus restrain themselves from committing another murder; however, after a number of murders, they will feel more comfortable with their behaviour and will intensify it, such that the cooling-off period gets shorter each time (Edelstein, 2014; Holmes & De Burger, 1988; Holmes & Holmes, 1998; Levin, 2008). The current study supports this latter explanation.

The second finding of these studies was that the time interval between murders may be the result of circumstances in the life of the serial killer (Lange, 1999). When the killer's life has been influenced by specific social, psychological, or biological factors, among others, there was found to be a significant change in the cooling-off period. While this is an important finding, Lang (1999) did not explain their findings in a coherent way, thus leaving it inconclusive.

The third finding was that there are three types of cooling-off periods: short (less than 14 days [14%]), long (more than 14 days [57%]) and a combination (some less than 14 days and some after 14 days [29%]) (Simkin & Roychowdhury, 2018). This determination of 14 days as the border between long and short cooling-off periods had not been mentioned in any previous studies and was thus new to the literature on serial murder. The researchers did not, however, offer any possible explanations for these different patterns.

The fact that different murders have different cooling-off periods demands us to address the theoretical aspects and interpersonal influences of this phenomenon (Lange, 1999). Our research questions are therefore: first, is there a pattern of cooling-off that is common to all serial killers or are there differences between them?; and second, can one serial killer have different cooling-off periods? Our hypothesis is that different killers have different cooling-off periods and, similarly, that one killer can have different cooling-off periods. These differences may have psychological, sociological, and geographical explanations among others.

The Current Study

Data File

Our data is based on the Encyclopedia of serial killers (Newton, 2006). We sampled every serial killer that there are stuffiest facts about time interval between his murderers and his age at the first murder. In total data on 53 serial killers were gathered, all of them are males. Their age at the time of the first murder ranged from 13 to 51 with an average of 26.98 years (standard deviation = 8.90). First murders took place between 1859 and 1965. For each killer, the date of the first and every subsequent killing was documented, and the period between every two consecutive killings was calculated.

Data Analysis

Data were analyzed using SPSS version 25. First, descriptive statistics were produced using frequencies for categorical variables and means with standard deviations for continuous variables (e.g., age). Differences between the periods of killings for every murderer were computed using repeated measures ANOVA. This procedure tracks each killer along his career and computes averages and standard deviations for the periods between killings. Correlations between periods of killings and also between age and periods of killings were computed using the Pearson correlation coefficient. The significant level for the relationship was below .05.

Results

Table 6 as well as figure 1 shows descriptive statistics (in months) of the periods between murders. As shown in this table, about half (49%) of the serial killers (26 out of 53) conducted 6 murders, 15% (8 out of 53) conducted 10 murders, 8% (4 out of 53) conducted 16 murders, and just one killer conducted 17 murders. Table 7 specifies the cooling off periods between the first series of the first four murders. Regarding the periods between murders, the longest period was found to be between the first and second murders (M=24.71, SD=41.15), followed by the period between the second and third murders (M=16.89, SD=35.21). The periods between the third and eighth murders ranged from 7.59 to 9.26 months on average. The period between all subsequent killings became shorter and ranged from 0.63 to 3.20 months. For the sole killer who conducted 17 murders, the period between the last two murders was 13 months.

Table 6: Means, Standard Deviations, and Periods (in Months) Between Murders.

	Number of Killers	% of Total Sample	Mean	SD	Minimum	Maximum
Murder 1 to Murder 2	53	100%	24.71	41.14	0.13	168.00
Murder 2 to Murder 3	52	98%	16.89	35.21	0.01	192.00
Murder 3 to Murder 4	45	85%	7.81	20.84	0.07	113.00
Murder 4 to Murder 5	34	64%	9.26	21.48	0.03	108.00
Murder 5 to Murder 6	26	49%	7.59	12.82	0.03	62.00
Murder 6 to Murder 7	22	42%	8.13	16.64	0.03	72.00
Murder 7 to Murder 8	18	34%	9.10	16.46	0.30	53.00
Murder 8 to Murder 9	12	23%	2.90	3.41	0.07	12.00
Murder 9 to Murder 10	10	19%	3.20	4.07	0.20	12.00
Murder 10 to Murder 11	8	15%	0.63	0.35	0.27	1.10
Murder 11 to Murder 12	6	11%	1.51	0.81	0.07	2.00
Murder 12 to Murder 13	5	9%	1.51	1.20	0.07	3.00
Murder 13 to Murder 14	7	13%	1.03	0.47	0.50	2.00
Murder 14 to Murder 15	4	8%	1.95	2.09	0.30	5.00
Murder 15 to Murder 16	4	8%	3.04	2.89	0.17	6.00
Murder 16 to Murder 17	1	2%	13.00		13.00	13.00

Figure 1: Average periods between killings in months

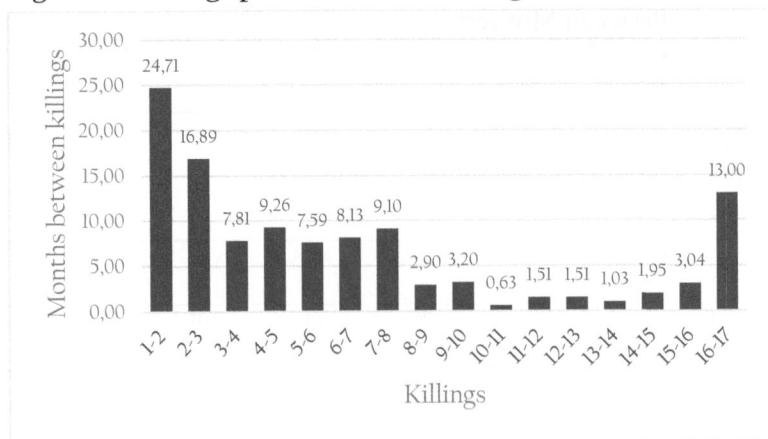

Figure 2 shows the association between consecutive murders and the level of heterogeneity between killers in their killing periods as expressed by standard deviations. As can be seen, there is a general negative trend between the levels of heterogeneity and the number of murders. In other words, serial killers who conduct more than 10 murders have relatively similar periods between consecutive murders (SD ranges between 0.35 to 2.09), while those who conduct fewer than 10 murders have a relatively high heterogeneity between their killing periods, meaning that they are less homogenous and demonstrate different killer profiles.

Figure 2:   SD between periods of killings

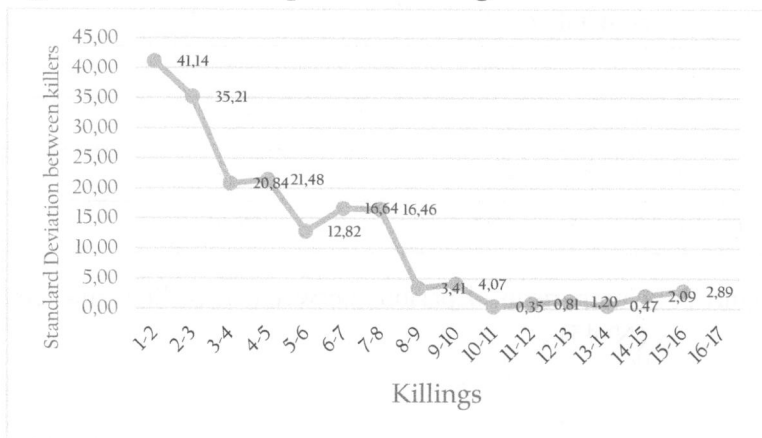

In order to assess the differences between killing periods, repeated measures ANOVA was conducted for 45 serial killers who had conducted 6 murders. This sub-sample was used since it provides the minimum sufficient data for this statistical procedure. This procedure tracks the series of each killer and computes averages and standard deviations for the periods between the murders. As can be seen also in Table 7 and figure 3, this analysis yielded a significant difference between periods of the first four murders (F=3.823, p<.05). That is, the period between the first and second murders (M=23.32, SD=40.79) was longer than the period between the second and third murders (M=17.15, SD=36.98) (p<.05); similarly, the period between the second and third murders was longer than the period between the third and fourth murders (M=8.03, SD=21.30) (p<.05).

Table 7: Means and SDs of Periods Between Murders of 45 Serial Killers.

	Mean	SD
Murder 1 to Murder 2	23.32	40.79
Murder 2 to Murder 3	17.15	36.98
Murder 3 to Murder 4	8.03	21.30

Figure 3: Comparison of periods between three first murders (N=45)

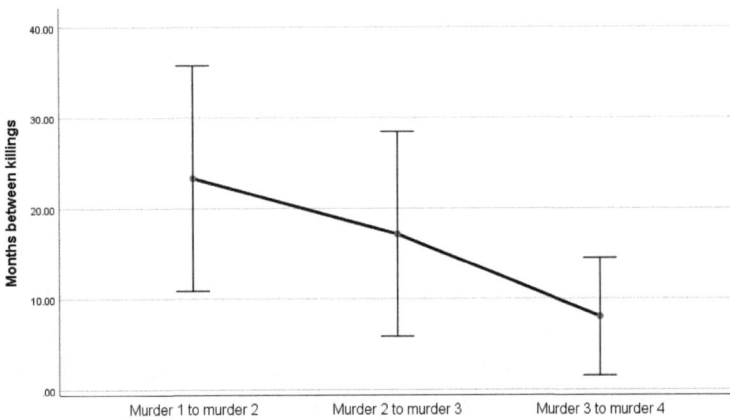

In order to predict the next murder according to the periods between previous murders, Pearson correlations were computed between the periods of the first ten murders (see Table 8).

As shown in Table 8, positive associations were generally found between the periods between past and future murders. Specifically, the period between the first and second murders positively predicted the periods between the second and third murders (r=.537, p<.01) and the fifth and sixth murders (r=.482, p<.05). It was also found that the period between the second and third murders positively predicted the periods between the seventh and eighth murders (r=.852, p<.01) and the ninth and tenth murders (r=.781, p<.01). Similarly, the period between the third and fourth murders positively predicted the period between the sixth and seventh murders (r=.855, p<.01), and the period between the fifth and sixth murders (r=.720, p<.01) positively predicted the period between eighth and ninth murders and also by periods between sixth and seventh killing (r=.835, p<.01).

Table 8: Pearson Correlations Between Periods of First Ten Murders.

	1–2	2–3	3–4	4–5	5–6	6–7	7–8	8–9
Murder 1 to Murder 2								
Murder 2 to Murder 3	.537**							
Murder 3 to Murder 4	.053	-.037						
Murder 4 to Murder 5	.244	.019	-.015					
Murder 5 to Murder 6	.482*	.076	.093	.091				
Murder 6 to Murder 7	-.019	.161	.855**	-.098	.255			
Murder 7 to Murder 8	.144	.852**	-.084	-.172	.077	.313		
Murder 8 to Murder 9	.118	-.017	-.088	-.001	.720*	.835**	.482	
Murder 9 to Murder 10	.244	.781**	-.045	.378	-.040	.235	.305	.063

*p<.05, **p<.01

Table 9 shows Pearson correlations between the age of the killer at the time of the first murder and the periods between future murders.

Table 9: Pearson Correlations between Age of the Killer at the First Murder and Periods between future murders.

	Correlation with age
Murder 1 to Murder 2	-.359**
Murder 2 to Murder 3	-.336*
Murder 3 to Murder 4	-.255*
Murder 4 to Murder 5	-.023
Murder 5 to Murder 6	-.085
Murder 6 to Murder 7	.160
Murder 7 to Murder 8	-.119
Murder 8 to Murder 9	.031
Murder 9 to Murder 10	.071

*p<.05, **p<.01

Negative correlations were found between the age of the killer at the time of the first murder and the periods between first and second murders ($r = -.359$, $p < .01$), second and third murders ($r = -.336$, $p < .05$), and third and fourth murders ($r = -.255$, $p < .05$). In other words, the younger the killer at the time of the first murder, the longer the time between subsequent first murders.

Discussion

In order to deal with the knowledge gap in the existing literature, our main research question was whether cooling-off periods among serial killers are common and have some general patterns or whether there are interpersonal differences. We also examined whether each serial killer has different cooling-off periods between the murders committed.

While Simkin and Roychowdhury (2018) found that the periods between murders were smooth without any peaks or change in pattern and got longer as the killers conducted more murders, our findings contradicted this smooth pattern. We found a longer period between the first and the third murders than with subsequent murders and the longest period between the first and the second murders.

In an attempt to explain this unique pattern which contradicts previous findings, we followed two existing theories on serial killers: escalation (Holmes & Holmes 1998; Edelstein, 2014) and dissociative identity disorder (Butler, 2006; Carlisle, 1988; Edelstein, 2014; Holmes Brown, Mansell, Fearon, Hunter, Frasquilho & Oakley.2005; Fox & Levin, 2005; Reinders et al., 2006; Van Der Hart et al., 2005). According to the former, serial killers escalate their lethal behaviour due to the frustration suffered when the murders do not fulfill their fantasies. The time interval between murders gets shorter and the killers become crueler (Homes & Holmes, 1998).

The latter explanation addresses fantasy and the existence of two identities of serial killers: those who suffered child abuse and those who are normative. In order for killers to commit their first murder, they enable a move into their post traumatic identity through which they fantasize about how they will kill their victims. Some of them call this identity the "dark side" of their personality via a technique of neutralizing shame and responsibility (Sykes & Matza, 1957). The killers are no longer satisfied by their fantasies and, like substance users, need a stronger stimulus. This theory explains the first murder. After the first murder, shock at their own deeds may enable the killers' normative identity to take control—a process that guarantees staying normative. However, after some time (the cooling-off period) the fantasies are back but they are no longer sufficient or satisfactory and the killers need the "real thing," namely, the next murder. As in other antisocial behaviours, the more a person engages in anti-social behaviour, the easier it becomes; each subsequent act is easier, and the loss of inner conflict enables them to act more quickly than before. This theory thus explains our finding that the period between the fourth murder and subsequent killings is shorter (0.63–3.20 months) than the period between the first, second, and third murders (24.71, 16.89, 9.26 months respectively).

An additional finding show that the younger the killer, the longer the cooling-off periods of the three first murders ($p<0.05$, $p<0.01$). This emphasize the difficulty of killers to commit their first series of murders and suggests its salience regarding younger killers as well. This topic can and should be examined in future studies.

Our results thus show the differences between serial killers regarding the number of victims during their criminal careers. Another difference is the fact that young killers have longer cooling-off periods between the first three murders they commit. There is, however, some universal or general trait which characterizes all serial killers. According to this pattern, the first three killings have longer cooling-off periods than the subsequent murders, a characteristic that may be attributed to the escalation and dissociative identity disorder theories discussed above. In other words the compulsion takes over after the second/third victim and the bloodthirst becomes more ravenous. This finding has a policy aspect. If we have a better knowledge, profiling or other tools to apprehend the killer after his first murder, we could have prevent him from becoming serial.

Limitations

When researching serial killers, it must be acknowledged that many are not apprehended, and thus we lack much information about their patterns of killing, including the cooling-off periods examined here. Of those apprehended, most have admitted to only some of their total killings. The data on serial killers are therefore partial and limit all studies on their patterns of behaviour.

A more specific limitation of this study is our finding that the periods between the first few killings can forecast the periods between future murders. While we showed that the periods between murders are longer in the beginning and get subsequently shorter, we are not currently able to explain these results, and it was not in the scope of this study.

It is clear to us that future studies on this topic would benefit from a much larger sample.

The next chapter deals with classification and typologies of serial murder and murderers, in which I will implement the integrative explanation for the known types of serial murderers. By so doing, we will be able to see to what extent the model explains the creation of serial murderers who are sometimes very different from one another.

Chapter Five
Typology of Serial Murders and Murderers

Different fields of knowledge have made many and varied attempts to establish typologies of behaviours, phenomena, and people within their field of knowledge. There is an outstanding example for it in psychology, in an attempt to characterize individuals according to the disturbances they suffer from. Another attempt has been made in the field of criminology in distinguishing between chronic criminals and career criminals (Edelstein, 2006). Attempts to classify serial murder have been made for understanding the variety and variance of these murders and murderers, in order to pour light on the different motives of the murderers, on the victim-criminal relationship, and other criteria. The existing typologies classify serial murderers on a basis of a mixture of characteristics, assumed motives, evidence from the scene of the crime, and background characteristics of the criminals. An additional problem is that these typologies combine definitions with an objective nature, like gender, age of murderer and victim, together with a subjective interpretation based on the motive of the felony.[134]

Regarding criminals in general and serial murderers in particular, it is important to distinguish between typologies which have been intended to serve the law enforcement authorities and more theoretical typologies.

Typologies in the Service of the Law Enforcement System

The tendency that seems to appear among law enforcement authorities is to establish relatively wide typologies based upon motives-reasons, as the FBI has suggested in the first typology of serial murder. According to this typology there are three types of serial murderers: The organized murderer, the unorganized murderer, and the murderer who integrates both ways of operation.

The organized murderer is exceptionally precise, brings the tool of the murder with him to the scene, and meticulously chooses the victim. After the murder he removes the body from the scene, and conceals every forensic piece of evidence. The unorganized murderer executes a "blitz attack" on the victim, with no planning, and leaves traces of a fast and brutal murder at the scene. The murderer uses what he finds at the scene as a weapon. After the murder he abandons the body, and the scene is full of legal (forensic) pieces of evidence. The integrative murderer integrates different components of the two types.

A wider typology that has been suggested in the field of law enforcement deals with the various motives of the serial murderer, although it is not clear how the division of the law enforcement authorities can help. Morton (2005) enumerates seven main motives: Anger, a criminal business, material benefit, ideology, power/excitement, psychopathy, and sex. Without entering into details of each of the categories, at first glance one can see an overlapping among part of the categories, for example, power and control and sexual basis, or a criminal business and material benefit. In addition, the motive of anger seems too general and suits several categories.

Morton (2005) presents an important perception, according to which the serial murderer does not choose the victim according to a specific category, but according to the conditions of the situation: Availability, vulnerability, and desirability:

- Availability means a connection to the victim's life style, or the circumstances in which the victims are involved that enables the murderer access to the victim.
- Vulnerability means the degree in which the victim is accessible to the murderer. Here, too, routine activity theory is highly suitable.
- Desirability means the attraction of the murderer to the victim, including many factors which are based on the motive of the murderer in relation to the characteristics of the victim, like race, gender, ethnic origin, age, or specific preferences of the murderer.

As we will see, an absolute majority of the serial murderers look for specific characteristics in the "ideal victim." In cases in which the impulse to murder is very high, the murderer would make do with a substitute of the "ideal victim" of his fantasies. The main innovation in this perception is that like other crimes which are executed by professional criminals, the murderer would choose a victim who would cause minimal risk in his being caught. In addition, the presented explanation establishes the importance of theories in criminology for the explanation of serial murder: The theory of routine activities and the theory of the rational choice.

A certain change in the method of classification was suggested by Keppel and Walter (1999), a classification that focuses more on a sexual murder. These scientists indicate four kinds of serial murderers on a sexual basis:

- Power-decisive: A motive of a strong masculine power versus a feminine or masculine victim.
- Ratification power: Looking for ratification through the victim that the murderer "pleases" him, or that he is "better" than other lovers.[135]
- Anger-vengeance: Vengeance of a specific woman or an alternative figure which, according to the perception of the murderer, has hurt him in the past.
- Anger-excitement: Causing pain and fear to the victim (man or woman) for the sake of sexual satisfaction.

Typologies Suggested by Theoreticians Outside the Law Enforcement Authorities

Vronsky (2007) claims that even today there is no agreed definition for a serial murder, and there is no one universal system that would establish categories of serial murderers. The wide range of the definitions and categories points to the fact that the phenomenon of serial murderers is wider and more varied than we thought (Ibid., p. 27). According to Vronsky, theoreticians who do not deal with investigating crimes tend to classify serial murderers according to a motive or motives for the murder, beyond the classification that is done for the bodies of law enforcement and investigative authorities. I will survey the different typologies which have been suggested according to their chronological order.

An attempted typology was done by Lee (1988),[136] who identified ten types of serial murderers according to a wide range of bio-sociopsychological categories: depressive, psychotic, brain injury, psychopath, passive aggression, alcoholic, hysteric, mentally handicapped, sexual deviant, and murderer of youth. The criteria for this typology are very varied and include a wide range of characteristics, and so distance us more from unequivocal criteria.

Another interesting typology of Lee (1988) refers to coining different labels aiming to differentiate among the serial murderers only by their motive: Benefit, passion, hatred, power and control, vengeance, opportunism, fear, contract, despair, ritual and mercy. The labels that were defined are not clearly differentiated, and it makes it difficult to distinguish unequivocally among the different types and motives.

Hickey (1992) describes early attempts for establishing typologies of serial murderers: One typology presented a classification from two up to 11 kinds of serial murderers, but there are inner contradictions. Some of the types deal with describing causativeness, while others describe the diagnosis of the murderers.

The Typology of Holmes and Holmes

Holmes and Holmes (1998) present one of the most organized typologies for classifying serial murderers, according to several criteria, through which we will be able to distinguish among the different types of murderers. It should be indicated that the different types of murderers that arise from these diagnoses are not significantly different from the ones of the previous typologies; the innovation is that the Holmes & Holmes (1998) created a clear system for classifying the different serial murderers. Here are the diagnoses suggested by these scientists for classifying serial murderers:

Motives

Internal motive—the internal motive is something very deep in the individual that is part of his personality, and pushes him to murder: There was something deep inside me, something that I couldn't control (the words of Ted Bundy, Ibid.). The concept of the "shadow" is connected to these words, a concept we dealt with in the previous chapter: This is an awful feeling. Something that eats you from the inside that threatens to take over from the inside and the only way to provide the meal is to murder a female who is trash and isn't worth anything ... (Ibid.).

External motive—a serial murderer who murders for the sake of material benefit, like someone who murders through a contract for the Mafia or a freelancer, or someone who murders for the sake of getting the life insurance of the victim (Blue Beard). Holmes & Holmes (1998) argue that the motive in this case is external to the personality, and there is nothing deep in his personality which demanded that he murders. It is my opinion that this claim of the scientist, that the motive is not part of the personality, is severe, since this is a distortion of all we know about motives and about the human soul.

Benefit

Psychological benefit—the psychological benefit can be a kind of sexual sadism which brings the murderer to satisfaction from a violent and fatal attack on a helpless victim. Another psychological benefit could be in avenging an innocent victim by displacing vengeance or hatred toward a hated object, or actually controlling the life of the other person. The benefit can be from the very action, planning it, and maybe even keeping souvenirs from the event.

Material benefit—material gain and money often moves serial killers. This serial murder can occur by murderers or assassins working as professional killers, murderers who kill their partners to receive insurance money, and more.

Location of the Murder

Geographical stability—the geographically stable serial murderer lives in a specific area, murders and gets rid of the body in the same area or close by. For example, John Gacy murdered 33 people, and buried most of them under his house or in his yard, and all the victims were local inhabitants. Such a murderer has a "convenience area" near his house or his place of work, and only there he is capable of operating (according to Holmes & Holmes, 1998) the area is about 19 km in diameter). Geographical mobility—the casual serial murderer moves from one place to another during his murderous career. For instance, Bundy murdered in ten different states in the USA, and the lack of information and cooperation among the law enforcement authorities made it difficult to catch him.

Choosing the Victims

Deliberate choosing—sometimes the murderer would choose an "ideal victim" according to physical characteristics, like body structure or a certain hair color, or according to age, gender or field of occupation. This category includes also a person who murders a specific individual by contract. Sometimes, the distinct characteristics of the victim appear in the fantasy world of the murderer, and in materializing the fantasy he would look for a victim who suits the same characteristics. Random choosing—there is no common denominator among the victims, and the only reason for choosing a specific victim was his location in the murderer's environment in the wrong time. This category suits the unorganized murderer.

Method of Murder

Focusing on the process—an organized event: The murderer plans, in an accurate and professional way, the entire process: He follows the intended victim, learns his habits and time table, plans how to kidnap him (sometimes using deceit and fraud), examines a location for the execution of the tortures and the murder, gets equipped with torturing instruments and the instrument of the murder, plans the times, the way of removing the body, and so on. The murderer draws enjoyment both from the planning and the execution. He elongates the duration of the execution, as he enjoys the reactions of the victim, from the various stages of the process.

Focusing on the action—an unorganized event—the murder is committed and terminates within a few minutes. But in defining this characteristic the authors did not pay attention to the fact that there may be a situation in which the focus will be on the action, but still, the event would be well organized. An example of this would be the case of a serial murderer who is a professional assassin. There may be a certain focus on the process in such a case as well, but the main focus in on the action.

The authors of this typology refer to four types of serial murderers, but this typology is an "ideal model" which would not necessarily be found exactly in reality. In addition, within each type of serial murderers there may be a certain variance.

Holmes and Holmes' typology (1998) received a few meaningful criticisms,[137] but I have thought it right to present it in length because this is one of the only typologies that presents clear criteria for classifying the different murderers. Part of the criteria is problematic indeed, like the reference to an internal and external motive, and moreover, the typology was attacked due to an overlapping among some of the categories. For example, between the hedonistic murderer and the murderer who acts out of a motive of power or control, and due to ignoring categories which are missing, such as a serial murderer with an ideological background. Regardless, it can be used for demonstrating how the integrative theoretical model explains the different types of serial murderers. Following are the four types of serial murder Holmes & Holmes (1998) present in their typology:

The Visionary Serial Killer

This murderer is defined as psychotic and with no connection with reality. He claims that he was pushed to a murderous behaviour according to the instruction of demons, angels, Satan or God, after having seen or heard them. It was found that sex is not an integral motive in the set of his motives. The scene of the murder in these cases seems to Holmes & Holmes (1998) as lacking any order or logic, but for the murderer it is perceived as "logical," expressing something unique for him. Due to his mental state, the scene is full of physical (forensic) evidence from which one can identify the type of the murderer.

For this murderer, the psychological benefit is: A sense of pleasure, of release and relief, and a sense of returning to balance. This murderer has no preferred type of victim,[138] and no physical, occupational or other characteristics can be seen as common for all his victims. The only common denominator for all the victims is the fact that they share space and time with the murderer.

The personality of the murderer prevents him from distancing from the geographical space in which he feels comfortable. The "comfort zone" is the place where he feels comfortable and familiar with the environment: The environment of living, working, shopping and entertainment. The murder is spontaneous and focused on the action rather than on the process. The murderer has no interest in choosing a specific victim, and at the scene of the murder there is no evidence of preparations and planning. The murderer would use an available weapon, including equipment he would find on the victim. Usually the tool of the murder would be left at the scene. The unorganized scene of the murder characterizes the personality of the murderer, and it would contain physical evidence, like fingerprints, blood stains, and so on. The evidence at the scene would point to the feelings of the murderer during the attack, like hatred, fury, or fear. From all these things it appears that this murderer suits the unorganized murderer who was described in the previous typology.

The Assignment-Oriented Serial Killer

This murderer, like the visionary serial killer, acts compulsively, but his primary motive is another. He is not defined as psychotic. He feels a necessity to murder all those people whom he "judged" as deserving to be executed. He murders a group of "unwanted" people—those who have been judged as such by the murderer himself. This verdict is executed following objective or subjective experiences of the murderer in relation to the victims. Perhaps part of his experiences that have to do with these people were real and even repeated themselves, and at the same time, it could be that the murderer suffers from a sense of injustice after being hurt by someone, and the victims serve as a substitution for the source of frustration, humiliation or injustice that has been done to the murderer in the past, since the origin of these feelings is not accessible for the murderer for various reasons.[139] The murderer makes a conscious decision to execute the murder. He chooses "to rid the world" of a selected group of people who do not deserve to live in our world, or more correctly, in his world. The murderer uses actions of neutralizing guilt,[140] by explaining that he releases the community from threatening, dangerous people. For example, if he decides to murder prostitutes, he would claim that he does a service to the community by preventing it from contamination of disease. Prior to the execution, there a fantasy occurs in which the murderer experiences an excitement that has to do with the planning of the murder and its execution.

The expected benefit is psychological. The murderer expects to achieve a sense of justice and self-worth since according to his perception, the murder would not only do well for himself, but he also makes the whole of society a better place to live in for the present and following generations. Unlike the visionary murderer, the murder act in this case is not perceived by the murderer as a decree of God, but as an instruction coming from his own sense of justice. The "correction" comes from his internal set of values (which are influenced, in turn, by sociocultural contents, AE).

The victims are chosen because they suit certain criteria that deserve to be exterminated, and in the stage of fantasy he identifies the preferred victim. The "ideal victim" does not fulfill a sexual fantasy; on the contrary, choosing the ideal victim focuses on not wanting the victim. The specific victim is chosen randomly out of the unwanted group (women, prostitutes, and so on), and the only condition the victim fulfills is having the undesired characteristic.

Like the visionary murderer, the assignment-oriented murderer also acts in his comfort zone, and is not mobile over a wide space. He is an established inhabitant in a certain place, and has built himself a good history in his working place. After the murder he does not feel a need to deal with the body (necrophilia[141] or mutilation). From the moment the victim dies, the mission is terminated for him, and he would leave the scene of the murder. Getting rid of the body would be done at the scene of the murder, and in this way, the chance that it would be discovered is diminished. At the scene of the murder there will be very little evidence, since in the stage of the fantasy the murderer had planned everything in advance, including avoiding leaving forensic evidence and being caught.

The method of murder: The assignment-oriented murderer works fast and focuses on the action itself. The action is well planned and therefore also highly organized. In as much as he is organized, less evidence would be left at the scene. Unlike the visionary murderer, he would bring the instrument of the murder with him and would take it with him at the end of the action. This murderer suits the pattern of the organized murderer, or the integrated one.

The Hedonistic Serial Murderer

The hedonistic serial murderer is attracted the attention of the media, probably because he connects between fatal violence and personal, sexual satisfaction. Hedonism is a movement for achieving pleasure, and in the case of a serial murder, it deals with a violent and fatal movement for the sake of achieving this goal. This type is divided into three sub-types:

The Lust Serial Killer—for this serial murderer, sex plays an integral role in the murder. Sexual satisfaction, with the killed victim as well (necrophilia), is the supreme goal, and it comes to him like an addiction to alcohol or drugs. Before going out to the act of the murder, he has a fantasy which includes choosing the victim and going through some kind of ritual—the way in which the victim is chosen, kidnapped, died and is removed, and the actions that the murderer would do with the body of the victim. From the moment that the border has been crossed[142] and the murderer has made a decision to commit a murder and sexual sadism, there is a very little chance that the murderer would hold himself from committing the murder. This serial murderer is motivated by sexual compulsiveness which pushes him to action aiming to satisfy this impulse. The expected benefit is psychological, when the murder fulfills an internal need of sexual satisfaction. The murderer is not defined as psychotic, and he is connected to reality. The satisfaction is achieved also by torturing and murdering of foreigners together with a sexual element, after the murderer has learned to link between murder and sexual satisfaction. Since the sexual component is part of the murder, the murderer looks for the "ideal victim," who has to be sexually attractive in the eyes of the murderer. If the compulsive impulse is very strong, the murderer may give up the ideal victim and find a substitute. The victim is unfamiliar to the murderer but is not random, since he has to meet the required characteristics.

This serial murderer kidnaps or persuades his victims in a relatively small area, but from there he is mobile, aiming to confuse the police. Therefore, one can define him as relatively stable geographically, but mobile in the spreading of the bodies. This murderer must have a physical contact with the victim. He may use various means, like strangling, stabbing with a knife, penetrating objects into the body of the victim, and rape. In addition, there are acts of necrophilia, and there might be acts like mutilation and dismembering of the body, preserving a certain organ at his disposal, and so on. The murderer is organized in his actions, since the fantasy that preceded the action serves as a behavioural script for him which was reconstructed and polished many times in his mind, and the focus is on the whole process, rather than the act of the murder.

The Thrill Serial Killer—for this serial murderer satisfaction is achieved through the reactions of the victim, and therefore he keeps the victim alive for a longer period of time. Like the lust serial killer, here, too, sex is an integral part. This murderer has to feel the excitement of the murder. The fact that the victim knows what happens to him brings the murderer a sense of satisfaction and fulfilling a purpose. Hence from the moment the victim dies, the murderer loses interest and plans how to get rid of the body. The expected benefit has to do, as has been mentioned, with a long process that only at the end of which the murder takes place. The murderer draws pleasure from the elongated process until the death of the victim, and not from the murder itself.

Like the lust serial killer, for this serial murderer the victim is an unfamiliar person, but he would be chosen meticulously and specifically since it has to meet certain physical criteria that fit the murderer's fantasy. For this end, the murder would follow a specific victim until getting him, and would not compromise on another victim.

This serial murderer tends to travel in his search for the right victim, and therefore he is considered geographically mobile. He tends to collect a victim in one state and get rid of the body in another state aiming to make it difficult for the police. Sometimes he decides on a place in which he wants the body to be found, and sometimes he does not want it to be found, and hides it well. The reason that the murderer wants the body to be found is that he passes a message that he is still alive and active.

The method of the murder is based on total control over the victim, as the pleasure and satisfaction of the murderer are drawn from the suffering the victim goes through. The sadist murderer does not get a sexual satisfaction from the pain he causes, but from the anticipation for the suffering the victim would experience in his tortures. Unlike previous types, the thrill killer is not characterized by "overkill"[143] of the victim due to lack of excitement of the murder itself and his being under control. There is no necrophilia and the murder weapon would not be found at the scene. The instruments of torture also would not be found at the scene, since the murderer would need them for the next murder. Some of the torturing instruments which serve the fantasy are penetrated into various opening of the victim's body before he dies.

It is important to distinguish between a serial murder for the sake of passion and the murderer for the sake of excitement. A murderer out of excitement is interested in leaving the victim alive in order to get full satisfaction, and therefore we would not find a necrophilic behaviour in this case. This serial murderer usually tends to be single, unlike the murder out of passion. The murderer for the sake of excitement tends to be more mobile geographically, and his being single or divorced makes it easier for him. He may have sexual relationships with women at the same time, but these are simple relationships with no sense of commitment, when the sense of compulsion gets stronger and he prepares for the next murder, his relationships with others become secondary.

The Comfort Serial Killer—this serial murderer was described as someone who murders for reasons of material needs: Money, business, or other material rewards. Later on, scientists refer to the professional assassin as suitable for this type of serial murderer (Schlesinger, 2001; Holzman, 1995). Unlike other serial murderers, the main goal of this serial murderer is to enjoy life, and his actions are done in order to achieve "the good life." These murderers do not behave blatantly with fatal violence. On the contrary, they murder quietly. This murderer is defined as a sociopath or a psychopath, and murders again and again, calmly, out of an interest of achieving or maintaining wellbeing. The act of the murder is random for him, versus the chase after goals which may be reflected in a material benefit. This is a rational and conscious motive, although the Holmes & Holmes (1998) think that his pattern of thought reflects a personality of a psychopath, for whom the lives of human beings are measured in terms of their financial worth.

This is the only type of serial murder in which the murderer hurts familiar people in part of the cases. The process of choosing the victim is not random. It is cautious and done generally by way of marriage or other kinds of relationships. In other cases, the victim can be a business partner. All the same, when it is a case of an assassination contract, the victim would be unfamiliar to the murderer. This serial murderer tends to live in one place and stay there. He does not wander in his murders, and in most cases, he murders his victims and gets rid of their bodies in the same area (the body would usually be found at the scene of the murder). When it is a case of a contract killing, the murderer would be mobile geographically, even over countries and continents.

This serial murderer kills in a planned and organized way, and he is focused on the action. First he chooses the victim whose death would fill the desired outcome. A long time is dedicated to choosing the method of murder which can be a slow poison or a fast murder. There is no focus here on the process, in which the murderer elongates the death in order to enjoy the suffering of the victim. The murder is focused, since through it, a material goal would be achieved. In a case of a murder according to a contract, there may be a process of surveillance. The scene is organized and there is no evidence, because if he is caught, he would lose his source of "income." There would be no signs of torturing found or any kind of sexual intercourse, no strangling of the victim and no mutilation of the body after dying. The authors claim that the murder weapon would be found at the scene, but they did not refer to the case of a professional assassin who shoots his victim from a riding car, for instance.

There are two types of serial murderers for the sake of bene-fit: Those who murder familiar victims, and those who murder strangers.

Murdering familiar victims—the typical one murders family members. The murderer may marry several times and accumulate the insurance money, or get hold of economic interests and family funds (Blue Beard/the Black Widow). The murder would kill the victim cautiously, after a period of time, usually through pills or poison. At first he would see to it that he is perceived as a caring and kind person who cares about the health of the victim and does everything in his power to save his life. One can see that choosing the victims does not involve specific characteristics except for the ownership of money and property, but the choice is absolutely not random.

Murdering strangers—the murderer acts out of a material motive and has to have a high level of professionalism. He is defined as having a criminal career since he works by contract. One can see how the theory of the rational choice suits this type of serial murderer as he considers the profit and loss of his actions.

Although the reference is to acquaintances and strangers, there may be a third type as well. I refer to the cases in which the victims are known to the murderer as they are dependents in an institution he manages, but beyond this there is no personal and intimate acquaintance. The murderer is interested in the social security money which he would collect after murdering his victims.

To sum up, this serial murderer kills acquaintances as well as strangers. Except this, he is different from the other serial murderers in the expected benefit which is material in this case. We can assume, though, that the murderer produces a certain psychological benefit from the enjoyment of achieving the material rewards which can be done only by murdering the victim.

I would like to expand the discussion on the professional assassin, beyond what the original scientists have written, since one can see the act of reframing or structuring in this murderer. Levi (1995) refers to the social organization of the murder and the professional assassin. The professional killer lacks the justifications and "supports" the law provides other murderers, like self-defense, insanity, or murder within the civil service. We deal here with a person who knows that murder is not normative, and consciously chooses to murder out of a calculated interest. In order to cope with his work, the independent murderer develops his own guilt-neutralizing techniques: Since the issuer is anonymous and a stranger, and so is the victim, the murderer executes "a denial of the victim." In addition, violating the contract would lead to punishment of the murderer by the issuer and damage his reputation, and therefore there is a kind of self-defense or denial of responsibility here. Another neutralizing way is denying the damage, since the professional murderer defines his actions as "a job that has to be done." The formulation is of a normal business action. An additional technique of neutralizing guilt is denying responsibility: The professional assassin focuses on his skills and a constant professional learning, and by so doing he emphasizes the technique and not the motives or the moral aspect of his actions.

After the first murder, the contract killer feels a tough dissonance. His self-image is broken, and he cannot share his feelings with others. As a result, he reframes his motives and activity. For example, he would emphasize for himself the financial aspect, refer to his action as a job, and create a distance between himself and the victim, and between him and the moral aspect of his work. For this end he needs to be restrained and emotionally distanced which would make the victim not another person, but a target. In other words, he depersonalizes the victim. It is obvious that such a murderer suffers from a severe antisocial personality disorder.

The Power/Control Serial Killer

Although the heinous necrophilic behaviour of this serial murderer points apparently to psychopathic lines in his personality, this person knows how to distinguish between good and evil and between reality and fantasy, even though it is fantasy that pushes him to this behaviour. This type of serial murderer is considered most fatal, due to his high capability of enchanting his environment. He is well aware of the risk he takes, for instance when removing the body, and as the risk is higher, his excitement strengthens. His high intelligence and great mobility make it difficult to catch him. His motive is to achieve full and dominant control over the destiny of the victim.

There is a similarity to the pattern of the serial murderer who acts out of passion and excitement. The murderer follows possible victims and chooses a certain kind of victim, but the victim is unknown to the murderer. The murderer has the ability to move from one place to another during his murders in order to make it difficult for the police, especially if there is no sharing of information among the police forces of different countries.

The method of the murder consists of bringing the victim to a deserted place in which he would not be able to call for help. After tortures that include deviant sexual behaviour, the murder takes place, and afterwards the body (or part of it) would be taken to the house of the murderer aiming to commit necrophilia which is a dramatic part of the ritual in this murder. As much as the process is longer, the enjoyment and satisfaction increases. The emphasis is on the process rather than on the action. The murderer enjoys the murder, because through it he can materialize his fantasies. Bundy kept a body under his bed or in the wardrobe for several days, and used to execute sexual experiments on it. This serial murderer is defined by Holmes & Holmes (1998) as a "master" in his work; a professional who improves his skills. Bundy claimed that the same mechanisms which are used in general learning are used also in learning how to kill efficiently and achieve the expected benefits. I think that this type of serial murder and murderer establishes duplicity in relation to the hedonistic types, and does not bring any significant innovation. As I have mentioned, this typology is important for understanding the classification of serial murder and murderers according to specific criteria which bear a theoretical and content significance.

As far as chronological order is concerned, we should refer here to the books of Vronsky (2004, 2007), in *Serial Killers: The Method and Madness of Monsters*, he refers to the classification conducted by the FBI, and therefore I do not see a point in repeating this classification. His second book deals with female serial murderers, and I will refer to it later on.

Since most of the serial murder cases in the USA have been committed out of a sexual motive, the typologies, beyond the one I have presented, referred mainly to the component of power and control as a central reason, while ignoring other categories of serial murder. The central categories that appear in the literature in the field of serial murderers are the following:

Power/control—An approach has been developed in recent years, according to which the central motive for a serial murder is a sense of power and control (Vronsky, 2007; Levin, 2008) whose extreme expression is in life and death. According to this approach, a serial murder that involves sexual activity is not connected to sex as a primary goal, and sex is just a means of controlling the victim.[144] The main goal is achieving the satisfaction that comes from full control over a human life, and for this end, serial murderers execute deceptive exercises to trick the victims, the public, and the law enforcement system.

Levin (2008) emphasizes the ambition for power and control, from his many years of experience and long acquaintance with serial murderers. According to Levin, these motives are most important for serial murderers, more than we have assumed in the past. Many serial murderers take the lives of other people just to feel the rush of power and control, or for re-establishing a control taken from them. By fully controlling their victims, up to the decision of who lives and who dies, the serial murderers feel a sense of superiority. In other words, they enjoy playing the role of God. The problem is that the feeling of power and control disappears relatively fast, and makes the murderer plan the next murder in order again to feel the satisfaction he has felt during the previous torture and murder. Levin (2008) refers to the fact that serial murderers lack the necessary self-control to prevent them from executing the next murder, and there is an inference to the psychoanalytic theory of the weakness of the superego and the sociological theory of the lack of self-control.[145]

Levin (2008) moves to another theory for explaining the serial murder for the sake of power and control—the theory that refers to the sociopath, the one who lacks conscience, empathy, and guilt feelings. The full control is expressed through sadism that provides enjoyment and satisfaction by causing pain and fear in others. Sadism is addictive, and therefore the sociopath needs increasing doses of sadism in order to be satisfied. When this need is accompanied by a need of power and control, the combination leads to a serial murder. This is the only way in which the serial murderer can feel successful. Since he is not capable of achieving what he wants in a legitimate way through the main stream, he crosses the border of what is considered proper and moral which is an inference the Levin (2007) makes toward Merton's theory (1958).

Many of the serial murderers suffered a lot in childhood. They have gone through abuse, sexual abuse, or have been neglected, and learned to take their anger out on others, for instance, by abusing animals.[146] They do this abuse mainly with their own hands, in a close and personal way that provides them a sense of power and control. Abusing a family member can also facilitate their sense of vulnerability and helplessness. But the violence and suffering they cause others are not just reactions to their abuse in childhood, but also a rehearsal toward a sadistic violence they would execute in the future against various people.

One of the common myths is that achieving power is always done through (sexual) sadism. This is a mistake. There are types of serial murderers who achieve power and control without using sex, like medical personnel who strangle or poison their patients out of a will to play God in determining who lives and who dies (Vronsky, 2007).

Levin (2008) refers to hate crimes as a kind of serial murder that is also motivated out of a will of power and control. Other scientists[147] called these murderers assignment-oriented murderer. These crimes are directed at individuals who are considered "different," in terms of race, religion, nationality, origin, sexual tendency, disability, status or gender. A serial murder of these individuals gives the serial murderer a sense of superiority, power and control he has not felt in the past, and so he reaches a sense of high spirits. He feels important, as he has the power to decide who suffers or not.

"Hate crimes" are learned by the murderers in their childhood from their parents, teachers, friends, working mates, culture, and the mass media. Among some of these individuals a prejudice might become a pathological hatred.

I think that this category is too wide because it includes serial murderers who operate out of motives of power and control which may come from totally different sources. This kind of generalization leads to ignore significant motives which are very different from one another. For example, serial murderers who operate for the sake of achieving appreciation and prestige, as in Munchausen Syndrome, experience a sense of control over the life of the victim which provides them with an ultimate sense of power. But they are different from serial murderers who operate out of a will to feel power and control in relation to a certain social sector, when it comes from vengeance or ideology ("the assignment-oriented killer").

Society—There are children who do not develop an attachment with their parents for various reasons, such as neglect and abuse, and this leads to a sense of helplessness, alienation and solitude. Their way to social relationships is distorted and murderous, and can reach a point of cannibalism and murder and keeping parts of bodies for the sake of "company." These murderers do not want the suffering of the victim, and the murder is done quickly, usually by strangling. For example, Dahmer murdered young and lonely men. He strangled them to death and executed necrophilia on them. By eating parts of his victims he hoped to make them a permanent part of him (Martens & Palermo, 2005).

In my opinon, creating a category for serial murderers of this kind seems redundant as a main category in serial murder today. It is true that one should not ignore either category, but it seems to me that considering the meager number of cases in this category it could have been presented as a subcategory.

Ideology—Part of the murderers who have been defined in the literature as serial murderers operate out of ideology. Such ideology can express a racial perception against minorities in society, like the murderers that have been committed by the Manson family in order to inflame a war between whites and blacks, or a view according to which certain sectors in society, like prostitutes, have no right to exist. While in a serial murder there is reference to this type within the mission killer, the literature deals with various sects in another kind of discussion of murder which I defined as mass-serial murder, and it was described and discussed in the relevant chapter.

Summary

As can be seen, due to the multiplicity of definitions of serial murder, there cannot be an agreement of the criteria for classifying serial murderers. Part of the typologies deals with the motive, part with the characteristics of the murder and the murderer, and still another part with both.

One of the outstanding problems in the suggested typologies is the will to include all kinds of murderers which make the typology too detailed up to the point that it includes sub-categories that are almost nonexistent, or two categories overlap one another. Alternately, the will to generalize creates too wide categories which express mainly a motive of power and control, and in this way one cannot learn about the various characteristics of the various serial murderers who belong to the same general category.

As I see it, one has to determine that the classification of serial murderers would include the motive as well as central characteristics, as has been done in Holmes and Holmes (1998), within an attempt to prevent overlapping among categories. In other words, the typology has to be exhaustive and exclusive. But the question is what should be the main criterion for classification— motive or characteristics?

This question seems simple, but the answer to it is the heart of the problem. If the main criterion for classification is the characteristics, or just one of them, then we would reach a situation of overlapping between serial murderers who torture and humiliate their victims sexually out of excitement, and those who operate in the same way out of passion or out of a will for power and control until the murder takes place, and then the categories would not exclude one another. Another problem that characterizes the existing typologies is the determinism that characterizes an ideal model for theoretical purposes which does not necessarily exist in reality. In my opinion, one can adopt the idea that different serial murderers are spread on different points between a sequence of motives and characteristics. Such perception enables greater flexibility and a reference to characteristics rather than to tough deterministic decisions.

The first step in classifying is mapping the phenomenon. One of the problems in this field is that there are no accurate statistics regarding the frequency of the different cases of serial murder. Even in the event that such statistics are provided, due to disagreement of the definition of some of the mass and mass-serial murder cases which were considered as a serial murder of a certain type. These include the murder of a family by one of the parents, or a mass-serial murder that is done for ideological reasons. In spite of what has been said here, the lack of accurate statistics on the frequency of the different types of serial murder does not have to be a hindrance in classifying the phenomenon, because the classification was meant to exhaust and exclude those types of existing serial murder. After the mapping of the types of murder, one has to try to suggest motives with the help of the theoretical model that has been presented, with reference to outstanding characteristics and the location of the serial murderer on different ranges of outstanding characteristics in the literature and in reality.

The suggested typology I have defined as mass-serial would not include murders such as the killing of a family by one of the parents, murder with an ideological background, murder that has to do with the activity of the organized crime, and murder by assassins in the service of the government.

If we examine the types of murder and murderers by taking into consideration this limitation, we can map the serial murder cases into some types according to motive and main characteristics. In addition, I will suggest an integrative explanation for each category and allocate the specific serial murderer in relation to outstanding characteristics in theoretical literature, as well as in some of the typologies.

Positions of Serial Murderers on the Sequence/ Range of Central Characteristics

1. Preoccupation with Sex

The small number of research findings about serial murder show that almost seventy percent of the serial murder cases have to do with sex between the criminal and the victim. Sexual intercourse can be part of an examination whether the victim is a prostitute or not—if the victim would agree to have sex so that the criminal would, allegedly, spare her live, then in the eyes of the murderer she would be defined as a prostitute, and therefore she does not have the right to live.

Furthermore, sexual intercourse can be part of the murderer's activity for the sake of satisfaction, sadistic enjoyment, and so on, and it can be physical, or the murderer might abuse the victim by penetrating objects into her body while masturbating. In addition, there may be acts of necrophilia: The serial murderer might have sex with the body at the scene, or keep parts of her body for masturbating it he future. That is to say, the occupation with sex can be absent or minimal as in the first type I mentioned, or highly dominant as described here.

2. Acquaintance with the Victim

While in individual murder cases, there is usually an intimate acquaintance between the murderer and the victim, in a serial murder there can be several options, unlike the myth according to which it is always an attacker lying in ambush for his stranger victim. Part of the serial murder cases call for a close and intimate acquaintance between the murderer and the victim. These are the cases in which the murderer acts for the sake of achieving a material benefit through killing his wife, lover, and so on (Blue Beard). When it is a case of women murderers, this phenomenon is called the Black Widow.

A similar case is called Munchausen Syndrome by Proxy. These are usually mothers who cause their children to be sick, aiming to achieve attention from the environment.[148] Moreover, there are cases in which there is a personal acquaintance between the murderer and the victim, but in a lower level and less intimate. For example, a woman who takes care of patients in a home for the aged, and murders them for the sake of a financial benefit.

Other cases are characterized by a total lack of acquaintance between the murderer and his victim. One example is of murderers who act out of a psychosis, murderers out of sado-sexual motives, murderers who act out of an "ideology to purify society," and professional assassins who murder strangers who happened to be in the wrong place at the wrong time, or those who belong to a group of the population which the murderer sees as unworthy of living.

3. Power-Control Games

This category refers to actions executed by serial murderers aiming to achieve a sense of power and control over the victim and his life. These actions bring the murderer sexual and psychological satisfaction in various ways and enable him to fill deficiencies which stem from his childhood, or retrieve feelings of power and control he has lost through childhood traumas. These murderers tend to elongate the games of control in order to enjoy the sense of power, and there are those who even go on holding pictures, films and organs of the body in order to go on feeling their control over the victim.

Other murderers, who are not motivated by the need to feel power-control, would hurry to murder the victim because this is their goal. In this way, for instance, a murderer who acts out of an ideology for purifying society, or a psychopath-paranoid who acts for the sake of releasing tension due to a sense of threat of super-natural forces. These murderers do not focus on actions of power-control. The very execution of the murder is their main goal, and they would hurry to terminate the action as fast as possible.

4.   Multiple Crimes

There are serial murderers who are motivated by a paranoid psy-chosis or an ideological perception that one has to eliminate peo-ple who belong to groups in society which are perceived as un-worthy of living, like prostitutes, homeless people, and so on. These murderers murder their victims as a mission, and by doing so, complete their mission. Usually they do not rape the victim or steal her money, but "just" murder her.

On the other hand, there are serial murderers who operate from a secondary motive than the murder. For example, sexual-sadist murderers who execute severe sexual felonies on the victim before his death, and sometimes even afterwards; or murderers with a power-control motive who torture the victim for a long time and finally murder him, and are, therefore, involved in felo-nies of severe attack other than the murder.

There are also serial murderers whose motive is materially driven and in order to succeed, must murder the victim. The victim in these cases can be familiar, or a total stranger to the murderer.

5.   Focus on the Action or Focus on the Process

One can distinguish between serial murderers who are focused on the act of the murder, and others who are focused on the process. For instance, murderers who act out of a paranoid psychosis, murderers who are motivated by a material motive, and murderers who are motivated by an ideology for purifying society and are focused just on the murder, and not on the process.

On the other hand, one can find serial murderers for whom the murder is part of a wider process, or its peak. They follow a potential victim, seduce him, and bring him to a place that has been prepared in advance, where they abuse him for satisfying sexual and psychological needs, while using torturing and killing instruments which have been prepared in advance, and later deal with the removal of the body, dismembering it, or in necrophilia and keeping parts of the body.

As I will show, each type of the serial murderers has similar or different characteristics out of the six characteristics that have been indicated. These characteristics can be allocated on a certain range or a sequence of different murderers, from different categories or from the same one.

There is no way of examining which are the most important characteristics or criteria for our case. They have been chosen because there is a lot of literature about them, and following an examination of each of the types of serial murderers. Other scientists may suggest other characteristics. All the same, when examining the typology and the main characteristics that stem from it, we can see that these characteristics, in my opinion, set an important index in distinguishing among the different serial murderers, and at the same time enable examining similarities among different types of serial murderers which do not overlap among categories. In this way, we will be able to find, for instance, that murderers of different types who operate from totally different motives, and are similar in part of their characteristics. In this manner, I will be able to specify the variety of existing possibilities in reality without categorizing reality according to the typology. As I will demonstrate, the categories are broad and include a wide range of murderers who operate from the central motive in the category. Therefore, not all murderers in the category have to meet exactly the same criteria. One can argue that it poses a theoretical problem, but it presents the complicated reality with its varied possibilities within each category.

A New Typology of Serial Murder and Murderers

1. A serial murderer of strangers and acquaintances following a felony for the sake of a material benefit

This category is similar to the organized murderer, in which the way of operation, planning, execution, and leaving the scene clean of evidence point to organizing the serial murder as a non-spontaneous event. This category consists of a few sub-types: (a) a murder of family relatives, like spouses for receiving the money of their life insurance and inheritance; (b) a murder of patients who live in a treatment institution for the sake of receiving the social security money or an inheritance; (c) murder by a contract killer; (d) a serial murder of a stranger while executing a robbery or for the sake of a robbery, as well as eliminating the witness of a robbery. In this context, it is important to remind the reader that every case of robbery in which there is more than one victim at a time was defined as another type of murder: Mass-serial murder.

There are scientists who defined this type of serial murder as a "crime-murder," whereas I think that this term is problematic, since murder is a crime by itself. This classification exhausts and excludes the category, since its definition relies mainly on the motive which is the outstanding characteristic for identification. There is no problem in this case to use the motive as the main criterion, because there are no other categories in this typology since there is a material motive for murder. In addition, this is the only category in which the murderer can know or not know his victims, unlike other categories, in which the murderer murders only strangers. The material motive is common to all four sub-types in this category, and knowing or not knowing the victim has to do with access, availability, and vulnerability of the victim, rather than to a personal sentiment toward him.

One of the criticisms of this category can be that it does not relate to all the cases, since there is a serial murder of rape victims, and this is also a murder that is connected to the execution of another felony. But since I have explicitly defined it as relating to cases of material benefit, then rape victims, for example, do not belong to this type of serial murder.

This category suits men and women alike, and most of the women murderers operate out of this motive (the Black Widow). Recently, there was a serial murderer woman found who worked as a prostitute and murdered victims for the sake of robbery.

Theoretical Explanation

The ability to murder a relative, like a spouse, for the sake of get-ting his/her money, as well as the ability to murder a person in cold blood who has never hurt the murderer in any way, just for the sake of receiving the money, is common to the murderers in this category. This serial murderer is characterized by an antiso-cial personality disorder. Three theoretical socioeconomic expla-nations suit this category.

One is Merton's anomie theory, in relation to the pattern of the "innovator"—individuals in society, who feel frustration and lack self-worth since they are incapable of materializing the dream of wealth, would choose deviant and criminal ways for achieving material benefits. A very small part of these individuals, who have a background of antisocial personality disorder, would use every possible measure for achieving their share of the cake, i.e., the end justifies the means, which is a guilt-neutralizing mean. For instance, American soldiers who served in Vietnam in special units which were intended for the elimination of North Vietnam-ese seniors, have not found their place after the war, and noticed that while they served their homeland, others were busy making money and accumulated a fortune. Some of these released soldiers have become serial contract killers.[149]

Another theoretical explanation which can be connected to these facts is the theory of rational choice—the choice to take the lives of people for making money is a rational choice. The murder-er chooses this way in order to maximize the profit and minimize the loss. When we speak about a professional assassin or a murderer who kills a relative who does his job professionally, the chance of being caught is very low. Therefore, a rational choice to make a fortune by using means that do not risk the freedom of the murderer seems attractive to this kind of person. One should bear in mind that people with antisocial personality disorder are capable of making rational choices, maybe even more so than the layman, since they can calculate, plan, and decide things with no emotional involvement.

Another theoretical explanation in this category belongs to the routine activity theory. The theory relates to the murder of strangers whose modern life has taken them out of their protected home. But this theory is well implemented in the murder of spouses as well. The routine of life of a couple enables a variety of possibilities of poisoning (through regular food at a regular time, or chronic medications) or strangling (the spouse goes to visit her mother or sister, and the murderer strangles her out of the house and prepares an alibi for that period of time, and later on, gives excuses for her disappearance by reporting that his wife is sick, is on a family visit, and so on).

As for the professional assassin, the extent of routine in the victim's life facilitates the possibility of hurting him during a business trip, at a regular time that he goes out to work, and so on. As for a robbery and murdering witnesses (victims), here, too, planning in advance enables knowing when the businessman or the employees finish their day's work, who manages the daily profit, and so on.

The argument that all it takes for executing such a murder is an antisocial behaviour disorder seems superficial. As we have seen in Merton's theory, such a murderer goes through a process of restructuring or reframing. From the moment he "decides" to fantasize how he would get the money and what he would do with it, the murderer has to go through a stage of neutralizing guilt, as he finds motives and justifications for his murderous act prior to executing it. These justifications can include a rational aspect of withdrawing from personal responsibility due to a previous exploitation on the part of the spouse or the dependents, so that there is a denial of the victim and the damage ("I made this money honestly," "He deserves it"); blaming society and addressing higher loyalties, like a concern for the future of the children. Another way of neutralizing can be done by depersonalizing the victim. All these enable the execution of the act and justifying it before and after the execution.

The reason why the murderer goes on with his murders is that the impulse for achieving a material benefit is never satisfied. He wants more and more, and is never satisfied. From this aspect, one can speak about an obsessive and maybe even addictive behaviour.

Allocating the Serial Murderer in Relation to the Six Central Characteristics
Sexual behaviour—Among serial murderers motivated by material benefits, there is lack of sexual behaviour. The goal of the murderer is to achieve material goods through murdering the victim, and sex is not a primary or secondary motive for the murder.

Acquaintance with the victim—Since this is a wide category with sub-categories, it has varied characteristics. Among some of the serial murderers of this category there is not any acquaintance with the victim, like in a case where the murderer robs the victim and murders him in order to conceal evidence, or when it is a case of a professional assassin.

On the other hand, another subcategory is of murderers who know the victim through a medium level of acquaintance. For example, nurses in a home for the aged who murder the victim for the sake of receiving his life insurance, national security, and so on. Since the victim is treated by the murderer, there is a certain kind of acquaintance between them, although not in a highly intimate level.

Another subcategory is a murder of spouses or lovers in order to receive life insurance, inheritance, and so on, and in this case the acquaintance is intimate and deep.

Power-control games—Apparently, this category seems irrelevant to power-control games since the murderer acts for the sake of receiving the money or property of the victim and nothing else. But on second thought, there may be a wider scope that characterizes this category. For instance, a man or a woman who poison their spouse in order to gain the inheritance or life insurance do not play power-control games in the regular way, as it is done in other categories, but all the same, one cannot argue that there are no power games at all in this case. The wife who feeds her husband with poisoned soup, poison she had bought and put there secretly. She takes care not to eat from the soup, and as her husband eats it, her thoughts are busy with the extent of the influence of the poison, and she might laugh in her heart or fantasize about what she would do with the money she would inherit. Therefore, one can say that in this category some serial murderers do not operate power-control games, while others do use them, but only within themselves.

Involvement of another crime—In this index one can also see two poles: Serial murderers whose activity is focused on murdering the victim, aiming to receive his money as heirs or legal beneficiaries. On the other hand, murdering the victim in order to take his property is a robbery, or a robbery and killing the victim in order to remove evidence.

Focus on the action or on the process—some of the serial murderers in this category focus on the act of the murder, as in the case of an armed robbery in which the businessman is murdered swiftly, the money is taken from the cash register and the murderer escapes from the scene, or alternately, in the case of the professional assassin. Some of the serial murderers in this category focus on the process for a short period of time, as in the murder of dependents in a home for the aged in order to receive their national security without reporting their death. On the other hand, mainly in murder of relatives, it is a process of long planning: Choosing the ideal victim (a rich husband), seducing the victim and establishing a relationship until the marriage, acquiring the poison, poisoning the victim, and so on. This is a process and only at its end would the victim die and the murderer achieve the financial benefit.

A serial murderer who acts from a paranoid psychosis
While the murderer, for the sake of material benefit, acts rational-ly and knows how to distinguish between good and evil, on the other pole of the sequence there is the serial murderer who acts from psychosis. This murderer suffers from a mental disease whose expression is a disconnection from reality, and a reference to his inner world as reality. He hears voices and sees sights which come from his psyche, and he refers to them as if they were real. Such a murderer is defined as one who is not aware of the quality of his deeds and does know how to distinguish between good and evil.

The only benefit he receives from executing serial murders is a relief of the threats on his life. The paranoia is expressed by hearing voices and seeing visions which instruct him whom to murder, threatening him that otherwise he would be hurt by su-perhuman powers, like Satan, God, and so on. When he obeys these instructions, his life is saved and he feels a sense of release and relief from the threat. In other words, from his subjective viewpoint which is objective as far as he is concerned, he murders for the sake of survival.

The instruction of who should be murdered comes, of course, from his sick psyche and can be explained by mental health pro-fessionals. This kind of murderer fits to the category of the unor-ganized murderer. He acts without planning, from the severe dis-tress of a threat on his life. He is not busy in rational choosing, but just attacks, aiming to kill his victim as fast as possible. As a re-sult, he does not prepare a weapon, but uses a weapon he finds at the scene, for example, strangling a woman with her bra. He leaves a lot of forensic evidence at the scene. Usually he does not deal with avoiding being caught. He is not afraid of the police, only the superhuman power which threatens his life. For this reason, he does not bother to hide the body and does not feel any need of contact with the victim or keeping a souvenir of him after his death. This category suits men and women alike, where the psychosis dictates the victims.

Theoretical Explanation

The theoretical explanation for this category is simple and relatively clear. We deal here with a mental illness that is expressed in the inability to distinguish between objective and subjective reality. In other words, reality and imagination are mixed in his psyche and perception of this type of murderer.

The psychosis under discussion is characterized by paranoia. The murderer feels he is persecuted by superhuman powers or by specific people who want, according to him, to kill him. In a case of a persecution of superhuman powers (demons, God, and others) they would try to kill him if he does not follow their instructions. The murderer is not aware of his illness, and he indeed hears the voices and sees the visions of these powers. He cannot distinguish between good and evil, and as far as he is concerned, he must follow the instructions in order to stay alive. There is no rational choice made by the murderer, but one can say that his behaviour is "rational" in relation to his "reality": He prefers to murder others rather than die. The murderer fears for his life and therefore executes the instructions quickly and with no hesitations or planning in order to facilitate the pressure and tension he is under in light of the threats on his life.

After the execution of the murder the murderer feels a relief and release of the state of threatening pressure, and calms down until the next time when he gets "instructions" to murder. He goes on murdering because after the cooling-off period, relaxation disappears, and he "gets instructions" to murder again.

2. Allocating the Serial Murderer in Relation to the Six Central Characteristics

Preoccupation with sex—For these serial murderers sex and sexual intercourse have nothing to do with the murder.

Acquaintance with the victim—It is customary to think that these serial murderers lie in ambush to total strangers, motivated by a paranoid psychosis. In fact, a major part of the murderers in this category murder total strangers who happened to be in the wrong time and place.

As I have argued, in a small part of the cases the psychosis dictates the serial murderer who to murder. When such a murderer says he has received an instruction to murder the son of his neighbour, and then his own children, it is obvious that his psyche determined the victims, and therefore he knows the victims in part of the cases.

Power-control games—It is not clear if power games are part of the paranoid imagination.[150] They act quickly to finish the murder with no planning, while leaving evidence at the scene. The psychosis is what prevents them from any kind of sophistication and a planned and controlled way of operation.

Involvement of another crime—Psychotic murderers murder in order to remove a threat of being hurt by super-powers. They are not interested in money or sexual relations with the victim, and their only ambition is to take the life of the victim under the instruction of these powers.

Focusing on the process or on the action—As has been said, these murderers cannot act "freely" due to their illness. They operate in the proximity of their place of work or living ("convenience area"), and focus on the action. They attack the victim suddenly, aiming to kill him as fast as possible. They do not plan the act, and do not prepare the weapon of the murder. After the attack they leave the body at the scene, as well as other evidence.

3. Ideological Serial Murder and Murderers Who Want to Purify Society

This category suits the category of the mission killer. One has to distinguish between a serial murder which is done by ideological groups, like the Manson family who murdered whites, trying to make the impression that the murderers were black people in order to arouse a racial war which I have defined as a mass-serial murder, and a serial murder executed by an individual or a team. In this category I will refer to a serial murder that is executed mostly by individuals against certain groups in society. Since this category has been discussed elaborately previously, I will indicate here just the central points.

We have to pay attention to the fact that unlike a mass-serial murder, most of the serial murder cases are done within the ethnic group and not among groups. As a rule, this category does not speak about a serial murder by black people or Hispanics by a white individual, or vice versa.

The serial murderer learned to label a certain social sector, or sectors, as unworthy. This learning can come from talks at home toward a certain group, prejudice he has heard from his peers, acquaintance with a member of this group, and attributing negative characteristics to the whole group following this acquaintance, and especially from the mass media which present these groups in a negative and maligning way. The mass media creates a depersonalization of marginal groups and present them as a threat or a danger to society.

The average civilized person who absorbs these messages would develop a prejudice toward these sectors, and may regard them as a threat in his heart. In more extreme cases, he would not employ people from a certain sector, complain to the police about prostitutes who stay in his neighbourhood, educate his children to contempt and hatred toward the people of a certain sector, and so on. Most of the people stop at this point in relation to their attitude toward sectors like minorities, immigrants, homeless people, prostitutes, disconnected youth, and so on.

But when such social messages fall on the ears of people with an "authoritative personality," who feel they have been hurt by people of a certain sector in a real or imagined way, the result might be a serial murder of people who belong to this category. The murderer would usually choose random victims who meet one condition: Belonging to the category that is considered by him as unworthy of living. The choice will be done according to availability and vulnerability of the victim.

The focus is on the act of the murder, and the murderer does not deal with fantasies and long-term planning, but looks for the most vulnerable victim, executes the murder and removes forensic evidence from the scene. He does not deal with dismembering the body or with necrophilia. Evidence of sexual intercourse usually is not found, as the victim is considered contemptible and repulsive as far as the murderer is concerned, except a case in which the murderer examines whether the woman in front of him is ready to have sex with him in exchange for her life, and by so doing, she confirms being a prostitute. A serial murder of this kind characterizes, in most cases, male serial murderers.

Theoretical Explanation

It takes learning to hate a whole sector of people just because of their occupation, origin, or skin color. This is a process of social learning, in which the individual learns to see people not only as contemptible, but even as unworthy of living. The whole sector is perceived by the murderer as a collection of potential victims. The murderer would not hurt a familiar person as a vengeance, but would choose randomly someone who belongs to this sector, just because he belongs, and not from any personal reason. That is, the ideal victim does not need to have any specific trait or act from the past for belonging to the population that the murderer has learned to hate. It is probable that he would choose the most vulnerable and available victim. One should indicate that in some sectors all the people of the sector belong to the vulnerable and available population for the serial murder, like street prostitutes, wandering youth, homeless people, and so on. There is nobody who would care for them or try to find out what happened to them, and nobody would notice their absence.

Beyond social learning and the influence of the media, it takes a personality that would make the social feelings of contempt, or the social condemnation into a call for the extermination of those deemed not worthy of living. One possibility is a personality with an antisocial disorder who does not feel empathy toward the other person. Moreover, this personality does not examine the results in the long run. Such a personality can regard those who belong to the contemptible category as sub-humans who do not deserve to live, and even refer to this group as causing all the personal and social problems of the individual.[151]

According to the neutralizing theories, the motives, and the social heroes, the murderer would be able to not only excuse his behaviour in a variety of neutralizing techniques, but also even feel like a "social hero," who fights the "public enemy." It would enable the murderer to operate, neutralize undesired feelings after the action, and repeat it again and again. An outstanding neutralizing technique is addressing higher loyalties, like the family and the community, as the murderer would argue that thanks to him his and the neighbourhood children would have healthy, pure and more deserving lives, with no prostitutes, homeless people or junkies around. This feeling of the murderer is most important if we remember the origins of the development of the antisocial disorder. The murderer who grew up with a significant sense of helplessness can feel, maybe for the first time, as powerful and as one who is known as such to others. Such a feeling can be intoxicating and addictive, and also explain the next murder.

The use of structuring or reframing would be done with the help of the techniques that have been presented above. The process begins with depersonalization of the victim. Later on, the murderer would use the neutralizing technique and the feeling of mission as a social hero. After the action, these techniques would serve for relieving "improper" feelings like guilt, and would pave the way to the next murder.

Furthermore, there is reference to the routine activities theory. In modern society, mobility is stronger, social control is weaker, and more people stay out of their homes or any controlling or supporting framework. The high mobility enables more young people to abandon their homes and move in the marginal areas of the big cities. A higher number of homeless people stay in parks and alleyways in defined areas; more women wander while working as prostitutes on particular streets and allies, cheap hotels and public parks, and, in addition, more young people move from one place to another by taking lifts with unknown strangers.

All these provide the serial murderer with a potential reservoir of victims who are defined in his eyes as undesired, with no supervision and no control. He can easily offer a lift to students in college who cannot afford to purchase a car, he can easily take a prostitute in his car or invite her to a hotel room where there is no registration, and he can easily seduce and kidnap youngsters and homeless people. These victims are characterized by very high vulnerability and availability which serve the goals of the serial murderer perfectly. It would take a long time, if at all, until someone would feel their absence, and even then it is not certain that the law enforcement authorities would allocate forces to search for the murderer since the victim is "unimportant."

Allocating the Serial Murderer in Relation to the Six Central Characteristics
Sexual behaviour—Among these murderers, there is no preoccupation with sex in general since the victims belong to a group considered improper. However, among some of them there is such an interest in a secondary way.[152]

Acquaintance with the victim—From what is known from the literature; there is no acquaintance between the murderer and the victim. The murderer does not choose for a target an acquaintance that belongs to a social category that is defined as unworthy, he randomly takes a victim who belongs to the same category. The only condition is having the occupational-social characteristics which are perceived as unworthy by the murderer. But there may be a situation when the murderer knows individuals who belong to the "unworthy group," and exactly for this reason develops an ideology that one has to eliminate the specific individuals, or other people (strangers and random) who belong to the group.

Power-control games—According to the literature, there are no control games between the murderer and the victim in these cases. The control of the murderer over the victim takes place, actually, by the very fact that the murderer exterminates the one who is defined by him as belonging to a group that is unworthy of living. The murderer is motivated to kill the victim quickly so that he would not exist to hurt or poison society. Therefore, he does not deal with power games and tends to finish his action quickly.[153]

Involvement of another crime—Although one could have assumed that the murderer would rape the victim who is perceived as unworthy, or rob his property, the very perception that the victim is unworthy makes him, and apparently his property as well, as untouchable in the eyes of the murderer. There is an option which I cannot examine, that there are cases of rape and robbery of unworthy victims in the eyes of the murderer. But as has been mentioned, from what is known even today, we have to determine that in this category no other crime is involved beyond the will to exterminate the victim.

Focusing on the process or on the action—This serial murderer aspires to murder victims who belong to a group that is perceived in his eyes as unworthy of living. There is no planning, seducing, transferring to another place that has been prepared in advance, abuse as well as actions of dismembering the body, or necrophilia. The murderer aspires to finish the act quickly, and the only thing that motivates him is the killing of the victim. Therefore, this is usually a case of a quick murder, with a relatively low extent of planning and tortures, focusing only on the act.

4. Serial Murderers Who Murder from Frustration/Humiliation

One could have combined this type of serial murder and murderers as part of the previous category of an ideological murder for the sake of purifying society. But since the motives in both cases are very different, it is desirable to separate between the two types. Although there may be similarities, there is no overlapping and in this way we achieve the goal of an exhaustive and exclusive category.

These serial murderers act out of a motive that is not self-explanatory, unless we know the history of the murderer. These are people who experienced frustration and humiliation in their childhood from parental figures, mainly the mother. Their lives were characterized by abuse and trauma which was expressed by sexual and physical abuse, neglect, criminal parents who used psychoactive substances and so on. In this situation there could not develop a positive attachment and relationships between parents and children.

Children who grow up in a family of this kind, and who have no alternative support group, like the expanded family, a foster family or something similar, might react to the childhood trauma with a behaviour that ranges from sorrow, solitude and depression and the development of significant psychological disturbances which are typical for post-trauma situations.

These children experience significant frustration and humiliation, accompanied by a sense of undermined self-esteem and severe helplessness. The child feels he cannot change his life because he does not control it, as the control is in the hands of the abusing parent. These children and adolescents are incapable of establishing a significant social attachment, and they find themselves rejected by their peers, and have difficulties achieving real goals in the educational system. Some of them try to unload the frustration feelings through abusing animals or hurting other children, but after a short period of time, these attempts of releasing the accumulated frustration are not perceived as efficient or sufficient.

One of the central problems these children and adolescents confront is the inability to unload their frustration against the frustrating factor since they are dependent on him physically and psychologically. The child and the adolescent develop a fantasy world in which they not only escape from the harsh everyday reality, but can feel excitement and relief while imagining the violent actions which would unload the accumulated frustration. The violent contents of the fantasy are absorbed from his surrounding culture that is soaked with violence. In addition, the culture emphasizes individualism and achieving happiness as supreme goals in society, and it strengthens the importance of fantasy in the eyes of these adolescents.

In their imagination, the ideal victim is a total stranger who has the characteristics of the abusing parent. In this respect, the adolescents execute a displacement and target the original frustrating object through an innocent victim. As has been said, the victim has to have characteristics which resemble the abusing parent, like color of hair, the eyes of the neglecting or abusing mother, her body structure and may be even her occupation. For this reason, I thought there is a certain similarity with the previous category—the future murderer chooses a victim who belongs to a certain sector, or a social group which has certain characteristics, and decides that this group with it members is not worthy of living. But unlike the previous category, in this case there is no ideology of any kind, only a will to release feelings of frustration and humiliation, and to renew balance in the individual.

The stage of fantasy fills the time of the youngster and young adult, and is a means of excitement and satisfaction for him. Over the course of time, this familiar excitement dwindles away, and a certain adjustment, getting used to, or endurance is established, just as a body gets used to a certain level of drug in the blood. Through various means which will be discussed later, the future murderer manages to break barriers and live out the execution his first murder. There may be a provocation that serves as a catalyst, or a pharmacological influence of psychoactive substances, but it is not mentioned in the research literature.

As has been said, the ideal victim has to meet similar characteristics of the abusing parent, but choosing the victim is incidental and the victim is unfamiliar to the murderer. The experience of the murder, including severe sexual abuse[154] of the victim prior to murdering him, is a means of releasing the frustration the murderer has accumulated over a long time. The abuse and the murder enable him to experience potency (power) and control which he has missed significantly throughout the years before the murder. After the murder he feels a renewed balance, and the in- ner order in his psyche is been restored. We may raise the ques- tion: Why does the murderer go on executing additional murders, and is not satisfied with the first one? This question has two an- swers. One possibility is that the murderer, in his imagination, has written a script and prepared the directing of the scene of the abuse and the murder, including positioning himself as the main actor, but in reality, the victim does not perform according to his plans, does not know to recite the lines of the text and does not behave according to the murderer's expectations. The deviation from the plan arouses frustration in the murderer, and pushes him to try to materialize the script in his head once more as he repeat- edly tries to perfect it.

The second explanation is that unloading the frustration to- ward a substitute cannot provide the murderer with the enduring satisfaction for which he had hoped. Since he cannot attack the original frustrating and humiliating source, he tries to achieve the expected satisfaction in the next murders, and his frustration is expressed by an escalation of his abusive and murderous behav- iour, sometimes including "overkill."

Such serial murder is characterized by murdering women as victims and, to a lesser degree, men, as well. In the case of murder- ing men, it has been found that the murderer was a homosexual or a bisexual. Among the cases of a male victim, there were cases of cannibalism, and scientists (Newton (2006), Ferguson et al. (2003); Schlesinger, (1998)) claimed that the goal of the murderer was some kind of immortal preservation of the victim. It is my opinion that this description is a romanticization of the murderer and the murder. According to my interpretation, the murderer who preserves parts of the body or performs cannibalism, does not want to preserve the victim, but rather looks for constant proof of his power as the body parts serve as a kind of medal.

Cannibalism does not always express a will of containing the victim, and it can testify of the murderer's power versus the victim as an act of hunting. Preserving parts of the body can serve, for the murderer, as a decisive proof of his power and control over the victim which symbolizes the imaginary attitude toward the abusive parent ("Not only can you not hurt me, but when I look at you, I know I've defeated you forever"). In this context we can mention a known phenomenon in the battlefield, when soldiers cut off parts of the body of the enemy, especially the heart or the head. This type of serial murder characterizes the absolute majority of men victims.

Theoretical Explanation

Two central explanations for the murderer's behaviour are taken from the fields of psychology and social psychology. One refers to the theory of *dissociative identity disorder* (DID). There is a background of a childhood trauma, and the child, and later the adolescent, disconnects part of the neutral identity and creates a dissociative identity where he preserves the memories of the trauma, a reference to the will of vengeance, or releasing the frustration that stems from his helplessness versus the abusive parent. It is not a repression mechanism, but a disconnection of part of the identity. The child cannot cope with the abusive parent and certainly cannot come up against him, and the disconnection enables him shift among several identities, since in the disconnected part of the identity he can create for himself a fantasy world. In the fantasy, the individual can construct a script of releasing the frustration and the humiliation he has experienced with no limits of morale and norms. Some murderers called this dissociative identity as the "dark side," the "shadow" or the like.

The literature about serial murderers refers to the individual's fantasy world, but it has not managed to explain what enables or makes the individual materialize the fantasy he has created for himself. There is accumulative evidence of a mutual awareness of identities, or at least that the neutral identity is aware of the existence and contents of the dissociative one, with a meaningful dynamics going on between the identities. Within the dissociative identity, the individual can feel potency, control and even satisfaction which are achieved through the introduction of violent contents into the fantasy. These contents are not invented, but exist in the world of the future serial murderer. They are part of his culture and of the messages coming through the mass media, through which he can establish a differentiated identity with other serial murderers who have become culture heroes, identify with them, imitate them or want to achieve greater publicity and acknowledgment than them.

But when the individual shifts from the dissociative identity to the neutral one, he feels an enormous emptiness. The very contents which brought him satisfaction and a sense of control over his life disappear, and instead he finds himself in the same tough reality of victimhood, a sense of helplessness, frustration and loneliness. With no tools to cope with the tough and frustrating reality, the individual shifts time and again to the dissociative identity which brings him satisfaction. As time goes by, the duration of staying in the dissociative identity would increase.

In the course of time the excitement and elation the individual feels from his dissociative identity fades away due to getting used to it, and he heeds stronger stimuli in order to feel the same satisfaction, just like a drug addict who needs greater quantities of drugs. On the other hand, in the dissociative identity he also encounters barriers in materializing his fantasy coming from the superego or the conscience which cannot contradict those of the neutral identity. Hence the individual starts operating techniques of neutralization, such as lack of responsibility and guilt, denying the victim and others, as well as using techniques of reframing which are reinforced by a culture that makes heroes out of serial murderers while depersonalizing the victims. In addition, the individual feels an immediate threat of his existence, at least in the psychological sense, and therefore creates a set of justifications for the future murder actions.

Only after having completed this process he is able to materialize his fantasy in reality. In the new situation the inhibition capability of the neutral identity is weak since it does not provide him with a sense of excitement and power, and causes him a sense of emptiness and helplessness. In the dissociative identity, on the other hand, the individual uses displacement and generalization of the victimizing figure, and finds satisfaction in a fantasy of murder and tortures of a stranger victim who has similar characteristics of the victimizing parent.

After the murder the neutral identity "takes the lead" of the individual after the shock of his actions. When the neutral identity is dominant, the individual would feel again an immense emptiness versus the satisfaction and power he had experienced before, during and after the murder. This feeling motivates him to move to the dissociative identity and try to enjoy the memories of this sense of elation. Moreover, the dominance of the neutral identity might cause the individual feel guilt feelings which are unpleasant for him, and this is an additional reason for his shifting to the dissociative identity. This dynamics between identities explains the cooling-off period he goes through until the next murder.

The next murder will come because the individual feels frustration, as the fantasy was not materialized in the way he had anticipated, and because he does not feel the expected release of the feeling of frustration and humiliation the original victimizer had caused him. This is why he would repeat his deeds with a certain escalation that can be seen in a shorter period of time between one murder and the next, in the level of abusing the victim, in preserving parts of the body, and other things. In the light of this explanation one can understand why there is a serialism of murders and why there is a cooling-off period between one murder and the next.

If we look at it through the psychosocial viewpoint, we can refer to the theory of the "broken identity." The individual who has gone through abuse feels stained and different from other children, rejected and broken. In addition to the trauma and as result of it, and the absence of a supportive attachment with substitute figures, the individual experiences difficulties in studies, social rejection, loneliness and emptiness. As a result of this situation his identity is cracked and broken into two identities: The virtual identity and the real identity which contains murderous contents. Such an individual feels distress from his inability to express his real identity in the social world, a world which would not be able to accept it, and therefore he murders victims who meet the requirements of the fantasy. Only in the situation of murder can he show safely his real identity with no fear. After the murder the individual feels a release and relief by being able to express his real identity, and returns to his virtual identity and normative behaviour. In the course of time, the pleasant memory of the authentic expression of his real identity through murder, together with the pressure to experience it again, would bring about additional murders in the future. This explains both the cooling-off period and the seriality of murders.

An additional important theory from the field of criminology, the theory of routine activity, deals more with the way of executing the crime rather than the reasons for doing it. As has been said, the murderer fantasizes of a figure with certain characteristics, like gender, occupation, look, and so on. Nowadays more women go out of their home to work or for recreation activity, and their home is not their castle any more. At the same time, we can find greater mobility among men, like wanderers, homeless, and people who look for their future in the big cities. In this state of affairs, it is easier for the serial murderer to find a victim who meets the criteria he looks for.

Allocating the Serial Murderer in Relation to the Six Central Characteristics
Preoccupation with sex—Among these murderers, unlike the next category, preoccupation with sex is usually in a low-medium level, if at all. Since the murderer develops a fantasy in which the

victim symbolizes the abusive parent, he has, even in this situation, a normative difficulty to fantasize having sex with a parental figure. But all the same, the fantasy can sometimes contain a sexual component in this category as well.

Acquaintance with the victim—One of the problems of murderers in this category is their inability to attack the original object of humiliation due to a physical and emotional dependency on him. Therefore, the victim is a symbol of the original victimizer. This is the reason for an absolute unfamiliarity between the victim and the murderer, as the victim has to symbolize in a certain way the abusive parent, for instance through body structure, hair color, belonging to a certain group in the population, and so on.

Power-control games—As previously mentioned, the murder serves as a way of releasing frustration or humiliation accumulated in the murderer's psyche for years. These feeling have been assimilated in his fantasies, and he acts according to the script that has gone through his imagination for endless times. He is not interested just in exterminating the innocent victim, but in transferring unto him the set of abuses that would enable him to re-experience control over the life of the victim, and through it over his own life. This is a process in which the victim becomes the murderer's punching bag who wants the victim to go through great sufferings as a reprisal for what the victimizer had caused the murderer. This is the reason why power-control games are a central motive among these murderers, through which they reach some kind of balance for the harsh feeling of helplessness they had experienced, since in this manner they experience a sense of justice and equilibrium.

Involvement of another crime—In addition to murder, there is an involvement in a serious attack which belongs to the stage of abuse. Referring to a crime of an attack when there is a murder can be seen ridiculous, but we have to bear in mind that the murder can come only at the height of the process of tortures in which the murderer may construct models of torturing instruments from various historical periods and try them on the victim. The murderer may cut off pieces from the victim's body while he is still alive as a goal, not just as a means of killing him. All the murderer's actions are done almost automatically, because he has repeated them again and again in his fantasies.

Focusing on the action or on the process—In order that a serial murderer of this type would be able to unload emotions of frustration or humiliation, he has to choose an unfamiliar figure, but one who symbolizes the original abusing or humiliating figure. For this end he has to find the ideal victim for him, first in fantasy, and then in reality. He may find the ideal victim and first fantasize of what he would do to him, and only later on go out to execute it in reality. In the stage of shifting to execution, the murderer has to allocate the ideal victim, follow him and seduce him to come with him to the place he has prepared. After a set of torturing the victim would go through, the murderer can dismember the body (but not in every case), and remove it from the scene.

All the above show us that there is focusing on the process, in which the murder is one part in a chain of actions that express for the murderer feelings of power and control. In other words, the death of the victim is, for part of the murderers, the peak of the sense of power, while for others the maximal sense of power and control is achieved while the victim is still alive, and death is only the end of the process.

5.   Sexual-Sadist Serial Murder and Murderers

This category contains types of serial murder and murderers which have been defined as "hedonistic." These are murderers for whom serial murder is part of the process and certainly not the main goal. In this category one can refer to a variety of sub-types of serial murderers, while the main difference between them is that part finish the process in the murder, and others keep parts of the body for necrophilic goals. This difference does not justify establishing a separate sub-type. Another difference has to do with the extent of sadism. While one serial murderer can enjoy "light" sadism, another would need dramatic tortures of the victim in order to feel satisfaction.[155]

All the serial murderers in this category have a common characteristic of a deficiency of a sense of power and control which is expressed through materializing power and dominance toward the victim, mainly through sexual sadism. The murderer has learned to connect violent and fatal sexuality with sexual satisfaction, and he sees the victim as a tool for materializing his sadist-sexual passions. The difference between the necrophiles and those who are not is in the will to preserve the experience and the exploitation of the victim as a tool.

Various scientists have mistakenly linked this category with the previous one which deals with the release of frustration and humiliation feelings on the part of the murderer and other phenomena. The current category deals explicitly with learning. The murderer has learned, as has been mentioned, to link between sexuality and murderous violence, and in a small part of the cases the murderer does not mean the victim would die, and death happens as a result of "extra" abuse of the victim. In addition, it can be that in a small part of the cases of this category the murder of the victim is done in order not to leave a living witness who would be able to incriminate the murderer. It is my opinion that murderers who belong to this category act with the aim to murder. It is not a mistake in the extent of abuse, and it is not an attempt to make witnesses to disappear. The murder is necessarily the central characteristic of the link between violence and sexuality; otherwise the murderer would not achieve sexual satisfaction.

A serial murder of this type is characteristic of men, and the absolute majority of the victims are women. There can be cases of murder of men by men, but they are almost unknown, unlike the previous category. There are cases which belong to this category that are executed with the help of women, when they are the spouses of the serial murderer. There are also cases in which there is a team of a few men who are usually relatives.

As I have mentioned, unlike other categories like murder out of motives of material benefit, an assignment murder, and others, the current category deals with serial murder as the focus of the murderer is not on the act of murder, but sometimes it is part of a long process, and it is the peak of the process or a central stage in it.

The process contains a surveillance of the victim and seducing him to come with the murderer to a place he has prepared in advance. In this place the murderer feels safe, and he operates severe tortures against the victim while producing sexual satisfaction from causing suffering to the victim, from knowing that he controls him and also from his pleas for mercy. The sadist satisfaction does not come only from the victim's pleas and the sense of superiority the murderer feels, but from his being able to cause pain and suffering. Some of the literature, such as Levin (2008), Wright et al. (2003), and DeFronzo (2007) claims that sadism takes place only when the victim pleas for mercy. I claim that sadism does not necessarily require an arousing verbalism, and it stems from the very sense of power the murderer experiences, maybe for the first time in his life, when he subjugates another person to his wills. At the same time there is no doubt that he feels satisfaction from the victim's behaviour which can be expressed in verbal pleas, tears, screams and other things which show him the extent of suffering of the victim. From this respect, there is similarity between this serial murderer and violent rapists who experience excitement not from the sexual act, but from the victims' suffering (Holmes & Holmes, 1998; DeFronzo, 2007).

In this respect there is similarity to the previous category, by the fact that the murderer experiences an immense feeling of potency.

This feeling is linked with the sense of helplessness of the murderer in his childhood, and establishing the connection between sexuality and violence. After the murderer has experienced satisfaction in his relations with the victim which can come through a direct sexual intercourse or through penetrating objects to the victim's organs, the murderer gets used to the situation and he escalates his sadist acts in order to feel the elation he has felt before.

There is an additional point to be clarified here. In previous typologies it was suggested that a serial murder of this kind was meant to confirm for the murderer his sexuality, and prove he is better than other men. This claim is not true, in my opinion, in relation to a serial murder, but in relation to cases of rape (the kind rapist, the smiling, and so on). A serial murderer is not interested in confirming his sexual capability, but in his absolute control over the victim which reaches its peak in the murder (Arndt et al. 2004).

In this context, Newton (2006) raises an argument according to which one should not distinguish between sexual felonies and violent felonies, because sexual attack is violent by definition. This argument refers to those scientists who claim that sex is not the issue here, and the felony is meant to provide the criminal with a sense of power and control. According to his opinion, a serial murderer with a sexual background develops out of other sexual criminals, where the murderer chooses victims according to his preferences: Children, youngsters, young women, adult or older women.

After the murderer experiences the sadist-sexual satisfaction he has looked for, he feels a temporary relaxation that explains the cooling-off period. In this respect he is similar to the serial murderers of the previous category. Part of the murderers continue the experience through necrophilia with parts of the body, while others enjoy looking at pictures and videos in which they commemorated the events, and others make do with using their memory.

Theoretical Explanation

The central explanation for this category is the combination of two personality disorders: Antisocial personality disorder and narcissism. The common characteristic for both of them is the inability to love the other person, and seeing him as a means for satisfying the individual's needs. These two disorders are attributed to a personal history of being a victim, abuse, neglect and trauma.

According to the professional literature of psychology, narcissism stands out by a preliminary stage of fantasies, and hence the explanation about dissociation is valid here as well. Since I have surveyed elaborately these explanations in relation to other categories, there is no need to repeat them here, but just to emphasize the inner world of the child who feels neglected, a victim, and so on.

The personality structure of the child and the adolescent who feels a helpless victim establishes in him a link which can be random in the first time, between satisfaction or sexual arousal and violence. After it repeats itself, we can say that the child has learned to link between the two in his mind.

At the same time, there is a claim that the exposure to pornography today, a pornography that contains violent aspects more than it did in the past, establishes a confirmation and positive reinforcement of the link between the two variables. The child tries to experience such a link between sexuality and violence in his environment, and if he indeed feels such satisfaction, he would develop sado-sexual characteristics within narcissism. All these are linked to the antisocial personality disorder in which the individual sees others as a means for achieving satisfaction. He does not feel empathy and caring for the victim and his goal is to achieve the satisfaction he is interested in. As has been mentioned the mass media might strengthen this link to a large extent, if the individual has a predisposition for it.

All the same, one cannot say that violent pornography is the cause for the link between sexuality and violence. Hundreds of thousands of people surf in the Internet into sex sites which offer a rich variety of pornographic contents, including sexual violence, and it does not make them serial murderers with a sadist-sexual background, but this link is strengthened when there is a predisposition for it.

Another theory that can explain this category is the dissociative personality disorder, according to which the dissociated part of the identity creates fantasy contents in which the future murderer abuses his victims and feels sexual satisfaction through the fantasy. Like in other cases, the intensity of the stimulus and satisfaction of the fantasy starts fading after getting used to it, and the future murderer needs to escalate the contents of the fantasy in order to get satisfaction.

The contents of the violent fantasy are not invented, but are taken from the murderer's sociocultural environment, as women are still presented as a means for sexual satisfaction of any kind (depersonalization). These contents exist in culture and society for years, and in part of the cases the message is that since it does not deal with human beings, especially in the case of prostitutes, then there is even covered legitimacy to act against them, like the category of the assignment murderer.

But the serial murderer would not be able to materialize his fantasy before executing an act of neutralizing and reframing, as we have found in other types of serial murderers. He would use the technique of denying the victim and the damage ("she is a whore, so she deserves it"; "I've done to her what she is used to get"), and so would pave his way to materialize the fantasy. After the murder the murderer would feel a retreat to the emptiness of his life, playing between the neutral identity and the dissociative one, until the next murder. In this category there is also room for the theory of the routine activities which explains how prostitutes, young women, women hitchhikers and other women are more vulnerable and available for the murderer because they are defenseless.

Allocating the Serial Murderer in Relation to the Six Central Characteristics
Preoccupation with sex—This is the most outstanding category in relation to preoccupation with sex, and there must be a sexual element. The only aim of the murderer is sexual satisfaction which stems from linking between sexuality and murderous sadism. This

fact distinguishes between this category and the previous one, as in all the other fields, there is great similarity between them. Pre-occupation with sex can be through a direct physical contact with the victim, or through penetrating objects into the victim's body and masturbating, necrophilia, preserving organs of the victim's body for future sexual use, and so on. The outstanding character-istic among these murderers is sexual sadism. The victim is an object for them, an object which was meant to satisfy their sexual motives in the ultimate way. After using them they can be thrown to the garbage bin and find a more interesting toy for satisfying their sexual sadism.

Acquaintance with the victim—Due to the murderer's diffi-culty to oppose an abusing or humiliating parent, the victim has to be a total stranger, although he symbolizes and resembles the parental figure. The symbolization can be in the body look, hair colour, eyes colour, or by belonging to a certain sector or occupa-tion.

Power-control games—This criterion refers to ranges of be-haviour. These serial murderers can be a sadist in a low level or an extreme level, but in any case they draw enjoyment and satisfac-tion from causing pain and suffering, as well as from the victim's response who knows or guesses what is going to happen to him. The murderer enjoys his demonstration of power and control over another person who begs for his life, and through sexual activity these feelings bring him high sexual satisfaction. Therefore, pow-er-control games are an inseparable part of the serial murderer who belongs to this category, and are his significant characteris-tics.

Involvement of another crime—This category refers to an ac-companied sexual attack to the serial murder. Such attack can contain a variety of sexual behaviours, like sodomy, rape, pene-trating objects to the victim's body and others. In addition, there may be necrophilic behaviour.

The motive for this serial murder is, as mentioned above, the link between sadism and sex, and therefore the murderer aspires to achieve sexual satisfaction rather than being satisfied with the murder itself. The murder can be the peak or part of the peak in a case of necrophilic behaviour and preserving parts of the body for future sexual intercourse. We may conclude that if there has not been found an evidence for sexual sadism, then the murder and the murderer are not suited for this category in which sadist-sexual relations are an integral part.

Focusing on the act or on the process—This type of serial murder, like the previous one, is a materialization of a fantasy. The murderer looks for the ideal victim in his imagination, or has con-structed in his mind a script for the plot after seeing such a victim. The murderer would allocate the victim, follow him, seduce him and bring him to a place in which he feels safe to act. The murder-er would imprison the victim in an abandoned place that has been prepared for this end, and there he would execute his sadistic tortures.

After the victim dies of the tortures, or the murderer feels he is not interested in him anymore, he may get rid of the body im-mediately after the murder, while some would prefer to have nec-rophilic relations with the body, or even dismember the body, remove parts of it and preserve others for the sake of enjoying the memories which arouse him sexually. Part of the murderers would keep parts of the body in the freezer in order to masturbate with this organ in the future. That is, for these murderers the fantasy leads the focus of the whole process.

6. Serial Murder and Murderers by Proxy

Serial murder and murderers in a medical context exist among physicians, dentists, nurses and other nursing personnel, and it exists among men and women (Newton, 2006).

I have described already, mainly in the context of the routine activities theory, the fact that serial murderers like the assignment ones have a convenient reservoir of potential victims among the populations which are in the margins of society. In the current case, the potential reservoir of victims is much more available and vulnerable. It refers to patients in hospitals, in old people's homes and children at home. This population is considered especially vulnerable for a few reasons: First of all, it is in a state of illness, old age or childhood, and needs an authoritative figure to determine the proper treatment, without having the option of knowing whether the treatment is right, proper and necessary. These are asymmetric relationships, a situation in which the parental or the medical authority can do almost anything, and this population is dependent on its caretakers, sometimes to the extent of its very existence. Secondly, when there is a death case of a patient in a hospital, particularly in a geriatric nursing institution, it seems quite natural. It is true, to a large extent, for children as well. Death is quite common in these populations, and hence it does not arouse a significant suspicion. Thirdly, even if there is a suspicion that death has not taken place in a natural way, these institutions would prefer to hush up the case in order not to damage their reputation.

Newton (2006) refers to several possible motives for serial murder in the medical field:

1. Murder for the sake of achieving a material benefit, like murdering patients in a home for the aged for having their life insurance or national security money.
2. Serial murder of hospitalized or helpless people for the sake of achieving satisfaction out a "divine" sense of power, as the murderer decides who would live and who would die. This is the ultimate power and control in a person's life, without any material benefit attached to it. This category includes nurses who murdered helpless people in order "to facilitate their work."
3. Munchausen syndrome by proxy—A case in which the mother or the nurse poisons a child or a patient in order to be the first to try to save him, and through this action would gain acknowledgment and appreciation. Unfortunately, many cases end up in death, when it is not clear whether the intention was to murder the patient. There are known similar cases among pyromaniacs as the one

who set the fire was the youngest fireman in the station, and he was the one who went out first to extinguish the fire, sometimes by endangering his life, and by so doing gained acknowledgment and appreciatio. It is difficult to know the extent of cases of this kind, since as has been said, in the environments in which a serial murder of this type takes place, it is an integral part of routine, in additi‐on to the policy of hushing up these cases. Most of the murder cases are done by nurses or mothers, aiming to gain attention and empathy. But this phenomenon exists, as has been mentioned, among men physicians as well.

4. Merciful murder—The will to put the patient out of his misery, when the physician knows he cannot cure the pa‐tient and wants to prevent the continuation of suffering.

5. Sexual sadism—This is quite a rare motive and this is why it has not received sufficient attention. For example, two nurses with a lesbian tendency used to kill their pati‐ents. It caused them great sexual excitement, and they used to go to a free room to have sex right after the mur‐der. In other cases, there were reports of women who we‐re murdered on the dentist's chair after receiving a high dose of anesthetic materials and have gone through sexual abuse prior to the murder (Newton, 2006).

Theoretical Explanation

There is apparently a great contradiction between the nursing and medical professions and murder. Physician's oath and the myth of the compassionate nurse present these figures as people who, to a large extent, sacrifice their private lives for the wellbeing of the patients. Hence the public has difficulty to receive the gap be‐tween the mythical image and reality. On the other hand, if we look at it rationally, people with a will to murder can do it very easily in locations like hospitals, so maybe a minor part of nurses and physicians have chosen rationally this occupation in order to be close to their potential victims without arousing any suspicion. It is like the situation with pedophiles who work in various func‐tions in kindergarten classes and schools. But it is difficult to accept the argument that a person invests many years of studying medicine just to have a convenient and safe place to materialize his murderous impulses.

The need of power and control is highly significant in human lives, especially in the globalization era in which the individual feels very small versus giant corporations and governments. But it does not make "normal" people become serial murderers. The lust for power directs people to choose occupations in which they can express power, as in politics, law, management, military, law enforcement and so on. The psychoanalytic theory would claim that there is sublimation of the impulse for power and control in a normative way. But in extreme cases the lust for power is not expressed, according to the perception of a very small part of the public, through the above-mentioned occupations. These people have a need to feel the ultimate power, the divine power.

A central motive in this type of serial murder is that these physicians and nurses feel satisfaction through the immense sense of power they have in their hands and by controlling others. The sense of power serves, for a small part of them, for rectifying deficiencies of control, or compensate for contempt of their skills and capabilities in their personal history. The sense of power among these people gets dull in the course of time due to getting used to it. These cases refer to the development of an antisocial/narcissistic behaviour personality. Since for these people others are perceived as instruments for fulfilling their needs, then after neutralizing guilt and reframing the circumstances they turn to serial murder which is of course the ultimate means of a sense of power. Part of the neutralizing guilt deals with the absence of personal responsibility due to history which necessarily led the murderer to do what he has done, while another part deals with denying the victim and the damage, since they deal with sick people, and part of the reframing would be that the murderer is not bad, he just wants to facilitate the patient's suffering, as some kind of mercy killing.

The serial murderer has a sense of power because he holds in his hands the decision who dies and who lives, but in fact, he does not make such decisions at all as he would kill his victims any-way. The murderer's intention is that he would be able to choose another victim but he spares his life. This argument is also incor-rect, because the murderer would choose the victim who is most available and vulnerable. The victims are usually unfamiliar to him, except in cases of mothers with Munchausen Syndrome in which the intention is to save the patient/child and gain acknowl-edgment and appreciation.

This explanation is true in almost all the cases in which we can find an aspiration for power and control, and therefore various scientists referred to the motive of power and control as an expla-nation for a comprehensive type of serial murder, mainly by sadists. As I have demonstrated, it is not true. The component of the need of power and control exists indeed in a few types of serial murder, but only in this category it is found in its most "pure" manifestation.

Another explanation of the way of operation of these mur-derers is the theory of routine activities which provides the mur-derer with a variety of defenseless victims who totally depend on their caregivers. From the point when the treatment of patients shifted from home to external organizations, there has been estab-lished a reservoir of highly available victims for serial murderers of this type. In addition, the routine of the "total institutions"[156] where victims stay enable the murderers act without arousing suspicion. Hence one can claim that there is a rational decision as far as considerations of benefit and loss are concerned.

Another explanation has to do with the personality of the murderer and psychosocial aspects, in this case, Munchausen syn-drome by proxy. This syndrome expresses a need by a parent, nurse or caregiver to receive social attention or acknowledgment which they cannot achieve in any other way. For example, there is a case in the literature of a pregnant woman who gained great attention during her pregnancy and delivery, but after giving birth, the atten-tion shifted from the woman/mother to the baby, and the mother murdered the baby. In doing so, she gained great attention as a be-reaved mother. The process repeated itself for five of her children.

Allocating the Serial Murderer in Relation to the Six Central Characteristics

Preoccupation with sex—In most of the cases which are known in the literature there is no involvement of sex in this type of serial murder. Sex does not play a role as a motive, as a means of satisfaction, and as a means for power-control. Only a few cases were found among dentists and lesbian nurses.

Acquaintance with the victim—Due to the variety of serial murderers in this category, one can distinguish between two groups. One group has a relatively low acquaintance with the victim, for example, a physician or a nurse who deal with a victim who has just arrived at the hospital. Either they cause him to die through a mercy killing, or Munchausen Syndrome, like a young nurse who wanted to get the acknowledgment of the nursing and the medical staff, poisoned a patient, and right away started in an attempt to save him and get the team's appreciation.

The second group is on the other side of the sequence. These are mothers, nurses, caregivers and physicians who know the victim thoroughly and intimately, and murder him in order to receive attention, empathy and even mercy. This process repeats itself time and again, and so the murderer gets repeated attention which, according to his perception, he would have not received in any other way.

Power-control games—In this category we can also see two significant extremes. On the one end there are mothers who act out of an aspiration to receive attention who murder their babies again and again for this end. There is nothing of the power-control games toward the victim here, but the will of his death in order to enjoy social benefit. On the other end, we can see a group of serial murderers, like physicians and nurses, whose sense of immense power in their hands regarding the question of who would live and who would die has to do with power-control games toward the victim, although these games are mainly in the caregiver's mind without making the victim aware of their intentions. At the same time, in certain cases, the victim may be aware of a murderous intention on the part of the care taking team, when the physician shares the patient with his intentions and the patient is not in a position to object, and so the murderer would achieve satisfaction out of the victim's helplessness who knows what is there for him. It is similar to power-control games that exist in the sado-sexual motive.

Involvement of another crime—When the serial murder is done for the sake of achieving a material benefit, like murder of patients in a home for the aged, then it is a case of involvement of another crime. It is true also when it is a case of a murder of patients for the sake of sexual enjoyment. But in most cases of the current category, there is no other felony involved except for murder which provides the murderer with a sense of power and control, or alternatively with attention and empathy from the environment.

Focusing on the act or on the process—Apparently, since this serial murder does not include control games between the murderer and the victim, but just between the murderer and himself, and since the victim is available and vulnerable, we can say that the focus is on the act of murder.

One cannot ignore the fact that sometimes there is a certain process in which the murderer executes repeated poisonings until a state of a critical situation. Therefore, we can say that the main focus is on the act, but to a certain extent there may be a focus on the process. Attributing serial murder and murderers to theoretical typology— After presenting the theoretical model for explaining serial murder, and the typology that classifies serial murderers according to their types, one additional assignment is required in order to have a complete picture. The intention is to present the new typology according to the six criteria which have been chosen for classification. But unlike the previous typologies, I will present the criteria by way of degrees or a sequence, rather than by a dichotomous way which does not suit the social sciences, including sociology and criminology.

One of the central problems with typologies and theoretical models is the rigidity with which we build an ideal model for social or psychological phenomena. I have mentioned already the problematic nature of the DSM which creates labeling and rigidity of symptoms for diagnosing mental disorders and illnesses. A similar problem exists in criminology and sociology which aspires to explain human behaviour in a very rigid way that borders on determinism. On the one hand, we aspire to create patterns in order to make it simple to identify, label and classify various phenomena, and on the other hand, the mental and social world is not molded into patterns. We aspire to create ideal models which are based on reality and can be implemented in the diagnostic and therapeutic field, and hence the suggested typology should be flexible and not rigid, keeping the condition of being exclusive and exhaustive.

For instance, instead of claiming that in a certain category of serial murderers there is or is not sado-sexual behaviour, one can say that a sado-sexual behaviour can exist in different degrees among different serial murderers. A serial murderer who is motivated by a sado-sexual impulse would have a high level of sexual sadism, while there will be no sexual sadism in another kind of serial murder, like a murderer who is interested in murdering the victim just for taking his money. Between these two cases, there may be types of serial murder with sexual sadism at a low and medium or high level.

Another example is a murderer who is motivated by a material motive in which the reflection of the power-control motive would be low, if any, while in a murderer who tortures the victim slowly and sadistically, we would see a high level of a power-control element. Holmes and Holmes (1998) were the first to refer to this issue, but the problem with their typology was the dichotomy of the criteria, like the one of an inner motive and external motive in the personality. At the same time, I found help in some of the criteria or the characteristics these scientists presented, like focus on the action versus focus on the process. In addition, I suggest additional characteristics, like involvement of sexual relations in the serial murder, or components of power-control as central motives.

Table 10: Classification of serial murder and murderers according to central criteria (Source: Edelstein, 2009)

Type/ characteristic	Preoccupation with sex	Acquaintance with the victim	Power-control games	Involvement of another felony	Focus on the action	Focus on the process
Following murder	nonexistent	nonexistent-high	Nonexistent-low	nonexistent-high	high	Nonexistent-medium
Murder out of a psychosis	nonexistent	nonexistent-high	nonexistent	nonexistent	high	nonexistent
Ideological murder for purifying society	nonexistent-low	nonexistent-low	nonexistent	nonexistent	high	nonexistent
Murder out of frustration-humiliation	low-medium	nonexistent	high	high	nonexistent-low	high
Sado-sexual murder	high	nonexistent	high	high	nonexistent-low	high
Murder in a treatment context	nonexistent-low	low-high	low-high	low-high	high	nonexistent-low

From the table above, one can learn how important it is to present the central criteria of serial murder in a flexible way, rather than in a dichotomous one. Profiling is also based on flexibility which enables determining the profile of a specific crime only after discussing it with reference to the ideal model. The scientists who works with the law enforcement system would have to determine where the specific case is located in relation to the suggested sequence. This determination would help, in turn, to decide the route of investigation taken, how to accuse and punish the criminal, and how to treat him, if at all.

There is some kind of criticism on the domain of profiling in felonies of this kind. The facts prove that the most elaborated American center on profile-making of severe delinquency reaches only a level of two percent of exposure and discovery of the executors. In my opinion, one of the outstanding reasons for this comes from the problematic typologies used by the Federal Bureau of Investigation (FBI), typologies whose characteristics are dichotomous, not allocated along a sequence, as is suggested here.

As I have mentioned, the social or behavioural sciences have always aspired to establish ideal models for personal and interpersonal phenomena, but due to the complexity of reality, part of these models missed their goal. On the other hand, there is something frustrating in typologies or models like the one suggested here, since we have no unequivocal criteria for understanding phenomena. As we have said, reality is more complicated and is not black and white, but has a variety of shades between the two ends. The phenomena move on a sequence of a certain field, and one cannot divide them into unequivocal units. But the advantage of such a model is that it enables referring to any range of possibilities of the phenomenon, and by so doing, it describes reality in a more correct and real way.

Summary of the Suggested Typology

When scientists are interested in creating typologies for a certain phenomenon, they have to keep in line with two criteria: The categories have to be exclusive and exhaustive. In other words, they have to include all the cases belonging to the phenomenon, but exclude cases which do not belong to the investigated phenomenon.

In previous typologies which have been suggested in the field of serial murder, there have been three main problems: Including cases of mass-serial murder under the classification of serial murder; overlapping among categories; and referring to the motive of power and control as a separate category, so it was impossible to distinguish among different categories which contained this common component. As has been said already, power and control are dominant components in serial murder, but they are a motive only in part of the categories of serial murder. Another problem is that part of the typologies mixed between motives and characteristics in serial murder.

The suggested typology presents separately the motives for serial murder and the characteristics of the different types of serial murder and murderers. Furthermore, the innovation is in presenting a psychological and social explanation for the motive and the way of operation. In this way, the typology meets two requirements I have posed, and, in addition, it presents for the first time an integrative theoretical explanation for the different serial murder and murderers in the various categories.

The question is whether there is overlapping among the types of serial murder and murderers in the suggested categories. The answer seems positive. For example, murder of inmates in nursing institutions was done mainly by women, and in this typology it appears twice: In the category of murder out of a material motive, in a felony which was meant to achieve a material benefit, and in the category of serial murder and murderers out of an aspiration for power. The critics would claim that his category does not meet the criterion of exclusion, but this is a superficial view. When examining the motive, we see two types of totally different murderers. One acts out of a material motive, while the other acts out of a psychological motive for power and control. This distinction undermines the criticism. The reservoir of victims is indeed identical in both cases, and there is an external similarity in the deeds of the murderer, but the motives and the way of operation are absolutely different.

An important conclusion appears from the typology, according to which there are common components for different types of serial murder both in background and causativeness. In many of the cases the murderers have a history of traumatic sexual and physical abuse in childhood, loneliness, and an inability to establish an attachment with parental figures, especially with the mother figure. These elements in the future serial murderer could have been removed in childhood, and instead of a murderer, he would have grown up as a child with impulses directed toward normative and legitimate channels. If versus the forces that have hurt the child in his childhood and adolescence there had been members of the enlarged family, there is a chance that at least part of the children would have grown to become normative members of society. Social services are needed or other factors defending the child by taking him out of the abusive home to a supportive family together with an appropriate psychological treatment. The accusers would claim that statistics show children who have grown up in a loving and warm family have become serial murderers (Vronsky, 2008). In these cases, the family has done everything in its power for the child and gave him warmth and love, and all the same, the future murderer developed a severe personality disorder. The answer to this claim is that statistics show that the majority of serial murderers have grown up in institutions, in adopting families, or in abusive families. Moreover, unlike an organic mental illness which develops in children and adolescents, no matter how much love and warmth they receive at home, personality disorders of the kind described here do not develop in a void, and are often influenced by the attitude of the primary caregivers. It is true, indeed, that not only the family influences the development of a serial murderer. The culture we live in is a source of norms, images, aspirations and impulses[157] of members in society. Socialization systems as well as the mass media transmit to children and adolescents cultural messages which establish normative perceptions of what is accustomed, proper and desired, and it is true in the material field, body image, gender relationships and almost any domain of our lives.

The mass media developed upon the invention of printing, and since then, it has grown at an increasing rate due to the development of technological means for transferring information, such as the Internet. As mass media gained greater audience, there have started arising apprehensions and claims about the immense power of the mass media, and suggestions have been raised to limit this power. Sometimes it happened as part of a process of creating a moral panic.

To return to our subject, one of the central claims was that the mass media increase the level of violence in society. Starting from animation films and up to action films for adolescents and adults, the contents of the media are soaked with violence. Numerous studies have been published on this issue throughout the years, and various ways have been suggested of how to overcome this dangerous influence, such as limiting the age of watching, the option of blocking channels and contents by parents, and so on.

On the other hand, the findings regarding the influence of the media on the increase of the level of violence in society often suffered from contradictions. Among other things, there was found a different influence on different publics. One of the significant findings is that the media do not create violence out of nothing, but can reinforce preliminary tendencies of aggressive behaviour through blunting emotions regarding the victim, "getting used" to watching bodies, looking for more violent contents, and so on. It is interesting to indicate that many of the studies have focused on movies, but ignored the news broadcasts in which violence is presented in quite a high frequency (murder, terrorism, beating old people). These contents have been perceived as "legitimate," because they represent reality.

One should pay attention to the fact that the term "mass media" is too general. Within this envelope there is a wide variety of tabloid newspapers which present, in a most blunt way, sexual and violent contents in order to arouse the curiosity of the public and sell more newspapers. On the other hand, there are newspapers which are considered as addressing a more intelligent public, and there we would not find a blunt expression of contents of this kind. This is true also for a variety of cable TV and radio channels, as well as for books and movies.

Whereas throughout the years there have been established bodies of supervision and control over the mass media channels, the development of the Internet has upset the option to do so in the worlds of content on the web. One can enter today any site and watch any kind of content as one chooses. Pedophiles can correspond with children and adolescents under a false identity and seduce them to meet, dates sites enable conversations among people about their different tastes, and there have already been many cases of encounters following an acquaintance on the Internet which have ended up in rape and murder. The Internet enables deviants of different kinds to impersonate as other people and seduce victims almost in any direction of their perversion. These deviants feel safe under their cover, and the other users have no safe way of certifying the identity of the people they talk to.

Mass media is not omnipotent, but under different circumstances, and personality and familial conditions, children and adolescents become a convenient audience for absorbing messages which do not fall in line with the values and norms accepted in society. In such cases, the child or his environment do not have the brakes which would examine and control the contents of the media, and therefore the child is exposed and might accept the messages as a proper and desired way of behaviour, especially if they meet his images, impulses and desires.

Another aspect of the mass media is by making loathsome murderers into culture heroes who gain great communication exposure, as well as commemorating their deeds in movies, in television series and books. A normative and mentally healthy youngster who is exposed to the glorification of criminals as culture heroes would obviously not identify with them, but when we deal with children and adolescents who have gone through traumas and suffer from severe psychological disturbances, the exposure to these contents might aggravate their deviant and delinquent behaviour, as I have shown above. That is to say, that there are consumers of communication who lack defense mechanisms against a variety of contents which might influence them, and at the same time the contents of the media meet a need of theirs to look for excitement, trying to be like the famous figures they watch. Mass media makes us believe that one can make any fantasy come true in a world which aspires to a goal without considering the legitimate means of achieving it. The stars on the screen that appear overnight transmit the message of living from one day to the next, demonstrating nihilism and power we lack in our personal and social life.

When individuals with certain impulses find a fertile ground for satisfying their needs, they become consumers of the media to a large extent. When the primary satisfaction fades away, they tend to look for sharper and sharper contents which they can find very easily. But at a certain stage, the media become limited in their ability to meet the needs. Then the needs and the will of the "real thing" paves the way from a reality of communication to communication of reality: Making the deviant individual into one of the culture heroes he had watched in the media who gains the big prize—becoming a celebrity (Goren, 1993).

To sum up, the media do not conjure their contents, or take them just from the allegedly distorted imagination of its creators. The American culture (mainly) encourages a violent response to actions that interrupt achieving individual and narcissistic desires. At the same time, the culture transmits a message according to which there are members in society whose lives are worth less than those of others ("the blood hierarchy"), and generally speaking, the price of human lives is quite cheap. These messages are transmitted through the mass media not only in fictional movies, but also through daily news broadcasts. When these messages are transmitted to people with the right background for absorbing the message at face value, certain individuals in society might act according to this message, while finding a variety of excuses and justifications one can find in the general "normative" culture.

Chapter Six
Serial Murder and Gender

In my previous book (Edelstein, 2006) I presented the typology which was suggested by Holmes and Holmes (1998) for classifying serial murder by women, and my criticism of this classification. The rate of serial murder executed by women has not been changed significantly since then, neither were there new explanations about it. If serial murder is considered a relatively rare phenomenon, then serial murder by females is even rarer.

Female Serial Murderers from Ancient History to the Early Modern Period

As a whole, women wanted to achieve through serial murder the same goals as did male serial murderers: Control, power and wealth. During the Roman Empire in the courts of the Caesars Caligula and Nero, there were female serial murderers who used poison (Vronsky, 2007: 72–92). The environment and the circumstances in which these women grew up shaped their murderous career. They murdered because they could do so, and because they had learned it from examples in their environment. Murder satisfied not only their passion for power, but also their emotional and material needs.

Similar examples can be found in the royal court of the Russian Tsar, as well as the court of Elizabeth I and Bloody Mary in England. But among these women, the sexual component was absent, and; therefore, they were not classified as serial murderers. This component appeared for the first time in the case of the Countess of Bathory who murdered from sado-sexual motives and out of a hedonistic passion rather than from political or any other reasons of a search for power. She has become known as the only female serial murderer who murdered with a sadistic background without a dominant male partner. She bathed in the blood of adolescent maids out of a belief that it would renovate her youth. She would torture the maids to death in sadistic ways, burn their organs, beat them with objects, dismember the bodies, throw them naked to the snow and skin them. In a period of thirty-five years, she murdered 650 women until she was arrested in 1610, at the age of fifty, when she started to murder women of the nobility.

Female Serial Murderers in the Pre-Industrial History

In this period, there is evidence of a few women serial murderers, for instance, La Toffania (1670–1719) in Italy who murdered 600 men. She gave the poison potion for free to women who wanted to murder their husbands secretly, and offered her customers to use each time a small amount in order to elongate the suffering. The motive that was attributed to her was hatred for men.

In France, the aristocrat Marie de Brinvilliers acted in the years 1664–1672 and murdered 50 men by poison. She volunteered to work at a hospital where she poisoned her patients. Among other things, she murdered her father and her two brothers who objected to her marriage. She conducted experiments on patients in order to determine the exact dosage of poison to cause death.

The Rise of the Modern Female Serial Murderer

The industrial revolution has brought with it immigration from the villages to the cities, and industrial cities have been built near the work plants. There was not a policy of wellbeing, not even public kitchens, so that situations of unemployment, poverty and morbidity often caused death. Women were much more vulnerable than men at that time, and only in the nineteenth century they have started to work in plants and factories as saleswomen and secretaries. At the same time, part of them worked in households, mainly young village girls who had left their homes aiming to look for work in town, and worked as maids under a very strict discipline. An undesired pregnancy used to bring about an immediate dismissal and death of hunger, and this led to the murdering of babies by their mothers. Many women found themselves dealing with theft which meant a death sentence, or prostitution, as they were exposed to the danger of murder or sickness. They were prostitutes of the lower class, like those murdered by Jack the Ripper, similar to the serial murderers of prostitutes known nowadays.

In England at that time, the press started to develop as most of the working class was literate (1830). Later on, "real crime" stories developed, and the public took interest in the crimes of women which were in harsh contradiction to the female ideal of the time. There started to appear reports about female serial murderers who kill by using poison, and the British Parliament hurried up to make rules for coping with the phenomenon (as has been done in the eighties, when there was an issue of an epidemic of serial murderers). The number of female serial murderers has increased consistently, and only in 1840 has it started to decrease (Ibid., pp. 97–134).

The Postmodern Female Serial Murderer

The one who is considered the first known postmodern female serial murderer is Aileen Wuornos (Arrigo & Griffin, 2004). In the past, the attitude toward male serial murderers was as monsters, while female serial murderers were perceived as "ladies." They were regarded as respectable and even attractive women who used their beauty and charm, as well as their manners, in order to entrap their victims and murder them by poison, while they continued to pretend to be mothers, wives, nurses, babysitters or widows. Wuornos tore up this stereotype. She was in a territory where so many women have been murdered, but she was different from all the female serial murderers before her. She dealt with prostitution, and shot to death seven of her clients and robbed their property (Ibid., pp. 139–180).

Vronsky (2007) presents a typology of serial murder and women murderers, although there is no innovation in it versus the typologies that have been presented before (Edelstein, 2006).

1. The Black Widow, a Female Serial Murderer for the Sake of Benefit

Betty Neumar, seventy-six, was suspected of murdering her five husbands in order to gain their inheritance. In 2008 in the USA, she was identified as a serial widow. The Black Widow enchants and seduces men until they become her lovers, then she marries them, and afterwards murders them for the sake of material benefit. Women murderers of this kind are analogous to male serial murderers who murder from a motive of material benefit. The label "Black Widow" describes their way of operation: Seducing men in order to make them helpless. A Black Widow is not motivated just by a material benefit, since taking the victim's property can be an expression of total control over him. Therefore, there are cases in which the Black Widow murders for the sake of small and ridiculous sums of money. Not all the female serial murderers who are motivated by a material benefit are Black Widows. Some of them appear as the Angel of Death, while others, with no classification, murder acquaintances and relatives from a variety of motives. There is a problem with this definition which actually contradicts the traditional and more correct definition of the Black Widow. As a matter of fact, such classification loses its meaning in the distinction between female serial murderers who act out of various motives and with different victims.

2. Serial Murder and Female Murderers—Angel of Death Type

Most of us perceive women automatically as a source of love, caring and feeding. We learn it through the caring of our mothers and, as we grow up, we get to know women in a variety of therapeutic roles: Nurses and teachers to name a few. Some female serial murderers use exactly this cover to execute acts of serial murder, especially nurses in hospitals. Some operate from the *Munchausen syndrome by proxy* (MSBP).

3. Female Serial Murderers as Partners of Men

According to the historical documentation, the female serial murderers who execute the most brutal actions usually act as a partner of a male serial murderer. It has been found that out of sixty-two female serial murderers who have been in the USA between the years of 1800–1995, about a third operated as partners, as part of a team or a couple (Vronsky, 2007). In most cases, women have not physically executed the murder, but participated in it by seducing the victim, helping in catching him, or torturing him, attacking him sexually, getting rid of the body or liquidating evidence. In most cases, the partner was a man who controlled the woman.

There are, though, unique cases of a female team or a pair of lesbians, but the common patterns is of a heterosexual couple who act as serial murderers. In these teams, the women are close to the stereotypical role of the male sexual-aggressor serial murderer. Until lately, the perception, and accordingly the punishment as well, was that the woman of the team was actually a victim of the man. The man is older than the woman; he has a rich history as a single sexual aggressor before meeting her, while the woman usually has no criminal record. These teams are highly organized, plan their crimes carefully, and choose their victims meticulously.

In this context, the FBI conducted a study of 20 wives or exgirlfriends of sadist serial murderers with a sexual background. Most of them grew up in broken families, and the common claim was that they acted out of love and passion to please their man. Most of them said that the serial murderer was tender and caring when they got to know him, gave them presents, and spent a lot of money on them. In responding to the question why they stayed with the serial murderer after discovering his real face, some answered that they were innocent or stupid and expected that he would change his behaviour, and the minority talked about love and financial or emotional dependency on the man. Some reported of a fear to leave him. Some women indicated that they obeyed as a substitution to attention and love, but another part has gone through socialization for such murders.

Vronsky (2007) found that since 1800 until 1995, 16 percent of the serial murderers were women, which means sixty-two women murdered about five hundred victims, including men, women and children. Out of them, three serial murderers murdered about two hundred victims. In addition, it was found that the majority of the female serial murderers appeared in the USA since the nineteen-fifties. As I have indicated in my previous book, gender roles had a great influence in shaping the fact that serial murder by women is a rare phenomenon, for two reasons. First, it is still uncommon that women would behave violently in general and in murderous violence in particular, and therefore, in the socialization process of women we find very little learning about violent behaviour in general and physical violence in particular. Second, in spite of the increase in the rate of women going out of their homes aiming to acquire an education, occupation, and leisure, most of the female serial murderers continue to act within the traditional framework of home and work, especially in the field of nursing.

According to Vronsky (2007), violence was perceived as something that has to do with man and manhood, and therefore when a woman acts violently, people tend to attribute it to something that is irrational which stems from the instinct of self-defense, a mental illness, depression or a hormonal imbalance. A murder of an individual by a woman is perceived as a result of an emotional outburst after an abuse of many years the woman has gone through by her husband, or by another figure. In other words, women can express themselves through expressive violence, but they do not use instrumental, planned violence. According to Vronsky (2007) this perception is incorrect. He indicates that in human history there were women in high political positions who gave orders for the execution of serial murders due to greed and passion. But as he indicates, these women are very far away from the modern American woman as far as time, class and culture are concerned.

In my opinion there is no doubt that society and culture have a significant role in shaping the serial male or female murderer. Except for the "traditional" movies and books about the wife who poisons her husbands, and the nurse who poisons her patients, there is no significant change in the social perception of the position of women in relation to a serial murder. The only change on this issue has to do with one serial female murderer, Wuornos, a prostitute who murdered and robbed seven of her clients for the sake of material benefit, using firearms and throwing their bodies to the side of the road. This change, that was accompanied by elaborate coverage on the news and in films, heralds that the cold-blooded serial murder of strangers can take place among women as it does among men. Alongside the change of the traditional perception and the image of the female serial murderer, a future change and increase is also anticipated in the rate of female serial murderers.

Vronsky (2007) refers to the feminist theory regarding serial murder and attacks it harshly. According to Vronsky, the second wave of feminism, the radical one, claimed that men conspire to murder women systematically, and therefore female serial murderers are in fact victims who have become aggressors. But Vronsky (2007) does not accept this perception and presents findings according to which more than half of the female serial murderers in the USA murdered at least one woman, and a third of them murdered at least one girl. That is to say that this is not the case of women who murdered those who had victimized them.

In my opinion, women's lib, that implied a "promise" of an increasing involvement of women in delinquency, including violent ones, is not expressed in serial murder. I assume that the progress in the field of women's lib and providing more equal opportunities in various fields would bring about the opposite outcome. Releasing the pressure would bring about a decrease in serial murders on the part of women, except in the material field. More women would learn to use firearms and would not hesitate to rob victims, men and women alike. Another approach on the feminist explanation is suggested by Clough et al. (1997). They claim that radical feminism posed the issue of female serial murder as a conspiracy of the patriarchal society in which women are eliminated due to their inferior status. For strengthening their claim, those who favor the feminist approach come out against the biological explanation, claiming that the biological theories lack a solid explanation, since "sexual murder is a cultural category." In addition, feminism attacked the psychological theories (at the micro level) claiming that they cover the responsibility of the murderer behind pathology. In other words, it is easier to blame the individual psychopath than to blame culture which normalized expressions of violence against women. The feminists claimed that a serial murder is composed of cultural aspects and social structure. According to them, the accepted perception among many scientists, a perception that says that a serial murder is a means for achieving power, must be evaluated in the context of gender roles as well, roles that are defined by the patriarchal structure. That is, according to them, female serial murder is a vengeance for social inferiority.

On the other hand, the scientists accuse the position of feminism as having a few defects. First, while the feminists came out against scientists who reduced the definition of serial murder to a few categories, they focused only in murder of women by men. Actually 15 percent of the serial murder cases are executed by women, but the feminist movement ignored this fact. It also ignored the fact that male serial murderers murdered men as well on the basis of status, sex, and other things. Furthermore, we would have expected that serial murderers would come only from the lower class due to their social position, but it is not so.

The conclusion of the scientists is that if we neutralize the criticism, then at the basis of the feminist theory there is an important innovation by regarding serial murder as a sociocultural phenomenon, as I have indeed referred to this issue among male serial murderers.

A Comparison Between Male and Female Serial Murderers

Vronsky (2007) claims that "female serial murderers can murder for the same reasons men do" (Ibid., p. 20). This claim is also supported by other scientists (Holmes & Holmes, 1998). All the same, there are several outstanding differences between male and female serial murderers: The female serial murderer does not document her actions and does not have sex with the victim, but do it just for the goal of murdering, with no torture or necrophilic relations. Her main satisfaction stems from the death of the victim. Scientists like Kenney & Heide (1994) have found that women serial murderers, like male serial murderers, had a childhood rife with physical and sexual abuse, and in many cases they grew up in families without two biological parents (80%), and in families in which there was a high use of psychoactive substances (71%). This reality led to loneliness, and the growth of fantasies that have become specific toward the murder. It has been found that female serial murderers operate for a longer time, until they are caught, than men, because the location of operation and the victims do not attract attention or any suspicion of them, especially because they operate within their traditional gender roles. One can point out a few statistical differences between female and male serial murderers:[158]

- Average number of victims: Among male serial murderers, the average number is 9.5 per murderer, while among female serial murderers it is eight victims per murderer.
- Age of the murderers: The average age of male serial murderers in their first murder is 27.5, whereas among female serial murderers it is 32.9. Women start murdering at an older age, and continue to do so up to their sixties and seventies.
- Choosing the victims: While most of the male serial murderers murder strangers, only a quarter of the female serial murderers murder strangers. Male serial murderers prefer

as their first choice single young women, children and single young men, while female serial murderers prefer spouses, children, friends, lovers, patients and inmates in hospitals and homes for the aged.

One of the typologies suggested for classifying female serial murderers was presented by Keppel and Walter (1999). These scientists presented profiles of women serial murderers, and the typology that characterizes them. According to this typology, one can refer to ten types of a female serial murderer:[159]

1. The Black Widow—Murders relatives for the sake of financial benefit.
2. Angel of Death—Murders patients, inmates, or children she takes care of, while the main motive is a material benefit or an unexplained impulse.
3. Member in a sect or a cult who is led to murder by a charismatic leader.
4. "A convenient partner"—A murderer who participates in a murder that is initiated by a husband or a lover.
5. A corrupted sadistic partner—A murderer who participates out of enthusiasm in a rape and a murder executed by her partner.
6. An explosive avenger—A murderer who is motivated to murder a certain kind of victim who remind her of someone who has abused her in the past.
7. Attacks for the sake of material benefit—A woman who murders strangers for the sake of material benefit. For example, assassins by contract who have been trained for this job during their service in the security services of regimes that have been exposed to their knowhow and professionalism, or women who are hired by other women for murdering a husband or a lover.[160]
8. Assignment-Oriented—A murderer with a social or a political agenda who tries to promote it through murdering certain victims who belong to a group that is defined as unworthy of living.

9. Looking for power—A woman murderer trying to achieve a certain extent of control or power in politics, or in her personal life.

10. Munchausen syndrome by proxy—Mothers and caregivers who serially murder their children or, nurses who murder their patients aiming to attract sympathy and attention.

This typology was influenced by the typologies suggested by the FBI, and it stems from profiling rather than from a systematic theoretical background. One can see the problematic nature of the suggested typology. There is a great overlap among a few categories, for instance, between category no. 2 and no. 10; 8 and 9; and 4 and 5. Another problem is that the third category does not refer to serial murder but to a mass-serial murder. The sixth, eighth and ninth have not received support in reality and there are no examples to demonstrate them, although they are not refuted on the theoretical aspect. In addition, the seventh category is based just on one murderer. This is an example of the difficulty of classifying female serial murderers due to their low number and the low rate of discovering them. From this respect, the typology suggested by Holmes and Holmes (1998) for female serial murderers was more clear and unequivocal, although it also had its problems.

Holmes & Holmes (1998) classified the female serial murderers into a few types:

- A female serial murderer out of a vision—A woman who suffers from a psychosis who usually murders her children.
- A female serial murderer out of benefit or convenience.
- The woman hedonistic serial murderer who links fatal violence with personal satisfaction which can be sexual as well.
- The one who looks for power—A woman who murders for the sake of getting a sense of power and social acknowledgment (Munchausen syndrome).
- A member in a sect or a cult.

The typology of female serial murderers is similar for Holmes & Holmes (1998) to the one of male serial murderers, due to their assumption that there is similarity between male and female serial murderers. There is also a will to create a common theoretical basis for both genders. All the same, one can see that the first category is a mass murder, whereas the fifth category is a mass-serial murder.

Vronsky (2007) tries to suggest an explanation for serial murder by women. He claims that the rate of women with antisocial behavioural disorder is significantly lower than that of men, and among women it is expressed mainly by deviant sexual behaviour. In addition, common behaviours among men, fire setting, abusing animals, physical aggression and harassment are rarer among women, although nowadays more women tend to present a more violent behaviour than they did in the past. Due to a gender bias, women tend to be classified as having a hysterical personality rather than as psychopaths. But Vronsky (2007) indicates that no research has been conducted on the connection between psychopathy and serial murder among women.

Regarding another theoretical explanation for serial murder by women, Vronsky (2007) claims that it is a mistake to think that murder is the ultimate fantasy of every serial murderer. Some serial murderers, especially those who act from a motive of power-control, lose interest in the victim from the moment the attack is over. Therefore, one has, according to Vronsky, to refer to power as a key. Today we begin to understand that female serial murderers can murder out of similar and even identical reasons to those of male serial murderers, although the way of expressing the motives for the murder are different (Ibid., p. 65). For example, a male serial murderer who acts from a motive of power-control would express his fantasy through sexual assault. On the other hand, female serial murderers would bypass the sexual expression and turn directly to murdering the victim. Hence, while a male serial murderer would get his satisfaction from controlling through rape and physical violence, the female serial murderer would get her satisfaction by the very death of her victim, or by taking his property.

In addition, while the man needs to kill the victim through the use of his hands and other means, the woman murderer makes do with killing the victim from afar by poisoning, manipulation, and so on. That is to say that what satisfies the woman in the act of the murder is the outcome rather than the process.

As a matter of fact, there rises again the assumption that there is no difference between the motives for serial murder between men and women, and the difference is in the tool of the murder, and the fact that the woman gets satisfaction from focusing on the murder (action), while the man gets satisfaction from the process.

In my opinion, there are some important insights in Vronsky (2007) argument. I think that the influence of a trauma and physical and sexual abuse among girls is not different, and maybe even greater than what boys experience. Therefore, one can assume that among girls there would also appear psychological disturbances which stem from the lack of attachment, like dissociation, antisocial behaviour, and a broken identity.

Due to the different socialization of women, one can assume that they would need a higher level and intensity of techniques of neutralizing guilt and responsibility than men. For example, if a woman uses violence, she would experience stronger guilt feelings than a man, since this behaviour is less accepted in society on the part of women, an issue which was dealt with in the socialization process.

At the same time, the fantasy women develop would deal more with avenging the original abusive object, using displacement and generalization to another innocent victim. In addition, the content of the fantasy among women is different from that of men, and it usually does not include sexual sadism, or sexual intercourse. The reason is, again, different cultural perceptions in relation to women's violence and the way of achieving satisfaction of power and control.

Summary

There is a greater difficulty to classify female serial murderers into categories due to the low number of women serial murderers. Theoretically, the same theories which have been applicable for the development of a male serial murderer suit the development of a female serial murderer as well. But the contents involved in men's fantasies would be different from those of women. Today, female serial murderers reflect to a lesser degree the stereotypical perceptions of the gender roles: Dealing with magic (potions, medicines and poison) for the sake of achieving a material benefit, while regarding the woman as a person who cannot be trusted. According to the stereotype, the woman hurts her children, husband and lovers, scheming in the dark against her closest ones.

The assumption is that today more women use arms for the sake of material and other benefits. In addition, the image of the female serial murderer who is attached to a male serial murder, like the reference to women in society as "the wife of ..." or "the daughter of ...," is changing, and the reference is to a more independent figure. Among male and female serial murderers one can find a will to correct a situation of deficiency and imbalance in the sense of having control over their lives. Among women, I think, these deficiencies are deeper, and the reason for it is not just the fact that more women are victims of abuse, but because such women do not have a sense of control and power in the patriarchal society, a pattern that still exists, to a large extent, in our time. Therefore, we would find among women the phenomenon of the Munchausen syndrome by proxy. The goal of the woman murderer in these cases is to achieve attention and social support. For example, nurses who hurt their patients and are the first to try to save them, in order to get acknowledgment and attention, or mothers who hurt their children. In other words, women would tend to attack a more accessible, available and vulnerable victim which corresponds to the routine activity theory.

In addition, we would find more and more cases of serial murders with a motive of vengeance which stems from abuse, as it is among men. At the same time, we have to be careful and distinguish between a single murder and serial murder in this respect, and not cling to the fact that today more women who have gone through abuse by their husbands, dare to attack them, and even murder them.

The mass media enables them to gain fame due to their exaggerated publication, since this behaviour contradicts the gender stereotypes. It is important to understand that the same psychological mechanisms I have described among male serial murderers operate among female serial murderers as well. We would find among them the negative impact of the lack of attachment with primary figures, the establishment of depersonalization toward the victim, psychopathy and violence (Arrigo & Griffin, 2004).

As I have demonstrated in my suggestion of the new typology, one can classify female serial murderers according to some of the classifications which refer to men serial murderers: Murder of strangers for the sake of material benefit (highly common); murder out of a paranoid psychosis; an ideological murder for the sake of purifying society (very rare today, and is done under the label of hatred toward men who belong to the "improper" groups); a sado-sexual serial murder (only as partners of a man or among lesbians, and even then it is very rare); and a serial murder by proxy (highly common).

Chapter Seven
Serial Murder Profiling: Our Contemporary Understanding

Though serial murder is a relatively rare occurrence, it causes great concern among the general public. The fact that most serial murderers are classified as sane (possessing antisocial personality disorders) is even more worrisome (Holmes & Holmes, 1998).

Movies, books, and television series (such as CSI and Criminal Minds) have generated a certain degree of public conception that forensics and the ability to think like a murderer can solve every occurrence of serial murder. It is important to remember that profiling (criminal profiling or offender profiling), in its different forms and contexts such as crime scene analysis, personality analysis, spatial analysis is at most an important tool for police investigations. Advocates of profiling relate to it as a science while critics of profiling refer to it as an art form (Fox & Levin, 2005).

The effectiveness of profiling in general, and profiling of serial murder specifically, has not been widely studied. Hodges and Jacquin (2008) argue that only two-thirds of murder cases in the United States have been solved, with the unsolved third of murders including at least some serial murders. They maintain that the efficiency and accuracy of criminal profiling has not been investigated sufficiently, although their findings suggest that law enforcement officials have a higher rate of accuracy using profiling than other investigative methods.

Other critiques include the fact that the Federal Bureau of Investigation (FBI) refuses to report on the efficiency of using profiling in solving cases of serial murder, which raises questions about the method (Snook, Cullen, Bennell, Tylor & Gendreau, 2008). Conversely, recently published books and articles attempt to identify the important tools that profiling uses, and their significance as investigative tools (Turvey, 2012).

This article proposes that the use of profiling as an investigative tool for murder cases, specifically cases of serial murder, is marked by many inadequacies, stemming in part from problematic criminology typology, as well as human error. However, continued development of the theoretical tools, empirical testing, and improved training, can change profiling into a more reliable and efficient investigative tool for solving murder cases in general, and cases of serial murder specifically.

Serial Murder

The exact definition of a "serial murderer" is a subject of discussion among researchers today. Whether the debate is academic or political (in order to allocate resources), it does not impede the ability to profile the phenomenon of serial murder. Serial murder can be defined as two or more instances of murder that are carried out by the same murderer (or group of murderers), with a period of at least three days, or even several years, separating the two instances of murder (Edelstein, 2006).

There are two primary problems encountered in investigating serial murders. The first is that the murderer and the victim are complete strangers. Whereas in a "typical" murder, the murderer is well known to the victim, in the majority of serial murder cases, there is no previous association between the two, which complicates locating the murderer. The second problem is that the majority of serial murderers are seemingly normal people; they have jobs, they are well-known neighbours, some even have families. Therefore, the likelihood that they would be suspected of criminal behaviour is rather low. For example, Robert Yates, a serial murderer who operated in Washington in the 1990s, was a married father of five, worked in the United States Air Force, and murdered 13 prostitutes; Gary Ridgeway, the "Green River Killer," was married three times, including at the time of his arrest. He was employed as a truck painter for 32 years, visited church frequently, and read the Bible at home and at work. He admitted to murdering 48 women over the span of 20 years in Seattle; Dennis Rader was a married father of two, he was a leader in the Boy Scouts, served in the United States Air Force, and was the president of his local church. He murdered 10 victims in Kansas (Morton, 2006).

Serial murder is one of the most severe crimes, and also one of the most publicized crimes, which has implications on the public sense of security. The severity of the crime and the widespread media reports about it establish "moral panic," and puts great pressure on the police department to solve the crime. The problem is that the odds of catching the killer are quite low, given the nature of the crime: an absence of previous association between the murderer and the victim; the absence of a missing person report, largely due to the fact that most victims do not have family ties because of their job, their status, or other circumstances; the murderer's double life as a person who works, learns, functions in a community versus his concealed criminal actions, makes it extremely difficult for him to be perceived as a suspect and arrested. For these reasons, profiling would be helpful in investigating serial murder crimes (Bartol & Bartol, 2013).

It is difficult to ascertain the exact number of active serial murderers that have not been caught, but different estimates indicate that the number of serial murderers that roam free in the United States at any given time ranges from tens to a few hundred (Hickey, 2010; Mitchell, 1997). In the same way, it is not possible to estimate the annual number of victims of serial murder, because many of their bodies have been intentionally hidden by the killer. For example, the aforementioned, Ridgeway, admitted to murdering 48 women victims. Hunter, who was nicknamed the "Happy Face Killer," was convicted of murdering eight women, but admitted to murdering 60. It is important to note that a conviction can be made only with the evidence of a body, and not solely based on admission. Therefore, it is unclear whether serial murderers boast of a high victim count or if the number is indeed correct (Bartol & Bartol, 2013).

Typology of Serial Murderers

Researchers generally seek to identify a number of shared characteristics of a certain phenomenon or problem in order to generate
an expansive database that would be useful in profiling. In cases
of serial murder, though, this is not possible. The primary reason
is that serial murderers differ greatly from one another, in personality (psychotic versus psychopathic), in motivation for murder
(power seeking, material gain), and whether they operate inde-
pendently or as contract killers. For this reason and in order to
improve our understanding of serial killers, many researchers have
attempted classifying and typologizing murderers and serial murderers (Edelstein, 2006; Fox & Levin, 2005; Holmes & Holmes,
2008).

Typology enables the classification of different serial murderers according to a variety of characteristics such as motivation,
the existence of a fantasy, the manner in which the serial murder
was conducted, the killer's psychological characteristics, as
shown at the crime scene, the killer's mobility, the geographic
span within which the killer commits his crime, and so on. Bartol
and Bartol (2013) define typology as "a particular system for classifying personality or other behavioural patterns. The typology is
used to classify a wide assortment of behaviours into a more man-
ageable set of descriptions, which can be useful" (pp. 41–42).

The classic problems that typology presents, and those that
specifically relate to serial murder are: overlap between categories;
a case that fits several categories; a case that does not fit into any
of the proposed categories; and lack of consensus as to the criterion or variable that will determine classification (motive, operating
patters, victim type). When profiling a serial murderer, most experts depend on the motivational and psychopathological aspects
deduced from information found at the crime scene (Canter &
Youngs, 2009).

Classifying Serial Murderers as "Organized" and "Disorganized"

The FBI was the first law enforcement agency to adopt a system of typology where killers are classified according to their degree of organization: organized or disorganized. Though this typology is the earliest in terms of chronology, it is still the most widely used and accepted practice, at least within the FBI for their work, and was even presented by two FBI employees (Hazelwood & Douglas, 1980). According to this typology, there are essential differences between these two personality types that are expressed both in behaviour patterns prior to the murder, such as choosing a victim and choosing a venue, as well as behaviour patterns after the murder. As the subject matter is beyond the scope of this article, we present these two classifications in brief.

The Organized Serial Murderer: The organized serial murderer plans his actions in advance. His normal social skills enable him to lure potential victims, who exhibit common features (e.g., gender, employment, socio-economic status). The organized murderer brings his weapons with him to the crime scene, and will take care to hide them or remove them after the crime, as well as clean the crime scene from all forensic evidence. The killer is well organized, in full control of his faculties and his actions throughout the entire process, and tends to tie up his victims in order to prevent them from hindering him in carrying out his fantasy (Bartol & Bartol, 2013).

Jeffrey Dahmer serves as an example of an organized serial murderer. This serial murderer would lure his victims into pubs and, after they were intoxicated, invite them up to his apartment for a "final drink," literally. This killer prepared a sedative for the victim's drink, as well as tools such as drills and surgical equipment, in order to drill open the victims' heads, dissect their bodies, and preserve some of their organs in jars of formaldehyde. These facts indicate that he was an organized murderer, who planned his steps ahead to achieve the outcomes that motivated him to perform the crimes. This killer was a serial murderer and a cannibal, and suffered from a combination of homosexual and murderous urges. He described each murder coherently, kept body parts in his home, acted in a relaxed manner; the crimes were deliberate and premeditated. A personality analysis determined that he suffered from repressed hostility, constant fear of social rejection, and severe isolation. All of these things caused him, in a symbolic manner, "to preserve" his victims. Sexual sadism and his need for control were the basis of his desire to have his victims in a submissive position while he abused them sexually. With that being said, the fact that he preserved his victims' organs in an unsuitable manner caused his neighbours to complain of a strong stench stemming from his apartment (Palermo, 2008). Another well-known example of an organized murderer is the infamous serial killer Ted Bundy.

The Disorganized Serial Murderer: This type of serial killer is diametrically opposed to an organized serial killer. He suffers from a lack of social skills, which makes it difficult for him to lure victims. The murder is committed without advance planning, and the disorganized personality of the killer will improvise a weapon with which to commit his crime at the location (for example, strangling the victim with their own clothing). The weapon will be left at the scene of the crime, as will a variety of other pieces of forensic evidence. At the murder scene, the killer operates on impulse, or in a rage, and is not in control of his faculties. His attack on his victim is instantaneous, an onslaught, not the fulfillment of a set fantasy, and therefore he is not likely to tie up his victim. The disorganized serial killer lacks clear criteria in selecting his victims, aside from their vulnerability and lifestyle (Bartol & Bartol, 2013; Davidovitz, 2013).

Herbert William Mullin serves as an example of a disorganized serial murderer. This killer operated without any advanced planning and without any attempt to cover his tracks. As an example, his first murder was committed when he traveled aimlessly on a rural road. When he spotted an elderly man, he requested assistance to fix a problem with his engine, and then beat him to death, leaving the body at the side of the road. Approximately ten days later, he picked up a hitchhiker, stabbed her in her heart, and threw her body to the side of the road. All of these things indicate the lack of advance planning, the lack of a specific process in selecting a victim, and the absence of any attempt to conceal the murder (Newton, 2006). Commenting on these two proposed categories, Newton (2006) points out that the dichotomy is not clear or simple given that some organized serial killers turn into disorganized killers with time. They begin to leave evidence, which facilitates in their capture.

Canter, Alison, Alison, and Wentink (2004) examine the typology empirically. They assessed 100 scenes of murder that were committed by 100 serial killers in the United States. They concluded that there was no correlation between the different characteristics of the crime that could point to the classification of the serial killer as an organized serial killer or a disorganized serial killer. In their conclusion, they argue that their findings have implications for serial killer profiling; where profiling may incorrectly classify a killer as an organized killer or a disorganized killer at the beginning of an investigation, the mistaken classification can lead to a faulty investigation, wasting valuable resources of time and money.

Aside from the two categories discussed above, researchers that examined the characteristics of different serial killers found that there is a third category that should be used in classification, the "mixed" serial killer, who exhibits characteristics of both an organized serial killer and a disorganized serial killer. Accordingly, the dominant typology was subject to sharp criticism, though its advocates tried to argue that there may be cases where the murderer begins to operate as an organized murderer, and changes with time to the stereotype of a disorganized murderer (Burgess., Hartman., Ressler., Douglas & McCormick, 1986; Edelstein. 2006; Hickey, 1997).

The simplicity of this typology was received enthusiastically by many researchers in academia, in the police sector, and in the field of profiling (Canter, 2004; Davidovitz, 2013; Holmes & Holmes, 2002). Conversely though, there was intense criticism of this typology and its capacity to serve as an investigative tool (Hickey, 1997; Kocsis., Cooksey & Irvwin, 2002). Additional criticism took it one step further and argued that there is no evidence to support the proposed typology (Snook et al. 2008). More complicated typologies were suggested by researchers attempting to discriminate between murder motives: physical as opposed to psychological; related to sexuality or unrelated; psychopathic as opposed to psychotic; and more (Hickey, 1992; Holmes& Holmes, 1998; Vronsky, 2007).

While the criticism of the earlier typology of a killer as an organized killer/disorganized killer was that the classification was too broad and general, the critiques of the later typologies were that they attempted to include all different types of serial killers, which led to the development of overly detailed typology, overlapping categories, and more. In other words, in their attempt to devise a typology that was clear and unambiguous, they developed a dichotomy that was at times problematic when classifying human beings. An example of this is the typology developed by researchers Holmes & Holmes (1998).

In this typology, the researchers classified serial killers according to five main groupings: visionary; mission-oriented; hedonistic (passion and lust), and power/control. This typology was tested empirically by Canter and his team of researchers (2004). They hypothesized that if this typology reflected reality, then all of the characteristics of each type of serial murderer would be noted among the characteristics of each killer classified in this category of serial murderer, and not be found among serial killers that are classified differently. Examination of the crime scenes did not produce empirical proof to support the proposed differentiation between serial killers or other murderers. With this, these typologies did facilitate an understanding of the broad range of types of serial killers, distinguishing between the psychotic and the psychopathic killer, and distinguishing between physical motives and psychological motives and, as such, contributed to important developments in understanding serial murder and in profiling.

The most current theoretical typology (Edelstein, 2006) seeks to prevent a dichotomy between the absence of and the presence of distinguishing criteria. Learning from critiques of earlier typologies, this typology assesses the characteristics of a killer and of the serial murder on a continuum, in accordance with statistically prominent features of one type of murder. In this way, an investigator or profiler can locate the characteristics of the murder and the killer on a continuum that includes: motivations; sexual relationships; power/control; degree of acquaintance with the victim; additional crime record; focus on the action, and the process. Another advantage of this typology is that it is relevant to different types of serial murder, and includes six different genres: serial murder related to romantic involvement; terror; organized crime; women who murder for profit; professional contract killers, and killers who murder for sexual and sadistic reasons (Edelstein, 2006). With this said, it is important to note that given that the research is relatively new, it has not yet been tested empirically to determine if the typology is in fact correct.

As mentioned, typology refers to a specific method for classifying personalities or other behaviour patterns. Over time, the two main criticisms of the typologies in general, and of typologies that deal with serial murder specifically, are that although they have a lot of theoretical importance, they fail to provide researchers with the necessary elements for analyzing a crime scene. Even more problematic, typologies lack the empirical research to ratify the proposed classifications (Kappel & Brines, 2003). Alternatively, later research indicates that the empirical value of typologies and their practical application in profiling is low or non-existent (Canter & Wentink, 2004; Canter, Alison & Wentink, 2004).

The debate among researchers regarding typologies in general, and typologies of serial killers specifically is not over. Some, primarily law enforcement officials, prefer the minimalist typologies while others, primarily academics, prefer those that are maximalist (Edelstein, 2006). It should be noted that typology was largely intended to classify the phenomenon from a theoretical perspective. Only afterwards can it be tested empirically. From the moment an analysis is made, it represents the reality that the investigators and profilers encounter. With this, the great challenge is that there are few serial killers but many different motivations, *modi operandi*, and signatures. It is possible that profiling a serial killer does not need to make use of a far reaching investigative tool such as typology but rather the "fingerprint" (signature) or the DNA of a specific criminal repeatedly found.

Profiling Serial Murders and Murderers

Holmes and Holmes (1996) define profiling as "an educated attempt to provide research agencies with specific information regarding the type of individual who commits certain crimes (p. 7). In their estimation, profiling is a critical investigative tool to be used at crime scenes that enables profilers to gain insight from the physical evidence and the pathology at the crime scene.

Snook et al. (2008) explain that "criminal profiling (CP) is the practice of predicting a criminal's personality, behavioural, and demographic characteristics based on crime scene evidence" (p. 1257). In their opinion, Holmes and Holmes (1996) determine that profiling has three primary components: one, sociological and psychological evaluation of offenders, for example, race, age, employment, religion, personal status and education, which will aid the police in reducing the range of suspects and conducting searches for relevant suspects; two, psychological evaluation of the objects in the suspect's possession, for example, possession of objects that could link the suspect to the crime that was committed such as a gun or pictures from the crime scene; three, suggestions for methods of interrogating the suspect, such as *via* interview or investigation, in accordance with the personality identified by the profiler.

An additional methodology of profiling emphasizes the importance of the typology of the offenders. According to this approach, the type of crime committed is correlated with the background of the offender, and therefore it is even possible to predict who will commit certain types of crimes (Ritter, 2013). Profiling is conducted in several stages. Initially, a police officer collects evidence from the crime scene, which is then passed along to the profiler, who makes predictions regarding the offender's character, behaviour and demographic characteristics. These predictions are then reported to investigators (Snook et al. 2008).

Canter et al. (2000), and Bartol and Bartol (2013) described profiling as a way of thinking through inferences from the crime scene or other characteristics, and the offender, who has yet to be found. Deductive reasoning in profiling is used when the police have a large number of suspects, or if the police have no idea who to search for and where to search for a crime suspect. This thinking pattern was developed in the FBI and inspired by the detective Sherlock Holmes and his deductive technique. As deductive reasoning, profiler attempts to build a criminal profile based on the different findings that were identified and analyzed, including sociological and psychological characteristics of the alleged killer.

Profiling has been subject to harsh criticism over the years in that it is not based on science and theory. Similarly, it has been charged that the FBI reports on its successes in solving crimes but does not provide information regarding cases where profiling failed to identify the offender. In the following sections, we examine the effectiveness of different profiling methods in cases of serial murder.

Crime Scene Profiling in Cases of Serial Murder: The assumption of investigators is that the crime scene reflects the killer's mental pathology, and therefore profiling based on the pathological physical evidence found at the scene can provide insight.

For example, the position of the body may point to the humiliation of the victim in a symbolic manner, taking physical memorabilia may indicate a form of psychological profit for the offender, use of duct tape may point to a murderer who served in the army or was interned in a prison, or these behaviours may be part of the killer's fantasy (Holmes & Holmes, 1996).

Motive: As mentioned, serial murder derives from many different motives. However, for the most part, serial killers are inclined to victimize population sectors they deem unworthy of living, largely because of abuse they experienced in childhood. Therefore, analyzing the victims at the crime scene can give the profiler a foundation for understanding the motive (Ask & Granhag, 2005).

Fantasy: Fulfilling a fantasy can include the killer's behaviour preceding the murder and in its aftermath, dismemberment of the body and taking "memorabilia" from the body. Such that in terms of evidence, it can be expected that in the murderer's home there may be photographs and videos, or body parts discovered in the freezer (Edelstein, 2006). An important characteristic in serial murder, primarily in murders that are sexual, is the existence of a fantasy that precedes the act of murder. The fantasy comprises a script that dictates to the murderer behaviour rituals and other rituals expressed that begin with luring the victim and end in his murder, or at times, even afterward (necrophilia).

Modus operandi (MO): Serial killers are likely to escalate their behaviour with time, to take memorabilia from the body and/or to act in a different manner so as to confuse the police. Therefore, even though one cannot ignore the killer's *modus operandi*, it is possible there might be severe mistakes made in the profile if the *modus operandi* is given too much prominence in trying to connect different cases of murder to the same murderer (Bartol & Bartol, 2013).

Signature: Serial murderers each have their own unique signature. This is their "business card," because it is important to them that they be identified with the act and thereby recognized, publicized, and made famous. For example, a killer will leave at the crime scene evidence of a repetitive behaviour, even ritualistic, a sketch or writing on the walls and/or on the body, and in that way it will be possible to connect this behaviour to a certain personality among those who have been arrested for interrogation. The signature is an important medium in profiling a serial murderer, primarily when it is necessary to choose a dominant suspect among several suspects and establish a case against him (Alison, Goodwill, Van den Heuvel & Winter, 2011).

With this, researchers have not found proof that serial killers operate in a consistent fashion over time, which casts doubt on the concept of "signature," and the ability to use it to connect different cases of murder Snook et al. 2008).

Staging of the crime scene: In a case of serial murder, as compared to other crimes, the setup of the crime scene is not meant to mislead profilers. In most cases, the staging of the scene of the crime scene derives from the symbolic motive of the killer, and the way in which he wants to portray his victim. For example, a female victim might be found with her legs apart and without her undergarments, even if there was no sexual offense committed, for the sole purpose of further humiliating her after her death. The staging of the crime scene has the ability to help in profiling a serial murderer, when the assumption is that primary elements of the setup will present themselves repeatedly.

Psychological Profiling of Serial Murderers: The preeminent assumption of profiling is that serial murderers develop severe personality disorders in their youth, primarily antisocial personality disorders, and that these disorders were evident in their youth and adolescence, and come to their full expression in their adulthood through serial murder (Vernon & Geberth, 1995). For example, investigators found a difference in operation pattern and crime scenes between sexual serial murderers who were childhood victims of abuse, and those who were not (Ressler; Burgess; Douglas; Hartman & D'Agostino, 1986).

Psychological profiling assumes that it is possible to build a profile of a serial killer in accordance with his personality as it is expressed in his behaviour patterns, such as rage expressed in "surplus killing," the degree of organization of a killer, or leaving the scene of a crime disorganized. Similarly, the evidence of sexual relations with the victim, or specifically recoiling from any physical contact with the victim and the use of an object to sexually penetrate the body, can also help build a psychological profile.

Psychological profiling of a serial murder assumes that if we understand the motive, the *modus operandi*, the signature, and the staging of the crime scene, we can locate the killer and/or identify him from among a variety of possible suspects.

One of the harshest critiques leveled against psychological profiling is that of Ritter (2013), who researched serial killers beginning in the 1970s. She asserts that as in all forms of profiling, profilers make certain incorrect psychological assumptions with regard to the emergence of the serial killer and his *modus operandi*. They then take care to adapt their perceptions to the reality, even if they are different.

Case Linkage in Profiling Serial Murder: One of the chief tools in all serial murder investigations is case linkage. In order for the case being investigated to be examined as a murder among a group of serial murders, it is necessary to correlate other murders to the same murderer, or to a murderer who has been arrested. This is done in accordance with the degree of similarity of the killer's behaviour in different murder cases. For example, the killer's signature is unique and appears in each of the crime scenes. This immediately helps to reduce the number of suspects (because it is not a single murder, which is much more common). On the other hand, incorrect linking of different murders to a specific murderer can lead to a mistaken conviction (Bartol & Bartol, 2013).

A profiler can link cases in one of two ways: the profiler can search a database of murders that have similar characteristics in terms of victims, signature and primarily by comparing DNA findings, even prior to locating and arresting the suspect; or the profiler will search murder cases committed by an apprehended killer that bear similarities to the current case (Morton, 2006; Tonkin., Woodhams., Bull., Bond & Palmer, 2011; Woodhams., Bull & Holin, 2010).

This objective is not simple, because a profile needs to be distinct and unique enough to reveal something about the motive, intent, or signature of a specific offender (Santtila; Pakkanen; Zappala; Bosco; Valkama & Mokros, 2008). These researchers examined 116 murders committed by 23 murderers in Italy. The stipulation was that each killer had committed at least two murders. They found 155 unique pairs of murderers and victims (case linkage). After encoding variables according to the degree of control of the killer, motive and *modus operandi*, they found that it was possible to use the independent variables to predict who the murderer was in 62% of the cases.

More researchers support this finding, and emphasize that the fact that the killer's *modus operandi* is not always consistent and can change in accordance with its efficiency in previous murders. The *modus operandi* can change from one murder to the next (Alison et al. 2011; Bennell; Snook, McDonald; House & Taylor, 2012; Canter & Youngs, 2009). An additional criticism is that the more murders that a murderer commits, the more likely it is that his *modus operandi* will not only escalate, but also change in order to mislead the law enforcement officials, as we stated earlier.

Another assumption that derives from this critique is that when a serial murder is in control of the situation, it can be assumed that he will operate according to the behaviour pattern that is familiar to him. This can be correlated with the model of the organized murderer and the disorganized murderer. However, the greater the degree in which the killer is not in control at the crime scene, and did not plan out his actions, the greater the differences between each murder case. This makes it more difficult, if at all possible, to attribute several murders to the same killer.

The great danger of profiling in this context is twofold. It might lead to mistakenly attributing incidents of murder to a specific offender who did not actually commit the crime, or failing to attribute different incidents of murder to a specific offender, even though he committed the crime. This difficulty intensifies when the serial killer tries to mislead the police by changing his signature, or when a serial killer copycats and mimics the *modus operandi* and the signature of a different serial killer.

In light of these critiques and others, and following the emergence of computers and technology in the field of profiling, the implementation of geo-profiling has been applied to serial murder.

Geo-Profiling: Geographic Profiling and Mapping in Serial Murder: In line with the principle of "the smallest effort" of spatial profiling, and in correlation with the theory of rational choice, the serial killer will consistently choose the shortest and most accessible route from his home to his victim (Magliocca, 2012; Snook et al. 2005). For example, the offender will choose the shortest route from his home to a place where street prostitutes, homeless youth, or others, are concentrated. With this, since a serial killer selects the most vulnerable victim within the category to which he is drawn, this principle is not necessarily correct in all instances. The killer might determine his route by tracking a specific victim, and not from an objective and rational decision of expending minimal effort.

According to centrality and spatial theories serial murderers commit their crimes close to home and do not travel long distances. They prefer to operate in a "safe" zone, or in an area that is comfortable to them, primarily for psychological reasons. This also stems from the motive. The greater the degree of an emotional or sexual arousal (expressive) motive, the shorter the distance between his home and the site of the murder (Bennell., Snook., Taylor, Corvey & Keyton, 2007). The researchers found that the murder site is limited to a relatively small radius, with the killer's home being in the center. One argument is that this radius becomes smaller as the number of victims rises, and eventually is reduced to a radius of about three kilometres [39]. These researchers noted that this phenomenon, "home dump site," characterized some of the better known serial murderers such as Gacy and Dahmer.

Other researchers noted different findings, but still support this theory, with the meeting between killer and victim ranging between 14 to 22 kilometres from the killer's home, and the dumping of the body ranging from 24 to 40 kilometres (Snook et al. 2005).

Geo-profilers assert that the simple way to determine the diameter of a serial killer's circle of activity is to identify the distance between the two murders that took place farthest from one another, and place the killer's home in the center of the circle that can be sketched between these points. This method was tested and found to be correct in 89% of cases of serial murder (Snook et al 2005; Bennell et al. 2007; Canter, 2003; Lundrigan & Canter, 2001). The researchers concluded that in cases of serial murder, this method can be used with a certain degree of security. With that, it should be taken into account that some serial murderers are mobile and likely to travel long distances in order to commit their crimes, at times traveling among many states in order to hide their tracks (Paulsen, 2007).

While the circle theory examined the location where bodies were found, a more sophisticated method posited that it is possible for the serial killer to begin in one location, commit the murder at a second location, and dispose of the body in a third location, making it difficult to profile (Canter & Youngs, 2009). For example, a murderer who is acting out a fantasy will murder and dismember the body at the crime scene. Conversely, other genres of serial killers might bury the body in their home, or alternatively, hide it in a cave, drown it in a river, abandon it in a mountainous area to be prey for wild animals, etc. The existing geo-profiling method will still relate to the place where the body was found, and in these instances, the chances of the profiling being helpful in finding the killer are lower.

With this, theories of geographic profiling assume that the greater the distance between the home of the serial killer and the specific location, the lesser the chance that he will commit another murder at the same location (Canter., Coffey., Huntley & Missen 2000; Rosmo, 1995). The most prominent example for our purposes is the killer's rational choice regarding disposing of the body. When the murderer distances himself from the area that is familiar to him, the dangers and stakes (arrest) are much higher. Therefore, some serial killers prefer to hide the bodies in their homes, in a storage area, in the freezer, or buried in the ground (Canter & Youngs, 2009). It is interesting that the importance of the geographic theory is precisely in cases where it is disturbed. In instances where the killer specifically concentrates his murders in only one area, the geographic profile loses its effectiveness (Rosmo, 1997; Quinet, 2007).

A General Critique of Profiling and a Specific Critique of Serial Murder Profiling

In this article, many different critiques of profiling in general are presented, and specifically in the context of its application to cases of serial murder. Yet, many articles and books publicized reviews of profiling and its efficiency in solving criminal offenses that were unsolved (Bartol & Bartol, 2013; Turvey, 2012). Alongside the attempt to present profiling as having a strong scientific basis, in the fields of psychology and sociology as well as other disciplines, there is a lot of criticism on the inherent professionalism of profiling as a field, specifically a field of proven scientific theory, with reviews of its methods of work in the criminal realm in general, and specifically with regard to serial murder.

The title of the article by Snook and his research partners (Snook et al. 2008) does not leave much room for doubt regarding their opinion on profiling, "The Criminal Profiling Illusion: What's

Behind the Smoke and Mirrors"? Books that describe profiling work also critique practices and failures in different domains, such as case linkage, ignoring certain facts that "ruin" the picture that has emerged of the person profiled, etc. It is important to remember that in serial murder, as in all serial crimes, case linkage is the cornerstone of the process of building a profile Holmes & Holmes, 1996).

Additional significant criticism of offender profiling that is relevant to serial murder is connected to inferences that the pro-filer makes. Inference demands logical thinking, critical thinking etc., which are not taught as part of profiling training programs Turvey, 2012). Turvey raised another critique in that profilers do not disconnect themselves emotionally from the crimes that they are investigating. This is especially correct with regard to cases of murder and serial murder. He ascertained that this can influence a profiler's objectivity, as well as his ability to produce a correct profile (Turvey, 2012). Turvey also determined that even after computer software was introduced to minimize human error, it is specifically human beings, who do not always correctly evaluate the information from a crime scene, who need to input the data into the computer system.

Beyond these critiques, the most significant criticism leveled against profiling, notably serial murder profiling, was the absence of credible statistical evidence as to the effectiveness of profiling in solving cases of serial murder, and/or other cases. Snook and others claimed (Snook et al. 2008) that the FBI refuses to publi-cize its success rate in using profiling to solve cases of serial mur-der, and even refuses to allow researchers access to the databases that they used. Additionally, the fact that there are many unsolved cases of serial murder in the United States raises questions about the reliability and effectiveness of the method.

The murder committed in 2009 in "Bar Noar", the gay and lesbian Tel Aviv club, though it relates to mass murder as opposed to serial murder, still serves as a local Israeli example of the prob-lematic nature of profiling. The police allocated many resources to

solving this murder, which remains unsolved even today. I estimate that this derives in part from mistakes and failures in the
profiling work that was done.

Summary and Conclusions

Profiling works backward in time, and attempts to understand
and explain events and characteristics of events that happened in
the past. In practice, it involves a team that reconstructs a mosaic
or puzzle of behaviours, characteristics, and motives of the killer.
The team's work extends from the murderer's childhood until the
most recent act of murder committed. This process includes a
variety of methods: analysis of the crime scene and the interaction
between the murderer and the victim; the crime scene dynamic;
the fantasy that guided the offender in selecting his victim and in
the way that he related to him; a victim profile; the manner in
which the murder was committed; and the disposal of the body.
The profile also relates to the time period after the murder and
includes components such as the killer's attendance at the funeral,
the killer offering condolences to the family in mourning, contact
with the police and media outlets, keeping body parts and more
(Geberth & Turco, 1997).

These points demand analysis and reconstruction of the
crime scene, of the geographic-spatial dimension, interviews with
relatives, criminal biography and general biography of the murderer, and so on. To complicate matters, in cases of serial murder
there is not high empirical confirmation for connecting different
murder cases to one killer, as the murderer's *modus operandi* is likely to change with the duration of time. All of this makes profiling
work difficult.

One of the important conclusions of this article is that building a profile of a serial murderer necessitates a variety of profiling
methods, and it is not possible to make do with only one method.
Seeing the offender, the victim and the crime scene as one holistic

form is quite important in building a good profile that will prove useful in the investigation.

The fact that each serial killer is different than other killers compromises our ability to generalize the information. Another significant challenge is that serial murder is a relatively rare phenomenon (one percent of all murder cases). This makes it difficult to generate statistics and find mutual characteristics of serial killers, and to employ deductive reasoning. Even worse, when generalizations are indeed made in terms of age, gender and race, they can actually move the investigation in the wrong direction (Geberth & Turco, 1997; Turco, 2008).

Beyond this, we saw that significant criticism has been expressed regarding the actual field of profiling and its work methods, in that it is influenced by subjective causes, and the investigator is not aware of the influence of this subjectivity on the profile that he builds. This critique is even more relevant when dealing with inductive reasoning, in which the pitfalls may be severe.

Profiling is often based upon typologies from the field of criminology. In addition to the claim that typologies are not properly formulated, that they contain too much or too little information and that their categories are not mutually exclusive or exhaustive, experimental study of the existing typologies has not found any empirical evidence of their accuracy. Consequently, they do not serve as a strong base for profiling.

Nonetheless, one cannot ignore the positive aspects of profiling. Despite their limitations, criminological typologies of serial murder aid in developing an understanding of the basic characteristics of serial murderers, even if there are different types of murderers. The typologies aid in understanding whether a serial killer is relatively stationary or mobile, if his motives are psychological (sexual) or material, whether or not he is psychotic, among other factors.

All these can aid the profiling, even if this does not mean 100% success. If we remember and properly understand that criminal profiling is just an additional tool among the various tools that can be used by investigators in order to solve cases of serial murder, we can see that it can make an important contribution to the investigation. For example, a consistent signature of the murderer, the motives that cause him to carry out the murders, use of certain items that are known only to some people, methods of murder or dismembering the body that require knowledge common only to certain occupations, and more. At the same time, other aspects of profiling, such as geographical-spatial profiling, can significantly aid the investigation with regard to location.

In conclusion, it is important to remember that profiling is not a substitute for a thorough investigation. Additionally, the profile is not able to identify a specific suspect for arrest, and it cannot remove a suspect from a list of suspects simply because he does not fit the profile. With this said, though, a profile can aid in identifying a suspect who was arrested through other methods of investigation (Fox & Levin, 2010; Holmes & Holmes, 1996).

There is a lot of room for the scientific development of this important field, for example: empirical examination of typologies, which will necessarily bring about their improvement; ongoing and deep familiarity with the serial killers who have been captured; examining the depth and length of the killers' resolve in leaving a "signature"; training profilers by learning from mistaken profiles; educating profilers in logical and critical thinking; and developing computer programs that will overcome human error in the profiling process. All of these things can be employed in order to advance the understanding and the information and thereby prevent wrongful convictions of innocent people, and vice versa.

Chapter Eight
Serial Murders and Murderers in Israel

At the time of writing this book, murders among criminal organizations in which mainly innocent citizens are hurt, have been almost routine. But since the issue here is mass-serial murder, referring to these crimes is not within our scope of discussion.

In Israel, there are about three or four known cases of serial murder which have been executed by new immigrants from the former USSR, or by foreign workers. The most famous case is that of Nikolai Bonner, described extensively in my previous book (Edelstein, 2006). There is an apprehension of the existence of additional serial murders in Israel, since quite a few murder cases have not been solved yet. In the Galilee, for example, there is a suspicion that there is a serial murderer who murdered five persons and has never been caught. This assumption can be right or wrong, and since I have no access to the investigation material, I cannot refer to it more elaborately.

The District Court in Haifa sentenced Nikolai Bonner to 120 years of imprisonment due to the murder of four homeless people and raping one of the victims. After a psychological observation, and in spite of the claim of drunkenness, the court found the defendant guilty. It has been proven that although his deeds had been done under the influence of alcohol, the defendant was not drunk to a degree that did not enable him understand his deeds. And indeed, he was well aware of his deeds, and planned his actions, like liquidating evidence by burning the bodies and the scenes of the murder (File 2049/05). In addition, the fact that he murdered several times, even if he was in a state of drunkenness, points to the fact that the influence of alcohol is not valid in this case.

The verdict does not shed new light on the facts that have been described in my previous book. The murderer knew his victims, but did not have very close relations with them. The murder acts were done after Bonner was angry with the victims, and under the influence of alcohol. The murderer was pedantic about burning the scene to destroy any incriminating evidence, and he would leave the bodies at the scene of the murder, assuming that the fire would consume everything.

It is impossible to find any evidence of planning or a decision to kill, though it is my opinion that the extent of fury Bonner demonstrated shows his preliminary attitude toward homeless people. It took a small spark, a catalyst, through a dispute or annoyance, to build up his anger into a murder. Although Bonner knew his victims, as has been mentioned, and did not plan the murder, the evidence strengthens my assumption that this is a case of an ideological murder for the sake of purifying society. This murderer killed people just because they belonged to a social sector which had, actually or imaginarily, hurt him, or did not deserve to live according to his opinion. In this case, they were homeless people who reflected for Bonner his own self. Bonner did not choose in advance a specific homeless person, but in the circumstances of this case, when one of these homeless people, a woman, refused to give him a lock for free, cursed his mother and refused to have sex with him, it was the accelerating factor for the execution of the murder. The psychiatric evidence shows a psychotic episode and general psychological problems.

Bonner murdered people who belonged to his sector—the homeless. Through them he saw himself and it made him angry and depressed. When they dared to disobey him or not comply with his will, and since they had been considered sub-human in his eyes, it led him to murder them violently in a manner that expresses an antisocial personality disorder, while trying not to be caught. Moreover, one can see the integration of the theory of rational choice together with the theory of routine activities. Bonner chose victims who met a central criterion—belonging to a despicable social category to which the murderer also belonged. But beyond this, he chose victims that nobody would look for who were defenseless since they stayed in the street at all hours of the day.

Examination of the Case in Relation to the Suggested

Classification

Preoccupation with sex—Low. Bonner tried to rape one of the victims. The other three victims were men and there was no sexual dealing with them of any kind.

Acquaintance with the victim—Low. He used to see them in his neighbourhood on a daily basis, but there was no friendship or any other close acquaintance.

Power-control games—The act of the murder was fast, following the catalyst of the confrontation between the murderer and the victim. There were no power-control games, and the murder was executed quickly like a Blitz attack.

Involvement of another crime—Bonner's murders were not for the sake of sexual satisfaction or a material benefit. After the murder he burned the scene, but it was meant, probably, to disrupt the investigation. That is, one cannot speak about an involvement of another crime, except the case in which he tried to rape one of the victims.

Focus on the action or on the process—These murders have not been planned. The murderer focused on the act of the murder, and no process can be seen there. After a quick murder, the murderer put the scene on fire and ran away. The conclusion that appears is that it is a case of a serial murderer who acts from an ideology of purifying society of a group which seems to him as unworthy.

Another case of a serial murder in Israel was published in an article in Haaretz newspaper (Esti Aharonovich, "A monster cat," 14.11.08).

This case is about Rostislav Boguslavsky, a new immigrant from Uzbekistan. The suspect slaughtered five hundred cats and later on murdered two homeless people and injured another homeless. The first victim was Listov. On 4.2.07 Listov was walking drunk near the market in Petach Tikva, and the suspect passed nearby and stabbed him in his belly. Listov was saved from death. Two weeks afterward, the suspect stabbed Vladimir Vefarb, sixty-eight, in the back of his neck, when the victim was drunk and sat on the curb of the pavement. The injured died of his wounds. Two months later, another male victim, fifty years of age, was murdered by the suspect when he was drunk. The murder took place at a building site not far from the market. The suspect stabbed the victim in his chest 14 times, with another eight stabs to the neck (overkill). In the pathological examination it was found that the suspect abused the body of the victim after his death, executing cuts in the area of the testicles a day after the event.

At the same time, the suspect, age 18, confessed to his father about the deeds described above. The suspect, 20 years old now, is accused of two murder cases, an attempt of murder and abusing hundreds of animals. The suspect admitted that since he was 13 he would kill cats and dismember their bodies. In his house cat skins and knives that served for these actions were found. The suspect said that he lived in the area of the market of Petach Tikva, and that he was angry at the alcoholics who used would defecate at night in the yard of his house. The suspect, who had immigrated to Israel at the age of eight, said that he was socially rejected and suffered from pupils' harassments. When he was in the fifth grade, he was sent to the psychological services due to anxieties and fears which he covered by a façade of self-confidence and the use of violence. According to him, at the age of 12, he started to smoke and drink alcohol. In spite of the recommendations of the psychological services to introduce him to psychiatric treatment, his parents did not do it due to economic problems. At the age of 14, the family moved from Nahariya to Petach Tikva. The suspect grew up with a feeling that the world hates him. In that year he was arrested for attacking another youngster because he wanted a game the other one had.

At the age of 16, he joined a neo-Nazi gang, and started believing in the supremacy of the Aryan race. In that year, he and his mates attacked two orthodox youngsters, and later on destroyed a

Yeshiva in Petach Tikva. The suspect was imprisoned for six months in Ofek Juvenile Prison.

After being released from prison, his mother sent him to a family in London, and when he came back he told his parents he did not want to stay in Israel anymore. Afterward, he asked to live in a monastery, but his Jewish father refused. After working with his father for two months, the suspect started to stay at home, closed the shutters and went out rarely. Later on he joined a devil worshippers' cult through the Internet. He claims that he did so in order to be strong and avenge his being a victim of abuse by the children of his childhood.

The suspect was released from military service on a psychological basis, after reporting to them that he sees and hears demons. He was addressed to a psychiatrist and received antipsychotic medication, but he did not bother to take them. A week before the meeting with the psychiatrist he stabbed his first victim (who was injured), and ten days after the meeting he murdered his second victim.

According to the suspect, he slaughtered cats at first in order to eat their flesh which was supposed to give him power, but stopped with this behaviour out of disgust. He claimed that he continued to kill cats in order to relieve pressures. He was turned in by his father and a friend, two out of the only three people in his world, before whom he had confessed his deeds.

The above facts were collected from an article in the newspaper, but beyond the commentaries of the writer, one can see them as solid facts, since they are backed up in the indictment and in his conversations with police investigators.

Allegedly, and according to the data at my disposal, we can refer to the suspect as suffering from a paranoid psychosis. He was allocated already in the fifth grade as suffering from psychological disturbances and was recommended to get psychiatric treatment. Later on, he reported delusions and hallucinations coming from demons, and was released from military service. A psychiatric evaluation was done following his initiation, showing a severe mental illness.

The fact that the suspect did not take the antipsychotic medication he had been given, showed that in spite of the suffering he had experienced by being exposed to these demons, it had its excitement and psychological benefit as well, which he did not want to stop by taking the medications. He argued that he wanted to hurt others because he had been hurt as a child from harassments of students in his class after he came as a new immigrant. His behaviour does not correspond to the description of the motive he gives. Although he could not avenge the same children, if indeed the motive was the will to avenge, he was supposed to hurt Israelis, as a displacement or symbolization of those who had hurt him in his childhood. In fact, he hurt only newcomers from the former USSR, where he came from, and only drunk homeless people. Although he does not admit to committing the murders, we can assume that if he did the deeds attributed to him, then those "demons" are the ones who directed him to the victims. The victims were unfamiliar to him, but had a common denominator: Newcomers from the former USSR, homeless and drunk. From this respect, the choice of the victims is random but specific.

To sum up, it is a case of a murderer who suffers from a paranoid psychosis who chose his victims from a sector which he perceives as unworthy of living, since somehow this sector reflects him.

Analysis of the Case According to the Suggested

Classification

- Preoccupation with sex—Nonexistent
- Acquaintance with the victim—Nonexistent
- Power-control games—Nonexistent
- The murder was committed quickly, and after stabbing the victim, the murderer left the scene. In one case, the murderer abused the body of the victim, but it was after the victim was already dead.
- Involvement of another crime—Nonexistent

- Focus on the action or on the process—The focus is on the act of the murder, without an early planning. The murder was executed very quickly. In one case, as has been mentioned, the murderer returned to the scene and abused the body.

According to the suggested classification, this is a psychotic murderer. It is interesting to indicate that this is a rare case in which the murderer brags and shares his behaviour with friends, and this information led to his relatively quick capture.

As we have seen, in cases of psychotic people, they do not murder haphazardly. Their sick psyche chooses the victims for them.

Summary

Multiple-victims murder has existed since the beginning of mankind. The question whether a deed under instruction or command is a murder (a suicide bomber, assassination issued by intelligence agencies, assassinating political opponents, obeying the instruction of any kind of leader) is a political issue rather than a criminological one.

This issue caused quite a few problems in the attempt to define multiple-victims murder in general and the mass-serial murder in particular. All the same, one can include murder of this kind as a multiple-victims murder provided that the context in which it was done is indicated. This kind of murder can be a mass murder, serial-mass murder or serial murder, depending on its unique characteristics.

Knowledge from the Past

The interest in the issue of multiple-victims murder is not new, but in the course of the two recent decades important academic books and articles on this topic have appeared. Most of the theoretical and research literature dealt with serial murderers and murders, while few studies have dealt with mass murder and murderers. There are several central reasons for this gap in the research literature: First, while the majority of mass murderers die either by their own initiative, or by the law enforcement systems, serial murderers stay in prison for long periods of time, and one can interview them to write their biographies.

Second, a mass murder, as shocking as it can be, is an event that is restricted in time and place, whereas a serial murder, on the other hand, has continuity and gains the media's coverage for a long time. In addition, a mass murder is a momentary event. One has to digest its outcome retroactively, and hence it is not frightening any more, while a serial murder is a continuous event, and certain sectors in the population are afraid to be the next victim. Thirdly, serial murder is more fascinating for the public than mass murder, mainly due to the way of presenting the murderer in the mass media and the connection to sex. While the mass murderer is perceived as someone who may be seized by an amok and temporary insanity and shoots indiscriminately, the serial murderer is perceived as a monster in a human disguise that behaves like the next door neighbour in everyday life, genteel, has a regular position at work, etc. In other words, the media make him one of us, even if monstrous, and these very characteristics arouse the public's interest and anxiety.

The professional literature on this issue suffered from an empirical difficulty and an inability to present full explanations to these phenomena and examine them in the research field. The main reasons for this situation are the small number of subjects, cases which are suspected to be cases of serial murder that have not been deciphered yet, the need to conclude, and even guess the motives of mass murderers who have been shot or committed suicide, and the problem of reliability of interviews with serial murderers.

The theoretical literature in this field has grown over the course of time, but has not presented, in my opinion, any new insights. The different theories have been reduced to the examination of the phenomenon on the basis of one theory which they tried to implement to serial murder. In this manner, many theories and explanations have been created indeed, but each one of them remained separated rather than integrated with the others.

Many typologies have been suggested in relation to mass and serial murder. In the field of mass murder, part of the typologies dealt with quite general motives, like the aspiration for power and vengeance. These concepts were not defined properly, both ver-bally and operatively, and have remained generally unclear. Other typologies, mainly regarding serial murder, have often been influ-enced by interests of the law enforcement system and less by the search for theoretical-academic knowledge per se. When im-portant typologies have been constructed, they suffered from sig-nificant defects due to the mixing of concepts of serial murder, mass murder, and mass-serial murder; duplicities in the categories of the typology, or using incorrect terms, like an "external motive" in relation to a material motive in a serial murder.

The main problem in the existing literature is the problem of definition. Even today, there has not been an agreed definition for mass murder, serial murder, and mass-serial murder. The defini-tion is the basis for the whole theoretical structure, and if there is no agreement about it, then it is relatively easy to attack the theo-retical aspects which are built on it, like typologies, and so on.

One of the central disputes in the professional literature is to what extent it is proper to use one concept to all cases of multiple murder, since the assumption at the basis of this suggestion is that there are no significant differences between mass murder, serial murder, and mass-serial murder. On the other hand, a claim materialized that each concept should be independent, due to its unique characteristics. This issue caused the confusion of con-cepts I have referred to here.

Limitations

In spite of the innovations the book suggests in the field of multi-ple-victims murder, one has to bear in mind the methodological and empirical problems in investigating this domain: There are no accurate data regarding murderers and victims; ethnographical research methods that have been found unreliable in this field; inability to gather data regarding mass murderers who have committed suicide or were shot by the security forces. All these damage the empirical research and for this reason, one cannot examine the suggested theoretical model, but only the direction of the investigation and the explanation it offers. Another central limitation stems from the fact that even today there is no agreed definition of serial murder and mass murder, and without an agreed definition it is very difficult to base typologies and explanations regarding these phenomena. But the theoretical model that is suggested in this book is not significantly influenced by this limitation. The explanation would be valid whether we define a serial murderer as one who murdered two or four victims. At the same time, it is difficult in the present situation to reach an academic discussion on an agreed basis.

Another problem in this field is that up to this day, there is no global objective database for these phenomena, one which would include the personal and familial background; the time intervals between one murder and the next (in a serial murder and a mass-serial murder), and other criteria. Since this is the case, the suggested explanations within the integrative model remain within the scope of a theory that has not been examined empirically, and we do not know now if it would be possible to examine the different variables operationally.

A Glance to the Future

I regard this work as a preface to a fertile and thorough discussion among scientists who are interested in the field of multiple-victims murder. It raises many questions, but cannot answer all of them. It is advisable that criminologists, sociologists, psychologists and experts from other fields of knowledge would reach an agreement on the definitions of mass murder, mass-serial murder, and serial murder for the sake of research.

Establishing international databases in the field of mass, serial, and mass-serial murder and murderers would enable scientists from all over the world to get help from the various data in order to develop explanations and theories in various fields of knowledge on an objective empirical basis, rather than only from conversations with the murderers and their family members.

Additional typologies, from different viewpoints, can be established beyond the ones that have been suggested here. In this manner, it would be possible to examine the similarities and differences among the different types of serial and other types of murderers. It would also enable refuting the existing myths which have been spread to a large extent by the mass media, and focusing on the more common fields of serial, mass-serial, and mass murder.

I do not think that one can prevent serial, mass-serial, and mass murders, but after it has been clarified that many of the mass-murder cases have to do with being dismissed from work, a method has been introduced in the USA, according to which upon receiving a person to work, the employer checks how it would be right to act in a case of dismissal, if needed, in a way that would not lead to an act of vengeance by the employee. Alternatively, one can think of a defense means for families who are in a process of divorce. Today there is a restraining order of the husband who beats up or threatens his wife (in a single murder), but a person who has decided to murder his family would not be deterred by a restraining order (Edelstein, 2011).

Another important issue has to do with the high access to firearms in a number of states, like the USA and Finland. There is no doubt that the fact that it is so easy to acquire weapons for the sake of a mass murder facilitates the execution of such felonies. Although it is very difficult to predict a mass murder on the basis of the history of the criminal, maybe certain checks would enable preventing a mass murder.

The FBI has already acted in this direction in instructions it has distributed to school principals. It seems probable that youngsters who have executed a mass murder at school would inform their schoolmates about it in advance. However, the culture of silence prevented this important information from reaching the authorities who might have acted to prevent such murders. (While writing these lines, a recent mass murder in a U.S. school has occurred, invoking this issue again).

Undoubtedly, beyond the specific psychological factor of every person, cultural and social factors influence, to a large extent, the shaping of serial, mass-serial, and mass murderers, mainly in a culture which makes heroes out of them. A suggestion of a cultural change is almost an impossible pretense. Though it is my opinion that the different kinds of mass media should act to stop the glorification of these murderers and present them in a negative light. Another way is to present the families of the victims and show what the murder has caused them, building identification in the public with the victims rather than with the murderers. It would reduce to a certain extent the carnival that goes on today, as these kinds of murderers know that they are glorified. An additional way of dealing with this phenomenon is not mentioning the name of the murderer at all. Again, claiming that it would deter or prevent the next murder would be too pretentious, but such a change could, in the course of time, hurt one of the central motives of such a murder, i.e., the motive of being famous, a problem that almost no theory deals with.

The issue of profiling appears in different circumstances, but most of the scientists who deal with this issue do not attribute great significance to it. The reason is the low rate of success of capturing violent criminals by the national profiling unit in the USA which is affiliated with the CIA. At the same time, some scientists still believe that profiling is the crux of the matter, and invest efforts and great budgets in this field. But as has been said, it has not proved itself until now. Since most mass, mass-serial, and serial murders have to do with secret planning and getting equipped with the instrument of the murder, while the murderer goes on behaving "as usual," it is very difficult to build a profile of a serial murderer, a mass-serial murderer, and a mass murderer and start implementing it in advance. In addition, it involves problems of freedom of privacy, since one cannot arrest a person just because he fits into a certain profile. In the same way that a psychological and psychiatric diagnosis is done retroactively, so it is with the diagnosis of mass, mass-serial, and serial murderers. Even if one could have built a profile of a serial murderer (in relation to a mass murderer it would be of little use), to find the murderer according to such a profile would be almost impossible. The only area that has any tools to prevent some kinds of mass and mass-serial murder is the intelligence community in regards to terrorism by people from inside and outside the country.

I have come to the conclusion that within the training of policemen, understanding the event and the scene by policemen, enables them to identify whether it is a case of a mass, mass-serial, or serial murder, and this distinction is important. Police forces which are called to an event that is a suspected mass murder must search the area of the murderer, while putting obstacles and barriers around the scene, and checking the means of escape by the murderer that are irrelevant. On the other hand, when there is a report of a single body, there is room to investigate possible eyewitnesses, conducting searches of the described vehicle by witnesses, and so on, whereas at the scene itself they have to work only with the lab for criminal identification and experts of the scene of the crime.

Therefore, better and more accurate knowledge of the three kinds of multiple-victims murder will help not only on the academic level, but on the practical level, as well.

Bibliography

Hebrew Sources

Edelstein, A. (2006). Criminal career and serial criminality, Ben-Gurion University, *Yediot Aharonot* newspaper, www.ynet.co.il as of 23.9.08.

Freud, A. (1977). *The self and the defense mechanisms*, Tel Aviv: Dvir Publication.

Goren, D. (1993). Communication and reality, Jerusalem: Keter Publishing House. *Haaretz* newspaper, Various articles (1994-2007).

The Knesset, (1977). *Penal Code Law 1977: Para. 298–304' 18–19* Mahshavot Publishing.

Peled, J., Saltzman, G., & Apter, A. (2001). Violence and murder of psychotic patients, *Medicine, Vol. 140*, (3).

P.H. 2049/05, *The state of Israel vs. Nikolay [son of Georgy] Bonner*, District Court, Haifa.

Schiff, M. & Benbenishty, R. (2004). Implications of terror events on high school students in Jerusalem, *Hebrew University: School of Social Work and Social Wellbeing*.

Shem-David, H. (2008). *Psychosis—The full guide*: www.ifeelgood.co.il/ profession.

Shkedi, A. (2004). *Words that attempt to touch: Qualitative research—Theory and practice*, Tel Aviv University: Ramot Publishing.

Yasur, Y. (1995). *The decision to murder*, Tel Aviv University: Ramot Publishing.

English Sources

Akers, R.L. (1973). *Deviant behavior: A social learning approach*, Belmont, CA: Wadsworth.

Akers, R.L. (1997). *Criminological theories*, CA: Roxbury Publishing co.

Alison, L. J., Goodwill, A. Almond, L., Van den Heuvel, C. & Winter, J. (2011). Pragmatic solutions to offender profiling and behavioral investigative advice. In: Ask, K. & Granhag, P. A. Motivational sources of confirmation bias in criminal investigation: The need for cognitive closure. *Journal of Investigative Psychology and Offender Profiling, 2*, 43–63.

Amsel, A. (1958). The role of frustrative nonreward noncontiguous reward situations, *Psychological Bulletin*, 55: 102

Amir, M. (1965). In Bryan, J.H. Apprenticeships in prostitution, *Social Problems*, 12 (3): 287–297.

Amir, M. (1966). In Bryan, J.H. Occupational ideologies and individual attitudes of call girls, *Social Problems*, 13 (4): 441–450.

Anderson, W.R. (1999). Can personality disorders be used as predictors of serial killers? *Futurics*, 23 (3/4): 34–43.

Arndt, W.B.; Hietpas, T; Kim, J. (2004). Critical characteristics of male serial murderers, *American Journal of Criminal Justice*, 29 (1): 117–131.

Arrigo, B.A. & Griffin, A.B.A. (2004), Serial Murder and the Case of Aileen Wournos: Attachment, Psychopathy and Predatory Aggression, *Behavioral Science and the Law*, 22: 375–393.

Ask, K. & Granhag, P. A. (2005). Motivational sources of confirmation bias in criminal investigation: The need for cognitive closure. *Journal of Investigative Psychology and Offender Profiling*, 2, 43–63.

Bartol, C. R. & Bartol, A. M. (2013). *Introduction to forensic psychology: Research and application*. CA: Sage Publications.

Beeghley, L. (2003). *Homicide: A sociological explanation*, N.Y.: Rowman & Littlefield Publishers, Inc.

Bennell, C., Snook, B., Taylor, P. J., Corey, S., & Keyton, J. (2007). It's no riddle, choose the middle: The effect of number of crimes and topographical detail on police officer predictions of serial burglars' home locations. *Criminal Justice and Behavior*, 34, 119–132.

Bennell, C., Snook, B., McDonald, S., House, J. C. & Taylor, P. J. (2012). Computerized crime linkage systems: A critical review and research agenda. *Criminal Justice and Behavior*, 39, 620–634.

Blackman, P.; Leggett, V.L.; Olson, B.L.; Jarvis, J.P. (1999). *The varieties of homicide and its research*, F.B.I. Academy, Quantico, Virginia.

Bowlby, J. (1969). *Attachment and loss*, N.Y.: Basic Books.

Brantley, A.C. & Hosky, R.H. (2005). Serial murder in the Netherlands, *Federal Bureau of Investigation Bulletin*, USA

Burgess, A., Hartman, C., Ressler, R. K., Douglas, J. E. & McCormick, A. (1986). Sexual homicide: A motivational model. *Journal of Interpersonal Violence*, 1, 251–272.

Butler, L.D. (2006). Normative dissociation, *Psychiatric Clinics of North America*, 29: 45–62.

Canter D. V., Coffey, T., Huntley, M. & Missen, C. (2000). Predicting serial killers' home base using a decision support system. *Journal of Quantitative Criminology*, 16, 457–478.

Canter, D. V. (2003). *Mapping murder: The secrets of geographical profiling.* London, England: Virgin Publishing.

Canter, D. V. (2004). Offender profiling and investigative psychology, *Journal of Investigative Psychology and Offender Profiling*, 4–6.

Canter, D. V., Alison, A. J., Alison, E. & Wentink, N. (2004). The Organized/disorganized typologies of serial murder: Myth or model? *Psychology, Public Policy and Law* 10(1–2), 71–101.

Canter, V.C. & Wentink, N. (2004). An empirical test of Holmes and Holmes's serial murder typology, *Criminal Justice and Behavior, 31* (4): 489–515.

Canter, D. V. & Youngs, D. (2009). *Investigative psychology: Offender profiling and the analysis of criminal action.* Chichester England: Wiley.

Carlisle, A.C. (1998). The divided self: Toward an understanding of the dark side of the serial killer. In Holmes, R.M. & Holmes, S.T. *Contemporary perspective on serial murder*, London: Sage Publications.

Castle, T. & Hensley, C. (2002). Serial killers with military experience: Applying learning theory to serial murder, *International Journal of Offender Therapy and Comparative Criminology, 46* (4): 453–465.

Cater, J.G. (1997). The social construction of the serial killer, *RCMP Gazette, 59* (2): 2–21.

Cleckley, H. (1941). The mask of sanity: An attempt to reinterpret the so-called psychopathic personality, St. Louis, MO: C.V Mosby.

Cluff, J; Hunter, A; Hinch, R. (1997). Feminist perspectives on serial murder: A critical analysis, *Homicide Studies, 1* (3): 291–308.

Cohen, L. E. & Felson, M. (1979). Social change and crime rate trends: A routine activities approach, *American Sociological Review, 44*: 588–608.

Cooley, C. (1902). *Human nature and the social order*, N.Y: C. Scribner's & Sons.

Davidovitz, A. (2013). *Lo magidatidot* (Will not foretell the future). Bitachon Pnim, 4, 8–11.

DeFronzo, J; Ditta, A; Hanon, L; Prochnow, J. (2007). Male serial homicide and structural variables, *Homicide Studies, 11* (1): 3–14.

Delisi, A; Scherer, A.M. (2006). Multiple homicide offenders, *Criminal Justice and Behavior, 33* (3): 367–391.

Dietz, P.E. (1986). Mass, serial, and sensational homicides, *Bulletin of The New York Academy of Medicine, 62*: 477–490.

Dollard, J. & Miller, N. (1950). *Personality and psychotherapy*, New York: McGraw-Hill.

Douglas, J., Burgess, A.W., Burgess, A.G. & Ressler, R. (2006), *Crime classification manual*, San Francisco: John Wiley & Sons

Douglas, J.E., Burgess, A.W.; Burgess, A.G. & Ressler, A.K. (1992). *Crime classification manual: A standard system for investigation and classifying violent crime*, N.Y.: Simon & Schuster.

Douglas, J., Burgess, A.W., Burgess, A.G. & Ressler, R. (2006), *Crime classification manual*, San Francisco: John Wiley & Sons

Dowden, C. (2005). Research on multiple murders: Where are we in the state of the art? *Journal of Police and Criminal Psychology, 20* (2): 8–19.

Durkheim, E. (1951), [1897]. *Suicide*, New York: Free Press.

Duwe, G. (2004). The patterns and prevalence of mass murder in twentieth century America, *Justice Quarterly, 21* (4): 729–761.

Edelstein, A. (2017). Case studies in multiple victims' murder, *Juniper Online journal of case studies*, Doi: 10.19080/jojcs.2017.02.55595

Egger, S.A. (1988). *The killers among us: An examination of serial murder and its investigation* (2 ed.), NJ: Prentice Hall.

Erdman, S.L. (2017). What is the difference between a serial killer, spree killer and mass murder? Cox media group.

FBI (2003). *Serial killers*, USA Government.

Felson, M. (2006). *Crime and nature*, London: Sage Publication.

Ferguson, C.J.; White, D.E.; Cherry, S.; Lorenz, M.; Bhimani, Z. (2003). Defining and classifying serial murder in the context of perpetrator motivation, *Journal of Criminal Justice, 31*: 287–292.

Flick, U. (1998). *Introduction to qualitative research* (2nd ed.), London: Sage Publication.

Fox, H. A. & Levin, J. (1994). *Mass murder and serial killing*, New York: Plenum

Fox, H. A. & Levin, J. (1998). Multiple homicide: Patterns of serial and mass murder, *Crime and Justice, 23* (3): 407–455.

Fox, J.A & Levin, J. (2003). Mass murder: An analysis of extreme violence, *Journal of Applied Psychoanalytic Studies, 5*(1): 47–64.

Fox, J. A.; Levin, J. (2005). *Extreme killing, understanding serial and mass murder*, London: Sage Publications.

Fox, J. A. & Levin, J. (2010). *Extreme Killing*, London: Sage Publications.

Gabbard, G.O. (1994). Psychodynamic psychiatry in clinical practice, the DSM—IV edition, American Psychiatric Press, Washington.

Gerberth, V.J. (1996). Practical homicide investigation: Tactics, procedures, and forensic techniques (3rd ed.), Boca Raton, FL: CRC Press.

Geberth, V. J. & Turco, R. N. (1997). Antisocial personality disorder, sexual sadism, malignant narcissism and serial murder. *Journal of Forensic Science*, 42(1), 49–60.

Giannangelo, S.J. (1996). *The psychopathology of serial murder: A theory in violence*, Westport, C.T.: Praeger.

Gibbs, J.P. (1975). *Crime, punishment, and deterrence*, New York: Elsevier.

Glaser, D. (1956). Criminality theories and behavioral images. *American Journal of Sociology*, 61: 433–444.

Goffman, E. (1961). *Asylums*, N.Y: Dubleday.

Godwin, M. & Canter, D. (1997). Encounter and death: The spatial behavior of U.S. serial killers. Policing, *An International Journal of Police Strategy and Management*, 20, 24–38.

Goffman, E. (1963). *Stigma: Notes on the management of spoiled identity*, NJ: Prentice Hall.

Greswell, D.M. & Hollin, C.R. (1994). Multiple murder: A review. *The British journal of criminology*, 34, 1–14.

Hale, R. (1998). The application of learning theory to the serial murder. In Holmes, R.M. & Holmes, S.T. *Contemporary perspective on serial murder*, London: Sage Pub.

Harbort, S; Mokors, A. (2001). Serial murder in Germany from 1945 to 1995, *Homicide Studies*, 5 (4): 311–334.

Hazelwood, R. & Douglas, J. (1980). The lust murder. *FBI Law Enforcement Bulletin*, 49(2), 18–24.

Hempel, A., Meloy, J. & Richards, T. (1999). Offender and offences, characteristics of a nonrandom sample of mass murderers, *Journal of the American Academy of Psychiatry and the Law*, 27 (2): 213–225.

Hickey, E.W. (1992). *Serial murderers and their victims*, Wadsworth Publishing Company.

Hickey, E.W. (1997). *Serial murderers and their victims*. Belmont, CA: Wadsworth.

Hickey, E.W. (2002). *Serial murderers and their victims*, Wadsworth publishing company.

Hinch, R. & Scott, H. (2000). Explaining female serial murders: Theoretical issues, Canada.

411

Hirschi, T. & Gottfredson, M. (1993). Commentary: Testing the general theory of crime, *Journal of Research in Crime and Delinquency*, 30: 47–54.

Holmes, R.M. & DeBurger, J.D. (1988). *Serial murder*, London: Sage Publications.

Holmes, R.M. & Holmes, S.T. (1994). *Murder in America*, CA: Sage Publications.

Holmes, R.M. & Holmes, S.T. (1996). *Profiling violent crimes*, London: Sage Publications.

Holmes, R.M. & Holmes, S.T. (1998). *Serial murders*, London: Sage Publications.

Holmes, R.M. & Holmes, S.T. (Eds.). (1998). *Contemporary perspective on serial murder*, London: Sage Publications.

Holmes, S.T., Tewksbury, R.; Holmes, & R.M. (1999). Fractured identity syndrome, *Journal of Contemporary Criminal Justice*, 15(3): 262–272.

Holmes, R. M. & Holmes, S. T. (2002). *Profiling violent crimes: An investigative tool*. CA: Sage Publications.

Holmes, R. M. & Holmes, S. T. (2008). *Profiling violent crimes: An investigative tool*. CA: Sage Publications.

Holmes, E.A.; Brown, R.J.; Mansell, W.; Fearon, R.P.; Hunter, E.C.M.; Frasquilho, F.; Oakley, D.A. (2004). Are there two qualitatively distinct forms of dissociation? A review and some clinical implications, *Clinical Psychological Review*, 25: 1–23.

Holzman, H.R. (1995). The serious habitual property offenders as "moonlighter." In Hobbs, D. (Ed.). *Professional criminals*, USA: Dartmouth.

Jenkins, R.L. (1960). The psychopath or antisocial personality, *Journal of Nervous and Mental Diseases*, 131: 318–334.

Jenkins, P. (2002). Catch me before I kill more: Seriality as modern monstrosity, *Cultural Analysis*, 3: 1–17.

Kappel, R. D. & Brines, W. (2003). *The psychology of serial killer investigation*. CA: Academic Press.

Kappel, R.D. & Walter, R. (1999). Profiling killers: A revised classification for understanding sexual murder, *International Journal of Offender Therapy and Comparative Criminology*, 43 (4): 417–437.

Kelleher, M. D. & Kelleher, C.L. (1998). *Murder most rare: Female serial killer*, USA: Praeger Publishers.

Kenney, B.T. & Heide, K.M. (1994). Gender differences in serial murderers, *Journal of Interpersonal Violence*, 9 (3): 383–398.

Kocsis, R. N., Cooksey, R. W. & Irwin, H. I. (2002). Psychological profiling of offender characteristics from crime behaviors in serial rape offences, *International Journal of Offender Therapy and Comparative Criminology*, 46, 144–169.

Kooistra, P. (1989). *Criminals as heroes: Structure, power & identity*, Bowling Green State University Popular Press.

Kraemer, G.G.D., Lord, W.D. & Heilbrun, K. (2004). Comparing single and serial homicide offences, *Behavioral Sciences and the Law, 22*: 325–343.

Lang, R. (1999). A Cusp catastrophe approach to the prediction of temporal patterns in the kill date of individual serial murderers, nonlinear dynamics, *Psychology and Life Sciences, 3* (2): 143–159.

Langton, M.L., Barbaree, H.E., Harkins, L., Arenovich, T., Peacock, E.J., Dalton, A., Hansen, K., Luong, D., & Marcon, H. (2008). Denial and minimization among sexual offenders, *Criminal Justice and Behavior, 35* (1): 69–98.

Laukkanen, M., Santtila, P., Jern, P. & Sandnabba, K. (2008). Predicting offender home location in urban burglary series. *Forensic science international*, 176(2–3), 224–235.

Levi, K. (1995). Becoming a hit man. In Hobbs, D. (Ed.). *Professional criminals*, Dartmouth, USA.

Levin, J. (2008). *Serial killers and sadistic murderers*, Prometheus Books, New York.

Levin, J. & Fox, J.A. (1991). *Mass murder: America's growing menace*, New York: Berkley Books.

Levin, J. & Fox, J.A. (2001). *Deadlines: Essays in murder and mayhem*, Boston: Allyn and Bacon.

Levin, J. & Fox, J.A. (2007). Normalcy in behavioral characteristics of the sadistic serial killer. In Kocsis, R.N. (Ed.). *Serial murder and the psychology of violent crimes*, Totowa, N.J.: Humana Press, Inc.

Levin, J. & Fox, J.A. (2014). *Extreme Killing*, L.A.: Sage.

Leyton, E. (1986). *Hunting humans*, Penguin Books.

Lofland, J. (1969). *Deviance and identity*, New Jersey: Prentice Hall, Inc.

Lundrigan, S. & Canter, D. V. (2001). A multivariate analysis of serial murderers' disposal site location choice. *Journal of Environmental Psychology*, 21, 423–431.

Magliocca, D. (2012). Geographical profiling: I'll find where you live. *International association for criminal psychology*, October, 14.

Martens, W. H. J. & Palermo, G.B. (2005). Loneliness and associated violent anti-social behavior: Analysis of the case reports of Jeffrey Dahmer and Dennis Nilsen, *International Journal of Offender Therapy And Comparative Criminology, 49* (3): 298–307.

Maruna, S., & Copes, H. (2004). *Excuses, excuses: What have we learned from five decades of neutralization research?* Chicago: University of Chicago.

Matza, D. (1964). *Delinquency and drift*, New York: Wiley.

Meloy, J.R. & Felthous, A.R. (2004). Introduction to this issue: Serial and mass homicide, *Behavioral Sciences and the Law, 22:* 289–290.

Merton, R. (1938), Social structure and anomie, *American Sociological Review 3:* 672–682.

Merton, R. (1957). Social theory and social structure, Glencoe, IL: Free Press.

Messing, J.T. & Heeren, J.W. (2004). Another side of multiple murder: Women killers in the domestic context, *Homicide Studies, 8* (2): 123–158.

Mills, C.W. (1940). "Situated Actions and Vocabularies of Motive," *American Sociological Review, 13:* 9–13.

Mitchell, E.W. (1997). *The aetiology of serial murder: Towards an integrated model*, University of Cambridge Press.

Mitchell, H. & Aamodt, M.G. (2005). The incidence of child abuse in serial killers, *Journal of Police and Criminal Psychology, 20* (1): 40–47.

Morton, R.J. (Ed.). (2005). Serial murder, multidisciplinary perspectives for investigators, *F.B.I.: Behavioral Analysis Unit.*

Mullen, P.E. (2004). The autogenic (self-generated) massacre, *Behavioral Sciences and the Law, 22:* 311–323.

Nelson, B. (2007). *Deviant crimes*, www.deviantcrimes.com Newton, M. (2006). *The Encyclopedia of Serial Killers*, Checkmark Books, N.Y.

Osborn, J.R. & Salfati, C.G. (2015). Re-conceptualizing "cooling off periods" in serial homicide, *Homicide studies, 19* (2): 188–205.

Palermo, G. B. (2008). Narcissism, sadism, and loneliness: The case of serial killer Jeffrey Dahmer, In: Kocsis, R. N. (Ed.), *Serial murder and the psychology of violent Crimes.* Totowa, NJ: Humana Press: Ch. 6

Paulsen, D. J. (2007). Improving geographic profiling through computer: Marauder prediction. *Police practice and research: An international journal.* 8(4): 347–357.

Petee, T.A.; Padgett, K.G. & York, T.S. (1997). Debunking the stereotype: An examination of mass murder in public places, *Homicide Studies, 1* (4): 317–337.

Pino, N.W. (2005). Serial offending and the criminal events perspective, *Homicide Studies, 9* (2): 109–148.

Porter, S., Birt, A.R., Yuille, J.C & Herve, H.F. (2001). Memory for murder: A psychological perspective on dissociative amnesia in legal contexts, *Law and Psychiatry, 24:* 23–42.

Quinet, K. (2007). The missing missing, toward a quantification of serial murder victimization in the United States, *Homicide Studies,* 11(4), 319-339.

Rappaport, R.G. (1988). The serial and mass murder: Patterns, differentiation, pathology, *American Journal of Forensic Psychiatry, 9:* 39–48.

Reinders, A.A.T.S., Nijenhuis, E.R.S., Quak, J., Korf, J., Haaksma, J., Panns, A.M.J., Skrapec, C.A. (2001). Phenomenology and serial murder, *Homicide Studies,* 5 (1): 46–63.

Reinders, A.A.T.S.; Nijenhuis, E.R.S.; Panns, A.M.J.; Korf, J.; Willesmen, A.T.M.; Den Boer, A. (2003). One brain, two selves, *NeuroImage, 20:* 2119–2125.

Reinders, A.A.T.S.; Nijenhuis, E.R.S.; Quak, J.; Korf, J.; Haaksma, J.; Panns, A.M.J.; Willesmen, A.T.M.; Den Boer, A. (2006). Psychobiological characteristics of dissociative identity disorder: A symptom provocation study, *Biological Psychiatry, 60:* 730–740.

Reisner, A.D. (2006). A case of Munchausen syndrome by proxy with subsequent stalking Behavior, *International Journal of Offender Therapy and Comparative Criminology, 50* (3): 245–254.

Ressler, R. K., Burgess, A. W., Douglas, J. E., Hartman, C. R., & D'Agostino, R. B. (1986). Sexual killers and their victims: Identifying patterns through crime scene analysis. *Journal of Interpersonal Violence,* 1, 288–308.

Ressler, R.K.; Burgess, A.W. & Douglas, J.E. (1988). *Sexual homicide: Patterns and motives,* Lexington, MA: Lexington Books.

Ressler, R.K. & Shachtman, T. (1992). *Whoever fights monsters,* New York: St Martin's Press.

Ritter, B. (2013). Why profiling is unlikely to work. (Extracted on 10.1.14), http://chicago.examiner.com/article/why-profiling-is-unlikely-to-work.

Rossmo, D.K. (1995). Place, space and police investigations: Hunting serial violent Criminals. In Eck, J.E. & Weisburd, D. (Eds.). *Crime and Place,* N.Y: Monsey.

Rossmo, D. K. (1997). Geographic Profiling. In J. L. Jackson and D. A. Bekerian (Eds.), *Offender Profiling: Theory, Research and Practice,* New York: John Wiley and Sons: 159–176.

Salfati, C.G. & Bateman, A.L. (2005). Serial homicide: An investigation of behavioral consistency, *Journal of Investigative Psychology and Offender Profiling*, 2: 121–144.

Santtila, P., Pakkanen, T., Zappala, A., Bosco, D., Valkama, M. & Mokros, A. (2008). Behavioral crime linking in serial homicide. *Psychology, Crime & Law*, 14, 245–265.

Schlesinger, L.B. (1998). Pathological narcissism and serial homicide: Review and case Study, *Current Psychology: Developmental, Learning, Personality, Social*, 17 (2/3): 212–221.

Schlesinger, L.B.(2001). The contract murderer: Patterns, characteristics and dynamics, *Journal of Forensic Science*: 46 (5): 1119–1123.

Schlesinger, L.B., Ramirez, S., Tusa, B., Jarvis, J.P & Erdberg, P. (2017). Rapid-sequence serial sexual homicide, *Journal of the American academy of Psychiatry and the law*, 45: 72–80.

Seltzer, M. (1998). *Serial killers*, New York: Routledge. Shoemaker, D.J. (1996). *Theories of delinquency*, Oxford: Oxford University Press.

Simkin, D & Roychowdhury V.P (2018). *Statistical study of intervals murders for serial killers*, arXiv. Org. Cornell University

Singer, S. D. & Hensley, C. (2004). Applying social learning theory to childhood and adolescent Fire setting: Can It Lead to Serial Murder? *International Journal of Offender Therapy and Comparative Criminology*, 48 (4): 461–476.

Skrapec, C.A. (2001). Phenomenology and serial murder, *Homicide Studies*, 5 (1): 46–63.

Snook, B., Cullen, R. M., Mokros, A. & Harbort, S. (2005). Serial murderers' spatial decisions: Factors that influence crime location choice. *Journal of Investigative Psychology and Offender Profiling*, 2, 147-161

Snook, B., Cullen, R. M., Bennell, C., Taylor, P. J. & Gendreau, P. (2008). The criminal profiling illusion: What's behind the smoke and mirrors? *Criminal Justice and Behavior*, 35, 1257–1276.

Sutherland, E.H. (1947). *Principles of criminology*, (4th ed.), Philadelphia: J.B. Lippincott.

Sykes, G. & Matza, D. (1957), Techniques of neutralization: A theory of delinquency, *American Journal of Sociology*, 22: 664–670.

Tonkin, M., Woodhams, J., Bull, R., Bond, J. W. & Palmer, E. J. (2011). Linking different types of crime using geographical and temporal proximity. *Criminal Justice and Behavior*, 38, 1069–1088.

Turco, R. (2008). Criminal profile construction and investigative procedures: A study of Western Dodd serial sexual murders. In: R. N. Kocsis (Ed.), *Serial Murder and the Psychology of Violent Crimes* (245–258). NJ: Humana Press: 245–258.

Turvey, B. (1999). *Criminal profiling: An introduction to behavioural evidence analysis*, San Diego, C.A.: Academic Press.

Turvey, B. E. (2012). (Ed.) *Criminal profiling an introduction to behavioral evidence analysis.* England: Elsevier.

U.S. Department of Justice. (1996). Homicide: Its impact and consequences, *National victim assistance academy*, Ch. 16.

Van Der Hart, O.; Nijenhuis, E.R.S.; Steele, K. (2005). Dissociation: An insufficiently recognized Major Feature of Complex PTSD, *Journal of Traumatic Stress*, 18(5).

Vernon, J. & Geberth, M. S. (1995). The psychology and psychodynamics of serial killers, *Law and Order*, 43(4), 1–6.

Vlahov, D.; Galea, S.; Resnick, H.; Ahern, J.; Boscarino, J.A.; Bucuvalas, M. et al. (2002). Increased consumption of cigarettes, alcohol, and marijuana among Manhattan residents after the September 11th terrorist attacks, *American Journal of Epidemiology*, 155(11), 391.

Vronsky, P. (2004). *Serial killers: The method and madness of monsters*, N.Y: Berkley Books.

Vronsky, P. (2007). *Female serial killers*, Berkley Books, New York.

Walsh, A. (2005). African Americans and serial killing in the media, *Homicide Studies*, 9 (4): 271–291.

Willesmen, A.T.M. & Den Boer, A. (2006). Psychological characteristics of dissociative identity disorder: A symptom provocation study, *Biological Psychiatry*, 60: 730–740.

Winter, D. (2006). Destruction as a constructive choice. In Manson, T. *Forensic Psychiatry: Influences of Evil*, Humana Press Inc. N.J.

Woodhams, J., Bull, R. & Hollin, C. R. (2010). Case linkage: Identifying crimes committed by the same offender. In: R. N. Kocsis (Ed.) *Criminal profiling: International theory, research, and practice* (117-133). NJ: Humana Press.

Wright, J., Hensley, C. (2003). From animal cruelty to serial murder: Applying the graduation hypothesis, *International Journal of Offender Therapy and Comparative Criminology*, 47(1): 71–88.

Endnotes

1 For expansion, see Edelstein, 2006.
2 This issue will be expanded later on.
3 There is disagreement among scientists regarding the required number of victims so that a murder would be defined as mass murder. A detailed reference to this issue will be presented later on.
4 A detailed reference to each of the types will be presented later on.
5 Scientists disagree about the number of victims that make it a serial murder. A detailed discussion about it will be presented later on.
6 This concept is essential in defining serial murder versus mass murder, and it will be dealt with in Chapter Three.
7 Some regard wrong generalizations like this one as the creators of myths, mainly in the mass media.
8 I will refer to this issue in details in the next chapter.
9 The fact that it is a continuous event that goes on incessantly is most important later on for the distinction between a mass murder and a serial murder.
10 In the chapter that deals with a serial murder I will present the sensation, anxiety and continuity which characterize such a murder versus a mass murder.
11 There is no intention, of course, to harm the value of the holiness of living and the suffering of the families, but to present the characteristics in the appropriate proportion.
12 Psychological and sociological characteristics will be presented largely later on.
13 Reference to gender differences in mass murders will be done later in this chapter.
14 See DeLisi and Scherer (2006), p. 370.
15 These aspects gained great attention in the literature in relation to serial murderers.
16 Most of the weapons are acquired legally in the US.
17 This issue will be presented extensively in the chapter which deals with serial murder and murderers.
18 It would be interesting to examine this explanation in the near future following the severe economic crisis that the US is going through.
19 A custom in which the individual blames himself, or is accused by others, for a contemptible behaviour, takes a sword and commits suicide in an attempt to regain his social respect.
20 For expansion, see: Shem-David, 2008.
21 Although it is not always clear what came first.
22 For expansion, see Sykes & Matza, 1957.
23 For expansion, see the chapter that deals with the integrative theoretical model for a serial murder.
24 The scientist dealt with serial murder, but the logic behind the explanation suits mass murder as well.

25   The first attempt to apply this theory to serial murder was done by Hale, 1993.

26   That is, knowing that the murder would end up with the killing of the murderer by the police forces.

27   Later on there will be reference to family annihilators and mass murderers who murdered a former employer and coworkers in the place they had been fired from.

28   See, for example, the book of Y. Yas'ur (1995), *The Decision to Murder*, in which the author demonstrates that murderers (though not mass ones) describe the circumstances in which the murder was executed when they felt they had nothing to lose.

29   These theories will be presented extensively in the next chapter.

30   For expansion, see Merton, 1957.

31   One of the four types of suicide defined by the sociologist Emile Durkheim.

32   For expansion, see Edelstein, 2006.

33   It is important to bear in mind that the percentage refers only to a mass murder in public places.

34   Ynet news site, 23.9.08.

35   Ynet news site, 23.9.08. It should be indicated that Finland, where there have taken place a number of events of this kind, stands out in its high level of suicides, and it is also relatively easy to get firearms there.

36   For reference to these concepts, see the chapter which deals with serial murder.

37   This is a chauvinistic approach of ownership of men over women.

38   For example, a student who murdered female students of engineering because he regarded them as too feminists.

39   A racial ideology can be accompanied also by an emotional aspect, since it integrates a kind of belief which involves emotions.

40   The working place is indeed defined as public, but it is a specific location which is not a shopping, entertainment or leisure center.

41   As we will see in the next chapter, serial murder is more salient in the US as well.

42   In the literary survey there is almost no evidence of a multi-disciplinary academic activity in this context.

43   For example, Ferguson el al., (2003), argued that a multiple murder would not include murder cases that took place within a political or criminal organization.

44   For expansion, see Merton, 1957.

45   These explanations will be dealt with thoroughly in the chapter which deals with serial murder.

46   This term will be presented in detail later on.

47   Regarding the definition of sequentiality, see the discussion later on.

48   It is important not to make a mistake in this context between a mass murder and a mass-serial murder.

49   This claim is somewhat problematic, since murderers sit in jail for many years, so they do not have the capability of murdering again, even if they would have wanted to do so.

50 There is no intention to claim that a murderer who murders for the sake of material profit does not suffer from pathology, but to distinguish between material and non-material aspects.

51 Due to the problematic nature of the division of multiple-victims' murder into sub-types, getting the empirical data is also deficient.

52 It should be indicated that in classifying felonies the term Predatory Crimes it is accepted nowadays.

53 For expansion, see: Skrapec (2001).

54 For expansion, see: Turvey, 1999, p. 287; Egger, 1998; Hickey, 1997; Holmes and Holmes (1996), p.108; Gerberth, 1996; Vronsky, 2007; Skrapec, 2001.

55 It should be indicated that the scientist confuse between mass-serial murderers and serial murderers.

56 Here we see again the confusion between the definitions of a serial murder and a mass-serial murder and among the scientists.

57 Criminal law does not define most of the felonies by referring to their motive as well.

58 Homes and Holmes (1998) also present similar assessments.

59 Harbourt and Mokros (2001) samples 61 serial murderers and found out that the average number of victims per murderer was 5.1.

60 Reference to these theories will be brought later on.

61 Reference to serial murderesses will be brought later on.

62 For expansion, see Mitchell (1997).

63 For expanding the subject, see Kraemer (2004).

64 As we will see later on, in part of the categories of serial murder there is an acquaintance, and there are even familial connections between the murderer and the victims, especially among serial murderesses.

65 Arndt et al. arrived to a little different conclusions, but since the differences are not significant, I do not see a need of presenting them.

66 One should bear in mind that the statistical model was based on post factum data, and the scientist did not prove the model on murderers who have not been arrested yet.

67 The issue of gender in relation to serial murder will be discussed elaborately later on.

68 We will discuss later on the correlation between this syndrome and serial murder.

69 A reference to serial murder committed by women will be presented later on.

70 A separate chapter will be dedicated to serial murder committed by women.

71 A detailed explanation will be given later on in the chapter.

72 The emphasis is in the original.

73 Unlike a variety of mental disorders which are not defined as mental illnesses.

74 The emphasis is in the original.

75 The first attempt to implement this theory regarding serial murder was done by Hale (1993).

76 Amsel's (1958) theory of frustration has also been discussed in the previous chapter, and therefore I will not present it again here, but just connect it to serial murder.

77 The idea is reminiscent of the Oedipus complex which Freud invented at his time.

78 Some claim that the blood is related to the woman's sexuality by commemoration the bleeding of the monthly period.

79 The scientist praises the theory and also claims that it can predict whether the child would become a serial murderer. He even tells us what kind of serial murderer he would be, but he does not speak about the scientists who composed this theory, and does not indicate even one empirical research that was done on this issue.

80 Holmes and Holmes (1998) objected to making the psychopath into a "supermarket" of psychology, as different disorders and behaviours for whom no formal or clear diagnosis was found, were put under the category of psychopathy.

81 The American book of definitions of disorders and mental illnesses.

82 See also Fox and Levin (1998).

83 We should pay attention to the fact that the theory of frustration-aggression and the theory of attachment come from the same circumstances of two almost contrary reactions in the child's personality.

84 In a conference of experts which the scientist summarized it is claimed that another common characteristic of serial murderers is impulsive behaviour. But as I have indicated, this behaviour characterizes just a little part of serial murderers, "the unorganized murderer" who is diagnosed as having a mental illness rather than an antisocial behaviour disorder.

85 See, for example, Anderson (1999), who claims that one can try to explain a serial murder by adopting some of the mental disorders presented in this manual, but his conclusion is that the manual does not provide us with a set of characteristics or criteria from which we will be able to predict a murderous behaviour (Ibid, p. 42).

86 Taken from a conversation with Sr. Mattar, May 2008, the Mental Health Center, affiliated to the Ben-Gurion University, Beer-Sheba.

87 Butler (2006).

88 A test which maps the body with the use of magnets, and serves as a central test for discovering tumors in the body.

89 Holmes et al., (2004) distinguish between dissociation and compartmentalization: dissociation is an alternative or other state of consciousness which is characterized by a sense of separation from the self and the world, while compartmentalization means inability to control cognitive actions or processes that controllable in a normal state. That is, emotional processes remain untouched, but the access to them is blocked, compartmentalized.

90 For expansion about the role of fantasy, see Vronsky (2004).

91 One has to refer cautiously to these descriptions. In the past there were found several serial murderers who tried to claim for insanity and forged a state of multi-identities.

92 See also Fox and Levin (2001).

93 Porter et al., (2001) claim that psychopaths cannot experience trauma and anxiety, and therefore this personality disorder cannot suit them. But the claim is that the psychopath is "created" following a trauma, and this contradicts their perception.

94 The emphasis is in the original.
95 We should relate to the murderer's words carefully and suspiciously in light of my comments of this research method.
96 An alternative explanation for this will be given within the sociological explanations for serial murder.
97 This suggestion of the scientists was made within the typology they suggested according to motive and benefit, and we will discuss it elaborately later on.
98 This is another example of the problematic nature of relying on a single case study.
99 In this context, it is recommended to look at Anna Freud's book about the defense mechanisms of the self.
100 The distinction between cultural and social explanations is artificial to a large extent, because society and culture are interwoven in one another. But for the sake of the discussion I wanted to separate between them in order to emphasize the different aspects of each of the viewpoints.
101 For instance, there are cultures in which violence is a legitimate way of solving inter-personal conflicts, while other cultures forbid any kind of inter-personal violence. One can see the custom of a duel as a violent way of solving conflicts, whether it is conducted between European gentlemen or between two hooligans in the American Wild West.
102 In this subject, the American literature does not deal with two historical events soaked in violence in the history of the US: The American Civil War and the conquest of Indian territories and exterminating a major part of them.
103 For example, the American response for hitting the Twin Towers, the conduct of the American army, mainly in Pakistan, the conduct of the Americans in the conflict in former Yugoslavia, establishing the Guantanamo prisoners camp for investigating and arresting suspects, so that they would not be subjugated to the American constitution, and others.
104 One can see that the suggested sorting resembles the central factor for mass murder.
105 In this context, see also Hinch & Scott, (2000).
106 See, for example, Hinch & Scott (2000); Levin & Fox (2007).
107 This is way of neutralizing guilt which will be dealt with later on.
108 This school of thought came up mainly during the seventies and claimed, in the spirit of the Marxist tradition, that part of the delinquency of the lower class against the middle and the upper classes expresses a rebellion against the exploitation of the lower class by the rich.
109 This is exactly the claim of the media, that it does not create violent contents, but simply presents the existing contents in the American cultural milieu.
110 See: Edelstein, 2006.
111 One can see here the connection between sociology and psychology.
112 There are updated developments of the theory, but it is important to present the original theoretical basis.
113 These techniques of justifications and excuses appear in Sutherland's differential association theory as part of the criminal learning. See later on.

114 This is unlike Merton's theory, according to which certain patterns of deviation stem from the rejection of society's values.

115 It does not mean that the criminal would verbally express regret, or confess his guilt, but an inner psychological feeling.

116 A later version of the theory, Matza (1964).

117 Although the language is not simple, I thought it was right to stay close as much as possible to the words of the scientist.

118 The emphases are mine, AE.

119 The emphases are mine, AE.

120 We have seen a similar problem in attributing a motive to the actions of mass murderers.

121 The emphasis is mine, AE.

122 The actor is the acting individual. Actor is a sociological term, and it means someone who is in a certain social situation who acts in a certain way.

123 A large number of the explanations of serial murder refer to the circle, in which the serial murderer's social solitude led him to turn to a fantasy state, and when he comes out of this state, he feels emptiness that can lead him to a greater social solitude.

124 An example for this we have seen also in the discussion about "mass murder and murderers among family annihilators."

125 For expansion, see: DeFronzo et al., 2007.

126 For expansion, see: Mitchell and Aamodt, 2005.

127 Norms are part of the cultural contents, but the meaning here is to the entirety of culture components.

128 From a conversation with Prof. Menachem Amir from the Institute of Criminology at the Hebrew University.

129 For example, there are significant lines of similarity between a narcissistic personality disorder and antisocial behaviour disorder. For expansion, see: Gabbard (1994).

130 Examples for this I have shown in relation to family annihilators in mass murder.

131 For example, Levin and Fox (2007).

132 For expansion, see: The rational choice theory (Gibbs, 1975).

133 For expansion, see: The rational choice (Gibbs, 1975).

134 For expansion and criticism about some of the more outstanding typologies, see: Canter & Wentink (2004).

135 This classification is based upon the FBI classification for rapists, and therefore this category seems inappropriate for serial murderers with a sexual background.

136 In: Hickey, 1992.

137 For expansion, see: Edelstein, 2006.

138 Later on I will refer to this point which has some problematic nature. Choosing the victims has to do with the murderer and his illness and is not totally random.

139 See the theory about frustration/humiliation-aggression.

140 One can refer to the theories which appear in the paragraph that deals with formatting/reframing.

141 Having sexual intercourse with the victim after his death—with the body or with parts of it.
142 As I have shown, crossing the border involves neutralizing guilt and shame prior to the action.
143 The meaning is stabbing the victims many times beyond what is needed for killing him.
144 This perception stands out in the theoretical and research literature in relation to other violent felonies, mainly rape.
145 Hirschi and Gottfredson (1992).
146 Levin (2008) found out that people who used to abuse animals, tended five times more to execute violent acts towards people, like rape, attack and murder (Ibid, p. 34).
147 For example: Holmes and Holmes, and Holmes and DeBurger.
148 For expansion, see: Reisner (2006). In addition, there were extreme cases in which a mother who received attention during her pregnancy and after the delivery felt she was ignored, since the attention shifted to the baby, caused her babies to get sick and die, and so she enjoyed the attention during the period of mourning and the next pregnancy, and so on over and over again.
149 Castle and Hensley (2002).
150 Dr. Matar indicated in a conversation I had with him that it is unknown whether paranoids are capable of power-control games, or not.
151 I have shown in the chapter about mass murderers that the murderer blames others for all his troubles and sufferings.
152 There is something to think about here. It is known that foreign armies that conquered other nations, including nations which had been perceived by them as hedonistic, sinful, unworthy, and so on, tended to rape the women and even the young girls of the conquered nation as a kind of a total conquest and control. In the literature on serial murder there is no such description regarding the victims.
153 We can see that when the murderer focuses on the action and not the process, there are no power-control games.
154 This is another significant difference which distinguishes between this category and the previous one.
155 The author deliberately avoids describing in full and graphic details the kinds of tortures involved.
156 Goffman, 1961.
157 Beyond the impulses of the id indicated by Freud.
158 For elaboration, see the study by Kenney & Heide (1994). These data have not been presented in my previous book.
159 For additional typologies, see: Kelleher, M.D. & Kelleher, C.L., 1998.
160 For elaboration, see Kelleher & Kelleher, 1998.